A Critical Account of English Syntax

Edinburgh Textbooks on the English Language – Advanced

General Editor
Heinz Giegerich, Professor of English Linguistics, University of Edinburgh

Editorial Board
Laurie Bauer (University of Wellington)
Olga Fischer (University of Amsterdam)
Rochelle Lieber (University of New Hampshire)
Bettelou Los (University of Edinburgh)
Norman Macleod (University of Edinburgh)
Donka Minkova (UCLA)
Edgar Schneider (University of Regensburg)
Katie Wales (University of Leeds)
Anthony Warner (University of York)

TITLES IN THE SERIES INCLUDE:

English Historical Semantics
Christian Kay and Kathryn Allan

A Historical Syntax of English
Bettelou Los

Morphological Theory and the Morphology of English
Jan Don

Construction Grammar and its Application to English
Martin Hilpert

A Historical Phonology of English
Donka Minkova

English Historical Pragmatics
Andreas Jucker and Irma Taavitsainen

English Historical Sociolinguistics
Robert McColl Millar

Corpus Linguistics and the Description of English
Hans Lindquist

A Critical Account of English Syntax: Grammar, Meaning, Text
Keith Brown and Jim Miller

Visit the Edinburgh Textbooks in the English Language website at www.euppublishing.com/series/ETOTELAdvanced

A Critical Account of English Syntax

Grammar, Meaning, Text

Keith Brown and Jim Miller

EDINBURGH
University Press

Edinburgh University Press is one of the leading university presses in the UK. We publish academic books and journals in our selected subject areas across the humanities and social sciences, combining cutting-edge scholarship with high editorial and production values to produce academic works of lasting importance. For more information visit our website: edinburghuniversitypress.com

© Keith Brown and Jim Miller, 2016

Edinburgh University Press Ltd
The Tun – Holyrood Road,
12(2f) Jackson's Entry
Edinburgh EH8 8PJ

Typeset in 10.5/12 Janson by
Servis Filmsetting Ltd, Stockport, Cheshire

A CIP record for this book is available from the British Library

ISBN 978 0 7486 9608 6 (hardback)
ISBN 978 0 7486 9610 9 (paperback)
ISBN 978 0 7486 9609 3 (webready PDF)
ISBN 978 0 7486 9611 6 (epub)

The right of Keith Brown and Jim Miller to be identified as the authors of this work has been asserted in accordance with the Copyright, Designs and Patents Act 1988, and the Copyright and Related Rights Regulations 2003 (SI No. 2498).

Contents

Introduction	1
Organisation and content	1
Why study the grammar of English?	2
What counts as the grammar of English?	4
The data	7
Grammaticality	9
Grammaticality and acceptability	9
Grammaticality and intuition	10
Grammaticality and power	13
Grammaticality: descriptive and prescriptive grammar	15
Grammaticality and language change	16
Adjectives and adjective phrases	19
Adjectives and adjective phrases: introduction	19
Adjectives and adjective phrases: adjectives and denotation	21
Adjectives and adjective phrases: adjectives and gradability	22
Adjectives and adjective phrases: adjectives as heads of noun phrases	23
Adjectives and adjective phrases: adjectives as a word class	26
Adjectives and adjective phrases: adjective positions in noun phrases	28
Adjectives and adjective phrases: reduplication	30
Adverbs and adverb phrases	32
Adverbs and adverb phrases: introduction	32
Adverbs and adverb phrases: adverbs and adjectives	34
Adverbs and adverb phrases: structure of adverb phrases	36
Adverbial clauses	38
Adverbial clauses: introduction	38
Adverbial clauses: time, condition, reason, concession	39
Adverbial clauses: less common types	40

Adverbial clauses: position in clauses and sentences	40
Adverbial clauses: spoken English	44
Adverbial clauses: subordinate clause or main clause?	45
Clause and text	**48**
Clause and text: introduction	48
Clause and text: clefts	50
IT clefts	50
WH clefts	52
Reverse WH clefts	53
TH clefts	54
Clause and text: cohesion	55
Cohesion: orientation	55
Cohesion: orientation in place	55
Cohesion: orientation in time	55
Cohesion: orientation in time: tense and aspect	55
Cohesion: co-reference and referent tracking	56
Cohesion: coordination and subordination	57
Cohesion: adverbials and conjunctions	57
Clause and text: cohesion – active, passive, middle	58
Clause and text: discourse markers	61
Clause and text: ellipsis	62
Clause and text: focus	63
Clause and text: focus: special syntactic constructions	64
Clause and text: focus: word order	67
Clause and text: given and new	67
Clause and text: non-finite clauses	71
Clause and text: spoken and written text	72
Clause and text: theme	75
Clause structure	**81**
Clause structure: introduction	81
Clause structure: constituents	81
Transposition	81
Substitution	82
Coordination	82
Clause structure: dependency relations	85
Clause structure: hierarchical structure	92
Clause structure: linearity and predicate-argument structure	95
Clause structure: linearity and grammatical functions	97
Clause structure: verb phrases	101
Clause structure: integrated and unintegrated syntax	103

Clefts	107
Clauses: clefts	107
Complement clauses	112
Complement clauses: complementisers	112
Complement clauses: embedded interrogatives	114
Complement clauses: mood and modality	119
Complement clauses: gerunds, infinitives and meaning	121
Complement clauses: noun complement clauses	122
Constructions	125
Constructions: overview	125
Non-finite clauses	128
Non-finite clauses: introduction	128
Non-finite clauses: infinitives	130
Non-finite clauses: free participles	131
Non-finite clauses: gerunds (Type 1)	133
Non-finite clauses: gerunds (Type 2)	134
Non-finite clauses: reduced adverbials	136
Non-finite clauses: reduced relatives	137
Non-finite clauses: verb stem	137
Non-finite clauses: *with* + NP	138
Non-finite clauses: eight types or four?	139
Nouns and noun phrases	141
Nouns and noun phrases: introduction	141
Nouns and noun phrases: common and proper	151
Nouns and noun phrases: count and mass	153
Countability: individuals and substances	153
Partitives	155
Number and agreement	155
Nouns and noun phrases: determinatives	158
Nouns and noun phrases: pronouns	164
Prepositions and prepositional phrases	170
Prepositions and prepositional phrases: introduction	170
Prepositions and prepositional phrases: prepositions and particles	171
Prepositions and prepositional phrases: prepositions, transitive and intransitive	173
Prepositions and prepositional phrases: prepositional phrases, their distribution	174
Complements of verbs	175

Complements (or postmodifiers) of nouns	175
Complements (or postmodifiers) of adjectives	175
Complements of prepositions	175
Prepositions and prepositional phrases: prepositions and meaning	176
Prepositions and prepositional phrases: prepositional verbs	178

Relative clauses 180
    Relative clauses: introduction 180
    Relative clauses: contact 182
    Relative clauses: free 183
    Relative clauses: infinitival 185
    Relative clauses: non-standard 186
    Relative clauses: propositional 187
    Relative clauses: restrictive and non-restrictive 188
    Relative clauses: shadow pronouns 190
    Relative clauses: th 193
    Relative clauses: unattached 195
    Relative clauses: unintegrated 197
    Relative clauses: wh 198
    Relative clauses: wh words as deictics 201
    Relative clauses: which as discourse connective 202

Sentences and clauses 206
    Sentences and clauses: introduction 206
    Sentences and clauses: clauses 208
    Sentences and clauses: complex sentences 210
    Sentences and clauses: compound sentences 211
    Sentences and clauses: main and subordinate clauses 212
    Sentences and clauses: sentence fragments 216
    Sentences and clauses: simple sentences 218
    Sentences and clauses: subordinate clauses: preposition or complementiser? 218
    Sentences and clauses: system sentence and text sentence 220

Verbs and verb phrases 224
    Verbs and verb phrases: tense and aspect: introduction 224
    Verbs and verb phrases: tense and aspect in English 227
    Verbs and verb phrases: future tense 229
    Verbs and verb phrases: middle construction 232
    Verbs and verb phrases: mood and modality 236
    Verbs and verb phrases: passive voice 243
    Verbs and verb phrases: present perfect and adverbs 245

Verbs and verb phrases: present perfect and resultative	249
Verbs and verb phrases: present perfect and simple past	252
Verbs and verb phrases: progressive aspect	254
Verbs and verb phrases: simple present	257
Verbs and verb phrases: situation (lexical) aspect	261
Word classes	268
Word classes: introduction	268
Word classes: major and minor	268
Word classes: gradience	270
Word classes: criteria	273
Word classes: semantics	275
Word classes: syntactic criteria and sub-classes	279
Notes	281
Bibliography	291
Index	294

Introduction

ORGANISATION AND CONTENT

When the proposal for this book was first submitted to the editorial committee for the English Language series, one response was a request for something different in format and content from the usual run of English Language textbooks. The authors lit on the idea of a format between dictionaries and encyclopaedias on the one hand and handbooks on the other, following the example of Swan (2005) and Carter et al. (2011). None of the entries is as long as a chapter in a handbook and none is as short as a dictionary entry. For the paper edition the entries are mostly in alphabetical order, with two major exceptions. The introductory sections and the entries on the general topic of grammaticality have been placed first. The entries relating to a given large topic, such as relative clauses, are grouped together but in each group the introduction comes first. The format offers several advantages. Students will easily find a given sub-topic, and the entries are linked by numerous cross-references so that they can follow a thread, say tense and aspect. We do not expect readers to work their way through the entries in alphabetical order. Thus, readers pursuing the topic of word classes can begin with the sections entitled 'Word classes', although these sections come last in the paper book, and then go on to the sections on individual classes of words. Some lecturers may omit one subset of topics, other lecturers another subset, and the format allows lecturers to decide the order in which they wish to discuss topics and to prescribe reading. The final advantage is that it is very suitable for the web-based version of the book.

Some explanation is called for as to what this book is and is not. It is not a teaching grammar of English, though students of English as an Additional Language will find that much of the discussion relates directly to the usages they hear and their understanding of English syntax. The book is not a reference grammar and does not try to emulate even the coverage in grammars such as Huddleston and Pullum (2005). Space simply does not permit such broad scope. Finally, the book is not a corpus grammar. A good number of the examples do come from corpuses but this does not make it a corpus grammar in the sense of analysing a particular corpus and listing the frequencies of particular items per 1,000 or 10,000 or 1,000,000 words, or the frequencies of the different types of noun modified by relative clauses introduced by *which*, and so on.

What is the book, then? It is a discursive and descriptive account of several major areas of English syntax, of the role of syntactic constructions in text and of the interaction between textual imperatives and the use of old or new structures, or of old structures with a new set of lexical items. (=> CLAUSE AND TEXT: COHESION – ACTIVE, PASSIVE, MIDDLE.) The book deals with problems of analysis (=> RELATIVE CLAUSES: FREE, SUBORDINATE CLAUSES: PREPOSITION OR COMPLEMENTISER?) but other major concerns are the variation that affects standard English and the fascinating constructions to be found in spoken English (standard or non-standard) and in non-standard English. (=> INTRODUCTION: WHAT COUNTS AS THE GRAMMAR OF ENGLISH?, GRAMMATICALITY: GRAMMATICALITY AND ACCEPTABILITY.) These constructions are generally ignored by reference grammars, proscribed by teaching grammars and not recognised in formal theories of syntax. Nonetheless, they must be taken into account by analysts developing usage-based grammars and they are essential to any attempts to trace ongoing change in English syntax. (=> VERBS AND VERB PHRASES: PROGRESSIVE ASPECT, VERBS AND VERB PHRASES: PRESENT PERFECT AND RESULTATIVE, VERBS AND VERB PHRASES: MIDDLE CONSTRUCTIONS, GRAMMATICALITY: GRAMMATICALITY AND ACCEPTABILITY.)

WHY STUDY THE GRAMMAR OF ENGLISH?

Who needs a knowledge of English grammar? And what English and what grammar? This book describes and analyses constructions from a number of varieties of English but does not prescribe this or that construction as 'good' English. (=> GRAMMATICALITY: DESCRIPTIVE AND PRESCRIPTIVE GRAMMAR, GRAMMATICALITY: GRAMMATICALITY AND ACCEPTABILITY.) On the theoretical side, linguists working on formal models of English grammar (and semantics) need a good knowledge of English in order not to make the mistake of declaring that such and such an example or structure is incorrect when it is typical of spoken standard English or of some non-standard variety or of some variety other than British or American English. (We comment here and there on judgements on data that contradict components of formal models.)

The most obvious set of consumers includes students taking degrees in English Language or Linguistics, whether senior undergraduate students or postgraduates on MSc or MA programmes. The set of senior undergraduate students is intended to include students at universities in English-speaking countries and students at universities elsewhere. (That dichotomy is nowadays disrupted by, for instance, universities in the Netherlands or Norway where degree courses are taught in English.)

Another obvious set of potential consumers, and perhaps the largest, encompasses teachers of English in primary and secondary schools and teachers of English as a Second Language (ESOL) or English as an Additional Language (EAL). A currently fashionable topic of research is English as a Lingua Franca and in particular what demands should be put on ESOL learners who require English for work but not for university study or professional qualifications in domains such as banking or insurance. A look at the constructions actually used by native speakers in spontaneous speech would solve some of the controversies over the content of English grammar courses.† Some of the notes refer to reference grammars aimed at the ESOL market, in particular contrasting the more prescriptive, rigid approach of Carter et al. (2011) with the more relaxed (and perceptive) approach of Swan (2005).

A third set of potential users includes students of speech and language therapy, who also need a broad, thorough knowledge of English grammar. Many of their clients (children and adults) are speakers of non-standard English, and many clients, even those who are speakers of standard English, use the constructions typical of spoken language that are commented on throughout this book. It helps if non-standard constructions and spoken constructions are not dismissed as errors or symptoms of some deficit in linguistic competence. The section on clause and text is also relevant to speech and language therapists, since they have to diagnose problems that their clients may have in producing coherent and cohesive text.

KB and JM hope that the book has something to offer colleagues. For example, scholars engaged in the typology of languages need a broad grounding. Analysis of formal written texts reveals many examples of relative clauses introduced by wh words such as *who* and *which* and examples of relative clauses introduced by *that*. Analysis of spontaneous spoken English reveals *that* relative clauses and clauses with no relativisers. Spontaneous spoken English also offers regular examples of relative clauses with shadow or resumptive pronouns. If the spoken data is taken seriously, we have to treat English as having at least three types of relative clause. (=> RELATIVE CLAUSES: WH, RELATIVE CLAUSES: TH, RELATIVE CLAUSES: SHADOW PRONOUNS, RELATIVE CLAUSES: NON-STANDARD.)

A broad descriptive grounding in English grammar has something to offer analysts working on applications of computational techniques to natural language, for instance theories of language evolution (spoken language preceding the appearance of written language), automatic parsing programs, and the development of digital grammar-checkers. Most, if not all, current grammar-checkers perpetuate the worst excesses of traditional prescriptive practices. And the users of grammar-checkers, and of prescriptive books such as Gwynne (2013) and Heffer (2011), need the grounding in order to assess the prescriptions. Some of them have no greater rationale than statements about preferred food or colours. The problem is that some of the prescriptions are held by many employers to be indispensable to correct writing, such as using *whom* or allowing only *that* as a relativiser in restrictive relative clauses. (=> RELATIVE CLAUSES: RESTRICTIVE AND NON-RESTRICTIVE.) The prescriptions are also regarded by many educated people as essential components of their social and cultural capital. (=>GRAMMATICALITY: GRAMMATICALITY AND ACCEPTABILITY, GRAMMATICALITY: GRAMMATICALITY AND POWER.) And any specialized area of activity has its own social and cultural capital; not just the obvious areas of medical or legal language or the vocabulary and style required for any area of academic activity (syntax, semantics, sociology, geology and so on) but the conventions for writing such documents as estimates and invoices, minutes and letters to the Inland Revenue.

WHAT COUNTS AS THE GRAMMAR OF ENGLISH?

This book reflects our experience of analysing and teaching syntax and our perception of the various audiences for accounts of English syntax. Several long-held ideas underpin the choice of content and the analyses offered. One is that spoken and written language are equally worthy of attention; not just the language of prepared speech events such as talks on radio or television, political speeches and sermons but also spontaneous or unplanned spoken language, that is, spoken language produced in circumstances that allow a minimum of planning time or in informal and relaxed conditions, such as domestic conversation (or domestic argument).

A second idea is that grammar and meaning are closely connected, to the extent that all grammatical morphemes carry meaning and that for most users of grammar, including non-native learners of any language, the most satisfying explanation of some grammatical point is a semantic one that applies to a good range of examples. This perspective is nowadays associated with the theory known as Cognitive Linguistics but the principle that grammatical differences signal differences in meaning long predates that theory.

A third idea is that it is essential to have insightful, reliable descriptive grammar as well as formal models. The term 'descriptive' is used pejoratively by some analysts, but the fact is that no description is possible without a theoretical framework and formal models go astray without solid descriptive support. The audience for good descriptive grammars and grammar is enormous; the market and range of applications for descriptive grammar is far bigger than the specialist market for formal models. And descriptive grammar does not stand still, just as formal models do not stand still. Good descriptive grammars draw on the vast amount of work that has been done inside and outside formal models over the past sixty years or so and a descriptive grammar produced in 2015 is not at all the same as a descriptive grammar produced in 1950.

A fourth idea is that it is vitally important to collect reliable data. One approach to data gathering is based on intuition: in its most basic form this method involves presenting examples to a number of native speakers of the language being analysed. The method can be beefed up by the use of statistical techniques, by recording the speed of response if examples are presented on computer, by getting informants to fill in gaps in sentences or to complete sentences. The second approach to data gathering is based on observations of usage. This can be done by analysing, say, essays by students on a particular topic, transcriptions of conversations or radio discussions and talks or the novels of a particular author. Nowadays, of course, the automatic searching of large digital corpuses yields information that was previously unavailable. In practice many linguists use both approaches. The important thing is not to rely solely on one's own intuition. For instance, many generative accounts contain statements to the effect that indirect questions must have the structure of *She asked where we were going*.† That is, the indirect question *where we were going* begins with the wh interrogative pronoun *where* but otherwise has the structure of a declarative clause – subject *we* + auxiliary verb *were* + main verb *going*. Such statements are observationally inadequate. Many examples such as *She asked where were we going* (with the structure of a direct question) are regularly found in both writing and speech. (=> COMPLEMENT CLAUSES: EMBEDDED INTERROGATIVES.)

Implicit in the previous paragraph is the idea that linguists describe usage, or the usages of particular groups of speakers and writers, but do not prescribe 'correct' usages nor proscribe 'incorrect' usages. Of course linguists have their personal prejudices and are well aware of the general conventions governing formal writing as well as the particular conventions applying to specific types of formal writing: research monographs and introductory textbooks; texts on literature or linguistics or history; detective novels and minutes of meetings. What is important is that in scientific work observer-describers set their prejudices aside and record and report all the patterns they come across. Of course, one swallow does not make a summer. Consider the example from the preceding paragraph *She asked where were we going*. If we had recorded just this one example we would not be justified in claiming that it represented an alternative indirect question construction. We could at most report that the example had been observed (whether in speech or writing). If no further examples were to be found by the same or other researchers, it would remain a curiosity but this indirect question construction is so frequent that it must be taken seriously.

The construction is relevant to another very important point: spontaneous spoken language and formal written language (to take the two poles of a continuum of text-types) are not just different but profoundly different. This affects core syntactic theory (no sentences; different ways of combining clauses; different constructions; and so on) and bears directly on the place of English in typologies of languages and on theories of first language acquisition, of complexity and of evolution of language. These topics are not discussed in this book but many of the comments on particular structures are relevant to them. We simply mention here that spoken language is central to most human activity. Humans spoke long before they began to write; typically, children control spoken language before they master written language. Even today, in spite of time devoted to social media, the majority of humans use spoken language more than written language. In any case, the language of social media communications varies from user to user, as can be seen from Twitter messages and the comments and discussions on the digital versions of newspapers. Some users write using the syntactic structures and vocabulary of informal spoken language while others use the syntax and vocabulary of formal writing. (=> SENTENCES AND CLAUSES: INTRODUCTION; SENTENCES AND CLAUSES: SENTENCE FRAGMENTS; SENTENCES AND CLAUSES: SYSTEM SENTENCE AND TEXT SENTENCE.)

In connection with spoken language, it is very worthwhile emphasising that while non-standard English is typically spoken, spoken

English is both standard and non-standard. Constructions that are typical of speech but not of writing are produced by speakers who speak some non-standard variety of English but also by speakers who otherwise speak standard English. (But note that standard English is not just BBC English. We can recognise a standard Scottish English, a standard Irish English (possibly two), a standard Welsh English, a standard Manchester English and so on. Many speakers of English speak a non-BBC standard or some non-standard variety but write standard written English.) If we are to understand variation in usage and changes in usage (language change), we have to take non-standard English and spoken English seriously. We have to take them seriously if we are to carry out reliable typological research, develop adequate theories of first language acquisition and literacy, and understand ongoing changes in English grammar. (=>GRAMMATICALITY: GRAMMATICALITY AND ACCEPTABILITY, GRAMMATICALITY: GRAMMATICALITY AND POWER, GRAMMATICALITY: DESCRIPTIVE AND PRESCRIPTIVE GRAMMAR, GRAMMATICALITY: GRAMMATICALITY AND LANGUAGE CHANGE.)

THE DATA

This is a relatively short and concise account of English syntax. At the centre of each topic is standard written British English, but there are also many examples from spoken English and some examples from non-standard English. The spoken examples illustrate constructions that are not normally included in grammars of English but are used frequently and have to be taken seriously by anyone interested in the full range of English syntactic structures and usages. In particular, there are some examples from New Zealand and Australian English.

The examples of written standard British English come from two sources. Some are invented by KB and JM but most have been collected by KB and JM over many years and come from digital corpuses, newspapers, novels, academic texts and student examination scripts. The examples of spoken English come from KB and JM's digital corpus of conversations collected for a project on the syntax of Scottish English, from a digital corpus of task-related dialogues, from data collected on the hoof from radio and television programmes (many examples were collected in the days before large corpuses of texts could be easily accessed) and from newspaper interviews. A very convenient journalistic practice over the past twenty years is to record interviews and to quote verbatim from them. Some examples of New Zealand English were collected by

JM during a four-year stay in New Zealand but most come from the Wellington Corpus of Spoken New Zealand English. The examples of Australian English come from articles in Burridge and Kortmann (2008) and from the Macquarie Corpus of Australian English.

An asterisk marks an unaccecptable sentence. A question mark preceding an example indicates that the example, while not downright unacceptable, is in some way peculiar. A dagger symbol (†) indicates that there is a relevant note in Notes at the end of the book.

Grammaticality

GRAMMATICALITY AND ACCEPTABILITY

Readers of this book will expect to find the analytical and theoretical points illustrated with examples. Readers with English as their first language will also expect the examples to be 'correct', and readers who are advanced students of English will expect that they can use the examples in their own writing without being penalised for using 'incorrect' grammar.

Unfortunately the concepts of 'grammatical' and 'grammaticality' are far from straightforward and many linguists prefer to use the terms 'acceptable' and 'acceptability'. These two terms highlight the fact that grammaticality is partly a social phenomenon. Very young children learning to speak English (or any language) do so in limited social contexts and acquire the morphological, morpho-syntactic and syntactic patterns of the speakers they are in frequent contact with. (The speakers may be adults or older children.) In the UK, children in social groups speaking non-standard English (the majority of the population, speaking different varieties) acquire different patterns from those acquired by children surrounded by speakers of standard English. What is grammatical for children in Chelmsford, say, is what their surrounding adults accept as grammatical, and similarly for children in other localities.

Children who have stories read to them are exposed to a different range of patterns (and vocabulary), and this exposure becomes more intense as the children move on to reading for themselves. These patterns are what people usually have in mind when they use words such as 'grammatical': following the patterns to be found in formal written English, particularly in texts that are carefully edited by the copy-editors working for publishers. This kind of grammaticality is also social, in that a particular, highly-educated, set of people determine what patterns are permitted in particular books and other publications. The set of patterns is surprisingly wide and written texts produced by highly-educated users of English show much variation in the syntactic constructions that appear. Even those whose task is to ensure what has been called verbal hygiene tend to focus on particular structures. (=> GRAMMATICALITY: DESCRIPTIVE AND PRESCRIPTIVE GRAMMAR.) The gatekeepers control only a small fraction of the material that appears in print, and exert no control over the patterns that appear in digital written texts, particularly in the social media, self-publications and a host of websites.

That grammaticality has a social basis does not mean that there are no objective linguistic correlations. There is a central core of structures that can be described as 'correct': in noun phrases, determiners such as *the* and *a* precede the head noun and relative clauses follow it; *all* and *both* precede *these* and *those*; the sequence of words in the verb group is Modal verb + Perfect Auxiliary + Progressive Auxiliary + V-ing (*might have been listening*). Such basic facts are indisputable; the difficulties begin with questions such as which relative clause construction to use in a given noun phrase. (=> CONSTRUCTIONS: OVERVIEW, RELATIVE CLAUSES: INTRODUCTION.)

GRAMMATICALITY AND INTUITION

When asked whether a particular example is 'correct' or 'grammatical' most speakers of English (and of any other language used in a literate society) call on the judgements that were inculcated at school. This means that the old shibboleths about split infinitives and hanging participles demonstrate their power. Worse, examples representing constructions in regular and frequent use in speech and writing are dismissed as 'incorrect'. (=> NON-FINITE CLAUSES: INTRODUCTION, NON-FINITE CLAUSES: FREE PARTICIPLES.)

For instance, during one syntax tutorial JM had occasion to discuss relative clauses in existential-presentative examples such as *There's one dog doesn't allow any stranger into the house*. The relative clause is *doesn't allow any stranger into the house*. The clause could have *which* as a relativiser (*which doesn't allow any stranger into the house*) and *which* would be the subject of *doesn't allow*. In most relative clauses a subject relative pronoun cannot be deleted, but relative clauses in existential-presentative sentences are the exception. The construction without *which* is very widespread, occurring in standard and non-standard English and in both speech and writing. It is also of very long standing, being attested in novels such as *Tom Jones* (1746). The students in JM's tutorial all declared that the construction was incorrect and that they had never heard any such sentences. (=> RELATIVE CLAUSES: CONTACT.)

The close connection between schooling and intuitions about grammaticality is particularly vitiating with respect to work on spoken language. There are a number of constructions that are frequent and typical in unplanned speech but are excluded from formal writing. An example of a proscribed relative clause is in (1).

1 a filing cabinet <u>that you can only open one drawer at a time</u>

The relative clause is introduced by the conjunction *that* and the body of the relative clause is simply a main clause with the main verb *open* and all the modifiers of that verb: the subject *you*, the direct object *one drawer* and a time prepositional phrase *at a time*. (=> CLAUSE STRUCTURE: DEPENDENCY RELATIONS.) When KB and JM were writing a dictionary of linguistics, they wanted to use the relative clause in (1) as an example of unintegrated syntax. (=> CLAUSE STRUCTURE: INTEGRATED AND UNINTEGRATED SYNTAX.) One referee commented that the example was ungrammatical. Since a dictionary is not the place to set out an argument about grammaticality and constructions that are typical and frequent in speech, the example was dropped.

Many constructions begin life in spoken language, make their way into writing but are not immediately accepted by educated users of written English. Consider the sentence *It is unreasonable what she suggests*. The referent of *what she suggests* is the unreasonable entity. Some analysts regard *what she suggests* as the subject of *is unreasonable*, and relate the example to *What she suggests is unreasonable*. The *what* clause is treated as being moved ('extraposed') to the end of the sentence. Another analysis takes *it* as the subject of *is unreasonable* and treats the subject as pointing forward to the *what* clause. The construction occurs regularly in speech, planned or unplanned, and in formal written texts such as letters to newspapers, which offered the example *It's unfair what they're doing to the union*. However, one major grammar of English dismisses the construction as incorrect.†

Another construction that is dismissed as ungrammatical (by proponents of the latest Chomskyan models of grammar among others) is the indirect question in (2) and (3).†

2 You have to ask <u>why is it necessary to raise this very delicate and difficult subject in the fraught and febrile context of a general campaign</u>.
New Zealand Herald, 17 February 2005
3 The biggest uncertainty hanging over the economy is <u>how red will things get</u>.
[Referring to map showing areas of house-price decreases in red]
The Economist, 10–16 May 2008, p. 97 'American housing. Map of misery'

The underlined indirect questions have the word order of direct questions, as opposed to *why it is necessary*... and *how red things will get*. The latter examples begin with wh words but otherwise have the word order of main clauses. It is these examples that are declared by grammars of English to be 'correct' and the structures in (2) and (3) that are 'incorrect'. Nonetheless, the construction exemplified in (2) and (3) is very frequent in planned and unplanned speech. For present purposes the important property of (2) and (3) is that they are *written* examples. (*The Economist*'s journalists are particularly conservative and meticulous in composing text that appears in print. That makes it difficult to class (3) as ungrammatical.) (=> COMPLEMENT CLAUSES: EMBEDDED INTERROGATIVES.)

Another area of grammar about which intuitions are unreliable is the use of *was sat* versus *was sitting* and *was stood* versus *was standing*. Some analysts took *was sat* and *was stood* to be Yorkshire dialect, with standard English requiring *was sitting* and *was standing*. It turned out that *be sat* and *be stood* are widespread. Analysts were unclear as to the status of the construction, some describing it as characteristic of a general non-standard or semi-standard variety of English. One dictionary of linguistics described <u>was sat</u> as 'colloquial British English' and <u>was stood</u> as 'regional British English'.†

In 1981 a handbook of usage for BBC personnel declared that *was sat there* and *was stood there* were unacceptable in any circumstances; thirty years on, the structure is widely used by, for instance, reporters on the BBC *News at Ten* (though not by the presenters, who read from autocues) and has reached newspaper writing, as shown by the examples in (4) and (5).†

  4 <u>Sat</u> between a beaming Tony Blair and Sir Bob Geldof, Ethiopia's Prime Minister, Meles Zenawi, pictured, could hardly have wished for a stronger endorsement.
  The Independent, 17 October 2007 'From West's favourite leader to gravedigger of democracy'
  5 The same could not have been said for John Fleck, <u>sat</u> alongside him on the bench.
  The Herald, Friday Sport, 23 May 2008, p. 5

(6) is from dialogue in a novel set and published in the early 1930s. The speaker is the wife of a Church of England vicar and definitely a speaker of standard English. (There is far more variation in <u>standard</u> English than the arbiters of usage imagine.)

  6 'My dear Hilary, how kind of you! Yes, indeed – I can do with all the white flowers I can get. These are beautiful and <u>what</u> a delicious scent!

Dear things! I thought of having some of our plants <u>stood</u> along there in front of Abbot Thomas, with some tall vases among them . . .'
Dorothy Sayers (1934), *The Nine Tailors*. London: Hodder and Stoughton, p. 59

There is a smallish core of constructions in English about which there is general agreement as to what is correct and what is not. As we move away from this core, more and more variation appears and the intuitions of individual speakers about grammaticality are regularly unsupported by data from very large corpora. Consider the verbs <u>rob</u> and <u>steal</u>. For many speakers the pair *rob* and *steal* are clearly distinguished: you steal valuables by taking them away illegally but you rob the owner of the valuables. A recent account of 'common errors' in English criticises the application of *rob* to the action applied to the valuables, as in this example from an undergraduate dissertation: *They'll probably end up going to jail or something or probably <u>robbing stuff</u>.*

This use of *rob* may seem new but is frequent enough to catch the attention of conservative speakers. The facts are not so straightforward, because the usage is old. In Johnson's *Dictionary* the third definition for ROB is 'to take away unlawfully'. An example is *fashion a carriage to <u>rob love from any</u>* (Shakespeare). This example highlights the ambiguity of the term 'grammatical'. For some, perhaps many, speakers, possibly younger speakers of English, *rob valuables from someone* is normal usage. It may represent a continuation of the original construction but it may be a modern development, quite independent of earlier usage. The construction *rob someone of their valuables*, may represent a usage that sprang up naturally among a particular group of speakers or a usage resulting from deliberate elaboration of the language by self-appointed arbiters of 'good' grammar. Given the frequency of *rob valuables from someone* and its long history, it is difficult to see why it should be labelled 'ungrammatical'.

GRAMMATICALITY AND POWER

The social concept of grammaticality is often bound up with struggles for linguistic, cultural and political power. The struggles take place in small and large arenas; the one we are about to discuss happened in a university setting. University X has an ethics committee, and every piece of research involving work with human subjects has to be approved. The convener of the Ethics Committee, a member of the management staff, announced that the grammar of many of the applications submitted for approval was unsatisfactory and that applications written in unsatisfactory language would be returned for revision. This is a good example of linguistic power being exercised, and of the would-be arbiter exposing gaps in their own knowledge. The first version of the Committee's regulations contained the following pieces of text.

> 1 The period data is to be kept will be commensurate to the scale of its research.

In the conventions for written English followed by JM and KB *commensurate* requires *with*.

> 2 It is expected that access to the Consent Forms <u>be restricted</u> to the researcher and/or the Principal Investigator.

The underlined part of (2) seemed peculiar, though another example aroused no misgivings (i.e., it matched KB and JM's intuitions): *It is required that Consent Forms <u>be stored</u> separately from data and kept for six years.* The peculiarity seemed to arise from the combination of *It is expected* and *be restricted*. Wondering whether their reaction was misguided, KB and JM checked a major reference grammar.† It listed the volitional verbs *command, demand, insist, order, propose, recommend, suggest*, and the volitional adjectives *adamant, keen* and *insistent*. (Note that *required* in the above example is a volitional verb.) The volitional verbs were said to require the subjunctive (*be*, not *is*). The comment on the volitional adjectives was that, expressing some command indirectly, they usually take the subjunctive in American English but *should* in British English. The grammar provided the examples in (3).

> 3 a I demand that he <u>leave</u> the meeting.
> b The editor insisted that this comment <u>be</u> taken out.
> c We proposed that the new Department <u>deal</u> only with postgraduate students.

The distinction between indirect commands and statements was highlighted by the examples in (4).

> 4 a The doctor was adamant that the person <u>leave</u> the surgery.
> b The doctor was adamant that she <u>prescribed</u> the correct medication.

A quick check on Google of 180 instances of the sequence <u>is expected</u> produced two examples with the subjunctive and 178 with <u>was</u> or <u>should</u>. That is, the syntax of (2) both failed to match KB and JM's usage and the data turned up by Google.

What is the explanation for (2)? It could be a case of hypercorrection, the writer of the document being aware of the construction Verb + *that* + Clause with subjunctive verb form. Semantics and pragmatics might have led the writer to the construction. *Expect* in its basic meaning and in many contexts is not a volitional verb: *I expect they will arrive about six*, *We expect her to take at least the silver medal.* Where the speaker is in a position of authority, *expect* can be used to signal a very indirect command: *I expect you to be here at 9 sharp* (employer to new employee). In (2) *expect* can be interpreted as part of an indirect command but, nonetheless, it does not normally combine with a clause containing a subjunctive verb. The moral of the tale is that pinning down exactly what is grammatical and what is not can be very tricky, and even highly-educated writers can go astray.

GRAMMATICALITY: DESCRIPTIVE AND PRESCRIPTIVE GRAMMAR

The distinction between descriptive and prescriptive grammar is crucial to serious linguistic work. Grammars that instruct readers in what is 'correct' and 'incorrect' grammar are prescriptive; their authors prescribe usage for their readers much as medical doctors prescribe medication for their patients. Descriptive grammars report all regularly occurring patterns and usages without attempting to characterise some as 'correct' and others as 'incorrect'. Descriptive grammars should in principle cover all and any type of spoken and written data and standard and non-standard varieties. Of course, a grammar providing the broadest possible coverage on paper would have to be in several volumes (probably many volumes) for ease of handling, and in digital form. The broadest coverage is necessary in order to understand language change. Structures that arise in spoken language, or even in non-standard language, find their way into the spoken and written standard. (=> GRAMMATICALITY: GRAMMATICALITY AND INTUITION.) Many of the clients treated by speech and language therapists are speakers of non-standard English. Therapists need to be aware that non-standard constructions are not a symptom of some cognitive deficit or difficulty with grammar. Using a structure with plural subject and singular verb, as in *The books was all ruined*, is not a symptom of a failure to grasp the concept of number (as a trainee therapist once suggested to JM).

The differences between the syntactic structures of spoken and written English and standard and non-standard English are important for schoolteachers and for many situations in which professionals such as doctors and lawyers interact with non-professionals. And the past twenty years or so have seen controversy in EAL (English as an Additional Language) circles about relaxing the standards of syntax required of learners who are not intending to train as teachers, lawyers or doctors at English-speaking universities. Large research projects have been undertaken in the search for a simpler English; answers are already available in the by now considerable body of work on informal and unplanned spoken English.

Prescriptive grammars tend to focus on a small set of shibboleths. Split infinitives such as *to boldly go* are either dismissed out of hand or held up as a pattern to avoid if possible. It counts for nothing that split infinitives are frequent and therefore a natural construction, and that they are often much more elegant than clunky unsplit infinitives. The use of *they* as in *Someone called to see you but they didn't leave their name* is proscribed, although *they* is neater than *he or she* and is a long-standing usage. Interestingly, the prescribers who worry about the use of a plural pronoun to refer to one person do not extend that worry to the use of *he* or *man* (as in *Man has developed complex mathematics*) to refer to male and female humans. A recent prescriptive grammar states that *that*, not *which*, is used in restrictive/defining relative clauses – *the book that Freya is reading, not the book that Katarina is reading*.† *Which* is used in non-restrictive/non-defining relative clauses – *I prefer James' book, which contains loads of facts about dinosaurs.* (=> RELATIVE CLAUSES: INTRODUCTION, RELATIVE CLAUSES: TH, RELATIVE CLAUSES: WH.) This proposed usage of relative clauses does not match JM's and KB's usage. It is however a usage recommended in American style guides, but many American academics produce restrictive relative clauses with either *that* or *which*. It is unfortunate that many people who worry about their control of written English or formal spoken English treat prescriptive grammars as setting out immutable rules that are somehow inherent in the language, when many of the prescriptions have as much justification as the prescriber's preference for particular foods or particular colours of shirt.

GRAMMATICALITY AND LANGUAGE CHANGE

The distinction between the terms 'grammatical' and 'acceptable' is useful when we examine language change. New patterns, or new usages of old patterns, become acceptable to speakers, though some speakers are more resistant to change than others. But the speakers who do accept a given change do so in the sense that they stop being surprised when they hear (or see) the pattern and then come to use it themselves. Over time the new pattern may even become 'grammatical' in the sense that writers use it and it comes to be recognised in reference grammars and possibly in prescriptive grammars.

One example of such change is the *hopefully* construction, as in *Hopefully the repairs will not cost too much.* It aroused great controversy in the UK in the late 1960s. JM resisted the pattern at first but now, in 2016, uses it without thinking in speech and writing. Its acceptance owes much to the parallel with examples such as *Sadly, the custom died out* and *Regrettably, the grant has come to an end.* (JM's late father-in-law resisted to the end.)

Another area affected by change is the set of verbs denoting the action of covering a surface with something or some things. There is an established alternation for verbs such as *spread, smear, spray*. *The child smeared chocolate over her face* and *The child smeared her face with chocolate, I spread jam on the bread* and *I spread the bread with jam, They sprayed weedkiller on the path* and *They sprayed the path with weedkiller*. Some verbs denote substances covering surfaces, while other verbs denote the surface that is covered: *cover* applies to the surface – *cover a wall with green paint* but not the substance that is spread – **cover green paint on a wall*. Some of these specialised verbs now occur in both constructions. KB and JM's usage is represented in *The trees scattered leaves on the lawn* (cf. *Leaves were scattered on the lawn* and *There was a scattering of leaves on the lawn*). But the following sentence occurred in a written text and suggests the construction *scatter the lawn with leaves*.

1 My fields <u>are scattered deep with</u> chestnut leaves.
Fidelma Cook, 'French leave'. *The Herald*, 17 October 2009, *The Herald Magazine*, p. 4

A general verb denoting the action affecting substances moved on to a surface is *apply*. KB and JM's usage is *apply paint to a door* but not *apply a door with paint*. But note the following example, which suggests the construction *apply soil with herbicides and pesticides*.

2 What they [= worms] dislike is wet, acidic soil which has been regularly applied with herbicides and pesticides.
Dave Allan, 'Binning mentality'. *The Herald*, 17 October 2009, *The Herald Magazine*, p. 37

Combinations such as *grant someone with funds* and *lavish the researchers with grants* are to be seen regularly. KB and JM's usage is still *grant funds to someone* and *lavish grants on the researchers*.

Often listed as mistakes are combinations such as *return back, reverse back, project out* and *reduce down*. They are considered barbaric by those who are aware of Latin etymologies, but such aware people are a small minority in the UK these days and the above combinations are very frequent. Speakers have changed their usage and the combinations allowed by the code have changed too.

A recent radio discussion of why children should read stories contained the examples *If Mum, or Dad or a babysitter or <u>whoever</u> reads the children stories, that's good* and *If they read Harry Potter or Enid Blyton <u>or whatever</u>, . . . Whatever* and *whenever* can be used as single-word responses that, depending on context, intonation and rhythm, may signal indifference but may simply be leaving a choice to the addressee. (5) sounds like a typical exchange between parent and uncooperative teenager.

   3 A: When can you come and help us with the painting?
        B: <u>Whenever.</u> (Just say what day and time suits you.)

   4 A: Will I cook potatoes or rice?
        B: <u>Whatever.</u> (I happily eat both.)

   5 A: Could you do what I ask you to once in a while?
        B: <u>Whatever.</u> (I'm not committing myself to any action.)

Whatever and *whenever* have long been unexceptional in examples such as *<u>Whatever you do</u>, don't buy that house* and *You can consult the books <u>whenever you like</u>*, and *I'll happily eat <u>whatever you're cooking</u>*. Sequences such as *Mum, or Dad or a babysitter or <u>whoever</u>* represent a new pattern, as do the responses (3)–(5). *Whatever* has changed from being just part of a semi-fixed phrase, *whatever you do*, or a determiner, *whatever books you like*; it has become a substitute for *and so on* and *etcetera*. It has also acquired the function of a response roughly equivalent to *anything you like, I don't mind*.

It has been suggested that the above uses of *whatever* do not count as a change in the grammar of English but as the exploitation of a possibility lying latent in the language before anyone thought to use it.† The uses have been invoked in support of the idea that the concept of grammaticality is unnecessary because it is impossible to set a boundary between word-sequences that will never have a use and those that currently have no use but will acquire a use at some future time. Predicting which word sequences will never acquire a use is indeed impossible but does not affect the concept of grammaticality. Given the social nature of grammaticality and what patterns are considered 'grammatical', different sets of patterns are 'grammatical' at different stages in the history of a given language. The concept of grammaticality does not rest on sand. KB and JM are aware from their experience over the past forty years that they and copy-editors share intuitions about grammaticality in written English. That is, as far as written English is concerned, KB and JM belong to a partly-real and partly-imagined community of educated users of British English.

Adjectives and adjective phrases

ADJECTIVES AND ADJECTIVE PHRASES: INTRODUCTION

An adjective phrase (AP) is one headed by an adjective, as in *interesting ideas, people eager to help, (We're) ready to leave*. APs occur in attributive position, preceding the noun in an NP, as in *the new proposal, some very attractive houses, those noisy crows*. APs also occur in predicative position, functioning as the complement of verbs such as *be, become, seem* and *appear. The children were sleepy, The sky became orange and red, The politicians seemed worried, She appeared unable to stand up.* The adjectives in APs are said to be used, or to function, attributively or predicatively.

There is a third position that can be occupied by APs, as shown in (1).

1. a Elegant and intelligent, Elizabeth had many admirers.
   b Worried about the interview, James came to ask our advice.
   c Pale and extremely thin, David could hardly walk.

Analysts who like the concept of a verbless clause can treat the underlined phrases in (1a–c) as clauses. One snag is that not only do these sequences have no verb but they have no subject either. Clauses without overt subjects are normally said to have resulted from ellipsis (=> CLAUSE STRUCTURE: VERB PHRASES.) or to have an understood subject that is controlled by a noun phrase (NP) in another clause. (=> NON-FINITE CLAUSES: INTRODUCTION.) The second snag is that clauses with understood subjects typically follow the clause containing the overt subject NP that permits the understood subject to be interpreted. In contrast, the underlined phrases in (1a–c) precede the clauses that contain the controlling subject. Analyses resting on ellipsis and/or controlling NPs turn out to be not straightforward, especially if thought of as a set of explicit procedures.

An alternative analysis is to take the underlined phrases at face value, as APs, allow them to apply to the subject NP of the following clause, and to treat them as denoting a property that is predicated of or assigned to that subject NP. Thus, in (1a) *elegant and intelligent* applies to *Elizabeth*, in (1b) *worried about the interview* applies to *James*, and in (1c) *pale and extremely thin* applies to *David*. The APs are adjuncts, being entirely optional. The term 'predicative adjunct' has been suggested; it captures the key properties of the phrases and will be adopted here.†

Whether an AP occurs in attributive or predicative position depends on the adjective that heads it. Many, possibly most, adjectives can occur in either position but some are restricted to one or the other. For example, *awake*, *ablaze* and *adrift* can be predicative but not attributive: **an awake baby*, **an ablaze house* and **three adrift yachtsmen* are not acceptable. Some adjectives are only attributive: *a major battle* but not **This battle is major*, *We were in utter despair* but not **The despair was utter*. A word of caution: forty years ago *major* could not occur predicatively but now many speakers do produce utterances such as *That decision was major*, *That battle was major*. Similarly, whereas *a key decision* and *a key component* were and are correct structures, many speakers now produce utterances such as *This decision will be key*.

In examples such as *The children were sleepy* or *The sky turned red*, *sleepy* and *red* are traditionally called subject complements. They are required by the verbs *were* and *turned* (in this meaning) and denote properties assigned to the referent of the subject NP. In other constructions, adjectives denote properties assigned to the referent of the object NP and are traditionally called object complements. Examples are in (2).

2 a We painted the walls (light) grey.
  b The committee considered his application (insultingly) frivolous.
  c The dog pushed the door open.
  d We bought this car new.

The underlined adjectives in (2) have been analysed and labelled in various ways. The simplest labels are the ones used above, subject complement and object complement. The labels 'subject predicative complement' and 'object predicative complement' are more complex but we adopt them.† The import of 'predicative', as in the term 'predicative adjunct' mentioned above, is that these adjectives denote properties that are predicated of (ascribed to) the referents of the object or subject NP. The term 'complement' is appropriate because, with particular meanings, certain verbs require them, as shown in (3a–c).

3 a I found the idea risible.
  b They consider this property suitable.
  c I take my coffee black.

I found the idea is certainly an acceptable clause but it suggests that the speaker had been searching for a statement of the idea. *They consider this property* (better: *They considered this property*) conveys the meaning of taking into consideration, which is not what (3b) means. *I take my coffee* is peculiar rather than unacceptable (compare *I take my* medicine). Now the notion of a property being predicated of some entity is associated with concepts such as propositions and the predicates of clauses, and some analysts treat the adjectives (and sequences such as *insultingly frivolous* and *light grey*) as clauses. The view taken here is that surface syntax should be taken as near as possible at face value (as in a contemporary theory of syntax called 'simple syntax' or 'natural language syntax'). The adjectives in (2) are APs functioning as object complements. In the semantic interpretation (whose details fall outside the scope of this book) they correspond to propositions. For instance, (2c) could correspond to the propositions 'The dog pushed the door' and 'The door became open' and (2d) to the propositions 'We bought this car' and 'At that time the car was new.'

ADJECTIVES AND ADJECTIVE PHRASES: ADJECTIVES AND DENOTATION

Adjectives typically denote properties belonging to the following types.

Human moods:	*sad, happy, kind, clever, jealous, funny, busy.*
Evaluations:	*splendid, ugly, slim, thin, horrible, wonderful, interesting, boring.*
Dimension:	*long, short, huge, tiny, small, big, hot, cold.*
Shape:	*round, square, oval, elliptical, pointed.*
Colour:	*red, blue, ochre, vermilion, turquoise, purple.*
Material:	*wooden, tin, cotton, woollen.*
Age:	*old, young, ancient, elderly.*
Speed:	*fast, slow.*
General properties:	*funny, hard, strong, clean, hot, beautiful.*

Another classification of adjectives splits them into those denoting inherent properties such as colour and size and those denoting non-inherent properties such as functional ones. Inherent properties apply directly to the referent of a given noun, such as *red* in *a red book* or *huge* in *a huge pumpkin*. The redness of the book and the hugeness of the pumpkin are visible to onlookers (with normal sight). Adjectives denoting inherent properties carry the same interpretation whether attributive or predicative: *the yellow tulip* is related to *The tulip is yellow* and *the large rat* is related to *The rat is large*. Adjectives denoting inherent properties fall into two further subsets: ones that are typically not context bound, such as colour adjectives, and ones that are typically relativised to contexts. For example, *a large rat* is not a *large animal*. The largeness is determined by a scale of size that applies to rats, while the largeness of any sort of animal is determined by a scale of size that applies to elephants and to shrews. A large shrew is a small animal but a large elephant is a large animal.

Adjectives denoting non-inherent properties do not apply directly to the referent of a given noun. *A poor dentist* is definitely someone whose skill at diagnosing dental problems and putting them right is not to be trusted but equally definitely is someone not in financial straits. There is no contradiction in the sentence *He weighs practically nothing at all because he's a very heavy smoker*. *An old friend* might be thirty. (Perhaps most users of this book regard that as old. KB and JM do not.)

Such adjectives typically occur only in attributive position: *the heavy smoker* is not related to *the smoker is heavy*. Often an adverbial paraphrase is possible: *She's a beautiful dancer* and *She dances beautifully*, *He's a heavy smoker* and *He smokes heavily*. Some adjectives are ambiguous between an inherent and non-inherent interpretation. *She's an elegant tennis player* may mean that the person wears elegant tennis outfits (*that elegant tennis player* and *that tennis player is elegant*) or that the person hits the ball with elegant movements (*that elegant tennis player* ≠ *that tennis player is elegant* but is equivalent to *That tennis player plays elegantly* or *That tennis player dresses elegantly*).

ADJECTIVES AND ADJECTIVE PHRASES: ADJECTIVES AND GRADABILITY

Gradability is a semantic concept to do with the possession of more or less of some particular property. The presence of the concept is typically signalled by the suffixes *-er* and *-est* or the words *more* and *most*: *a long snake, a longer snake, the longest snake, a fearsome snake, a more fearsome snake, a most fearsome snake*. In spoken English the two types of marking gradability are occasionally combined: *a more longer snake, the most longest snake*. Such examples are not acceptable in writing, and may be commented on if they occur in speech in formal situations, such as television interviews.

Gradability rests on the action of comparing two or more entities. Two entities can be presented as equal with respect to some property: *Fiona is as clever as Angus*. The goal of the comparison need not be mentioned. If Angus has been the object of discussion, *Fiona is as clever* (and *Fiona is cleverer*) is easy to interpret. Similarly, if several people have been under discussion the sentence *Fiona is the cleverest* is easily interpreted.

Sentences such as *Fiona is the cleverest student in the class* raise interesting problems for constituent structure and dependency relations. (=> CLAUSE STRUCTURE: CONSTITUENTS, CLAUSE STRUCTURE: DEPENDENCY RELATIONS.) The phrase *in the class* modifies *cleverest*. Some analysts have suggested recognising discontinuous constituents. For instance, in the sentence *The cleverest in the class is Fiona*, the head *cleverest* is immediately next to its modifying phrase *in the class*. The two underlined sequences can be transposed: *Fiona is the cleverest in the class*. Here *the cleverest in the class* is a constituent (a phrase). In *the cleverest student in the class* can we treat *the cleverest in the class* as being split into two parts by the insertion of *student*? We suggest that nothing is gained by this analysis. The important thing is to recognise that in *the cleverest student in the class* the phrase *in the class* is dependent on/modifies *cleverest* and that a head and its modifier need not be right next to each other.

The degree to which an entity possesses some property can be intensified or attenuated. Intensifying modifiers are words such as *highly* (*highly embarrassing*), *deeply* (*deeply offensive*). Attenuating words and phrases are *slightly* (*slightly cheeky*), *not really* (*He's not really impolite, just a bit unsubtle*).

ADJECTIVES AND ADJECTIVE PHRASES: ADJECTIVES AS HEADS OF NOUN PHRASES

Prima facie, certain NP structures appear to have an adjective as their head. Examples are in (1). The relevant adjectives are underlined.

1 a Her first film was not outstanding but her <u>second</u> was.
  b The party members dislike the leader but even the <u>boldest</u> hesitate to challenge him.
  c Caring for the <u>old</u> should not be impossible.
  d Targeting the <u>obese</u> is the thin end of the wedge

One way to handle all the examples is to assume that the NPs containing the underlined adjectives also contain a dummy noun. These structures are shown in (2).

2 a her second $_{NP}$[her second $_N[Ø]_N]_{NP}$
  b the boldest $_{NP}$[the boldest $_N[Ø]_N]_{NP}$
  c the old $_{NP}$[the old $_N[Ø]_N]_{NP}$

In (1a)/(2a) the dummy N is interpreted via the corresponding NP in the first clause, *her first film*. In (1b)/(2b) the dummy NP is interpreted via the NP *the party members*. *Party members* can be taken as a compound noun; that is, in both cases it is the noun in the NP in the preceding clause that controls the interpretation of the adjective. This analysis handles the fact that in its internal structure the word *boldest* has the superlative *-est* suffix and it allows (1a) and (1b) to be given the same analysis. (Another approach would be to treat both as resulting from ellipsis. *Her second* would derive from *her second film*, with *film* being ellipted and *the boldest* from *the boldest party members*, with *party members* being elided.)

How is (1c) to be treated? Ellipsis is not an attractive option because there is no preceding NP, say *the old people*, that would permit ellipsis on the basis of context. Could *old* be a noun? It couldn't, because of severe restrictions on the structure of the NP. It can only have the definite article; the combinations **caring for some old*, **caring for an old*, **caring for old*, **caring for this old* and so on are unacceptable. Also unacceptable is a plural form after numerals or *many*: **caring for many olds*. The syntactic and morpho-syntactic evidence indicates clearly that *old* in (1c) is an adjective. A solution to the problem lies in another restriction: phrases such as *the old* or *the poor* (as in *The poor are always with us*) or *the great unwashed* (as in *the army of the great unwashed*) always refer to human beings. This allows us to say that the dummy noun in (2c) has a special interpretation, always being interpreted as *people*.

There is another construction that bears on the question of adjectives and nouns. We begin with the example in (3).

3 The phonetics orals will be held next week.

Oral by itself, say in *His PhD oral was yesterday*, might be taken as an ellipsis of *oral examination*, that is, as an adjective. In (3) the form of the word is *orals*, a plural and indisputably a noun. It is an instance of conversion, a process whereby a word form belonging to one word class also becomes a member of another word class. In a dictionary *oral* has an entry as an adjective and an entry as a noun. *Oral* is different from *old* in (1c)/(2c) precisely because in (3) it is in the plural and because it occurs in combinations such as <u>this oral</u> *(will be a nightmare)* and <u>many orals</u> *(take place this week)*. Other examples of adjectives converted to nouns are given in (4)–(6), the adjectives in the (a) examples and the nouns in the (b) examples. These adjective/nouns are so common that they probably pass unnoticed by most users of English.

    4 a   an encyclopaedia of <u>ancient</u> languages
             The <u>ancients</u> developed a sophisticated mathematics.

    5 b   That's a <u>very intellectual</u> approach.
             <u>Many intellectuals</u> read detective novels.

6 c Their reaction was <u>absolutely classic</u>.
    She has <u>many classics of French literature</u> on her shelves.

The conversion of adjectives to nouns (or the use of adjectives as nouns, as it might have been put in earlier times) is not new, as shown by (7), from Charlotte Brontë's novel *Shirley*.

7 Let a woman ask me to give her <u>an edible</u> or <u>a wearable</u>... I can at least understand the demand...

Since *an edible* can only be something to eat and *a wearable* a garment to wear, no problems of interpretation are posed by this usage. Similarly, in the context of washing machines words such as *woollens* and *delicates* can only be interpreted as referring to clothes made of wool or delicate materials. In the same context *cottons* and *linens* do not denote types of cotton or linen (=> NOUNS AND NOUN PHRASES: COUNT AND MASS.) but clothes made of cotton or linen. Notices in hospitals urge staff to dispose of *sharps* in special containers. More opaque is the word *smalls*, a now-obsolete euphemism for underwear. On the outside of a packet of fancy biscuits the word *thins* in *almond-studded butter thins* can only refer to the biscuits and in (8), heard on the BBC World Service, *unfashionables* must refer to teams or players. (Words with the suffix *-able* or *-ible* lend themselves to use as (plural) nouns. An academic paper contained *inferrables* and the *Radio Times* (16–22 August 2014, p. 34) carried an article entitled 'Join the unbeatables'. It may be significant that the early examples in (7) have these suffixes.)

8 It offers a rare chance to one of <u>the unfashionables</u> to reach the final.

As this paragraph was being written, the British cyclist Sir Chris Hoy announced on a television programme that he never expected to find himself standing on a platform with *the greats*. The plural contrasts with the singular in the fixed phrase *the great and the good* and can be seen as indicating that a change is underway, a greater use of adjective-noun conversion. Another example from the domain of food is the word *crisps*, denoting, in the UK, the extremely thin slivers of potato that are cooked till they are crisp and brown; what in North America are known as *chips*. (But in the UK, at least for older speakers, *chips* denotes the small chunks of fried potato known as *French fries* in North America. A change in usage may be underway, thanks to supermarket packaging.)

Other examples are not tied to a specific context but have a highly conventional interpretation. *Heavy*, as in (9), refers to large blokes who are not averse to using physical force to persuade people to comply with some instruction or demand.

9 If you don't pay up, we'll send the heavies round.

And a *nasty* is something that makes life unpleasant in some way for a given person. A parent perusing a maths paper might say *Question 3 is a real nasty* (but not **Question 3 is a really nasty*, which would be acceptable if *nasty* were an adjective).

Past participles, a sub-type of adjective, occur in the plural too, as in *Indian handknitted's* (in a catalogue and with the 'grocer's apostrophe'). The interpretation is not a problem, as the phrase can only denote garments and the catalogue made it clear what sort of garments. Two more examples, too tempting to leave out, are Donald Rumsfeld's *known unknowns* and *unknown unknowns*.†

ADJECTIVES AND ADJECTIVE PHRASES: ADJECTIVES AS A WORD CLASS

Various criteria distinguish adjectives from other word classes, although some adjectives are good central members of the class while others are peripheral.

Criterion 1: Adjectives occur in NPs modifying the head noun. Most adjectives precede the head noun but some pronouns require the adjective to follow them (=> NOUNS AND NOUN PHRASES: INTRODUCTION, ADJECTIVES AND ADJECTIVE PHRASES: ADJECTIVE POSITIONS IN NOUN PHRASES.): *this red dress, infinite space, absolute zero, something wonderful.*
Criterion 2: Adjectives occur as the complement of copula verbs such as *be, become* and *seem*, and other verbs such as *turn. The weather is awful, They became rich, They seem friendly, He turned pale.*
Criterion 3: Adjectives can be modified by words such as *very, amazingly*, etc.: *very reluctant, amazingly skilful, exceedingly large, astonishingly clumsy.*
Criterion 4: Many adjectives have comparative and superlative grades. The grades are signalled either by means of the endings *-er* and *-est* or by means of syntactic constructions with *more* and *most. tall – taller – tallest, reluctant – more reluctant – most reluctant.*

Words such as *tall* meet all the criteria and are central (prototypical) members of the class. In contrast *utter* meets only criterion 1 – *utter darkness* but not **The darkness is utter, *very utter darkness* or **the utterest darkness* – and *asleep* meets only criterion 2 – *The children are asleep* but not **the asleep children, *very asleep children* or **the asleepest children. Utter* and *asleep* do not meet the criteria for other word classes (=>WORD

CLASSES: INTRODUCTION.) and the adjective criteria that they do meet are the major ones. They are therefore put into the class of adjectives.

Two semantic distinctions correspond to different syntactic behaviour, occurring with the progressive form of *be*, *is being* or only with the simple form, *is*. The first is between stative and dynamic, which essentially has to do with the type of situation a given adjective can be applied to. Stative situations involve no change and no use of energy or will-power: *The dog is very hairy, Celia is pretty, Our son is afraid of the dark*. Dynamic situations involve change (they can begin, stop and evolve), expenditure of energy and the exercise of volition. Verbs typically denote dynamic situations, as in *The children are playing in the garden, We drove to Brussels, She is training for the Olympic Games*. Some verbs denote stative situations, as in *James knows that they are on their way, Jennifer understands the theory*. (=> VERBS AND VERB PHRASES: SITUATION (LEXICAL) ASPECT, VERBS AND VERB PHRASES: PROGRESSIVE ASPECT.)

Adjectives are typically applied to stative situations (or to properties that appear in stative situations), as in the examples above, *hairy*, *pretty* and *afraid*. Some adjectives can be applied to both stative and dynamic situations. For example, *Jacob is helpful* denotes a permanent, stative situation, but *Jacob is being helpful again* denotes a dynamic situation. (Who knows how long he will continue in helpful mode?) Note the use of the progressive *is being helpful*. Similarly you can say *The dog is very friendly*, describing a permanent characteristic of the dog, or *Don't worry. The dog is just being friendly* (as it barks and leaps up at the person). The latter, with the progressive, denotes a dynamic situation. It is worth noting that even adjectives such as *sad*, which might seem to be completely stative, can be given a dynamic interpretation and dynamic syntax in an appropriate situation. Thus, an actor (or a child) might say *I'm being sad*, meaning they are imitating a sad person.

Another semantic distinction that has syntactic effects is between adjectives denoting permanent properties and adjectives denoting temporary properties. Examples are in (1)–(2).

1 a The team surveyed the country's <u>navigable</u> rivers.
  b The team drew up a list of the rivers <u>navigable</u> (at this time of year).

2 a The <u>visible</u> stars are very bright.
  b Our telescope increased the number of stars visible (that night).

(1a) and (2a) denote permanent situations, or situations presented as permanent. (1b) and (2b) denote situations presented as temporary.

ADJECTIVES AND ADJECTIVE PHRASES: ADJECTIVE POSITIONS IN NOUN PHRASES

In prototypical basic NPs, APs precede the head noun, as in *a warm pullover* and *reckless drivers*. Less basic NPs are affected by two complexities: some APs follow the head noun and where two or more APs precede the noun their ordering is not free.

APs (typically just one word) follow their head noun in certain fixed phrases that came into English from French when French was the language of the court and the aristocracy. Examples are *court martial, blood royal* (*She is a princess but not of the blood royal*), *heir apparent* (the person recognised as the heir to the throne), *lord lieutenant* (the person holding the place of the monarch in counties in the UK), *notary public (You need to have the document validated by a notary public*). There are other fixed phrases that have the order noun-adjective phrase but are not connected with royalty or government. Examples are *the body politic, from time immemorial, (The killer is) a devil incarnate*.

NP heads such as *someone, something, anyone, anything, nobody* and *nothing* can be modified by APs but the latter follow the pronoun, as in (1).

1 a   Did you meet <u>anyone interesting</u>?
  b   <u>Nothing good</u> will come of this!
  c   There's <u>something nasty</u> in the woodshed.
  d   <u>Someone special</u> is spending Christmas with us.

A noteworthy feature of the underlined phrases in (1a–d) is that they have non-specific reference. The speaker may know what the nasty item in the woodshed is but does not reveal the information to the addressee. When used with specific reference such phrases show the order AP + someone/something. *Buy this for the <u>special someone</u> in your life, That <u>nasty something</u> was just a hedgehog.*

The head adjective in an AP may be modified by a prepositional phrase, as in *younger <u>than me</u>, popular <u>with teenagers</u>, specific <u>to this rainforest</u>*.† Consider the examples in (2).

2 a   She married a <u>man younger than me</u>.
  b   I occasionally read <u>books popular with teenagers</u>.
  c   The team is researching the <u>fauna specific to this rainforest</u>.

The order of adjectives preceding the head noun is complicated. Much research remains to be done and attempts to state general patterns of adjective order in APs have been unsuccessful, although there are partial patterns. For instance, intensifying adjectives such as *certain* and *sheer* come in first position: *certain uncooperative firms* but not *uncooperative certain firms, a sheer silly costly proposal* but not *a silly sheer costly proposal*. Despite these difficulties, the current major reference grammar of English offers a template that allows us to set out the major points.† Consider the NPs in (3).

3 a entire huge deserted Russian coalmines
   b certain angry retired American generals
   c feeble amusing working economic theories

NPs are held to have four zones for adjectives. Not all the zones have to be filled in a given NP. Into the first zone, the precentral zone, go words such as *certain, pure, absolute, entire, feeble*. Into the second, the central zone, go typical adjectives (=> ADJECTIVES AND ADJECTIVE PHRASES: ADJECTIVES AS A WORD CLASS.) such as *small, fast, thick, peaceful*. The third, the postcentral zone, is for participles and colour adjectives such as *amazing* and *vermilion*. The fourth, the prehead zone, contains, inter alia, adjectives derived from proper nouns and denoting nationality, provenance and style. Examples are *Swedish* and *Palladian*.

The zones, especially the second, third and fourth ones, allow more than one adjective and questions of ordering arise inside a particular zone. For example, the second zone contains basic adjectives such as *cold, long, short, huge, round, large, rainy*. Such adjectives combine in preferred orders. Thus, *a huge round pond* is preferred to *a round huge pond* (the latter definitely peculiar) and *a small square garden* to *a square small garden*. Adjectives of size precede adjectives of shape. But things are not always so clear-cut; adjectives denoting size and adjectives denoting temperature can occur in either order. For instance, the sequences *short cold winter days* and *cold short winter days* are equally acceptable. Adjectives of colour precede adjectives of material: *a red cotton pullover* but not **a cotton red pullover, a blue woollen dress* but not **a woollen blue dress*. Adjectives denoting evaluations precede those denoting size or age: *wonderful tall trees* is acceptable, *tall wonderful trees* is not; *beautiful old houses* is acceptable, *old beautiful houses* is not, or at least requires a greater effort of interpretation. (=> ADJECTIVES AND ADJECTIVE PHRASES: ADJECTIVES AND DENOTATION.)

The preceding two paragraphs merely offer a brief summary of a very complex phenomenon. An important point to make is that sequences of three or four attributive adjectives in an NP are quite rare in spontaneous spoken language but not in formal writing. A humorous postcard from the early 1990s showed two women sitting at a table drinking wine and smoking. The text below the picture conveyed the words spoken by one of the women: *then he said why was I always trying to CHANGE him and I said probably because he's such an obnoxious thoughtless selfish overbearing self-righteous hypocritical arrogant loud-mouthed misogynist bastard.* The humour lay in the fact that in relaxed circumstances such as those shown in the illustration most people do not produce NPs containing more than one attributive adjective, never mind nine.

Another important point is that, even in written text, NPs containing a noun modified by one or more adjectives, a PP, a participial phrase – *the book lying under the desk* – or a relative clause are typically direct objects, oblique objects or complements. That is, in a given clause they typically occur after the main verb or the copula, as in the humorous example in the above paragraph. (The first sentence in this paragraph is not typical: the subject NP in the complement clause extends from *NPs* to *relative clause.*) They typically do not occur as grammatical subject in clause-initial position. It was demonstrated in the early 1990s that in British newspapers the complexity and positioning of NPs correlate with the intended readership. Upmarket newspapers had the largest proportion of complex NPs and the largest proportion of these as subjects. Downmarket newspapers had the smallest proportion of both, and middle-market newspapers were in between.†

ADJECTIVES AND ADJECTIVE PHRASES: REDUPLICATION

The phenomenon of reduplication is usually associated with languages other than English. It occurs in languages as far apart geographically and typologically as Classical Greek – *luō* 'I am washing' versus *le-lu-ka* 'I have washed' – and Maori – *mare* 'to cough', *mare mare* 'to cough many times'. It also occurs in English, though it is not mentioned in reference or teaching grammars. The examples in (1) were noted on the hoof in television programmes.

    1 a It's a big big fish.
          (From a fishing programme, referring to the effort needed to land the fish.)
      b There's still a long, long way to go.
      c That was a bad bad decision.

In (1a–c) the reduplication of the adjective has an augmentative function: it signals a more than average quantity of some property. The fish is huge, the distance is very great and the decision was not just wrong but terribly wrong. Anticipating the examples in (2), we can say that suitable paraphrases are *It's a really big fish, There's still a really long way to go* and *That was a really bad decision*. Consider now the examples in (2).

2 a My brother isn't rich rich (just comfortably off).
  b The car isn't expensive expensive (but it isn't cheap either).
  c The test won't be difficult difficult but you'll need to keep your wits about you.

The examples in (2a–c) are used to deny that an entity has an extreme amount of some property but also to deny that the property is at the opposite end of some scale. The brother is not exceedingly rich (no yachts on the Med or Rolls-Royces in the garage) but he does not have to worry about the cost of heating his eight-roomed house or going on holiday to a luxurious hotel. The car is not going to ruin you if you decide to buy it but it does cost a considerable sum. The test will not be so difficult that you cannot possibly pass it but you will have to pay great attention as you work through the problems.

It is worthwhile mentioning here that adverbs also reduplicate, as in *Do you really really like me?* (That is, *are you just saying you really like me to keep me happy?*) Verbs too can reduplicate, as in (3).

3 A: Do you have anybody you like at school?
  B: Do you mean 'like like'?
  A: No, just somebody you get on with.

Adverbs and adverb phrases

ADVERBS AND ADVERB PHRASES: INTRODUCTION

We will apply the label 'adverb' prototypically to adjectives plus the suffix *-ly*, with the proviso that these forms modify verbs, adjectives or other adverbs. Thus, *easily*, *quickly*, and *efficiently* are adverbs that modify verbs, as shown in (1). *Amazingly* and *really* are adverbs that modify adjectives, as shown in (2), and other adverbs, as shown in (3). In contrast, words such as *deathly*, *friendly* and the archaic *goodly* are adjectives, as shown in (4).

1.   a She solved the crossword easily.
    b The police quickly set up roadblocks.
    c The gymnasts performed amazingly.
    d Fiona runs the company efficiently.

2.   a Your sister is amazingly clever.
    b This proposal is really idiotic.

3.   a The engine runs amazingly quietly.
    b He dealt with the matter really competently.

4.   a A deathly silence ensued.
       I miss her friendly advice.
       A goodly sum of money went missing.

Word forms such as *easily* are adverbs; their function in clauses is adverbial. The distinction in terminology is important, because other words also have an adverbial function. Noun phrases (NPs) such as *last month* and *next week* are not adverbs but have an adverbial function, as in *We met last month* and *The manager is retiring next week*. Similarly, prepositional phrases (PPs) such as *in Norwich*, *after the storm*, *with enthusiasm* and *out of kindness* modify verbs, have an adverbial function but are not adverbs: *She works in Norwich*, *The engineers repaired the damage after*

<u>*the storm*</u>, *I accepted the offer <u>with enthusiasm</u>, They helped <u>out of kindness</u>*. NPs and PPs like the above can be called adverbials. That is, the term 'adverbial' applies to a function in clauses and also to types of constituent. The *-ly* words have an adverbial function but constitute the word class of adverbs.

The *-ly* adverbs and the other types of phrase that have an adverbial function – in traditional terminology, adverbs of manner, time, place and reason – are all optional constituents in clauses. Directional PPs denoting goals, such as *to the square* as in *The demonstrators proceeded to the square*, may be obligatory, as with *proceeded*, and particular verbs allow or exclude them. Various types of finite and non-finite clause have an adverbial function, most obviously the various adverbial clauses. (=> ADVERBIAL CLAUSES: INTRODUCTION.)

It is worthwhile mentioning that we need to refine the traditional view that adverbs modify verbs. There is a grain of truth in the traditional view with respect to which types of adverb are permitted in a given clause. Adverbs of manner such as *easily* in (1a) and *efficiently* in (1d) are licensed by verbs, or at least by clauses containing main verbs as their head. Such adverbs are not licensed by clauses containing a copula verb and a degree adverb such as *absolutely, totally*, or *slightly. The children were absolutely impossible, He was totally charming, The chairman is slightly arrogant.*

Consider now the interpretation of (1b). What has the property of being quick? Not just the action of setting up or setting up roadblocks, but the whole situation of the police setting up roadblocks. That is, from the perspective of the semantic interpretation, *quickly* applies to the whole clause (with the exception of the adverb itself). Adverbs of place, time and reason also apply to whole clauses; more accurately, the interpretation of such adverbs affects the interpretation of the whole clause. To take one of the examples above, in *The engineers repaired the damage after the storm*, the interpretation of *after the storm* relates not just to *repaired* or *repaired the damage* but *The engineers repaired the damage*.

Note that the above comments on the interpretation of adverbs are not affected by clauses such as *Watch carefully* or *Sit quietly*. Prima facie, the adverbs *carefully* and *quietly* appear to modify the verbs *watch* and *sit*, but this is only because these are imperative clauses consisting of just the bare verb. These adverbs are to be treated as modifying the whole clause. If the clause were *Watch carefully as I mix the ingredients* or *Watch the demonstration carefully*, the adverb *carefully* would modify *Watch as I mix the ingredients* and *Watch the demonstration*.

Adverbs of another type also modify whole clauses and sentences but the scope of the modification is signalled by the position of the adverb preceding or following the clause. The traditional label for these is 'sentence adverb'; examples are *regrettably, sadly* and *frankly*, shown in (5).

 5 a Regrettably, this proposal is unworkable.
   b Sadly, she did not survive the accident.
   c Frankly, I think you're a fool.

Sentence adverbs express the speaker's or writer's attitude towards some state or event or towards their action in stating some proposition or holding some view. In (5c) *I think you're a fool* conveys a statement and *frankly* conveys the information that the speaker is stating exactly and openly what they think. In *Stupidly, I lent him some money* the adverb *stupidly* conveys the speaker's judgement on his or her action in lending the money.

Sentence adverbs typically precede or follow an entire clause or sentence; (5a–c) can be rephrased as *This proposal is unworkable, regrettably, She did not survive the accident, sadly* and *I think you're a fool, frankly*. If a sentence adverb occurs in the middle of a clause it is marked off from the clause by commas in writing – *I think, frankly, you're a fool* – and in speech by brief pauses. The label 'sentence adverb' is not entirely satisfactory for analysts who distinguish between clause and sentence. In the examples in (5) the sentence adverbs modify a single clause but they can modify combinations of clauses, as in *Regrettably, the proposal, although it is otherwise very welcome, does not specify when the regulations will be applied.*

ADVERBS AND ADVERB PHRASES: ADVERBS AND ADJECTIVES

The entry on adverbs deals with word forms consisting of a stem that can occur on its own as an adjective and the suffix *-ly*: *easy – easily, simple – simply, continual – continually, regular – regularly* and so on. In standard written English there are adverbs that are identical in form with adjectives. There is no form *fastly* derived from *fast. She drives very fast, Finish the report as fast as you can. Finely* modifies adjectives and participles, as in *a finely balanced match, a finely judged choice.* Verbs (or clauses – see the entry on adverbs) are modified by *fine: The clock is working just fine, The new curtains go fine in the dining room.*

Comparative and superlative 'adjective' forms also occur as adverbs: *Easier said than done* (fixed phrase), *The traffic went slower and slower, Who runs slowest/fastest?* While **She spoke clear* is not acceptable as standard English, *Speak clearer* and *Who speaks clearest?* are. There is variation among speakers as to what counts as acceptable standard forms: speakers who accept *The traffic went slower and slower* or *Drive slower, you're too close to the car in front* reject sentences such as *He drove very slow into the garage*. The same speakers might well utter sentences such as *Come quick, there's been an accident*, or *You'll have to walk quicker*.

Note that the above paragraphs bring out an ambiguity in terms such as 'adjective', 'noun' and so on. For example, 'adjective' applies to a particular set of forms; some such as *pretty* have no marking announcing that they are adjectives, and others such as *likeable, beautiful* or *snowy* have the suffixes *-able, -ful* and *-y* that signal 'adjective'. In this usage 'adjective' denotes a lexical class. 'Adjective' is also used syntactically, being applied to words that occur in particular positions in a phrase or clause, that is, to words that have a particular distribution. These words also have a particular function, the modification of nouns. Like 'adjective', the term 'adverb' is used lexically and syntactically. In the statement '*quickly* is an adverb', 'adverb' is used lexically. In the statement '*quick* in *Come quick* is an adverb' the term 'adverb' is used syntactically. The statement can be unpacked by saying that *quick* is in a position that can be occupied by words such as *immediately* or *promptly* and modifies the verb *come*. It is identical in form with the adjective *quick* as in *a very quick response* but is quite different in its syntax. The required treatment of *quick* and other such words in a dictionary is to have two entries, one for the adjective and one for the adverb, thus recognising that the adjective and the adverb are homophones.

One major reference grammar of English states that in non-standard or very familiar English the use of the adverb for the adjective form is widespread and gives examples such as *She pays her rent <u>regular</u>* and *They played <u>real good</u>*. (The latter sentence has two examples of adjective-adverb homophones, the adverb *good* modified by the adverb *real* and the combination *real good* modifying *played*.†) The phrase 'very familiar English' is rather vague: who are the speakers producing the very familiar English? However, the statement does allow that the usage in question is very widespread: the majority of speakers of English speak non-standard varieties and many speakers of standard English vary their usage depending on whether they are speaking or writing and on the degree of formality. From a typological perspective the usage is quite unsurprising, since English is a Germanic language and in Germanic languages adjective-adverb homophony is the norm. The usage has long been excluded from standard English prescriptive grammar but is long-standing and very resistant. Examples from Trollope are in (6), (6a) from a speaker with only a modicum of education but (6b) from Trollope himself. (7) is from a letter to a British gardening magazine in 2010.

6 a 'Well; and we can't help ourselves now. That's where it is, Mr Sowerby. Lord love you; we know what's what, we do. And so, the fact is that we are <u>uncommon low</u> as to the ready [= uncommonly short of ready money] just at present, and we must have them few hundred pounds ...'
Trollope, A. (1860–1861), *Framley Parsonage*. (Folio Society 1996, p. 332. Text based on Penguin edition, 1984)

b On the present occasion Scelestum felt that his Nemesis had overtaken him. Lame as she had been, and <u>swift</u> as he had run, she had mouthed him at last ...
Trollope, A. (1860–1861), *Framley Parsonage*. (Folio Society 1996, p. 379. Text based on Penguin edition, 1984)

7 The recent cold snap went largely unnoticed within the conservatory, as the temperature remained at an equable level. Prior to installing the Solar Shield we would have had to wear several layers of extra clothing to sit <u>comfortable</u>.

(7) and (8) raise a question of analysis. (8) is from the *New Zealand Listener*, a serious, intellectual magazine.

8 Americans are using the net to find pharmacies in countries such as Canada where they can buy their drugs much <u>cheaper</u> because of price controls.

KB and JM have the usage *to sit comfortably* and prefer *buy their drugs much more cheaply*. The question of analysis is this: are *comfortable* and *cheaper* adverbs modifying *buy* or complement adjectives? *Comfortable* could be seen as a subject complement modifying *we* and *cheaper* as an object complement modifying *drugs*. If the latter analysis is accepted, then the different usages reflect, not an adjective-adverb homophony, but different constructions, V O Object Complement and S V Subject Complement versus S V (O) Adverb. JM and KB use the last construction in preference to the first two.

ADVERBS AND ADVERB PHRASES: STRUCTURE OF ADVERB PHRASES

Adverbial phrases have as their head an adverb, defined as an adjective plus the suffix -*ly*, or an adverbial, PPs denoting place, time, manner and reason. (=> ADVERBS AND ADVERB PHRASES: INTRODUCTION.) In addition we must take into account the set of sentence adverbs such as *hopefully*. (=> ADVERBS AND ADVERB PHRASES: INTRODUCTION.) Adverbs and adverbials allow a range of premodifiers, as in (1a–d):

1 a The firm collapsed <u>very</u> suddenly; <u>a bit</u> suddenly; <u>rather</u> suddenly.
  b <u>unexpectedly</u> quickly; <u>horrifyingly</u> quickly; <u>amazingly</u> quickly; <u>remarkably</u> quickly.
  c <u>right</u> after two o'clock; <u>immediately</u> after two o'clock; <u>long</u> after two o'clock;
  d They didn't play <u>that</u> badly; We thought they would resist <u>much more</u> determinedly.

Adverbs and adverbials also take a range of complements, as in (2).

2 a The decision will be taken independently <u>of what the staff think</u>.
  b One lot of books arrived separately <u>from the other lot.</u>
  c This example can be analysed analogously <u>to the previous one</u>.

Sentence adverbs also allow premodifiers and complements. A naturally-occurring and quite complex premodifier is in (3). The sentence adverb *surprisingly* is modified by the phrase *perhaps not altogether* in which *altogether* is modified by *not* and *not* in turn is modified by *perhaps*.

3 <u>Perhaps not altogether</u> surprisingly the 993 ... quickly assumed the role among many enthusiasts of some sort of defender of the air-cooled faith ...
Chris Horton, 'Defenders of the Faith'. *911 & Porsche World*, 84. July 2009.

(4) offers an example of a sentence adverb, *sadly*, with the complement *for the whole family*.

4 <u>Sadly</u> for the whole family, he did not survive what was a risky operation.

Adverbial clauses

ADVERBIAL CLAUSES: INTRODUCTION

Adverbial clauses modify other complete clauses. This distinguishes them from relative clauses, which modify nouns, from noun complement clauses, which also modify nouns, and from verb complement clauses, which modify verbs. In their syntax adverbial clauses differ from the other types of subordinate clause in being introduced by a set of special subordinating conjunctions such as *although, though, because, before, after, as soon as.* (=> SENTENCES AND CLAUSES: SUBORDINATE CLAUSES: PREPOSITION OR COMPLEMENTISER?) With respect to the constructions allowed in adverbial clauses, we will see that some adverbial clauses are more subordinate than others and indeed that there are grounds for asking if some sequences that traditionally have been treated as subordinate clauses are in fact, if not main clauses, at least non-subordinate. (=> ADVERBIAL CLAUSES: SUBORDINATE CLAUSE OR MAIN CLAUSE?)

The underlined clauses in (1a–d) are examples of adverbial clauses modifying complete clauses.

1 a <u>When the snow fell</u>, the major roads were blocked.
  b The road will be empty <u>if we leave before seven o'clock</u>.
  c <u>Since/because you've spent all your money</u>, you won't be able to top-up your mobile.
  d <u>Although my brother is going</u>, I'm staying at home.

The label 'adverbial' suggests that adverbial clauses modify verbs, but they modify whole clauses. In (1a), *when the snow fell* denotes one situation and *the major roads were blocked* denotes another situation. The clause *when the snow fell* specifies the time at which the second situation came about. It does not just modify *were blocked* but *the major roads were blocked*.

ADVERBIAL CLAUSES: TIME, CONDITION, REASON, CONCESSION

Consider the examples in (1).

1 a <u>When the snow fell</u>, the major roads were blocked.
  b The road will be empty <u>if we leave before seven o'clock</u>.
  c <u>Since/because you've spent all your money</u>, you won't be able to top-up your mobile.
  d <u>Although my brother is going</u>, I'm staying at home.

In (1a), the main clause *the major roads were blocked* refers to one situation and the clause *when the snow fell* specifies the time at which that situation came about. Such adverbial clauses are called adverbial clauses of time.

In (1b) *if we leave before seven o'clock* denotes one situation, the speaker and other(s) leaving before seven. The other clause, *the road will be empty*, denotes another situation. This other situation will come about if the first situation comes about. The clause *if we leave before seven o'clock* sets out the conditions or circumstances in which the travellers will find the road empty. It is known as an adverbial clause of condition.

In (1c) the clause *Since/because you've spent all your money* describes one situation: the person spoken to has spent all their money. The second clause, *you won't be able to top-up your mobile*, denotes another situation: the person addressed is unable to buy time for their mobile phone. The first clause provides the reason for the second situation and is called an adverbial clause of reason.

(1d) is slightly trickier than the others. As before, one clause denotes one situation and the other clause denotes another situation. The speaker uses the clause *I'm staying at home* to state one situation. The speaker uses the first clause to concede a point in the discussion. The clause *although my brother is going* can be glossed 'OK, I'll concede one point: it is true that my brother is going.' Such clauses are called adverbial clauses of concession. (Analysts often just talk of time clauses, conditional clauses or conditionals, reason clauses and concessive clauses or concession clauses.)

Adverbial clauses of time can be introduced by other subordinating conjunctions: *as* (<u>As we got out of the car</u> *we noticed the ants*), *while* (<u>While Jacob was in Prague</u>, *Barnabas delivered his newspapers*), *before/after* (<u>Before/after she went to New Zealand</u>, *she sold her car*), *as soon as* (*We'll have the meal* <u>as soon as they arrive</u>), *till* (*Stay there* <u>till I come back</u>).

ADVERBIAL CLAUSES: LESS COMMON TYPES

(1)–(7) exemplify types of adverbial clause other than those of time, condition, reason and concession.

1. The buildings were put up *so that* travellers could get shelter.
   Adverbial Clause of Purpose

2. He fell so awkwardly *that* he sprained his ankle.
   Adverbial Clause of Result

3. He was such a rogue *that* nobody employed him.
   Adverbial Clause of Result

4. James is taller *than* Katarina was at the same age.
   Adverbial Clause of Comparison

5. James is as tall *as* Katarina was at the same age.
   Adverbial Clause of Comparison

6. *Even if* it rains, we'll still be able to visit the castle.
   Adverbial Clause of Concession-Condition

7. Peter is ideal for the job, except that he wants to move to Canada.
   Adverb Clause of Exception

(4) and (5) could be exceptions to the statement that adverbial clauses modify complete clauses, since the clause *than Katarina was at the same age* can be interpreted as modifying either the clause *James is taller* or the adjective *taller*, and the clause *as Katarina was at the same age* can be interpreted as modifying the clause *James is as tall* or the word *as* in *as tall*. Informal spoken English has a construction with *what*: *James is taller than what Katarina was* and *James is as tall as what Katarina was*. These examples can be analysed following the account of free relatives. (=> RELATIVE CLAUSES: FREE, RELATIVE CLAUSES: WH WORDS AS DEICTICS.) That is, *than* in *taller than* and *as* in *as tall as* can be analysed as prepositions whose complement is the pronoun noun phrase *what*. *Katarina was* can be analysed as resulting from ellipsis, say of *that tall*: *than what [Katarina was that tall]*.

ADVERBIAL CLAUSES: POSITION IN CLAUSES AND SENTENCES

Adverbial clauses of time, reason, condition, concession, concession-condition and exception can precede or follow the clause they modify. Adverbial clauses of purpose usually follow the clause they modify, while adverbial clauses of result, comparison and exception always follow the clause they modify. The position of *because* and *when* clauses turns out to have implications for the constructions that can occur inside the clauses and even for their status as adverbial clauses as opposed to main clauses. We adopt the treatment of adverbial clauses as not embedded in the clause they modify. For instance, the sentence *When we arrived, they left* has the arrangement of clauses

$_S[_{AdvCl}[\textit{When we arrived}]\ _{MCl}[\textit{they left}]]_S.$

This arrangement allows us to show that the adverbial clause of time applies to the entire main clause. This arrangement differentiates adverbial clauses (Figure 1) from (restrictive) relative clauses (Figure 2) and noun complement clauses (Figure 3), which are embedded in noun phrases (NPs), and from verb complement clauses (Figure 4), which are embedded, along with the verb they modify, in a matrix clause. (=> COMPLEMENT CLAUSES: COMPLEMENTISERS, COMPLEMENT CLAUSES: NOUN COMPLEMENT CLAUSES, RELATIVE CLAUSES: RESTRICTIVE AND NON-RESTRICTIVE.)

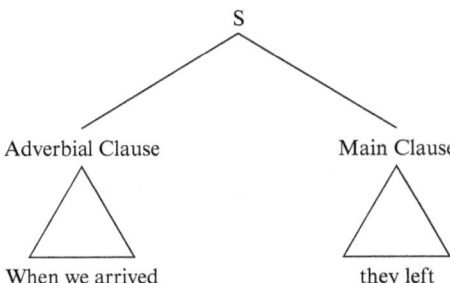

Figure 1

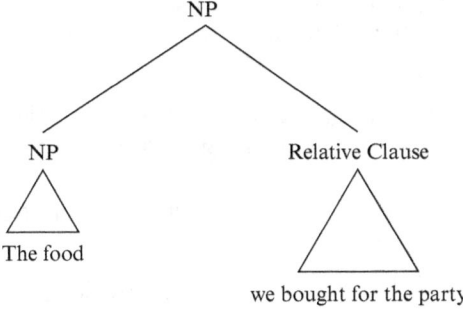

Figure 2

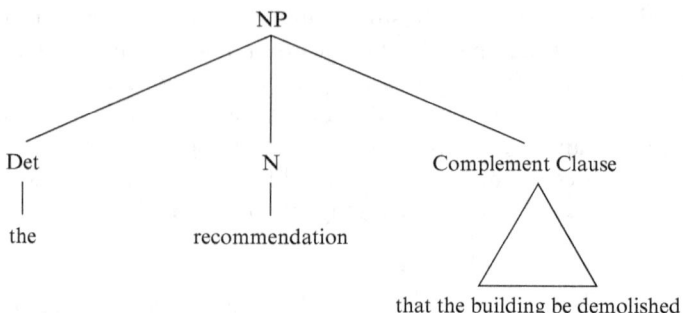

Figure 3

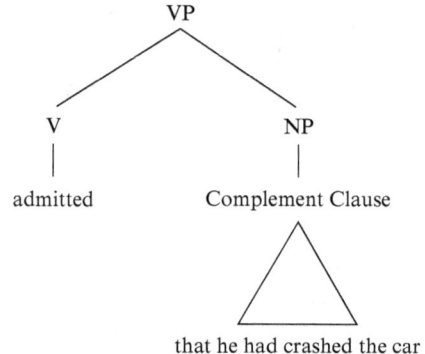

Figure 4

Typical examples of sentences consisting of a main clause and an adverbial clause have an adverbial clause followed by a main clause, as in the preceding paragraph. That main clause is declarative, but the adverbial clause could be followed by a declarative or an interrogative main clause, as shown by (1)–(3).

1 When they arrive, <u>show them into my office</u>.   [**imperative**]
2 Although they have capital to invest, <u>do they understand the business?</u>
    [**yes-no interrogative**]
3 If the chairman can't come, <u>who will address the meeting?</u>
    [**wh interrogative**]

Adverbial clauses of condition pose a particular problem: there are dependency relations between the adverbial clause and the main clause. This relationship was recognised in Classical Greek times, when special technical terms were created for the two clauses; the protasis is what is stretched out in front of the listener, i.e., the proposition expressed by the adverbial clause, and the apodosis is what is 'paid back', i.e., the proposition expressed by the main clause. The dependencies affect the verb tenses and are illustrated in (4)–(6).

    4 If they <u>agree</u>, we <u>(will) move</u> in right away.
    5 If they <u>agreed</u>, we <u>would move</u> in right away.
    6 If they <u>had agreed</u>, we <u>would have moved</u> in right away.

(4) presents the protasis as quite possible. The present tense signals that the speaker regards an event as located in (their) present time; events located in present time are close and have a high degree of probability and may even be happening as the speaker speaks. (5) presents the protasis as less probable in the speaker's estimation. Past time is further away from speaker and hearer than present time and events presented as located in past time are thereby presented as further away with respect to possibility. (6) presents the protasis as so far away in time that it cannot now happen. Using the past perfect, the speaker places the event even further away than past time, and so far away with respect to possibility that it cannot happen. The dependencies are present tense in both clauses, past tense in the adverbial clause and *would* + verb stem in the main clause, past perfect tense in the adverbial clause and *would* + *have* + past participle in the main clause.

There is a conditional construction that is typically used only in formal written English. Examples are in (7)–(9).

    7 <u>Should you require further information</u>, please contact us in writing.
    8 <u>Were the weather to break</u>, the harvest would be badly affected.
    9 <u>Had they not interfered</u>, the project would now be completed.

(7)–(9) can be described as examples of a conditional construction, since they have a protasis and an apodosis. The protases are expressed by the underlined clauses, all with the word order of yes-no interrogatives and all containing a modal verb (*should*) or a copula (*were*) or the auxiliary *have*, all in the past tense. Whether these clauses should be labelled 'conditional clauses' is a moot point, but the whole construction, embracing both clauses, can justifiably be labelled 'conditional'. The protasis clause may well have developed from a yes-no interrogative. Indirect support for this speculation comes from current usage in informal spoken English, in which speakers ask a question, thereby establishing in the discourse a condition from which another event follows. Consider (10).

    10 <u>Is the boss going to be at the party?</u> OK I'm staying at home/In that case I'm staying at home.

(10) could be uttered in two different contexts. In one the speaker has already been informed that the boss is going to the party, checks the information using the underlined question and makes a statement. In the other, the speaker asks the question, someone replies affirmatively, and the speaker then states that they will stay away.

The protasis can also be expressed by an imperative clause joined to a following main clause by *and*. (11) is an invented spoken example, (12) is a real written example.

11 <u>Allow damp to get a hold</u> and before you know it we'll have wet rot.
[= If you allow damp…]
12 <u>Factor in, say, a patchy service history</u>, …and you could be looking at rather less than £10K
[= If you factor in, say,…]
Porsche Magazine

The clause *Factor in, say,…* is hardly a conditional clause but the whole sentence does represent a conditional construction.

Other adverbial clauses can occur both in speech and writing but in informal spoken English adverbial clauses of time, reason and condition occur regularly whereas concession clauses with *although* are rare. One reason for this is the alternative way of expressing concessions with a main clause ending with *though*. Consider the contrast between (13) and (14).

13 Although he's very small, Jimmy is an outstanding footballer.
14 Jimmy's an outstanding footballer; he's very small though.

In uttering either (13) or (14) the speaker concedes the proposition 'Jimmy is very small' and asserts that, in spite of his size, Jimmy is an outstanding footballer. The two constructions have very different pragmatic effects. (13) expresses a positive judgment and can quite naturally be followed by *He must be in the team for the cup match*. (14) expresses a negative judgment; speakers who uttered (14) and followed it with *He must be in the team for the cup match* would be asked to explain themselves. If (14) were followed by *There's no way he can play against Tufftown Rovers*, the speaker would be thought quite consistent.

ADVERBIAL CLAUSES: SPOKEN ENGLISH

Investigations of informal spoken English reveal subordinating conjunctions that do not turn up in writing. Typical of spoken English, standard or non-standard, is *only* (= *except that*) as in *I'd to meet you for lunch, <u>only I'm going to be in France that week</u>*. Two of them are very widespread but not acceptable (yet) in spoken standard English: *without* as in *You can't buy that without you buy the whole set* and *on account of* in *He's not here today on account of he has a meeting in Grimsby*. More restricted are *from* (=*since*), as in *I haven't seen her from I left school* (attested in Scottish and Irish English) and *while* (= *till*) as in *You'll have to wait while she comes home* (attested in Northern English). Subordinating conjunctions can change their original meaning. For instance, the temporal subordinating conjunction *till* has acquired a purpose interpretation that is more or less strong depending on the context. *Wait there till I come back* (spoken to a child) can only have a time interpretation; *Hold the plank steady till I get the screw in* has both a temporal and a purpose interpretation (= *so that I can get the screw in*); *Put the TV on till we hear the news* has only a purpose interpretation.

ADVERBIAL CLAUSES: SUBORDINATE CLAUSE OR MAIN CLAUSE?

We turn now to a phenomenon that has been called 'insubordination', namely subordinate clauses becoming, if not full-blown main clauses, at least non-subordinate. ('Insubordination' carries the metaphor of clauses refusing to obey the rules, a metaphor that is not entirely appropriate. A blander and more obviously technical term would be 'desubordination', which does have the merit of reflecting the nature of the phenomenon, whereby clauses originally subordinate lose the properties of subordinate clauses.) We begin with adverbial clauses of reason introduced by *because*. In general, adverbial clauses preceding the clause they modify are clearly subordinate. Like relative and complement clauses, they exclude interrogatives and imperatives. (1) and (2) are unacceptable.

1 *Since/because/if do you have a driving licence, you can borrow my car
   [Since/because/if you have a driving licence, ...]

2 *If/when pay a deposit, you can take the laptop away.
   [If/when you pay a deposit, ...]

The fronting of adverbials and negatives is not allowed either, as shown by (3) and (4).

3 *When/because into the room dashed the dog, our guests screamed.
   [When the dog dashed into the room, ...]

4 *When/because/if never have I been in Glasgow, how could I have met her?
   [When/because/if I have never been in Glasgow, ...]

Because clauses can follow the clause they modify, as in (5).

> 5 Juliet was annoyed <u>because the electrician did not turn up</u>.

Such clauses are more flexible in their syntax than the ones in (1)–(4), allowing fronted adverbials and negatives, as in (6) and (7).

> 6 Juliet was annoyed because into her clean kitchen came a very muddy dog.
> 7 Juliet was annoyed because never had she seen such poor work.

(6) and (7) are indications that following *because* clauses are less subordinate than preceding ones. Particularly in speech, it is possible to find *because* clauses containing wh interrogatives, as in (8) and (9), and, but only in speech, following *because* clauses can contain tag interrogatives, as in (10).

> 8 Just take the rest of the cake – because who's going to know?
> 9 I'm not going to the party, because when's it likely to finish?
> 10 We're not inviting him – because he was nasty to Katarina, wasn't he?

The weak subordinate nature of following *because* clauses can be seen as linked with the usage exemplified by (11).

> 11 We're having a day out tomorrow because I heard the boss saying he was sending us to the Manchester office.

The *because* clause does not modify *We're having a day out tomorrow*; the speaker is not providing a reason for having a day out. Rather the speaker is giving the reason why they are able to make a confident statement about the day out: 'I know this because …'. The contrast between the strongly subordinate status of preceding *because* clauses and the weakly subordinate status of following *because* clauses has also been linked to a difference in discourse function. Preceding *because* clauses act as signposts to the upcoming text, whereas following *because* clauses convey comments on the preceding text. Comments are not so closely integrated with the preceding text, and in fact following *because* clauses can be paraphrased as 'and the reason is/was that'. The paraphrase with *and* brings out the status of following *because* clauses as ones that are being added on.

Preceding and following *when* clauses likewise differ in that preceding ones are strongly subordinate and following ones are weakly subordinate, as indicated by the latter allowing adverbial fronting, as in (12).

> 12 Freya was reading when in through the open window flew a wasp.

Note the contrast between (12) and (13).

> 13 When a wasp flew in through the open window, Freya was reading.

(13) (or at least the speaker who utters it) uses the entry of the wasp as an orientation in time: at that point in time, here is what Freya was doing. If anything (12) is the other way round: the event of Freya reading is the background for the main event, the entry of the wasp. That is, the *when* clause in (12) looks rather like a main clause and *when* functions less like subordinating conjunction and more like a connective linking two chunks of text. Constructions such as that in (14) give further support to this view. The first clause contains a simple past tense verb and the two clauses present two events, one following on from the other rather than one being the background for the other.

14 Freya opened the wardrobe door when out flew several moths.

(JM once had occasion to examine narratives written by 13- and 14-year-old school students. One student had written *She shone the light along the dark passage when suddenly she saw a rat.* The teacher corrected this to *When she shone the light along the dark passage she suddenly saw a rat.* The correction is an indication either that the teacher did not recognise the construction or thought it unacceptable in writing. Its practical effects were to destroy the flow of the narrative and the effect of the adverb fronting in the second clause: *she suddenly saw* is, in this sentence, rather bland in comparison with *suddenly she saw*.) (=> CLAUSE STRUCTURE: INTEGRATED AND UNINTEGRATED SYNTAX.)

(11)–(14) are examples of the standard conditional clause in English introduced by *if. If* clauses have other uses in English. In spoken English they are regularly used to issue instructions in institutions such as hospitals, banks, and dental surgeries. Examples are in (15)–(17).

15 If you'd just like to roll up your sleeve (I could take a blood sample).
16 If you'd just sign this box (the loan agreement will be complete).
17 If you could open your mouth wider (I could get a better grip with the pliers).

In informal speech and writing *if* clauses can be used to express wishes, as in (18) and (19).

18 If only she would see the advantages of our proposal!
19 If only we didn't have to catch a plane at 5am!

(18) and (19) look like discourse developments from complete conditional constructions: *If only she would see the advantages of our proposal, she would change her mind*, and *If only we didn't have to catch a plane at 5am I would enjoy going off on holiday.*

Clause and text

CLAUSE AND TEXT: INTRODUCTION

Most of this book is given over to an analysis of word classes, phrase constructions, major types of clause, and clause constructions. Whether invented or taken from real texts, the examples used in the account have been kept as simple as possible: a phrase, a single clause and clauses combined into a sentence. In the sections labelled 'Clause and text' we look at how clauses are put to work in text and texts. This topic is anticipated in other sections; for instance, it is suggested that sentences can be most usefully thought of as low-level discourse units (or text units) strongly linked to written text. The labels for the fundamental different types of clause – declarative, interrogative, imperative and exclamative – reflect directly the uses to which the clauses are put: making statements, asking different sorts of questions, issuing commands, advice and suggestions, making exclamations. The point emerging from the 'clause and text' sections is that all the different clause constructions play a role in creating texts and their meanings, and that where clause syntax offers alternatives, the choice of one structure over another is not random but based on differences in meaning and textual effect.

The construction of a text is not so tightly controlled as the construction of a clause. While there is scope for different intuitions about clause syntax (given *They stopped tourists going into the tombs* and *They stopped tourists from going into the tombs* do you accept one or other, or both?), many of the structures of clause syntax are tightly controlled. *Where you did see the snake?* is definitely incorrect, as is *We advised them leaving early* (compare *advised them to leave early*). When the principles of text construction are flouted, the results may be judged peculiar rather than incorrect but the text produced may be very difficult to follow. Consider the following versions of a text adapted from a concert programme, the original in (1a) and a rearranged version in (1b).

1 a 1   As a child prodigy on the concert circuit around Europe, Mozart was almost always greeted with astonishment and admiration.
     2   That a boy of only six should play so well brought delight to members of the nobility.
     3   When an older Mozart took six months to try his fortunes in Paris, he was surprised by his understated welcome.

  b 1   When an older Mozart took six months to try his fortunes in Paris, he was surprised by his understated welcome.
     2   That a boy of only six should play so well brought delight to members of the nobility.
     3   As a child prodigy on the concert circuit around Europe, Mozart was almost always greeted with astonishment and admiration.

The problem with (1b) is that it presents later events before earlier events (though (3) would be acceptable with a pluperfect *had ... been greeted* instead of the simple past *was ... greeted*) and introduces the main character in a random fashion. To count as a text, a collection of words (written or spoken) must have the essential properties of coherence and cohesion. Cohesion is the name given to a range of options that allow addressers to signal their intention that a series of sentences or utterances is to be interpreted as a cohesive unit – a text. These options are both grammatical and lexical.

Cohesion is concerned with language internal choices for the creation of a text, with the linguistic devices that signal the organisation of a collection of words into a text. Coherence has to do with language external factors, with the content of the narrative, using 'narrative' in the broadest sense: novels, newspaper articles, academic books and papers and so on all have narratives. A given narrative deals with particular events, processes and states and the participants in them. (A 'participant' can be a person, a country, an idea, a political policy. The range is unlimited.) Events must be related in such a way that the reader or listener can construct an interpretation of the order in which things happened. The participants in the events must be introduced or reintroduced so that readers or listeners can track them through the events without suddenly being faced with a participant that they cannot place in the events or relate to the other participants. (In novels readers might puzzle over a human participant; the listeners to, say, a sermon might puzzle over a quotation whose relevance to the view being expounded has not been stated.)

Coherence is supplied by the succession of events and states; a narrative can be moved on or delayed for some background to be supplied. Novels allow authors to interweave narratives with flashbacks. New participants and circumstances are brought in to join older participants and circumstances. New topics are opened up as discussions proceed. The control of given and new information is successful insofar as it allows readers and listeners to put together a clear interpretation of a given text. Intersecting the control of given and new information is the use of focus, the highlighting of new information and the downgrading of old information, and the need from time to time to make pieces of information salient, whether they are old or new.

The presentation of events, processes and states and the progression of a narrative are achieved by the use of different tenses and aspects. (=> VERBS AND VERB PHRASES: TENSE AND ASPECT: INTRODUCTION.) The handling of old and new participants involves the use of definite and indefinite noun phrases and the contrast between lexical nouns and pronouns. The highlighting of information, the placing of some element in focus position, is marked in spoken English by major shift in pitch – the tonic stress or tonic syllable. In written English, but also in spoken English, various syntactic constructions allow constituents to be put into focus position or to be the initial element in a clause: IT cleft, WH cleft, extraposition, double object construction. (=> CLAUSE AND TEXT: CLEFTS, CLAUSE STRUCTURE: LINEARITY AND GRAMMATICAL FUNCTIONS.) The interplay of the active and passive constructions plays an important role in the downgrading of information and the contrasting of old and new information. (=> CLAUSE AND TEXT: COHESION, CLAUSE AND TEXT: FOCUS, CLAUSE AND TEXT: THEME.)

CLAUSE AND TEXT: CLEFTS

The four cleft constructions play an important role in English grammar, functioning to highlight pieces of text and the information they carry and to present pieces of information as given or new. (=> CLAUSE AND TEXT: GIVEN AND NEW.)

IT CLEFTS

Perhaps the most frequent construction is the IT cleft. IT clefts are used to present information as new and to put new information into focus (alternatively, to make it salient or to highlight it) and typically to contrast it with something else. (=> CLAUSE AND TEXT: GIVEN AND NEW, CLAUSE AND TEXT: FOCUS.) IT clefts are also used in narrative to set the time and place of an action (sometimes to introduce a participant). The information not highlighted is presupposed (taken for granted) by the speaker or writer. These properties are illustrated in (1).

> 1 All the staff were stunned when the fire broke out. It was Jennifer who activated the alarm and tackled the blaze with an extinguisher.

The IT cleft in (1) picks out one person from the set of staff members; *Jennifer* carries new information. It also conveys a contrast – Jennifer and not one of the others. Similarly, the IT cleft *It was* + *John* + *that/who cooked duck in our kitchen at Christmas* (=> CLEFTS: CLAUSES: CLEFTS.) presents *John* as new information and as contrastive, 'John and not somebody else', or 'John and not the person stated to have been the cook by a previous speaker'.

A very typical example is in (2), with *the drive* clearly new information and contrasting with *looks*. *Which* rather than *that* is unusual in IT clefts.

> 2 The Scirocco's looks have improved with age but it's the drive which will sell you the car.
> *The Herald* (Scotland), 10 October 2014, Drive section, p. 10

Another common highlighting use of IT clefts is to give salience to times and places but with no or very little contrast, and often in the opening sentence of a narrative, as in (3).

> 3 It was in 1941 that the Germans invaded the Soviet Union. The Soviet Government was taken by surprise.

(3) contains the opening sentences of a newspaper article, this use of IT clefts being typical of such texts, possibly to catch the reader's attention.

In conversation and other types of informal English (spoken and written), the *that* clause may be omitted because it would be repeating information from a previous utterance. This is exemplified in (4).

> 4 a Is he the murderer?
> b No no it's the man that owns the garage

(4) is from a discussion of a television soap. The full IT cleft could have been *it's the man that owns the garage that's the murderer* but the underlined clause is omitted because it would repeat information given in A's utterance.

The final example of an IT cleft shows that in certain conditions, here asking for confirmation of the route to be followed on a map, given information can be repeated as part of a complete cleft and can even be put in focus. See the underlined chunk in (5). The word in capitals carries a focal accent and is in focus.

5 a See the side where the cliffs are? Go along till – go straight along then down till you're about a cm above the picture of the waterfall.
   b so it's the side nearest the CLIFFS I've to go?

WH CLEFTS

As discussed in the section on thematisation (=> CLAUSE AND TEXT: THEME.), the wh clause in a WH cleft can be considered the theme of the entire cleft construction. As theme, the wh clause conveys given information and points forward to new information. Consider (6), adapted from a real text.

6 But the idea that Pytheas "discovered" Britain is doubtful; he happened on a collection of islands that had flourishing industries and trading posts. <u>What is beyond doubt</u> is that he ventured very far north indeed and wrote down what he saw.

The wh clause (underlined) in the WH cleft picks up *doubtful* from the first sentence and provides a bridge to it and also a contrast, *beyond doubt*. The free relative clause points forward to the new and focused information *he ventured very far north indeed and wrote down what he saw*. (=> RELATIVE CLAUSES: FREE.) The new information relates to an entire clause and the proposition it expresses but it can relate to just a phrase, as in (7).

7 The rain we can cope with, it's often welcomed, but <u>what we dread is the hail</u>.
   Le Chai Insider (*Laithwaite's*), Autumn 2014

(7) presents a contrast between the rain and the hail. *The rain* is in theme position in the first clause. (=> CLAUSE AND TEXT: THEME.) It is given information, as the previous sentence introduces the topic of storms, and at the beginning of the sentence, neatly balancing the hail, which is in final position in the sentence. What allows *the hail* to be put in final position is the WH cleft. The property predicated of the hail, that the writer and his colleagues dread it, is made the theme of the final clause, *what we dread*, and *the hail* is given prominence by then being put in final position where it carries a focal accent.

One use of WH clefts, illustrated in (8), is to draw a line under a stretch of discussion and point to a new topic or a new set of instructions. (In (7) the hail is a new topic, as the writer goes on to discuss the damage inflicted by hail the previous year.)

8 A1: Right. Okay em right, have you got a start point right down near the bottom of the page which is above Crest Falls?

B1: Yeah.
A2: Right. The start point's about half an inch above it?
B2: Yeah.
A3: Okay. Right, <u>what we need to do is draw a line towards the</u> poisoned stream.

(8) is adapted from an exchange between participants in an experiment requiring them to draw a route on a map with landmarks. Neither participant was able to see the other's map. The underlined WH cleft draws a line under the opening dialogue establishing that the start point is in the same place on both maps and points forward to the next stage in the task, drawing the first part of the route up towards a landmark labelled 'Poisoned Stream'.

The property of pointing forward to a new topic is regularly exploited by speakers and writers at the beginning of a text or a section of text. A lecturer might start by announcing *What we're going to look at this morning is mapmaking and politics.* This WH cleft is the classic standard construction as described in reference grammars. (=> CLEFTS: CLAUSES: CLEFTS.) In spontaneous speech a much less integrated construction is often used, consisting of a wh free relative clause followed by a complete main clause, as in (9).

9 <u>What will happen</u> – she'll be raised using two ropes.

(9) was uttered by a radio reporter discussing the raising of a ship from the seabed. He had been asked if the weather would allow the operation to take place. He replied that a weather-window was expected and that the salvage crew hoped to raise the ship in that window. He then used (9) to introduce an explanation of what would happen.

In spontaneous conversation speakers may avoid WH clefts by turning the wh free relative clause into the direct object of a verb of saying and by putting the new topic – in (10), the dense population – into a completely separate clause. An example, from real recorded conversation, is in (10). (The transcription has been 'tidied' to make the example easier to read.)

10 I tell you <u>what surprises you</u>. As I say – it's marvellous how many people lived in such a really small area

REVERSE WH CLEFTS

In WH clefts information is made the theme of a clause in the shape of a free relative and the speaker can focus on new, possibly contrasting information. This is highlighted by being signposted by the free relative clause and by being put in final position, as in (7), where *what we dread* does the signposting and *the hail* is new information. WH clefts can be reversed, that is, the free relative clause and the final noun phrase can change places; (7) becomes *the hail is what we dread*, a reverse WH cleft.

TH CLEFTS

The construction known as a TH cleft is exemplified in (11), which comes from the same sort of task-related dialogue as (8).

11 a Follow that bit up vertically – right? – till it stops.
   b Uhuh.
   c That's what I mean.

In dialogue TH clefts are used to drive home a particular point and to draw a line under a section of text. They do not point forward to upcoming new instructions or to a new topic. They enable the speaker to, for example, draw attention to some entity in one clause or combination of clauses and to make an important point about it in a separate clause, making the point prominent by means of the demonstrative. Thus, instead of saying *I'd like to buy that villa* a speaker can establish the villa in the addressee's attention by saying *You see that villa?* and following it with *That's what I'd like to buy*.

The construction is not confined to dialogue. The following examples are from written text on the BBC news website, an article about uranium.

12 These decay elements produce other forms of radiation – beta and gamma – which can penetrate the human body. As they smash into cells they can kill them – that's what causes radiation sickness.
13 ... damaged cells start to proliferate wildly – that's what causes cancer.

The writer could have written *As they smash into cells they kill them and cause radiation sickness*. This version leaves it open whether radiation sickness has other causes, but it has two other disadvantages. It reduces *cause radiation sickness* to the status of second conjoined verb phrase and third-mentioned event after *smash into cells and kill them*. (12) splits off the first two events into a separate bundle, while the TH cleft makes it clear that these events, and no others, cause radiation sickness and makes that information very salient.

The above example of TH clefts are introduced by *that*, because the demonstrative points back to earlier items in the texts that are, so to speak, receding and relatively distant from the speaker/writer. Where TH clefts point to items that are perceived as relatively close to the speaker, *this* is used. The speaker who says *Listen to the next part of the speech. This is what really bothers me*, treats the next part of the speech as relatively close, as approaching the speaker.

CLAUSE AND TEXT: COHESION

Cohesion is one property of sets of phrases and/or clauses that form cohesive units or texts. Cohesion is produced by various linguistic devices, both syntactic and lexical, though here we focus on the syntactic.

COHESION: ORIENTATION

A range of devices allow readers or listeners to locate events in place and time, to identify the participants, and to relate one sentence/utterance to another.

COHESION: ORIENTATION IN PLACE

Directional complements, such as *travelled to Armenia* and *returned from New York*, and location adjuncts, such as *worked in her library, stayed dry under his enormous umbrella*, are primary devices promoting orientation in place. They are supported by deictics such as *here* and *there*.

COHESION: ORIENTATION IN TIME

Orientation in time is signalled by prepositional phrases such as *before Tuesday, for three months* and *in April*, and by noun phrases such as *all year, this week* and *that particular Wednesday*. These phrases are adjuncts with an adverbial function. (=> ADVERBS AND ADVERB PHRASES: INTRODUCTION.) The ordering of events and states is signalled by various adjectives and adverbs. An earlier location in time is expressed by adjectives such as *former, preceding, previous* and by adverbs such as *already, first*. Simultaneity is expressed by adverbs such as *meanwhile, now, simultaneously*. A later location in time is expressed by adjectives such as *ensuing, later*, and *next*, by adverbs such as *afterwards, then* and *next* and by prepositional phrases such as *after the tsunami, since last week*.

COHESION: ORIENTATION IN TIME: TENSE AND ASPECT

Tense and aspect are central grammatical categories and play a central role in the temporal orienting of events, processes and states. *The striker scored a magnificent goal* presents the event as happening before the time of speech. *The striker scored a magnificent goal but the other team had scored three* relates two events. The striker scoring took place at some time before the event of speaking, but the event of the other team scoring took place even earlier. Similarly, two events can be presented as related in future time: *The striker will score but the other team will have already scored three goals.* (=> VERBS AND VERB PHRASES: TENSE AND ASPECT: INTRODUCTION.)

The use of the progressive allows speakers to, as it were, place one event inside another. In stating *Jacob was driving across the bridge when the storm struck*, the speaker places the event of the storm striking inside the event of Jacob driving across the bridge. In using the perfect the speaker presents someone as, metaphorically, possessing the result of an event, thereby allowing some other event to happen. The speaker who says *I've finished the report and e-mailed it* to you is letting the addressee know that they can read the report whenever they are ready. (=> VERBS AND VERB PHRASES: PROGRESSIVE ASPECT, VERBS AND VERB PHRASES: PRESENT PERFECT AND SIMPLE PAST.)

The range of tenses and aspects allows speakers to present events, processes and states in different orders and ways depending on the requirements of a given text. Thus a speaker can say *The wind was blowing hard and it was pouring with rain so we didn't go out* or *We didn't go out. The wind was blowing hard and it was pouring with rain.* A series of events can be presented in the order in which they happened, as in *The fire alarm went off. Someone banged on my door and shouted.* Alternatively, the banging may be given prominence by being mentioned first and the ringing of the fire alarm is referred to by a past perfect verb: *Someone banged on my door and shouted. The fire alarm had gone off.*

COHESION: CO-REFERENCE AND REFERENT TRACKING

To count as a text a collection of clauses and/or sentences must be about a stable set of participants, circumstances and places, with the changes of participant, etc. being clearly signalled so that the listener or reader can interpret the information being conveyed and appreciate that they are indeed dealing with a text. The continuation of a participant (human being, inanimate object, abstract entity), event, place and so on is conveyed by special words called 'proforms', which include the traditional class of pronouns. Consider the sentences in (1).

1 a The residents were very upset when they heard about the new road.
  b The residents were very upset when the council announced the new road.

In (1a) the residents continue from the main clause to the adverbial clause of time and are mentioned in the latter by means of the pronoun *they*. In (1b) the adverbial clause introduces a new participant, the council, mentioned by means of a full noun phrase. A change of participant, but not of type of participant, can be signalled by *one*, as in *We have a German car but my sister has a Japanese one*. The proform *there* applies to continuing locations, as in *We wrote to the school but nobody there was interested*. The proform *do (so)* or *so do* applies to events, as in *They said they would rebuild the house and they did* and *He worked in Paris and so did his sister*.

Participants can, and regularly do, continue from one sentence to another and proforms can reach across sentence boundaries, as in (2a–d).

2 a   The residents were very upset. They had just heard about the new road.
  b   We have a German car. However my sister has a Japanese one.
  c   We wrote to the school. To our dismay, nobody there was interested.
  d   They said they would rebuild the house. After a long delay, they did.

Continuity of participants is signalled by understood subjects, as in *Katarina promised to visit us*, where the understood subject of *visit* is *Katarina*. It is also signalled by ellipsis, as in conjoined clauses, whether active, as in *Ayala went to the ball and [Ø] danced with Jonathan*, or passive, as in *Ayala was invited to the ball and [Ø] was asked to dance by Jonathan*. (=> NON-FINITE CLAUSES: INFINITIVES.)

Certain proforms are used to point backwards and forwards in texts. Anaphoric proforms such as *the latter* and *the foregoing* point backwards, cataphoric proforms such as *the following* point forwards.

COHESION: COORDINATION AND SUBORDINATION

We simply note that coordination and subordination are central syntactic devices whose purpose is to connect individual clauses into clause-combinations, in informal speech, and sentences, especially in writing.

COHESION: ADVERBIALS AND CONJUNCTIONS

A large set of different kinds of adverbials and conjunctions are available for explicitly marking which segments of a text are connected and the type of each connection. For example, there are additives such as *furthermore, in addition*; adversatives such as *but, however, nevertheless*; causals such as *for, as a result*; and temporals such as *while, subsequently*. Texts can be structured in different ways and the type of structuring can be signalled by different sets of adverbials. For instance, progression is signalled by the adverbials used in (3), general-to-specific by those in (4).

 3 <u>First</u> prepare the chicken by chopping it into small pieces. <u>Then</u> mix with the sauce ingredients. <u>Next</u> heat the oil until smoking and <u>then</u> add the chicken. <u>Now</u> stir until cooked.
 4 Dogs react in different ways. <u>For example</u>, Rottweilers may attack without provocation, pitbull crosses are notorious and even common pets such as the Jack Russell are not reliable with children.

CLAUSE AND TEXT: COHESION – ACTIVE, PASSIVE, MIDDLE

We analyse the active, passive and middle constructions as syntactic structures but also paying attention to the semantic and pragmatic factors governing which construction is used in which situation: presenting an agent affecting a patient (active), downgrading or omitting the agent (passive), attributing control of the situation to an inanimate entity (middle). In this entry we look at how, in particular, the choice of active or passive contributes to the cohesion of a text, carrying the listener or reader from one clause or sentence to the next. The middle can also play a cohesive role, but a limited one. (=> VERBS AND VERB PHRASES: PASSIVE VOICE, VERBS AND VERB PHRASES: MIDDLE CONSTRUCTIONS.)

Consider the (invented) example in (1), spoken say by a guide.

 1 Welcome to the Ring of Brodgar. The Ring is the most northerly circle of standing stones in Britain. It was erected between 2500 and 2000 BC.

The topic of the three clauses/sentences in (1) is the Ring of Brodgar. (=> CLAUSE AND TEXT: GIVEN AND NEW, CLAUSE AND TEXT: THEME.) It is first mentioned in the first clause by means of the noun phrase *the Ring of Brodgar*. It is referred to in the second clause by the noun phrase *the Ring*, which is the grammatical subject of *is* and, as given information, theme of the clause. The Ring is referred to in the third clause by means of *it*, the Ring now being firmly established in the text and the minds of the listeners. As given information and continuing topic of this chunk of text, *it* has to be in theme position, and the passive construction allows this without disruption to the text: *was erected* ... The passive is also appropriate because the builders of the Ring are unknown, but it would be possible to have a third clause of the form *The inhabitants of this island built it between 2500 and 2000 BC*. This alternative text is acceptable but the flow from the second to the third clause/sentence is less smooth.

(2) is from *The Glass Room* by Anne Cleeves.

2 a Nina took him to a small coffee shop in a back street...
  b It was dark, like walking into a Victorian parlour at dusk.
  c The place was run by an elderly man.
  d He baked great cakes and scones...

Sentence (2a) introduces the coffee shop. (Nina is well-established in the preceding text.) The coffee shop is the topic of sentences (2b) and (2c) and, as given information and continuing from one sentence to the next, it is referred to by the subject noun phrases *it* and *the place*. *The place* can be made subject noun phrase because of the passive construction, *was run by an elderly man*. As in (1), the author could have written *An elderly man ran the place* but that would have broken the flow from sentence (2b) to sentence (2c). Sentence (2d), however, cannot be passive; *Great cakes and scones were baked by him* sounds a little absurd, with new information in theme position (cakes and scones not having previously been mentioned) and given information in final position, *him*. As it stands, sentence (2d) recognises that the topic of the text has changed from the coffee shop to the elderly man, who is referred to in sentence (2d) by *he*, grammatical subject of *baked* and theme of the clause. The choice of *he* as grammatical subject precludes a passive.

The need to have textual cohesion, and the typical organisation of given and new information and reference tracking, are so powerful that verbs not typically found in the passive construction are coerced into it. (3), with the verb *confer*, is from a newspaper article. The normal pattern is *confer something on someone*, but not *confer someone with something*. But the latter is exactly what occurs in (3).

3 Next month the trio return to their roots, Aberdeen University – the place they first met and got together as students – where they will be conferred with honorary degrees.

The topic of the text is 'the trio', and in the first clause *the trio* is the grammatical subject of *return* and the theme of the clause (and indeed the whole sentence). *They* is the theme of the relative clauses with *first met* and *got together*. 'The trio' continue as topic of the text and *they* (co-referent with *the trio*) is theme and grammatical subject of the final relative clause. But this calls for a passive, and a passive is created, *will be conferred with honorary degrees*.

(3) has a dynamic passive, describing an event, but the same textual pressure is exerted on stative passives. Consider (4), from a BBC broadcast.

4 The council thought the trees might be sold as timber, but they were found to be useless for this. They were still embedded with war-time shrapnel and bomb fragments.

The normal structures are *Bomb fragments were embedded in the trees* or *The blast embedded bomb fragments in the trees* or even *The trees had bomb fragments embedded in them.* **The trees were embedded with bomb fragments* is not (yet) acceptable but is the pattern imposed by the need for a passive structure in order to have *the trees* (or *they*) as theme, being given information.

Two final examples. A newspaper article on the Trades Union Congress in which the major topic was the general secretary Norman Willis, contained the sentence in (5), with the noun phrase *Norman Willis* as theme of the clause. The possible patterns are *delivered a snub to Norman* or *a snub was delivered to Norman*, but not *Norman was delivered a snub*. Nonetheless, the sentence in (5) is what was written and published.

5 Norman Willis, the Trades Union Congress general secretary, has been delivered a snub only days before the opening of the annual Congress.

(6) is from a gardening article in a newspaper. It is the final (relative) clause that is of interest, *which has been regularly applied with herbicides and pesticides*. The verb *apply* normally occurs in the patterns *applied herbicides to the soil* or *herbicides were applied to the soil*, but not **The soil was applied with herbicides*. The author of the article got as far as *What they dislike is wet, acidic soil* and opened a relative clause modifying *soil*. Having chosen the relativiser *which*, the abnormal passive structure follows. The author could have written *to which herbicides and pesticide have been regularly applied*, but perhaps that structure was deemed too complex for a Saturday newspaper supplement or perhaps the author was hurrying to meet the deadline.

6 A compost heap or box in an organically managed garden is a magnet for worms. What they dislike is wet, acidic soil which has been regularly applied with herbicides and pesticides.

Attentive readers and listeners will find many examples of textual pressure producing unusual passive patterns, especially with verbs of spreading (in the broadest sense) such as *be lavished with gifts, be incised with her initials, be scattered with fossils* and so on.

Like the passive, the middle construction is occasionally at the service of textual cohesion and the conventional ordering of given and new information, as in the question-answer pairs in (7)–(9).

7 a What do you think of the course?
  b It jumps as well as it walks
    [A real utterance produced by a member of the New Zealand Olympic horse-jumping team]

8 a How is the Open course? [Golf]
  b It's playing really well in spite of the wind.

9 a Are these cars popular?
   b They're selling really well at the moment.

CLAUSE AND TEXT: DISCOURSE MARKERS

What are discourse markers? Typical lists include single words such as *and, because, but, indeed, now, oh, so, then, hence, therefore, well*; phrases like *after all, as a result, by the way, I mean, in other words, to sum up* and *y'know*. Examples of some of these are in (1).

1 a <u>Now</u>, tell us what you think of the exhibition.
   b <u>Indeed</u> I agree with what you've just said.
   c I agreed with Angus. <u>Well</u>, I didn't agree so much as not disagree.

We note at this point that some analysts talk of adverbials while others use the term 'discourse particles'. Since the term 'particle' is applied to words such as <u>up</u> in *They've eaten all the food up* we use the term 'discourse marker'. (=> PREPOSITIONS AND PREPOSITIONAL PHRASES: PREPOSITIONS AND PARTICLES.)

There are some syntactic properties that distinguish discourse markers from other word classes. As shown by (2a–c), discourse markers cannot be the focus of a cleft construction.

2 a <u>Nonetheless</u> you should send her the agenda.
   b It is the agenda you should send her.
   c *It is <u>nonetheless</u> you should send her the agenda.

Discourse markers are sometimes said to be entirely optional. From the a theoretical and descriptive perspective that is true, but the speaker who fails to use discourse markers in speech is not a native speaker, and discourse markers in writing make an important contribution to the cohesion of a text. (=> CLAUSE AND TEXT: COHESION.)

Discourse markers can typically occur in various positions, though not *and* or *but*. (3a–c) show variations on (2a).

3 a You should <u>nonetheless</u> send her the agenda.
   b You should send her the agenda <u>nonetheless</u>.
   c ?You should send her <u>nonetheless</u> the agenda.

Discourse markers are multifunctional; *but*, for example, can signal that speakers are introducing a proposition, disagreeing with the listeners, rebutting arguments or establishing themselves as the current speaker in an exchange. *Indeed* emphasises the truth of a proposition and gives salience to an upcoming utterance. *Now* can signal that the speaker is about to express a contrary opinion: *Now, I think you're misinterpreting the situation*. *Then* can be used to issue a challenge: not just *What are you going to do about that?*, which can be a neutral question, but *What are you going to do about that, then?*

Discourse markers signal relationships between pieces of text (*and, but*), relationships between speakers and listeners (*then, now*), and the attitude of the speaker to some piece of text and the proposition(s) it expresses (*after all, I mean*). Some analysts emphasise that discourse markers signal the relevance of an utterance to some situation rather than some preceding piece of text. A wife observing her husband taking delivery of a large parcel of books might comment <u>*So*</u>, *you've been spending a lot of money on books* or *I see you've been spending a lot of money on books* <u>*then*</u>.

CLAUSE AND TEXT: ELLIPSIS

Ellipsis is the deletion of text that repeats material in the same or preceding sentence. The clearest examples are question–answer pairs of the sort in (1) and pairs of utterances of the sort in (2).

1 A: Who's working at the airport?
   B: John
2 A: I'm going to throw out all these books that are lying around.
   B: No, you mustn't.

The full answer in (1) would be *John's working at the airport*. The chunk *'s working at the airport* is a repetition of material in A's question and is deleted. Elliptical constructions are grammatically defective in that they lack a constituent or constituents that are normally obligatory. In B's utterance in (2) the sequence *throw out all these books that are lying around* has been ellipted leaving behind the modal verb *mustn't*. *You mustn't* is grammatically incomplete because modal verbs require a complement consisting of a main verb with object noun phrases and adverbial prepositional phrases as appropriate.

It is generally accepted that the type of ellipsis illustrated in (1), known as textual ellipsis, is governed by certain criteria.

i   The ellipted words are precisely recoverable, as in (1).
ii If the missing constituents are restored, they yield a complete clause.
iii The missing words can be restored from the preceding text.
iv The missing words are present in the text in exactly the same form.

If criteria (i)–(iv) are met, the ellipsis is known as 'strict ellipsis'. If criterion (iv) does not apply, the ellipsis is known as 'quasi-ellipsis'. (3) and (4) are examples of quasi-ellipsis.

3   A: Who's driving you to the airport?
    B: Hamish.

4   A: Have you done your homework yet?
    B: I am.

The missing material in (3) is *is driving me to the airport*, with *me* instead of *you*, and in (4) it is *doing my homework*, with *doing* instead of *done* and *my* instead of *your*. Textual ellipsis is a common way of handling constituents conveying given information. (=> CLAUSE AND TEXT: GIVEN AND NEW.) Some entities may be treated by the speaker as given because they are salient in a particular situation. Such ellipsis is known as 'situational ellipsis'. Neither criterion (iii) nor criterion (iv) applies, as shown by (5)–(7).

5   Looking for somebody?
6   Hi! Glad you could come.
7   Tastes off to me.

In the situation the listeners will instantly interpret (5) as *Are you looking for somebody*, (6) as *I'm glad you could come* and (7) as *It tastes off to me* or *The meat tastes off to me* and so on. Situational ellipsis is very common in face-to-face conversation.

CLAUSE AND TEXT: FOCUS

The concept of focus is applied in various ways but all the applications have to do with highlighting words, phrases or clauses, making them stand out from the surrounding constituents in a clause or sentence. By means of various focusing constructions speakers and writers emphasise the information carried by given constituents, contrast one piece of information with another, introduce new information (that is, information that the speaker or writer chooses to present as new) and make sure it is firmly established, reintroduce information, or shift the listener's attention to another entity or topic of conversation. Note that focusing has its converse, namely defocusing or making constituents less prominent, usually because they convey information that is treated by the speaker as given. (=> CLAUSE AND TEXT: GIVEN AND NEW.)

This textbook deals with the syntax of English but of course the central focusing device in spoken English is pitch, specifically the placement of what is called the focal accent. In a neutral sentence a non-focal or tonic accent goes on the last major lexical item. The question *What's been going on?* might elicit the answer *Michael went to the cinema with Freya yesterday*, with the tonic on Freya. The question *Who did Michael go to the cinema with yesterday?* might elicit the answer *Michael went to the cinema with FREYA* yesterday, with the focal accent on FREYA, carrying the new information. The question *Who went to the cinema with Freya yesterday?* might elicit the answer *MICHAEL went to the cinema with Freya yesterday*, with the focal accent on *MICHAEL*, carrying the new information. (In real conversation, the most likely answers to the last two questions are just *Freya* and *Michael*.)

An important point is that we are not going to describe the preceding examples with focal accent as contrastive; Michael and Freya are not overtly contrasted with other individuals, and we keep the term 'contrastive' for examples where a contrast is overt. (See the discussion of different types of focus below.) This point is relevant to the analysis of IT clefts. (=> CLAUSE AND TEXT: CLEFTS.)

Focal accents are a phenomenon of spoken language. In written language writers can either use an alternative font to represent focal accents, such as the capital letters above, or italics or underlining, or they can use syntactic constructions such as IT clefts: *It was FREYA that Michael went to the cinema with* and *It was MICHAEL who went to the cinema with Freya*. But speakers do not just rely on focal accent but also exploit word order, particles and syntactic constructions such as clefts. We first discuss various types of focus and then the focusing or highlighting devices available in the grammar of English.

Speakers and writers choose which pieces of text they want to put in focus. They can focus on single words or phrases realising arguments of the verb in a clause. Thus, the question *Did you meet the Chairman?* may be answered by *I saw his DEPUTY* or *It was his DEPUTY I saw*. The focus is on the noun phrase *his deputy*. The focus may be on a word or phrase referring to some property of an argument. *I thought your car was NEW*, with focus on the supposed property of the car as being new, may get the response *It's actually SECONDHAND* or *No, it's SECONDHAND*. (Note the discourse marker *actually*. (=> CLAUSE AND TEXT: DISCOURSE MARKERS.)) Instead of individual arguments or properties of individual arguments the focus may be on a complete sentence and the proposition it conveys. The question *What happened?* requests the addressee to describe a complete situation (to utter a statement about a complete situation): *The horse bolted, The referee awarded a penalty*.

CLAUSE AND TEXT: FOCUS: SPECIAL SYNTACTIC CONSTRUCTIONS

The classic focusing constructions, handled in all major reference grammars of English, are the clefts. (=> CLAUSE AND TEXT: CLEFTS.)

Here, in connection with the distinction between argument, predicate and sentence/proposition focus, we add only that IT clefts typically involve argument and predicate focus, whereas WH clefts can involve all three types of focus. (=> CLAUSE AND TEXT: FOCUS.) In *What happened was that Ken and Karen had a huge row* the whole underlined clause and the proposition it conveys are in focus. In *What I do like is haggis* just the underlined noun phrase and the argument it realises are in focus. The naturally occurring example in (4) focuses on a noun phrase denoting a property of a car.

> 4 At £28, 320 it's not cheap. But what it is, is a sensible choice with a surprisingly lively performance.
> *The Herald* (Scotland), 24 October 2014, Drive p. 12

Note the comma in (4) separating the initial free relative clause *what it is* from the remainder. The structure converts to a straightforward reverse WH cleft: *A sensible choice with a surprisingly lively performance is what it is.*

Two constructions typical of both standard and non-standard spoken English have the property that constituents that could be part of a straightforward clause occur first in the construction, followed by a complete clause. In (5) the constituents are adjectives (adjective phrases), and in (6)–(8) the constituents are noun phrases.

> 5 Holly had a sheet of paper in front of her. Vera could see a list of names, a neat tick by each one. <u>Organized and efficient</u>, that was Holly.
> Anne Cleeves, *The Glass Room*, p. 267

The normal main clause *Holly was organized and efficient* provides insufficient highlighting. A WH cleft, *What Holly is, is organized and efficient*, would work if there had been a discussion about Holly's characteristics, but there has not. To achieve the highlighting, the author has put the adjective phrases in their own piece of structure (and with their own intonation envelope, if the text is being read aloud). This is followed by a complete clause beginning with *that*, which points back at the adjectives, and increases the highlighting.

(6)–(9) offer examples of what we will call the NP Clause construction. The underlined NP in (6) is followed by a complete clause. This example comes from a formal speech reported in *The Herald*.

> 6 <u>The areas of industry that were being hit quite hard</u> – the one that stood out was the food industry.
> *The Herald* (Scotland), 27 October 2007

It has been suggested that the NP Clause construction is the result of poor syntactic planning: the speaker becomes tangled in a complex noun phrase, breaks off the syntax at the end of the noun phrase and begins a new construction. The sequence NP Clause is certainly convenient for speakers who lose their syntactic way, but in the vast majority of instances the NP is quite simple. In (7) there are two instances of the construction, one with *the driver* as the NP, the other with *the boy that's full time* – which is more complex. In (8) the NP is *my eldest*, which is not at all complex.

  7 <u>The driver</u> he's really friendly . . . and <u>the boy that's full time</u> he gives you a lot of laughs

  8 "My youngest daughter gets embarrassed when she sees me on television," says Stewart. "<u>My eldest</u>, she doesn't mind so much because it gives her extra street-cred at school."
The Herald (Scotland), 13 November 2007, p.17. Dr Iain Stewart being interviewed by Susan Swarbrick – 'Preparing to rock your world'.

  9 "You know, it's an amazing building. <u>The one that was never built</u>, that would have been even more amazing. It was going to be over 550 feet in height, an unbelievable sight."
Sir Terry Leahy, interview in *The Tablet* by Chris Blackhurst. 22–29 December 2007

The NP Clause construction serves two purposes in the production and organisation of text. It allows the speaker to establish a new entity, or re-establish a given entity, in the listener's attention. (=> CLAUSE AND TEXT: GIVEN AND NEW.) And it allows the speaker to contrast one entity with another: Stewart's youngest daughter is contrasted with his eldest, the cathedral (in Liverpool) that was never built is contrasted with the one that was.†

The construction is not new. (10) is from Charles Dickens' novel *Bleak House* (chapter 4), first published in 1852–1853. The speaker is not addressing Mr Jarndyce. *Mr Jarndyce* is in apposition to *Your cousin*.

  10 'Your cousin, Mr Jarndyce. I owe so much to him. Would you mind describing him to me?'

It is worthwhile mentioning another construction with the order Clause NP, as in *They're still here, the people from next door* and *It's a dangerous pastime, reviewing*. The construction is not used to establish a new entity or re-establish a given entity but to clarify the reference of the pronoun, *they* and *it*. The reference is highlighted by the noun phrase being outside the clause and having its own intonation envelope.

Such examples are regularly labelled 'right dislocation', and the construction in (6)–(10) is labelled 'left dislocation'. The labels create the impression that the 'dislocated' noun phrases move from inside the clause. It is reasonable to describe an example such as *That guy* I just loathe as involving movement. The underlined direct object is at the front of the clause and there is no extra direct object. In contrast, in (6)–(10) the underlined noun phrases are followed by complete clauses with their own subjects. It is worth noting that a pause between the NP and the clause is possible. The analysis assumed here is that the original constructions are NP Clause and Clause NP and that they are not derived by any movement of constituents. (=> CLAUSE STRUCTURE: INTEGRATED AND UNINTEGRATED SYNTAX.)

CLAUSE AND TEXT: FOCUS: WORD ORDER

English main clauses have a neutral or unmarked word order (or constituent order): SVO, Subject-Verb-Object. Any deviation from that order is marked and gives salience to whatever constituent is out of its neutral position. Consider the pairs of examples in (1) and (2).

1 a I can't stand this programme.
  b This programme I (just) can't stand.

2 a I don't support that club.
  b Support that club I don't.

(1b) and (2b) have marked word order, with the direct object *this programme* at the front of (1b) and the verb phrase *support that club* at the front of (2b). In copula clauses the complement of the copula may be fronted. Such fronting may occur in a single clause as in *We flew with X Airline. Wonderful it wasn't.* Or it may occur in two conjoined clauses to give salience to a contrast, as in (3).

3 Don't let your granny tell you: "What's for you, won't go past you." Charming she may be, but a 21st century career councillor she isn't.
  The Herald (Scotland), 24 October 2014, p. 22

CLAUSE AND TEXT: GIVEN AND NEW

A major role in the production of coherent and cohesive text (=> CLAUSE AND TEXT: INTRODUCTION, CLAUSE AND TEXT: COHESION.) belongs to the interplay between new and given information. A text opens with new information but as soon as the next chunk of text is being produced the speaker or writer has to treat that first information as given and add new information to it. (The very young repeat statements and questions and are treated indulgently, most of the time, by their adult carers. Many of the very old, especially those with failing faculties, repeat themselves but are not always treated indulgently.)

Speakers decide whether to present information as given or new. What counts as new is information that, in the speaker's judgement, the addressee does not know and cannot infer from a given situation. Suppose a tourist asks a native of a town for directions to some shop. The local might reply with (1).

> 1 Go straight down this street. You'll come to <u>a statue of a man on a horse</u>. Turn left. You'll see <u>a shop painted bright yellow</u>. That's what you're looking for.

The street in which the two are standing is treated as given. The statue and the yellow shop are treated as new. The speaker assumes that the tourist does not know them and not only refers to them by means of the underlined indefinite noun phrases but leads up to the noun phrases with *You'll come to* and *You'll see*. The noun phrases carry new information when first uttered, but once uttered the information they carry can be treated as given. The first mention of the shop is by means of a full noun phrase conveying an additional property with the reduced relative clause *painted bright yellow*. (=> NON-FINITE CLAUSES: REDUCED RELATIVES.) The second mention is by means of the demonstrative pronoun *that* (=> NOUNS AND NOUN PHRASES: PRONOUNS.), which is devoid of information about what kind of entity is pointed to.

Clauses typically convey a mixture of given and new information. In the first clause/sentence in (1) *this street* carries given information; the speaker and the addressee are both standing in the street. *Go* and *straight down* convey new information, or information that the speaker probably thinks is new to the addressee, since the latter has asked for directions. Clauses/sentences can convey only new information, especially at the beginning of texts. The typical construction used is the existential-presentative, as in (2).

> 2 a There's a nasty storm coming.
> b There's a famous cathedral in Barcelona that is still being built.

Such clauses/sentences are labelled 'thetic'. The metaphor is that the speaker uses them to place new information before the addressee; 'thetic' derives from the Classical Greek ti-the-mi ('I place'). It would be possible to use a basic declarative clause with an indefinite subject, *A nasty storm is coming*, but the existential-presentative construction is most frequently used for this purpose. The existential-presentative construction is obligatory for copula clauses describing location, as shown in (3).

3 a There's a tube of superglue in the garage.
  b There's a very old longcase clock in my mother's house.

Of course there are other ways of expressing the information. *A very old longcase clock stands in the hall in my mother's house* is perfectly grammatical but sounds very bookish, and one could say *You'll find a tube of superglue in the garage* and, humorously, *A tube of superglue lives in the garage*.

More formal types of text, such as lectures and written documents, require other ways of introducing new entities, from concrete objects to propositions: *I'm going to move on to an even better example of free indirect speech, I'm going to project another image onto the screen, Let me introduce you to one of our interpreters, This evening we are going to present our new economic Plan B*.

What do speakers typically count as given? The most obvious candidates are entities that are physically present in a given situation or entities (whether concrete or abstract) that have just been mentioned. Thus, if two people are sitting at a table on which there are laptops, notebooks and a dictionary, it is normal for one person to ask the other, e.g., *Could you pass me the dictionary?*, using the definite noun phrase *the dictionary*. One of the people may mention that they have seen a new edition of the dictionary. The other person may ask immediately or after a couple of minutes *Are you going to buy the new edition?*, using the definite noun phrase *the new edition*. If the conversation is renewed the following day, the other person may consider it necessary to reintroduce the new edition, e.g., *You mentioned a new edition yesterday. Are you going to buy it?*

An entity can be considered given if it is central in the culture shared by the participants in some exchange. (Some analysts call the participants 'interlocutors'.) Students at some universities can talk without any preliminaries of *the library*, meaning the university library. In a more restricted context, students in the final year of a particular degree progamme in a department with its own library may use *the library* to refer to the departmental one. In the UK, interlocutors can use the phrase *the Prime Minister*, confident that they will be understood as referring to the British Prime Minister. Interlocutors in Brussels would have to make the reference clear: the British Prime Minister as opposed to the Belgian/French/Dutch/Spanish Prime Minister.

An entity may be treated as given if it is reckoned to be a piece of generally-known encyclopaedic knowledge. A speaker might announce *It's very exciting, the Higgs boson*, assuming that everyone has heard of the Higgs boson. It is a reasonable assumption, but it is possible that an addressee will respond *What's the Higgs boson?*, or even *What's a Higgs boson?*

In any linguistic interaction the speaker and the hearer are at the very centre and therefore highly salient in any situation. Particularly in informal speech (domestic conversation, conversation between friends), the first and second person pronouns are omitted in both questions and statements. Invented examples are in (4).

    4 A: Find what you were looking for?
        B: Yes, got it in the kitchen.

(4A) is missing *Did you* and (4B) is missing *I*. Third person pronouns can be omitted if the third person(s) or some inanimate entity are salient, as shown by (5).

    5 a Not looking very happy. [Speaker looks or nods at person]
        b Seems very expensive. [Speaker in restaurant]

As remarked in the first paragraph above, information that is new when first mentioned is already given on its second mention. Consider the examples in (6).

    6 a The students went into the examination hall. They wrote their names on the script books and began to read the questions.
        b Freya went to the exhibition. Katarina couldn't.
        c I was ill yesterday. So was my wife.

In (6a) *the students* is replaced by *they* in the second sentence and reduced to zero in the second clause of that sentence, *[...]began to read the questions*. In (6b) *went to the exhibition* is replaced *by couldn't* [go to the exhibition], the negative *n't* adds new information – and in (6c) *ill* is replaced by *so*.

The ellipsis of constituents carrying given information can extend over various turns in a conversation. (7) is a classic excerpt from real conversation with the ellipted constituents in square brackets and underlined. The boy mentioned in A1 is a certain Richard, who has been under discussion.

    7 A1: what's he going to do, that boy, anyway?
        B1: [<u>that boy is going to</u>] play golf
        C1: [<u>that boy is going to</u>] be a professional golfer
        A2: is he [<u>going to be a professional golfer</u>]?
        B2: he would [<u>be a professional golfer</u>] if he could [<u>be a professional golfer</u>].
             I think he's applied for a scholarship

The actual transcription is in (8).

8   A1: what's he going to do, that boy, anyway?
    B1: play golf
    C1: be a professional golfer
    A2: is he?
    B2: he would if he could. I think he's applied for a scholarship

The examples in (4)–(8) prima facie contradict general statements on the lines of 'All English clauses consist of a subject, verb and object' and 'English clauses always have a subject'. The contradiction is not serious. As remarked above, the omission of subject pronouns is typical of informal speech but not of other text-types, such as formal written texts. The contradiction is actually helpful, because it draws attention to the need to establish complete clauses that can be used to account for the data that turns up in real spoken and written texts. In the case of examples (4)–(8) we can account for the data by appealing to ellipsis, the deletion of repeated, and therefore given, material.

CLAUSE AND TEXT: NON-FINITE CLAUSES

We recognise eight major non-finite constructions, not counting the sub-types of infinitives and gerunds. (=> NON-FINITE CLAUSES: EIGHT TYPES OR FOUR?) These constructions play two roles in the organisation of text: they bring together in one piece of syntax two or more events that are presented as part of a larger event, and they aid the production of dense, well-integrated text.

The two most frequent non-finite constructions, the to-infinitive and the simple ing- gerund (*I intend to visit my friends in New Zealand* and *We love sailing*) present events as closely connected – having an intention and visiting friends, loving something and sailing. The close connection is reflected in the integrated syntax: the infinitive and gerund have no subject (there is an understood subject, determined by the subject of *intend* and *love*) and no tense and they cannot contain a modal verb. (=> NON-FINITE CLAUSES: INFINITIVES, NON-FINITE CLAUSES: GERUNDS (TYPE 1).) Infinitives and gerunds function as subject or object of the verb they modify; *to visit my friends in New Zealand* is the direct object of *intend* and *sailing* is the direct object of *love*. In *To visit my friends in New Zealand is not easy*, the *to* phrase is the subject of *is*.

There is another gerund, the Type 2, as in *We heard the dog barking in the garden*. This sentence could be rephrased as two sentences: *We heard the dog. It was barking in the garden.* The two separate sentences present the hearing and the barking as separate events, and the degree of separateness can be increased by the insertion of another sentence to give, e.g., *We heard the dog. It was barking in the garden. But we didn't realise this right away. We thought it was in the house.* The speaker who uses the sequence *heard the dog barking in the garden* leaves no room for doubt.

Reduced relative clauses allow the production of complex but well-integrated noun phrases: instead of *the theory that was explained in the lecture* we have *the theory explained in the lecture*. Reduced relative clauses are not typical of informal conversations or impromptu speeches and interviews, doubtless because they require more planning than just a full relative clause introduced by *that*. They are quite common in formal written texts of all kinds, especially ones in which a lot of information has to be conveyed in a minimum of syntax. (=> NON-FINITE CLAUSES: REDUCED RELATIVES.)

Free participle clauses allow two or more events to be presented as part of a single larger event. The sentence *She opened the door of the car, jumped out and ran off into the darkness* presents three separate events that took place one after the other. *Opening the door of the car and jumping out, she ran off into the darkness* presents opening the door, jumping out and running off as a single complex but fast-moving event. Participial clauses can replace adverbial clauses or a main clause: *Knowing the area well he easily found an alternative route* is a more compact piece of text than *Because he knew the area well . . .* or *He knew the area well and so easily found an alternative route.* (=> NON-FINITE CLAUSES: FREE PARTICIPLES.)

(At the University of Auckland one of the examination papers for final-year students in Business Studies requires them to read a report (usually on the problems faced by some firm) and write a 100 word précis of the report. The course is taken by many students whose first language is Chinese. A doctoral candidate was investigating whether these students faced any linguistic problems, expecting to find that they had difficulty with complex relative clauses and various kinds of adverbial clauses. Instead she discovered that they found it difficult write a précis in 100 words or less because they did not control the necessary non-finite clause constructions.)

CLAUSE AND TEXT: SPOKEN AND WRITTEN TEXT

Like any natural language, English has many different constructions, more than forty, not taking into account the question of whether to count given sequences of words and phrases as one or more constructions. (=> RELATIVE CLAUSES: INTRODUCTION.) These are not distributed evenly over different types of written text, never mind different types of spoken and written text. Constructions such as NP Clause (*The driver, you get a good laugh with him*) and V DO Complement Clause

(*Everyone knows Helen Liddell, how hard she works*) and the discourse marker *like* are almost never found outside informal spoken language such as conversation and impromptu discussion. Other constructions are rarely found outside formal written texts: adverbial clauses of concession introduced by a complement noun phrase or adjective phrase – *Learned lawyer though she is, Skilful and intelligent though she is* – relative clauses with pied piping – *the desk, the mahogany veneer of which was badly damaged*. (=> CLAUSE STRUCTURE: INTEGRATED AND UNINTEGRATED SYNTAX, CLAUSE AND TEXT: DISCOURSE MARKERS, RELATIVE CLAUSES: WH.)

The above examples might lead readers to think that there is a clear-cut distinction between spoken and written text. This would be a mistake. There are many types of spoken text: conversation (by telephone or face-to-face), enquiries at airports, discussions with doctors and dentists, exchanges with waiters and shop assistants, sports commentaries on radio and television, lectures, formal meetings and so on. Equally there are very many types of written text, such as personal letters, diary entries, e-mails, text messages, newspaper reports and articles (and different newspapers with different styles of text), novels, poetry, academic textbooks, academic monographs, official documents and so on.

Analyses covering the whole range of spoken and written texts have failed to find a set of properties shared by all types of spoken text and excluded by all types of written text. But there is one type of spoken text that is very different from all other types, and that is face-to-face conversation. It is different in the constructions that are used, the vocabulary and the organisation of text. These properties have been observed by analysts of British English and American English (and by analysts of other languages such as French, German, Italian and Russian).

Analysts can rarely say '95% of the instances of such-and-such a construction occur only in such-and-such a text-type'. Usually the distribution is much more nuanced and affects unexpected constructions. For example, attributive adjectives (*an enormous meal*) are relatively rare in face-to-face conversation (6% of the words in one 1,000-word excerpt, 4% in another) and interviews (5.5%), and distinctly more frequent in formal written texts of all types (8% in book reviews in newspapers and official documents, and 7.6% in professional letters). Reduced relative clauses (*the books lying on the floor, the books bought by the library*) are very rare in informal conversation but more frequent in formal written text-types such as academic papers and monographs and official documents (but nowhere near the 8% for attributive adjectives). Free participle clauses are found in tiny numbers in romantic fiction, adventure fiction, academic prose and official documents, but not at all in face-to-face conversation and interviews.

Wh relative clauses are very rare in face-to-face conversation but occur in slightly greater numbers in interviews and prepared speeches. Th relative clauses are also rare; contact relative clauses are more frequent (but not numerous). Adverbial clauses in general are even rarer. The most frequent types (relatively frequent, that is) are adverbial clauses of condition and time, but, e.g., adverbial clauses of concession are missing. In academic prose and official documents all types of adverbial clause occur.

The special properties of conversational texts are not mysterious. Speakers produce speech in real time with little opportunity to revise and edit their text before it is uttered, and listeners have to process the text just as rapidly. Speakers do not just transmit information via words, phrases and clauses but exploit a number of back-up systems: pitch, amplitude, voice quality, gestures, facial expressions, eye gaze and body posture. Speakers are constrained by the limitations of short-term memory. The consequences for the text are that words, phrases and clauses are shorter, each conveying a small amount of information; there is less subordination and more coordination; syntactic chunks are less well integrated with each other. (CLAUSE STRUCTURE: INTEGRATED AND UNINTEGRATED SYNTAX.) A major difference is that spontaneous spoken language does not lend itself to analysis in terms of sentences, which can be treated as low-level units in written text. (=> SENTENCES AND CLAUSES: INTRODUCTION, SENTENCES AND CLAUSES: SYSTEM SENTENCE AND TEXT SENTENCE.)

The constructions that occur only in conversation and interviews are NP Clause (=> CLAUSE AND TEXT: FOCUS: SPECIAL SYNTACTIC CONSTRUCTIONS.), V DO Complement Clause (=> CLAUSE STRUCTURE: INTEGRATED AND UNINTEGRATED SYNTAX), relative clauses with shadow pronouns and clauses introduced by the 'discourse marker' *which* (=> RELATIVE CLAUSES: SHADOW PRONOUNS, RELATIVE CLAUSES: *WHICH* AS DISCOURSE CONNECTIVE.). These clearly contribute to the ease of production and interpretation of spoken utterances. The NP Clause structure allows the speaker to produce a noun phrase, which may be quite simple or relatively complex, and then to produce a clause with a pronoun subject but a more complex verb phrase. The listener has time to process the noun phrase and work out the referent before having to process the information about properties of the referent. Similarly, the V DO Complement Clause structure allows the noun phrase to be produced and interpreted before the properties of the referent are mentioned via the complement clause. Shadow or resumptive pronouns occur in simple relative clauses but they also allow speakers to avoid the complexities of pied-piping (=> RELATIVE CLAUSES: WH.): structures such as *the theft <u>that we knew nothing about</u>* occur regularly in spontaneous speech and appear to pose no difficulties in production, whereas structures such as *<u>the theft about which we knew nothing</u>* are very rare in spontaneous speech and appear to be too complex for easy online production. The relative clause with the shadow pronoun has the word order and structure of an ordinary main clause, whereas the other relative clause has a fronted prepositional phrase.

We close this entry with a word of caution. The above comments on whether a given construction is rare or very rare in a particular type of text are based on large-scale frequency studies over the past thirty years. These studies look at large collections of written and spoken texts but pay no attention to the individual speakers and writers. A given individual speaker may produce quite complex syntax even in very relaxed face-to-face conversation. Conversely, a given writer may produce quite simple syntax even in an official document or an academic monograph. Note that such individual cases do not contradict the evidence of the large-scale studies of text. The general patterns are clear.

CLAUSE AND TEXT: THEME

The terms 'topic' and 'theme' are used by different groups of analysts to refer to the first phrase in a clause. In a basic clause the typical topic or theme is the grammatical subject noun phrase but in non-basic clauses other phrases can occupy topic or theme position. The movement of other phrases into that position is known as topicalisation or thematisation. (The first clause in the previous sentence but one has a prepositional phrase as theme: *In a basic clause*.)

Here we put the terms 'topic' and 'theme' to different uses. Every coherent text is about something, and the technical term, and indeed the relatively everyday term, for this something is 'topic'. This is the only use to which we put the term. We talk about the topic of a book, a chapter, a paragraph, a newspaper article. Communications in speech and image have topics (television and radio programmes, items on news broadcasts and informal discussions and conversations). In written texts the topic is signalled by a special layout. Books have titles, as do the chapters inside them. Titles state the general topic and are prominent; book titles are spread across the dustjacket and are on the spine, while chapter titles are typically in large type and possibly also in bold. Topics of conversation can be introduced by phrases and clauses such as *Can we discuss whether Jennifer is to be allowed to go on holiday with her friends?*, *How do I use the maps app?*, *We need to talk about our trip to Uzbekistan.*

The topic of a text is not associated with one particular construction or one position in a clause. The three sentences in (1) offer three different constructions, different items in theme position – *There, Many species of mammal* and *This reserve* – and a change of vocabulary, *numerous* replacing *many*, *is home to* replacing *live*, which replaces *There are*. Nonetheless the three sentences have the same topic, the large range of mammals in the reserve.

1 a There are many species of mammal in this reserve.
  b Many species of mammal live in this reserve.
  c This reserve is home to numerous species of mammal.

English clauses/sentences have two relatively prominent positions – the beginning and the end. The first phrasal constituent is prominent by virtue of being in first position and being the starting point of the speaker's message. Whatever is in first position is the theme: this is often, but not necessarily, the grammatical subject NP. (=> CLAUSE AND TEXT: THEME.) The concept of theme is defined in syntactic terms – the first phrasal constituent, but the theme of a clause or sentence is important as the starting point of a message and is not chosen at random. (The final position in the clause is called end-focus.)

Speakers and writers choose the starting point of their message. The most frequent theme is the grammatical subject, whether the clause construction is active, passive or middle. (=> VERBS AND VERB PHRASES: PASSIVE VOICE, VERBS AND VERB PHRASES: MIDDLE CONSTRUCTIONS.) The themes in (2a–c) are underlined.

2 a <u>The child</u> swallowed the medicine with difficulty.
  b <u>The medicine</u> was swallowed by the child with difficulty.
  c <u>This medicine</u> absorbs very quickly. [A real example]

Also regularly occurring in theme position in clauses are phrases denoting location and time. They act as a frame for the event described by the clause and can play an important role in giving cohesion to a text. (=> CLAUSE AND TEXT: COHESION.) Examples are in (3).

3 a <u>In August 1941</u> Germany invaded the Soviet Union.
  b <u>At six o'clock in the morning</u> Cecilia Macwhirter got up.

(3a) could be the beginning of an article in a newspaper or periodical, while (3b) could be the first sentence in a novel. The underlined phrases are prominent but not in focus, although in other contexts they could be, as in (4). The focus comes from the contrast between the various time phrases, and in (4) the time phrases are also cohesive, signalling the succession of events and states.

4   <u>At the beginning of the week</u> Fred decided to have it out with his tenants. <u>On Tuesday morning</u> he began to wonder if that was a wise course of action. <u>By Wednesday evening</u> he had severe doubts. <u>On Thursday morning</u> he decided to ignore the problem.

Less typical clause themes are direct objects, as in (5), and directional phrases, as in (6). These are known as marked themes, 'marked' because they are connected with less-frequent and non-normal word orders. The most marked themes are direct objects as in (5), directional phrases as in (6a and b) and complements of copulas, as in (7b) and (8b). Passive clauses in which the *by* phrase is at the front of the clause are particularly marked: *By the Greeks were the Persians defeated.* The typical clause theme, the grammatical subject noun phrase, is said to be unmarked.

5   <u>The letters</u> she handed to the manager.

6   a   <u>Into the room</u> lolloped two retrievers.
    b   <u>To Roger</u> she bequeathed her collection of garden gnomes.

Adjective phrases that are the complements of copulas are also unusual as theme. In (7) and (8) the 'a' examples have typical, neutral order and the 'b' examples have untypical order.

7   a   <u>This book</u> is very soporific; I read it in bed at night.
    b   <u>Very soporific</u> this book is; I read it in bed at night.

8   a   <u>The lack of central heating</u> is particularly noticeable.
    b   <u>Particularly noticeable</u> is the lack of central heating.

There is usually a textual reason for untypical theme phrases. (5) is suitable for a text in which a contrast is made, as between what the secretary did with the letters and what she did with the parcel: *The janitor gave the morning post to the secretary. The letters she handed to the manager, the parcel she put in her cupboard.* (6a) is a special construction that allows a directional phrase to be clause theme and the grammatical subject to be in final position. In (6a) *the room* is given and the phrase *two retrievers* is new and prominent because it is in end-focus position. A suitable text might be the one in (9).

9   There was a bump at the door. Juliet opened it. <u>Into the room</u> lolloped two retrievers.

In (7b) the phrase <u>very soporific</u> is new information and very prominent. The construction is one that is typical of informal speech and a typical situation would be one in which the speaker holds up the book and makes the comment. The book is salient in the situation and given. (8b) is more typical of written text, such as the (fictitious) surveyor's report in (10).

> 10 The house requires serious modernisation. The electric wiring is old-fashioned and unsafe. Sinks, handbasins and baths are in poor condition. Particularly noticeable is the lack of central heating.

In the text in (9), *Into the room* connects the final sentence with the preceding text, a typical function of theme phrases.

Because theme noun phrases typically convey given information, many of them consist of pronouns. New information is typically introduced by full noun phrases, that is, by noun phrases containing at least a lexical noun, very possibly an article, and possibly other modifiers such as adjectives, prepositional phrases and relative clauses. When mentioned a second time in a text the new information has become given and is typically referred to by means of a pronoun. In informal speech a third and fourth mention may involve no overt noun phrase at all. As shown in (11) (=> CLAUSE AND TEXT: GIVEN AND NEW.) in informal speech phrases conveying given information are often ellipted.

> 11 A1: what's he going to do, that boy, anyway?
> B1: [that boy is going to] play golf
> C1: [that boy is going to] be a professional golfer
> A2: is he [going to be a professional golfer]
> B2: he would [be a professional golfer] if he could [be a professional golfer].
> I think he's applied for a scholarship

(12) is an invented example of the interplay between full and pronominal noun phrases in the expression of new and given information.

> 12 <u>Elizabeth</u> took the letters from the postman. Two letters were addressed in a handwriting that <u>she</u> did not recognise. <u>She</u> handed the bundle to **her father** and[Ø] returned to the garden. **He** went into his library and [Ø] shut the door.

The mentions of Elizabeth are underlined. The references to her father are in bold. The first mention of Elizabeth is by means of the proper noun *Elizabeth*. The second and third mentions are by means of the pronoun *she*. The fourth mention is not a mention at all, since *she* is ellipted in the clause *returned to the garden*. The first mention of her father is by means of the full noun phrase *her father*, the second one is by means of the pronoun *he* and the third one involves ellipsis before *shut the door*.

Not all second and third mentions are by means of pronouns. In (13) the first mention of the briefcase is by means of the noun phrase *the case*.

The second mention is by means of another, much longer, full noun phrase, *The battered black case with gold initials*. The reason is simply that the author is supplying more information about the case.

13 The lawyer came downstairs carrying <u>his case</u>. <u>The battered black case with gold initials</u> was looking as though it had been stuffed full of gold bars.
Val McDermid, *Crackdown*

This use of full noun phrases for second or third mentions is found in newspaper articles, where a lot of information is packed into a small space. The typical pattern is for the first mention to be a proper name and the second mention a full noun phrase, as in (14).

14 For sheer theatrical effect it is hard to beat <u>Arnaud Montebourg</u>. Tall and elegant, <u>the 50-year-old Socialist politician</u> is as shameless bossing about global companies as <u>he</u> is at charming old ladies at trestle-table picnics ... in his wineland constituency.
The Economist, 8–14 December 2014, p. 41 'Enfant terrible'

Guidebooks afford good examples of the use of theme phrases as bridges from one piece of text to the preceding piece. In guidebooks these bridging themes have the additional function of leading visitors through a building. The passage in (15) is taken from the National Trust guide to Lindisfarne Castle and the relevant phrases are underlined.

15 The Entrance Hall
<u>This room</u> takes its character from the sturdy columns and rounded arches which divide the room into three. <u>The single column on the right</u>, carrying two arches, has an octagonal capital, in contrast to the two plainer columns on the left, which support three arches ... <u>Above the fireplace</u>, a decorative map of Holy Island has a wind direction indicator as its centre.

The phrase *this room* refers back to the title (specifying the topic) of the section 'The Entrance Hall', which is where visitors begin their tour of the castle. *The single column on the right* picks out one of the sturdy columns mentioned in the first sentence. *Above the fireplace* orients the visitor by means of a very salient feature of the room.

We close this account of theme by indicating complexities that appear to be required by applying the concept to naturally-occurring texts. The concept was developed with respect to clauses such as <u>*The Duke*</u> *gave this teapot to my aunt*, <u>*My aunt*</u> *was given this teapot by the Duke*, <u>*This teapot*</u> *was given to my aunt by the Duke* and <u>*This teapot*</u> *the Duke gave to my aunt*.† The themes are easily picked out and are underlined. What about the examples in (16) and (17)?

16 a <u>Personally</u>, I'm going to avoid this airport in future.
   b <u>Strictly speaking</u>, the bearded tit is a separate species.

17 a <u>Regrettably</u>, Angus had to sell the business.
   b <u>To my surprise</u>, they all came to visit us.

Phrases such as *Personally, Strictly speaking, Regrettably* and *To my surprise* convey comments by speakers on their attitude to some event or statement or on the content of some statement. *Personally* signals that the following clause simply presents the speaker's view; *Strictly speaking* signals that some other classification is less accurate; *Regrettably* signals that Angus' selling the business is viewed negatively by the speaker; and *To my surprise* signals that the speaker was expecting something else to happen.

How should such examples be analysed with respect to textual organisation? In (16b), for instance, is *Strictly speaking* part of the clause *the bearded tit is a separate species*? If it is not, we can say that *the bearded tit* is the theme of the clause. If it is, then the definition of theme – the first phrase in a clause – forces us to say that *Strictly speaking* is the theme. On the other hand, these comments/disjuncts apply to the whole clause that follows.† Indeed they apply not just to single clauses but to whole compound sentences, as in (18), and to clauses with marked theme phrases, as in (19). (=> CLAUSE AND TEXT: THEME.)

18 <u>Regrettably</u>, they had to sell the house they had bought forty years before but their son bought it and allowed them to stay on.

19 a <u>Astonishingly</u>, rugby they don't like.
   b <u>Regrettably</u>, in the garden he planted cabbages.
   c <u>To my surprise</u>, above the fireplace hung my brother's picture.
   d <u>Understandably</u>, to Roger she left her collection of garden gnomes.

A solution to the difficulty is to recognise a special type of theme, an outer theme, the name reflecting its occurrence at the outermost edge of clauses (and indeed sentences). *Astonishingly, To my surprise, Strictly speaking* and so on can be treated as outer themes. This allows us to keep the concept of clause theme for the body of the clause: *I* in (16a), *the bearded tit* in (16b), *above the fireplace* in (19c) and so on. It also allows us to apply the concept of marked theme and to analyse the role of marked themes in creating contrast, as in (4), emphasis, as in (10) and acting as a bridge to previous text, as in (15).

Clause structure

CLAUSE STRUCTURE: INTRODUCTION

On the paper page or computer screen a written clause consists of a string of words running from left to right (in the writing system of English and other languages). In speech a clause is a string of words following one after the other. For our purposes we ignore various facts: that a written chunk of language consists of marks on paper, that a spoken chunk of language consists of vibrations of air, and that words and clauses belong to the interpretations of such sequences of marks or vibrations constructed by the users of a given language.

Strings of words can be interpreted as arranged into groups (phrases), the individual words as differing in status (heads and modifiers) and clauses as a whole as having central and less central components. Some analysts talk of heads and the phrases that modify them or modifiers; others talk of heads and the phrases that are dependent on them, or dependents. Here we use 'modifiers'. The grouping of words into phrases is dealt with in the sections on different types of phrase. (=> ADJECTIVES AND ADJECTIVE PHRASES: INTRODUCTION, ADVERBS AND ADVERB PHRASES: INTRODUCTION, NOUNS AND NOUN PHRASES: INTRODUCTION, PREPOSITIONS AND PREPOSITIONAL PHRASES: INTRODUCTION, CLAUSE STRUCTURE: VERB PHRASES.)

CLAUSE STRUCTURE: CONSTITUENTS

How can we tell when two or more words hang together to make a phrase? There are two major criteria: transposition and substitution.

TRANSPOSITION

The term 'transposition' refers to the idea of groups of words being moved around when a given example is rearranged. For instance, we can think of (1) as being rearranged to give (2).

1 <u>The extravagant promises of politicians</u> never deceive these intelligent voters.
2 These intelligent voters are never deceived by <u>the extravagant promises of politicians</u>.

(1) and (2) convey the same propositional meaning (it is represented as DECEIVE (PROMISE, VOTER), DECEIVE being the predicate and PROMISE and VOTER the arguments) but do so using different constructions. We can think of active sentences as being dismantled and put together as passive sentences; in this context, transposition essentially has to do with the same words turning up in the same order in different constructions. To form the passive sentence from the active one, the words *the + extravagant + promises + of + politicians* are moved to the end of the sentence all together. You can't leave any of them behind and you can't change the order of these words. And the words *these + intelligent + voters* are moved to the front of the sentence all together. Similarly, the examples in (3) all show transposition at work.

3 a I give no credence to <u>the extravagant promises of politicians</u>.
  b I ignored <u>the extravagant promises of politicians</u>.
  c It is <u>the extravagant promises of politicians</u> that annoy intelligent voters.
  d There are <u>the extravagant promises of politicians</u> in every election leaflet.
  e Never mind <u>the extravagant promises of politicians</u>, the local council claims to work miracles.

In all of these examples, the group of words *the extravagant promises of politicians* functions as a coherent unit – a phrase.

SUBSTITUTION

The second criterion is simply whether one word can be substituted for a group of words. In (4), *They* in (4b) is substituted for *the extravagant promises of politicians* in (4a) and *her* or *him* in (4b) is substituted for *that intelligent voter* in (4a). This is good evidence that in (4a) each of these groups of words forms a phrase.

4 a <u>The extravagant promises of politicians</u> annoyed <u>that intelligent voter</u>.
  b They annoyed <u>her</u>/<u>him</u>.

COORDINATION

A minor test for phrases is coordination. Consider (5).

5 The agency owned <u>the land</u> and <u>the rights to any minerals</u>.

The phrases coordinated by *and* are *the land* and *the rights to any minerals*. If the sentence is made passive, the entire sequence *the rights to any minerals* has to move, as in (6).

6 The land and the rights to any minerals were owned by the agency.

No part of the phrase can be left behind, as shown by the incorrect version in (7).

7 *The land and <u>the rights</u> were owned by the agency <u>to the minerals</u>.

Conjunctions such as *and, but* and *or* typically coordinate phrases of the same type, two (or more) noun phrases as in (5), two (or more) prepositional phrases as in (8). The coordinated phrases make up a single larger phrase, as shown by the movement of *the land and the rights to any minerals* in (6) and the two prepositional phrases, as in (9).

In (8), two prepositional phrases are coordinated.

8 Fiona went to the office <u>with her application form</u> but <u>without her passport</u>.
9 <u>With her application form</u> but <u>without her passport</u> Fiona went to the office.

Similarly, two adjective phrases can be coordinated, as in (10), and two adverb phrases, as in (11).

10 The countryside was <u>golden in the autumn sunshine</u> and <u>amazingly peaceful</u>.
11 Seonaidh swam <u>very quickly</u> and <u>very silently</u> out to the yacht.

(12) could be analysed as having coordinated verb phrases but the verb phrase is not a unit with much support (=> CLAUSE STRUCTURE: VERB PHRASES, CLAUSE STRUCTURE: DEPENDENCY RELATIONS.) and an alternative analysis takes (12) to be derived by ellipsis from (13). *Margaret$_2$* is deleted.

12 Margaret <u>has finished the sudoku puzzles</u> and <u>is now solving the crossword</u>.
13 Margaret$_1$ <u>has finished the sudoku puzzles</u> and Margaret$_2$ <u>is now solving the crossword</u>.

We finish this discussion of tests for constituent structure by noting that they connect with the distinction between clause and sentence. (=> SENTENCES AND CLAUSES: INTRODUCTION, SENTENCES AND CLAUSES: CLAUSES.) The tests apply most easily and productively to single clauses.

All the above examples, apart from (12) and (13), consist not just of single clauses but of single main clauses. If you go through textbooks and even advanced research papers on formal syntax you will find that this is typical. The exception, and it is a very important exception, lies in studies of complex sentences and the movement of constituents within them. The sorts of questions addressed by such studies are the unacceptability of *What Margaret has finished the sudoku puzzles and is now solving? (compare Margaret has finished the sudoku puzzles and is now solving what?) and the acceptability of She accepted the proposal that they appoint who? versus the unacceptability of *Who did she accept the proposal that they appoint? Who cannot be moved from final position in the sentence to initial position, the one normally occupied by wh pronouns in interrogatives.

The test of movement does apply to complete clauses. Adverbial clauses, for example, can occur before a main clause, as in When the train drew in he made for the platform and He made for the platform when the train drew in. Complement clauses can likewise be moved, as in The committee accepted that the building would have to be demolished and That the building would have to be demolished was accepted by the committee. Even relative clauses can be moved, as in A laptop that contained her research data was destroyed in the fire versus A laptop was destroyed in the fire that contained her research data.

The coordination test applies to clauses, as in When Gordon reports to them and if his report is adequate, they will give him a permanent post (adverbial clauses), I told her that she was being transferred and that the transfer was not a promotion (complement clauses), I've lost the book that you recommended and that you asked me to take to Kirsty (relative clauses).

The substitution test does not apply well, at least in the substitution of a single word for a whole clause. In When Gordon reports to them, they will give him a permanent post, the adverbial clause might be replaced by then, but in initial position then sounds more contrastive or placing emphasis on a sequence of events: Gordon reports and only after that is he given a permanent post. In final position, They will give him a permanent post then, then is more acceptable as a substitution for the adverbial clause, but only if the adverbial clause too is in final position. Other types of adverbial clause do not have convenient single substitute words. (=> ADVERBIAL CLAUSES: INTRODUCTION, ADVERBIAL CLAUSES: LESS COMMON TYPES.)

Complement clauses look as though they can be replaced by single words such as this, that and it. He regretted that he had rejected the offer and He regretted it or He regretted this. The difficulty is that the sentences with it and this have a different function in text from the sentence with the complement clause. Instead of being a straight substitution, the pronouns function as anaphors in text, pointing back at a previous chunk of text (on one analysis) or pointing at the same proposition as a previous chunk of text (on another analysis): *He rejected the offer. He regretted it/He regretted this.* Such questions of analysis do not arise when substitution tests are applied within a single clause.

In a noun phrase the head noun can be modified by a relative clause or a single adjective, as in *the windows that he had painted* versus *the painted windows*. The difficulty here is that we are not dealing with a straightforward substitution, since the relative clause follows the head noun but the adjective (or participle) precedes it.

To return to the general point: tests for constituency apply easily and productively within single clauses, especially single main clauses. The coordination test applies to whole clauses; the movement test applies to all types of subordinate clause, giving particularly smooth results for adverbial clauses; the substitution test either does not work or raises problems. These general problems do not affect the analyses offered in the other sections of this book but it is worth making two points. One is that there is on the market an approach to syntactic analysis, known as radical construction grammar, in which the analysis of constituent structure is carried out on individual constructions and not on a whole language.† In this approach an analysis of constituent structure for one construction does not necessarily carry over to any other construction. The second is that the problems outlined above not only support the distinction between clause and sentence but support the idea that a hierarchy of clause types (or construction types) is required. Constituent structure and dependency relations are established for the basic type (or types) and paths are constructed from the basic clause types to less basic types. Information about constituent structure and dependency relations travels along the paths, so to speak.†

CLAUSE STRUCTURE: DEPENDENCY RELATIONS

It is generally, but not universally, accepted that the head of a given clause is a verb. This analysis applies very straightforwardly to languages, such as Turkish, in which finite verbs have a complex structure, including morphemes corresponding to modal verbs in English, to the passive auxiliaries and to markers of tense and aspect. The syntax of English clauses is not as accommodating but the analysis nonetheless has much solid support.

Note first that different verbs have different powers of control. (1a–c) show that some verbs exclude direct objects; (2a–c) show acceptable combinations. (3a–c) show that other verbs require a direct object;

acceptable combinations are in (4a–c). (5a–c) show that a third set of verbs allow a direct object but do not actually require one. (Here we talk of verbs controlling other items in various ways; many analysts employ the term 'license' and talk of verbs licensing particular items.) Modifiers that are required or excluded by verbs are called 'complements';† modifiers that are optional are called 'adjuncts'. Where a direct object is allowed but not required, as in (5a), it is still treated as a complement because many verbs exclude direct objects and many verbs do require them. (The term 'complement' derives from a Latin verb 'to fill'; a complement expression fills out the verb (or noun, etc.), completing its syntax but also its meaning. The term 'adjunct' derives from the Latin verb 'join' or 'add' and simply means 'something adjoined', tacked on and not part of the essential structure of clauses.)

1 a *The conjurer vanished the rabbit.
  b *Alan was sitting his guests.
  c *Jennifer departed her friends.

2 a The conjurer made the rabbit vanish.
  b Alan was seating his guests.
  c Jennifer sent her friends off/saw her friends off

3 a *The workmen erected.
  b *That snake scared.
  c *The tree crushed.

4 a The workmen erected scaffolding.
  b That snake scared us.
  c The tree crushed two cars.

5 a Pavel will cook (the meal) tonight.
  b Who's cleaning up (this horrible untidy mess)?
  c If you hold (the log), I'll saw (it).

The above examples are clauses with main verbs and subjects, and some also have direct objects. Some verbs combine with direct objects and oblique objects, as in (6a–e). (=> CLAUSE STRUCTURE: LINEARITY AND GRAMMATICAL FUNCTIONS.) The construction will be labelled the 'DO-OO construction'.

6 a The students baked a cake[**DO**] for Margaret[**OO**].
  b Jacob kicked the ball[**DO**] to Rene[**OO**].
  c Andy hit the ball[**DO**] to Roger[**OO**].
  d We forwarded the letter[**DO**] to Philippa[**OO**].
  e The firm presented a gold watch[**DO**] to the foreman[**OO**].

Some verbs exclude oblique objects, as in (7a), while others control the particular preposition that occurs in the oblique object, as in (8).

7 *The tree crushed the car to Juliet.

8 a *Pavel cooked a meal to Jennifer (... for Jennifer).
   b *Many put the blame to Ed (... on Ed).

(7) excludes *to Juliet*. In (8a) *for Jennifer* is possible but *to Jennifer* is not. *We put this question to Ed* is acceptable but *put the blame to Ed* is not. The required preposition is *on*: *put the blame on Ed*.

Related to the DO-OO is the 'second object construction', exemplified in (9a–d).

9 a The students baked Margaret a cake.
   b We wrote Philippa a letter.
   c I sent Barnabas books.
   d Pavel cooked Jennifer a meal.

Some verbs that allow the DO-OO construction do not allow the second-object construction. Consider (10a–c).

10 a ?Andy hit Roger the ball. (hit the ball to Roger)
    b ?The firm presented the foreman a gold watch. (presented a gold watch to the foreman)
    c ?Katarina forwarded James the letter. (forwarded the letter to James)

The second-objects are *a cake* in (9a), *a letter* in (9b), *books* (in 9c) and *a meal* in (9d). Because some verbs exclude second objects and indirect objects, it is clear that these types of object are controlled by verbs.

Verbs also control or license the occurrence of directional phrases, as exemplified by (11).

11 The deer bounded <u>into the forest</u>.

The verb *bounded* requires a directional phrase, here *into the forest*. *?The deer bounded* is at best a peculiar sentence. Some verbs of movement do not absolutely require directional phrases but merely allow them: the clauses *We were walking to the post office* and *We were walking (not cycling)* are both acceptable. Nonetheless the directional phrase *into the forest* is treated as a complement because such phrases are excluded by verbs that do not express movement, as in **The dog is <u>lying onto</u> the good sofa* versus *The dog <u>jumped onto</u> the good sofa*.

Some modifiers of verbs are optional, such as adverbs of time and adverbs of location (as opposed to direction). In (12) *on Sunday morning* is an adverb of time and *in Ponsonby Road* is an adverb of place.

12 I was having brunch on Sunday morning in Ponsonby Road.

Either adverb or both adverbs can be omitted and the remainder is an acceptable clause: *I was having brunch on Sunday morning*, *I was having brunch in Ponsonby road* and *I was having brunch*. There is one exception, and that is the copula *be*, which requires some modifier in addition to the subject. In *I was <u>in a café on Ponsonby road</u>* the underlined adverb of location is required by *was* and is a complement. This exception does not vitiate the idea that adverbs of time and location are optional. *Be* is an unusual verb. Not for nothing do we have the special technical term 'copula' and recognise special copula construction(s).

In clauses the verb can be seen as controlling syntactic linkage, that is, agreement and government. Traditionally a structure was said to show agreement if two constituents had the same property, such as a noun and a verb both being plural (and having plural suffixes) or, in languages such as Italian, a noun and an adjective having the same gender and the same suffix. Government was said to apply when one constituent required another constituent to have some property. Thus, a verb might require an object noun to have an accusative case suffix but would not itself have a case suffix. From a dependency perspective there is no distinction between agreement and government; all syntactic linkage is government. In a clause, verbs require their noun modifiers to be of a particular type and number. For example, *were* requires a plural subject noun as in (13), or conjoined nouns as in (14), or a collective noun, as in (15).

13 The students were agreed that the examination is too long.
14 The chairman and the manager were agreed that production must be increased.
15 The committee were agreed that the decision was wrong.

To take a simpler example, *believes* requires a third person singular subject noun, *believe* (present tense) requires a third person plural noun, as in (16a and b).

16 a His sister believes things are going to improve.
   b His sisters believe things are going to improve.

Clearly the above view runs contrary to the traditional account of verbs agreeing with nouns in number. The contradiction disappears if we think of the traditional account as based on a model of speech production. Speakers decide what they are going to talk about, pick a suitable noun, say a singular third person noun (in the nominative case if the language being used is one such as Russian), and then pick a suitable verb and make it agree with the noun already chosen. All this fits in very well with the perspective of information structure and language use, but the dependency perspective is not directly related to either language use or information structure. (=> CLAUSE AND TEXT: INTRODUCTION, CLAUSE AND TEXT: COHESION.)

Verbs control the other constituents in a clause. For example, some verbs can have adjective phrases as complement: *seemed unhappy, turned yellow, grew tall*. Many verbs exclude adjective phrases. Other verbs require or allow a direct object noun phrase and a prepositional phrase: *inserted the keycard into the slot, hurled a boomerang at the wallaby, blamed the pilot for the crash/blamed the crash on the pilot*. Note that the verb may require particular prepositions: *blame* requires *for* in *blamed the pilot for the crash* and *on* in *blamed the crash on the pilot*. We can also say that *blame* allows either structure, whereas other verbs require one particular structure.

The examples discussed so far all consist of a single main verb plus modifiers. What about the clauses in (17a–c), which all contain combinations of auxiliary verb and main verb?

17 a The general <u>is</u> blaming the politicians for the disaster.
    b The general <u>has</u> blamed the politicians for the disaster.
    c The general <u>might</u> blame the politicians for the disaster.

The auxiliary verbs in (17a–c) are underlined. They illustrate the two major classes, the modal verbs such as *might, will, can*, and *should*, and the remainder, *be, have* and *do*. (=> CLAUSE STRUCTURE: VERB PHRASES.) The label 'auxiliary' reflects the view that these verbs are mere helpers, carrying negation and tense in negative clauses: *The dam can't/couldn't hold; The inspector wasn't coming* (versus *The inspector came not); Sarah didn't apply* (versus *Sarah applied not.) Be, have* and *do* are easily treated as mere helpers because they denote neither concrete nor abstract entities. (=> WORD CLASSES: SEMANTICS.) Modal verbs, in contrast, do denote different modalities, such as possibility and necessity.

An alternative analysis regards auxiliary verbs as heading the phrases in which they occur. The major reason is that each type of auxiliary verb requires a particular type of complement: *Is* in (17a) (and other forms of *be*) requires a verb + *ing, has* in (17b) (and other forms of *have*) requires a verb + *ed* (or some irregular form, such as *written, brought, taken); might* in (17c) (and other modal verbs) requires the bare verb stem (*might blame* but not **might to blame*). In (17a) *blaming* is a dependent of (or modifies) *is*, but in turn is the head of the remainder of the clause, allowing a direct object and a prepositional phrase and, in this construction, requiring the preposition *for*. Similarly for *blamed* and *has, blame* and *might*. This analysis does not destroy the distinction between main verbs and auxiliary verbs. *Is*, etc. are still auxiliary verbs in that they control only a small part of the constituent structure of a clause and their contribution to the meaning of a clause does not bear on the type of situation or the type of participants. *Blaming*, etc., is still a main verb, controlling the bulk of the constituent structure and making a major contribution to the meaning by determining the number and type of participants and, with them, the type of situation. (=> CLAUSE STRUCTURE: LINEARITY AND PREDICATE-ARGUMENT STRUCTURE.)

It is very worthwhile commenting that the distinction between head and modifier/dependent is important for the construction of meaning. Consider the clause *Margaret drove her car to Brussels*. The head of the clause, *drove*, signals the general type of situation conveyed by the clause. *Her car* narrows down the situation: not just driving in general but driving a car. *To Brussels* narrows down the situation even more: not driving around aimlessly but driving a car to a specific goal. *Margaret* completes the specification of the situation: whoever Margaret is, she was the agent who carried out the driving of the car to Brussels.

The relationship between verb and subject is equally important in constructing the semantic interpretation of a clause. For instance, a verb such as *flow* requires a subject noun denoting a liquid; if in a given clause it has a subject noun denoting some other kind of entity, *flow* imposes an interpretation of that entity as a liquid. (Of course, some entities can be either liquids or solids; molten steel flows, solid steel does not.) Thus people talk of a crowd flowing along a road, of traffic flowing smoothly or of ideas flowing freely. Such talk offers a view of the crowd moving along a road held in by the buildings on either side and propelled by a mysterious motive force, just as a river moves along in a mysterious fashion held in by its banks. This distinction between literal language and figurative or metaphorical language will not be explored here but it is important to be aware that many of the constraints which linguists discuss apply to literal language but dissolve in figurative language.

Dependency relations, the relations between heads and their modifiers, are independent of direction in two senses. The first is simply that, when representing such relations on paper (or computer screen), we can choose different layouts. The head of a clause could be at the top of a page with the modifiers below it, the head could be at the bottom of the page with the modifiers above it, the head could be at the left-hand side of the page with the modifiers to the right. We could even have a quasi-3D representation as a cube, with the head on the back wall of the cube and the modifiers projected in front of the head. The second sense is that, whatever diagrammatic representation we choose, the representations of dependency relations correspond to representations consisting of words and phrases in a line, from left to right as in English and many other languages, from right to left as in Semitic languages, and from top to bottom as in some Chinese texts and even in a spiral, as in old documents in Arabic written in Yemen. Working with a specific language, we can indicate dependency relations directly on a linear representation of a clause, as in Figure 5, or we can have a separate representation for dependency relations, as in Figure 6. Note that in Figure 6 there are no phrases, just words. It does not show any constituent structure: *my*, *five* and *energetic* 'hang from' the node for *friends* but the arrangement simply says that *friends* is the head and they are dependents or modifiers. The arrangements of dependents is separate from word order. It so happens that *my*, *five* and *energetic* precede *friends*, but *concert* precedes *the*, which precedes *after*. The separate representations of dependency relations have to be connected with representations of constituent structure, but that task lies far beyond the scope of this book.

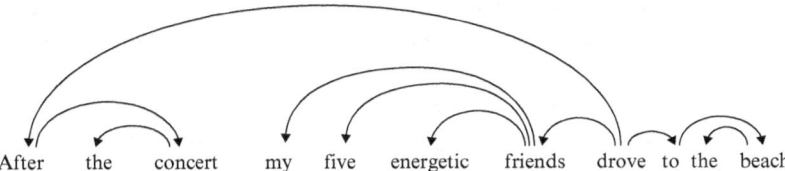

Figure 5

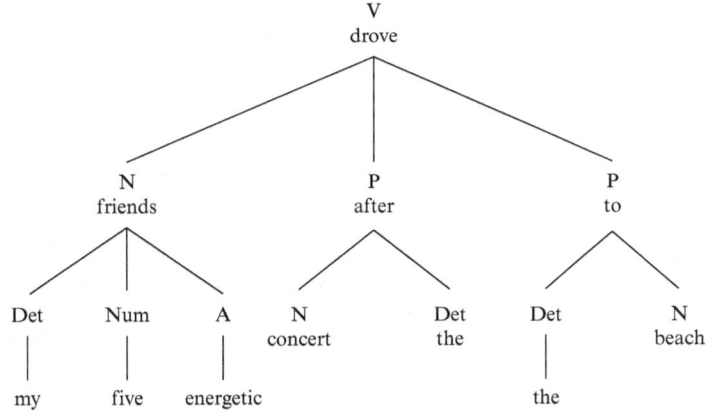

Figure 6

We finish this account by pointing out a connection between dependency relations and the distinction between clause and sentence. A small number of dependency relations cross clause boundaries, such as the relation between the relative pronoun *which* and inanimate nouns (*the wall which collapsed*) and between *who* and human nouns (*the children who were injured*). But by far the largest number of dependency relations hold within single clauses, and this supports the distinction between clause and sentence.

CLAUSE STRUCTURE: HIERARCHICAL STRUCTURE

This section addresses the question, again briefly, of how the structure of a clause or sentence can be represented in diagrams. (=> CLAUSE STRUCTURE: CONSTITUENTS, CLAUSE STRUCTURE: DEPENDENCY RELATIONS.)

Analyses of syntax (for any language) can apply the concept of hierarchical structure and the type of diagram known as a hierarchical structure diagram. The concept of hierarchical structure is straightforward. The basic idea is that, in a given clause, the smallest syntactic units are words, that words combine into phrases, and that small phrases can combine into bigger phrases and so on until the clause is complete. That is, constituent structure is a hierarchy, with the smallest units at the bottom and the biggest units at the top, and with the very biggest unit, the clause, at the very top, as shown in Figure 7.

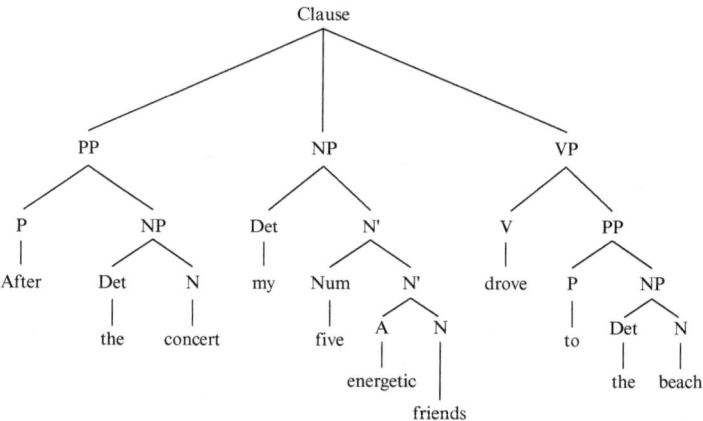

Figure 7

(This conception of syntactic structure as hierarchical works for English, other Indo-European languages, and many non-Indo-European languages. There are also many languages in which the establishment of words is not at all straightforward. However, since our focus is on the syntax of English, we can ignore that difficulty, although it is an important problem for general linguistic theory.)

One preliminary question is this: should we work with diagrams representing both constituent structure directly and dependency relations directly? Such an approach is the one on which X-bar theory is based. Originally diagrams of constituent structure displayed only the hierarchical arrangements of constituents, as in Figure 7. A growing interest in dependency relations led to the development of diagrams showing both constituent structure and dependencies. This was achieved by abandoning labels such as NP, AP, PP and VP and replacing them with N", A", P" and V". (The symbol "'" is known as a prime. The term 'bar' was used, and is still used, because the original notation used N, A, etc. with two horizontal bars above them.) The symbol N" indicates that the head of a given sequence of words is a noun, possibly but not necessarily accompanied by complements and specifiers, and similarly for A", P" and V". In the original theory specifiers are words to the left of a head and complements are words, or phrases or another clause, to the right of a head. N" dominates N', which represents N and a complement, and analogously for A', P' and V'. The lowest level in a diagram contains just N, A, P or V, which are the heads of phrases. Figure 8 shows an illustrative structure.

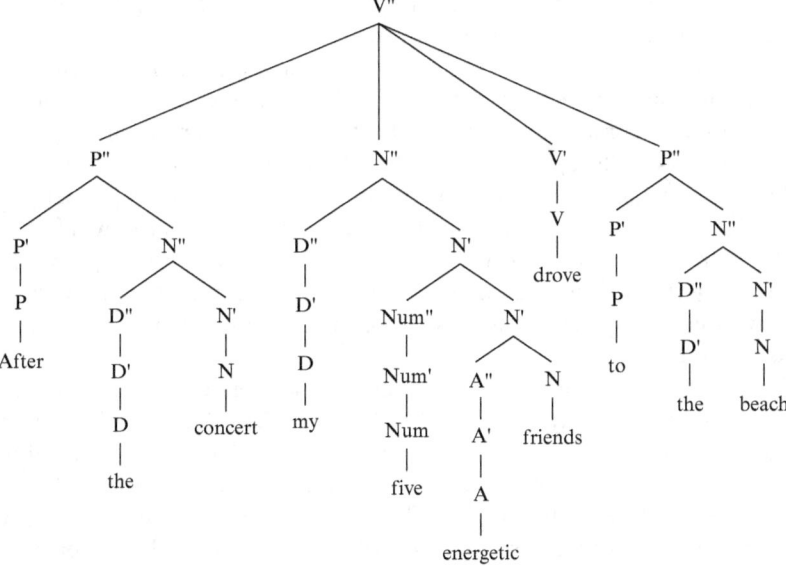

Figure 8

A second question is what sorts of elements should be represented in constituent structure diagrams. In the section on constituent structure (=> CLAUSE STRUCTURE: CONSTITUENTS.) we assume that constituent structure includes words, phrases and clauses. But words also have a structure, and in a phrase such as *is complaining* the main verb consists of two parts, *complain* and *-ing*, that are also constituents, but inside a given word. The word *is* can be seen, more abstractly, as realising the verb *be*, the aspect Progressive, the tense Present and the number and person Third Person Singular. One set of formal models (known collectively as Chomskyan generative grammar) takes these abstract properties to be constituents represented in constituent structure diagrams as I (for inflection) and Agr (for Agreement, that is Number and Person), PerfP for Perfect Phrase and so on. KB and JM hold the view that inflectional morphology is best excluded from constituent structure and handled in the lexicon.

A third question has to do with levels of structure. As can be seen from Figure 8, X-bar representations, even of relatively simple phrases, have many levels. If KB and JM were writing a different book, one focusing on explicit constituent structures for each construction they discuss, they would limit the number of bars to one and avoid many more levels by handling inflectional morphology in the lexicon by means of features. (Complexity has to go somewhere. Handling inflectional morphology in the lexicon makes the lexicon complex but the authors prefer that to complex hierarchical structure.)

The above discussion has to do with representations of structure that combine dependency relations and arrangements of constituents in a single diagram. Analysts who hold that dependencies are basic in syntax work with representations that show these relations directly but leave the arrangements of constituents to be inferred. Dependencies can be shown either by having curved arrows linking a head word with the words dependent on it (see Figure 5) or by adapting representations originally designed for constituent structure but which now show dependencies by having head words dominating the dependent words, as in Figure 6.

In principle, dependency relations are independent of linear order. The sentences *She seldom wears that dress* and *That dress she seldom wears* have the same network of dependency relations – *wears* as the head of the clause, modified by the dependent noun phrases *she* and *that dress* and the dependent adverb *seldom*. The same dependency relations apply to the interrogative clause *Does she seldom wear that dress?* The interrogative clause does bring a complication: should we treat *does* as the syntactic head of the clause, requiring a verb stem, here *wear*, that is the head of the remainder of the clause? Or should we treat *does* as dependent on *wear*? Exploring these questions would take us beyond the remit of this book and in any case they do not affect the statement that the same set of dependency relations applies to the three clauses and that dependency relations are independent of linear order. (=> VERBS AND VERB PHRASES: MOOD AND MODALITY.)

CLAUSE STRUCTURE: LINEARITY AND PREDICATE-ARGUMENT STRUCTURE

Representations of predicate-argument structure derive from logic. Examples in the literature usually offer a verb as predicate, although in logic predicates also relate to properties that are expressed by adjectives and nouns. The arguments of predicates are noun phrases (NPs) and prepositional phrases (PPs), but marked for the roles that the predicate assigns to them. For instance, TAKE, as in *John took the phone from Jennifer*, requires a subject NP with an Agent role, a direct object NP with a Patient role, and a PP containing an NP with a Source role.

A traditional term is 'participant role'. It captures the idea that roles are played by participants in situations. A more recent term is 'theta role'. This comes from Chomskyan formal models, where the concept of thematic role was (re)introduced in the 1970s. These thematic roles were represented by the Greek letter theta, θ, and came to be known as theta roles. Below we simply use the term 'role'.

The concept of role has aroused controversy since the late 1960s but for the purposes of this book the details of the controversy are not relevant. The key issue is whether a reliable and restricted set of roles can be established. They can, provided three points are observed. One is the relationship between grammatical differences and meaning (=> INTRODUCTION: WHAT COUNTS AS THE GRAMMAR OF ENGLISH?). The account of English syntax presented in this book is informed by the principle that differences in grammar signal differences in meaning. In an application of this principle, different roles are recognised only when there are differences in grammar. The second point is that roles should be as general as possible, and the third point is that a distinction must be made between roles and role-players.

The above points can be illustrated with reference to the role of Agent. Consider the examples in (1).

1 a My neighbour planted this tree.
  b The tree overshadowed our garden.
  c My computer performed the calculations.

d   This buttress held up the wall.
e   The earthquake destroyed many buildings.

All of (1a–e) answer the question *What did X do?* – *She planted this tree, It overshadowed our garden, It performed the calculations, It held up the wall, It destroyed many buildings* are acceptable replies. All of (1a–e) have corresponding WH clefts (=> CLEFTS: CLAUSES: CLEFTS.) – *What my neighbour did was plant this tree, What this buttress did was hold up the wall,* and so on. They all allow the progressive but this is a much weaker criterion, as a number of non-Agent verbs also allow the progressive. (=> VERBS AND VERB PHRASES: PROGRESSIVE ASPECT.) Accounts of roles have been proposed in which *neighbour* in (1a) is an Agent, *buttress* is an Instrument, *earthquake* is a Natural Force. The approach taken here is that all the subject nouns in (1a–e) are Agents but *My neighbour* denotes a prototypical Agent, exerting its volition, using its own energy, initiating an action and producing an effect. *The tree* uses its own energy and produces an effect, and *the earthquake* denotes a peripheral Agent that just produces an effect. Information about natural forces, plant life, digital machines and so on, belongs in the lexical entries for individual lexical items.

Paying attention to grammatical differences, we say that, e.g., *Ken bought the car from Kate* and *Kate sold the car to Ken* involve different assignments of roles, although the 'common sense' view would be that the two sentences describe the same situation. In the first one *Ken* is presented as Agent and *Kate* as the Source (from which the car moves), while the second one presents *Kate* as Agent and *Ken* as Goal (to which the car moves). Note the clefts *What Ken did was buy the car from Kate* and *What Kate did was sell the car to Ken.* As a corollary, we note that in a sentence such as *The ball rolled into the bunker* [golf] *the ball* is often assigned a role of Theme, which is the role played by entities that are located in a place or moving. This role is not supported by any grammatical evidence; in the above example *the ball* denotes a peripheral type of Agent player. The label 'Agent' is justified by the acceptability of the WH cleft construction: *What the ball did was roll into the bunker.*

Verbs can be subcategorised in terms of the number and type of constituents they require or allow – NPs, adjective phrases, PPs, the kinds of nouns they take as subjects or objects – in non-figurative language *flow* requires a subject noun denoting a liquid, *grow* requires a subject or object noun denoting an animate or vegetable entity; the particular prepositions they require – *collide* requires *with* but not *into* or *against*. Verbs can also be subcategorised in terms of the roles they require or allow. For each individual verb, all that information together is known as its valency. Some examples are given below.

CLAUSE STRUCTURE

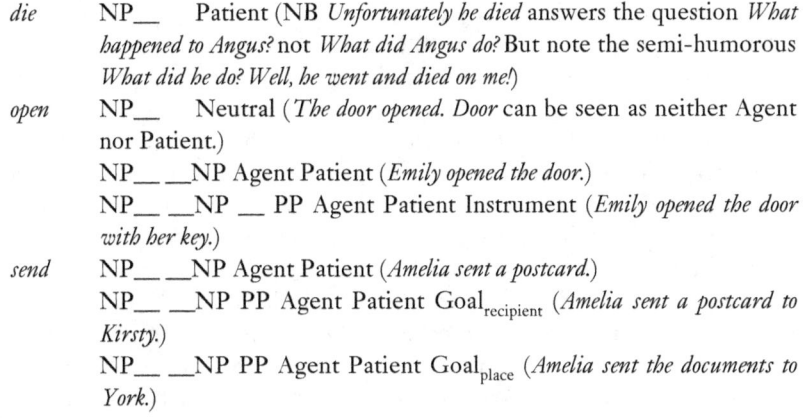

die NP__ Patient (NB *Unfortunately he died* answers the question *What happened to Angus?* not *What did Angus do?* But note the semi-humorous *What did he do? Well, he went and died on me!*)

open NP__ Neutral (*The door opened. Door* can be seen as neither Agent nor Patient.)

NP__ __NP Agent Patient (*Emily opened the door.*)

NP__ __NP __ PP Agent Patient Instrument (*Emily opened the door with her key.*)

send NP__ __NP Agent Patient (*Amelia sent a postcard.*)

NP__ __NP PP Agent Patient Goal$_{recipient}$ (*Amelia sent a postcard to Kirsty.*)

NP__ __NP PP Agent Patient Goal$_{place}$ (*Amelia sent the documents to York.*)

Note that Kirsty is one type of Goal player and York is another.

smash NP__ Patient (*The bowl smashed.* NB *What happened to the bowl? It smashed.*)

NP__ __NP Agent Patient (*The vandal smashed the bowl.*)

hear NP__ NP__ Experiencer Neutral (*Anne heard a noise.* NB Not a reply to *What did Anne do?* Anne did not carry out an action but had an experience. Compare *Anne listened to the noise*, which is an appropriate reply to the question.)

go NP__ PP PP PP Agent Source$_{place}$ Goal$_{place}$ Path$_{place}$ (*We drove from Essex to York via Cambridge.*)

receive NP__ NP__ PP Agent Patient Source$_{giver}$ (*Kirsty received a postcard from Amelia.*)

look NP__ PP Agent Goal$_{place}$ (*Emily looked into the box, Emily looked at the photographs.* Goal$_{place}$ and movement because Emily directs her gaze.)

CLAUSE STRUCTURE: LINEARITY AND GRAMMATICAL FUNCTIONS

A given dependency structure can be in correspondence with two representations of linear structure. It corresponds directly with the basic constituent structure of the clause, as in Figure 7 and the clause in turn corresponds with the constituent structure of a sentence, that is, a clause arranged and possibly extended so as to fit into a particular text with a particular discourse effect. The dependency structure, e.g. as in Figure 6, corresponds indirectly with the linear structure of the sentence, e.g. as in Figure 5. Two other structures with linear representations are exploited in syntactic analysis. One is lexical-conceptual structure and the other is predicate-argument structure. (=> CLAUSE STRUCTURE: LINEARITY AND PREDICATE-ARGUMENT STRUCTURE.) The development, extension and application of lexical conceptual structure is of central importance in linguistics but is not essential to this book and is not discussed. All that need be said is that it is a representation of universal cognitive-semantic structures constructed from ontological building blocks such as events and states; things and places or paths; going, staying or being; causing.

In order to describe the linear structure of clauses we focus on the basic type – active, declarative neutral clauses with no one constituent more salient than the others. The simplest and most concrete structures can be analysed using the various word classes (=> WORD CLASSES: INTRODUCTION, WORD CLASSES: SYNTACTIC CRITERIA AND SUBCLASSES.) and the concept of grammatical functions. The grammatical functions deployed in this book are subject and object (direct object, oblique object and second object).

Subject NPs typically precede the verb in active, declarative clauses: *The dog was gnawing a bone.* They are involved in number and person agreement with the verb: *The dog is barking* but *The dogs are barking.* They are replaced by the subject form of pronouns: *The dog was barking* à *He/She was barking* but not *Him/her was barking*. In connected text, subject NPs are typically, but not necessarily, the theme (topic, for many analysts) of a sentence. (=> CLAUSE AND TEXT: THEME.) The subject NP plays an important part when clauses are conjoined. (1) and (2) can be conjoined to give (3).

1 The flood wrecked the houses
2 The flood carried off many cars.
3 The flood wrecked the houses and [ ] carried off many cars.

During the conjoining, *the flood* in the second clause is deleted, as indicated by the square brackets. Only the subject noun can be deleted, precisely because it is central in both clauses.

In active, declarative clauses direct object NPs typically come immediately after the verb: *The dog gnawed its bone.* They are replaced by the object form of pronouns: *The cat scared the dog* → *The cat scared him/her.* They become the subject NP of the corresponding passive clause: *The wind turbine delighted the inhabitants* → *The inhabitants were delighted by the wind turbine.*

Oblique objects are any NPs preceded by a preposition: *She gave the brooch to her granddaughter, This is for you, We were amazed by the results.*

The concept of indirect object is needed for clauses such as *My brother left Ian the books. Ian* is an object. It immediately follows the verb *left* and becomes the subject of the corresponding passive: *Ian was left the books by his brother.* That is, the basic syntactic criteria indicate that *Ian* in this construction (the double object construction, see below) is a direct object. Many analysts are reluctant to treat it as a direct object, partly because it denotes a recipient and not a patient (but this is controversial, (=> CLAUSE STRUCTURE: LINEARITY AND PREDICATE-ARGUMENT STRUCTURE.) and partly because it corresponds to an oblique object in *My brother left the books to Ian.* We adopt the generally accepted view and call *Ian* an indirect object. (NB Traditionally the term 'indirect object' was applied to nouns such as *Ian* in *left the books to Ian.* This use of indirect object has been generally abandoned in favour of 'oblique object'.)

In the double-object construction, as in *left Ian the books,* the NP *the books* is known as a second object. The concept applies only to the double-object construction. In *left the books to Ian, the books* is a direct object and *Ian* is an oblique object.

In order to describe the linear structure of clauses we focus on the basic type – active, declarative neutral clauses with no one constituent more salient than the others. Descriptions that focus on dependency relations do not devote much time to the arguments for and against verb phrases. The simplest structures are in (1)–(3).

1   NP:S V   The tree fell.
2   NP:S V NP:O   The forester felled the tree.
3   NP:S V NP:O PP [NP:OO]   The forester loaded the tree-trunk onto the truck.

(1) is to be read as 'The clause consists of a Noun Phrase with the grammatical function of Subject, followed by a Verb.' (2) is to be read as 'The clause consists of a Noun Phrase with the grammatical function of Subject, followed by a Verb, followed by a Noun Phrase with the grammatical function of direct Object.' (3) is to be read as 'The clause consists of a Noun Phrase with the grammatical function of Subject, followed by a Verb, followed by a Noun Phrase with the grammatical function of direct Object, followed by a Prepositional Phrase containing a Noun Phrase with the grammatical function of Oblique Object.'

Other possible structures are in (4)–(9).

4   NP:S V NP:C   Fiona is a lawyer; Her brother became a criminal.

(4) is to be read as 'The clause consists of a Noun Phrase with the grammatical function of Subject, a Verb and a Noun Phrase with the grammatical function of Complement.' (=> CLAUSE STRUCTURE: DEPENDENCY RELATIONS.)

5   NP:S V AP:C   The children seem restless; Ishbel sounded very tired.

(5) is to be read as 'The clause consists of a Noun Phrase with the grammatical function of Subject, a Verb and an Adjective Phrase with the grammatical function of Complement.'

6   NP:S V NP:O AP:C   The painter painted the door dark-green; The critics consider this novel outstanding; The machine crushed the car flat.

(6) is to be read as 'The clause consists of a Noun Phrase with the grammatical function of Subject, a Verb, a Noun Phrase with the grammatical function of direct Object, and an Adjective Phrase with the grammatical function of Complement.'

7   NP:S V NP:O NP: C   The committee made Fiona president.

(7) is to be read as 'The clause consists of a Noun Phrase with the grammatical function of Subject, a Verb, a Noun Phrase with the grammatical function of direct Object, and a Noun Phrase with the grammatical function of Complement.'

8   NP:S V PP:OO   The car is at the garage; She is working in her garden; The roof was destroyed by the storm; We're driving to Granada.

(8) is to be read as 'The clause consists of a Noun Phrase with the grammatical function of Subject, a Verb, and a Prepositional Phrase with the grammatical function of Oblique Object.'

9   NP:S V NP PP:OO   David Cameron became Prime Minister in 2010.

(9) is to be read as 'The clause consists of a Noun Phrase with the grammatical function of Subject, a copula, Noun Phrase with the grammatical function of complement, and a Prepositional Phrase with the grammatical function of Oblique Object.'

10 NP:S V AP:C PP:OO   I am busy on Saturday; The car was crushed flat by the machine; I was made very unwell by the deep-fried Mars bars.

(10) is to be read as 'The clause consists of a Noun Phrase with the grammatical function of Subject, a Verb, an Adjective Phrase with the grammatical function of Complement, and a Prepositional Phrase with the grammatical function of Oblique Object.'

CLAUSE STRUCTURE: VERB PHRASES

In the section *Clause structure: linearity and grammatical functions* the structures in (1)–(10) are not analysed as containing verb phrases (VPs). The difficulty is that the criteria for recognising verb phrases do not apply straightforwardly to English clauses. The strongest criteria are transposition and substitution. For all other types of phrase these criteria apply without difficulty inside clauses and in common constructions. (=> ADJECTIVES AND ADJECTIVE PHRASES: INTRODUCTION, NOUNS AND NOUN PHRASES: INTRODUCTION, PREPOSITIONS AND PREPOSITIONAL PHRASES: INTRODUCTION.) But they do not apply easily to sequences of finite verb plus object(s) of some kind. Consider the occurrence of *do so*, which used to be counted a criterion. An example is in (1).

    1 David Lemming jumped off the cliff and George Lemming did so too.

Did so indeed substitutes for *jumped off the cliff*, but two words are involved and it seems that *did* substitutes for *jumped* while *so* substitutes for *off the cliff*. The normal construction in British English is the one in (2a). The substituting sequence is *so did*, which is an even less plausible substitution of *did* for *jumped* and *so* for *off the cliff* because the verb and its complement would have to be transposed, as in (2b). *So* could then be substituted for *off the cliff* and *did* for *jumped*.

    2 a David Lemming jumped off the cliff and so did George Lemming.
        b David Lemming jumped off the cliff and <u>off the cliff jumped</u> George Lemming.

The one structure from spontaneous spoken English that might be a criterion is shown in (3).

    3 Came right in he did without so much as a knock.

Unfortunately the structure of (3) is not clear. *Came right in he did* could be seen as a rearrangement of *He did come right in*, except that the latter has *come* while (3) has *came*. Moreover, new electronic bodies of spoken English are yielding examples such as *They complained about it all the time they did*, which has two clauses, *They complained about it all the time* and the tagged-on clause *they did*. So (3) can be analysed as having a two-clause structure in which the first clause, as happens regularly in spontaneous speech, is lacking a subject. That is, it can be analysed not as a basic construction but as resulting from ellipsis. (The type of ellipsis known as 'situation ellipsis', in which a word or phrase is ellipted because its referent is salient in the situation. In the case of the situation described by (3) we can assume that the person who came right in has been mentioned very recently.)

Examples such as *He cannot resist eating lokum* and *Eating lokum he cannot resist* have been proposed as supporting the concept of verb phrases. *Eating lokum* is said to be a VP and it can be transposed from final position in a clause to initial position. The trouble is that *eating lokum* is a non-finite clause, a gerund (=> NON-FINITE CLAUSES: GERUNDS (TYPE 1).), and gerunds are a different construction from finite clauses. They cannot take tense or modal verbs and have a different distribution from finite clauses. Gerunds such as *eating lokum* occur in clause positions typically occupied by NPs, as in *I enjoyed eating lokum*. Protoypical VPs do not occur in NP positions.

Other arguments for VPs turn on examples of the sort in (4)–(6).

4 Jim couldn't solve the problem but Margaret could.
5 What Margaret did was solve the problem.
6 Solve the problem is what Margaret did.

The argument runs that in (4) the phrase *solve the problem* has been ellipted – *could solve the problem* is reduced to *could*. Ellipsis is usually taken to delete single constituents, which would make *solve the problem* a single constituent, a VP. In (5) *was* has as its subject the wh clause *What Margaret did* and *solve the problem* as its complement. In (6), *Solve the problem* is the subject and in first position; that is, the sequence *solve the problem* has been moved (transposed) to the front to give (6). The difficulty is that in (5) and (6) *solve the problem* cannot take tense or aspect, and, like the gerunds mentioned above, has a different distribution from finite VPs.

One piece of data that looks more promising for VPs is conjunction, as in (7).

7 Jennifer checked the oil level and topped up the windscreen wash.

(7) can be analysed as having a subject NP, *Jennifer*, and two phrases – VPs – connected by *and*: *checked the oil level* and *topped up the windscreen wash*. But there are alternative analyses that treat supposed VPs as clauses whose subject NP has been ellipted, and other analyses try to handle conjunction in terms of heads and their dependent modifiers rather than in terms of phrases. Although many analyses employ VPs, the evidence is much weaker than for other types of phrase and not strong enough for us to abandon the view that the verb is the head of the clause. (=> CLAUSE STRUCTURE: CONSTITUENTS, CLAUSE STRUCTURE: DEPENDENCY RELATIONS, CLAUSE STRUCTURE: HIERARCHICAL STRUCTURE.)

CLAUSE STRUCTURE: INTEGRATED AND UNINTEGRATED SYNTAX

The syntax of formal written language is said to be integrated, while that of spontaneous spoken language is typically (but not necessarily) unintegrated. Consider the following examples.

1. If you've got some eggs about whose age you are not sure here's a useful test
2. if you've got some eggs you're not sure about their age here's a useful test
   [cookery programme on New Zealand television]

In (1) the noun *eggs* is modified by the relative clause *about whose age you are not sure*. *About whose age* is the complement of *sure* but is at the front of the clause. The relative pronoun *whose* connects the relative clause to *eggs*. Crucially, the relative clause immediately follows the head noun *eggs* and is held to be embedded; that is, the basic NP is *some eggs*, the direct object of *'ve got*. Into that NP is inserted the relative clause, *about whose age you are not sure*.

In (2) the relative clause is replaced by *you're not sure about their age*. This looks like a main clause; there is no relative pronoun and the clause is linked to *eggs* by the personal possessive pronoun *their*. *About their age* is the complement of *sure*. All the evidence indicates that *you're not sure about their age* is a main clause which is adjacent to *some eggs* but not embedded in it. The differences are summed up by saying that in (1) the second clause is integrated into the NP *some eggs about whose age you are not sure*, but not in (2).

(3) is an example of a relative clause embedded in an NP but with no overt pronoun linking it to the head noun.

3. I only wear shoes that I'm not thrown forward on my toes
   [BBC radio discussion]

The relative clause is *that I'm not thrown forward on my toes*. It modifies the head noun *shoes* and is linked to it by the complementiser *that*. But inside the relative clause there is no wh pronoun or even an ordinary pronoun linking with *shoes*. A formal written English equivalent is *shoes by which I am not thrown forward on my toes* and a possible spoken version is *shoes that I'm not thrown forward on my toes by them*. In the former *which* provides the link, in the latter *them*. But in (3) the relative clause is not completely integrated into the syntax of the main clause. (=> RELATIVE CLAUSES: SHADOW PRONOUNS.)

The example in (4) does have integrated syntax.

4 Only Nato forces stand between what that man is doing and a huge tragedy.

The integrated syntax lies in the complement of *between*. The noun phrase [*what* [*that man is doing* Ø]] is coordinated with the noun phrase *a huge tragedy*. The actual spoken version of (4) is in (5).

5 Only Nato forces stand between that man <u>what he's doing</u> and a huge tragedy.
[BBC radio discussion]

In (5) the basic complement of *between* is *that man and a huge tragedy*. Interpolated between the two NPs is the free relative clause *what he's doing*. The free relative is not embedded in another constituent; it is simply adjacent to *that man*. Its subject, *he*, is co-referential with *that man*. (5) puts the human protagonist at the centre of the event, *that man* being the 'direct object' of *between*; he is mentioned first and then the relevant characteristic is mentioned, what he is doing.

Other examples are ... *Everybody knows Helen Liddell <u>how hard she works</u>* [radio discussion] and *I've been meaning to ask about the new baby and <u>Alan how they're getting on</u>* [conversation]. A written example, from a recent non-trivial novel, is in (6).

6 I remembered Rossi, how he'd listened so modestly to the cheers and speeches.
Elizabeth Kostova, *The Historian*, 2005

The construction is far from new; (7) is from the Authorised Version of the New Testament and is a straight calque of the New Testament Greek.

7 Consider the lilies of the field <u>how they grow</u>.

Later groups of translators seem to have considered the unintegrated syntax of (7) unsuitable for writing. The *Good News Bible* has *Look at how the wild flowers grow* and the *Revised English Bible* has *Consider how the lilies of the field grow*.
The classic WH cleft construction offers a good example of integrated syntax, as in (8).

8 <u>What they will do</u> is <u>use this command to save the data</u>

Is links the clauses *what they will do* and *use this command to save the data*. The second clause can be thought of as integrated into the overall structure by losing its subject and its tense. The typical WH construction in spontaneous speech is exemplified in (9). No integration has taken place; the clause following *is* has a subject and its own tense. (=> CLAUSE AND TEXT: CLEFTS.)

   9 right, well, what you're doing is <u>you're drawing</u> a line

As a final example of unintegrated syntax consider the examples in (10).

   10 a it's unfair what they're doing to the union [radio discussion]
           b it has been well documented the effect "phONEday" had on both business and domestic users [article in *The Independent*]

It is the subject of *is unfair* in (10a) and of *has been well documented* in (10b). What is unfair or well documented is conveyed by the free relative clause *what they're doing to the union* and the NP *the effect*... In formal writing, and this is why (10b) is surprising, we would expect the free relative clause and the long NP to be the subjects: *what they're doing to the union is unfair* and *the effect "phONEday" had... has been well documented.*

(11) shows another construction typical of spontaneous speech but not of (planned and edited) writing. (=> CLAUSE AND TEXT: FOCUS.)

   11 <u>this older woman in the class</u> she likes to kid us all on

(11) begins with the NP *this older woman in the class* and continues with the complete clause *she likes to kid us all on.* The subject of the clause, *she*, is co-referential with the initial NP. The explanation of the NP–clause structure as a way of dealing with complex subject phrases looks plausible for examples such as (12) but not at all plausible for (13), with a very short NP.

   12 <u>the people who are listening to this</u> many of them will not understand the complexities [radio discussion]
   13 <u>the driver</u> you get a good laugh with him [recorded conversation]

Occasionally the construction is used to contrast two referents, as in (14), from a road report on Classic FM. *That* in *that's now been cleared* is a demonstrative pronoun, as was clear from the non-reduced pronunciation and the slight pause between *A28* and *that.*

   14 there's been an accident in Kent on the M26 but <u>the earlier accident on the A28</u> that's now been cleared

Speakers could use the construction to escape from a syntactic mix-up but most examples do not display any signs of syntactic breakdown such as hesitations and repetitions. The primary function of the structure is to establish referents and make them salient; its secondary function is to enable speakers and listeners to handle complex referring expressions. (12) enables listeners to establish the referent of *the people who are listening to this* and then to decode the clause *many of them will not understand the complexities*. *Them* provides the link to *the people who are listening to this*.

Classic indirect question clauses are integrated with the main clause.

15 I asked where the new form came from

The WH complement of *asked* conveys a question. It begins with the interrogative *where* but the rest of the clause, *the new form came from*, has declarative constituent order. Compare (16a and b), in which the WH complements have the word order and structure of a WH interrogative clause with subject-auxiliary inversion. (16a) is from conversation and (16b) is from a university final examination script. This type of indirect question is generally ignored in discussions of English syntax, but note the written example (17) from a newspaper article. (=> COMPLEMENT CLAUSES: EMBEDDED INTERROGATIVES.)

16 a I can't remember now <u>what was the reason for it</u>.
    b The question centres on <u>where did this new form come from</u>.

17 No one is sure <u>how long are the passages leading off from this centre</u>.

This section concludes with examples of a further three spoken constructions: relative clause with shadow pronoun in (18), clause with preposed PP and shadow pronoun in (19), and in (20a and b), clauses in which what look like conjunctions (indeed, a subordinating conjunction in (20b)) are separated from the rest of the clause by a comma (presumably indicating a pause in speech).

18 I'm one of these people that <u>I</u> don't like to be surprised. [Conversation]

19 out of the twenty four traditional medicine shops they visited rhino horn was for sale in nineteen of <u>them</u> [BBC radio report]

20 a <u>Plus</u>, the lack of ordered rules means that OT analyses are not burdened with various intermediate levels of representation. [PhD thesis]
    b <u>Although</u>, English has been the most successful language in becoming a lingua franca.

Clefts

CLAUSES: CLEFTS

English has four cleft constructions, the IT cleft, the WH cleft, the reverse WH cleft and the TH cleft. They each have particular functions in discourse (=> CLAUSE AND TEXT: CLEFTS.) and are used frequently in all sorts of texts from informal conversations to extremely formal written documents. This section focuses on the structure of clefts.

Strictly speaking, the cleft constructions all consist of two clauses, and on an even stricter view, only the IT and WH clefts merit the label 'cleft'. Why 'cleft'? The idea behind the label is that an IT or WH cleft can be thought of as created by taking a single clause, cutting or cleaving it in two, and stitching the two parts together again in a different arrangement. Consider (1).

1 John cooked duck in our kitchen at Christmas.

The initial chunk of any IT cleft is *It be*. This is followed by a constituent, which is highlighted. The second part of the IT cleft is a relative clause. Assume the first part of our cleft is *It was*. The next step is to cleave (1) into two parts and turn one of the parts into the complement of *was*. Let us say that this part is *duck: It was duck*. The second part, the remainder of the clause – *John cooked in our kitchen at Christmas* – is turned into a relative clause modifying the complement of *was*. Thus we obtain *It was + duck + that John cooked in our kitchen at Christmas*. Any of the other constituents in (1), apart from *cooked*, can be converted into the complement of *was*, as in (2)–(4).

2 It was + John + that/who cooked duck in our kitchen at Christmas.
3 It was + in our kitchen + that John cooked duck at Christmas.
4 It was + at Christmas + that John cooked duck in our kitchen.

The final component of IT clefts was described above as a relative clause. This categorisation is plausible for examples such as *It was John* _that/who cooked the duck_. It is even possible to have _It was John cooked the duck_, with a contact relative clause. (=> RELATIVE CLAUSES: CONTACT.) This construction may look odd because _John_ is the understood subject of _cooked the duck_ and contact relative clauses are supposedly only possible with non-subjects. Thus, _the book I read_ is acceptable because _book_ is the direct object of _read_. But _It was John cooked the duck_, while highlighting _John_, also serves to introduce him as the cook; that is, it is one of the existential-presentative constructions, which do allow contact relative clauses without an overt subject noun.

Sentences such as (3) and (4) are the ones that raise doubts about the analysis as a relative clause. After all, relative clauses modify nouns, not prepositional phrases such as _in our kitchen_ and _at Christmas_. Nor do they modify adverbial clauses, such as _because he was ill_; but note the example _It was because he was ill that we decided to return_. (Relative clauses introduced by _which_ can modify clauses, or the propositions expressed by clauses, but such relative clauses are excluded from IT clefts: *_It was because he was ill which we decided to return_.) Because of examples such as (3) and (4) the term 'annex clause'† has been proposed instead of relative clause. (=> RELATIVE CLAUSES: PROPOSITIONAL.)

There is an alternative construction to the one in (3) and (4) that does not require the concept of an annex clause. See (5) and (6).

  5 It was in our kitchen _where_ John cooked duck at Christmas.
  6 It was at Christmas _when_ John cooked duck in our kitchen.

Instead of the 'annex clause' introduced by _that_ there is what looks like a free relative clause. (=> RELATIVE CLAUSES: FREE.) (5) can be assigned the structure in (7).

  7 $_{Clause\,1}$ (It was at Christmas)
     $_{NP}$ ($_N$ (when) $_{Clause\,2}$ (John cooked duck in our kitchen then))

When points to a time, specific in this case, and _then_ points to the same time. On this analysis the combination of clauses is unintegrated, the two clauses simply being juxtaposed and _then_ being deleted. The structure for (5) is shown in (8). _When_ is replaced by _where_ and _then_ by _there_.

  8 $_{Clause\,1}$ (It was in our kitchen)
     $_{NP}$ ($_N$ (where) $_{Clause\,2}$ (John cooked duck in our kitchen there))

(See the account of reverse WH clefts below for a construction in which the clauses in (7) are more integrated.)

When did the construction in (5) and (6) come into use, and in what types of text? KB and JM became aware of the construction in the mid-1990s, which means it was almost certainly in use (possibly limited use) before then. It is the regular construction in informal conversation but has spread to scripted spoken English such as news broadcasts and to written texts such as newspapers and public notices, as shown by (9)–(12).

9 It was five years ago when Nelson Mandela realised his prison number could be put to another use.
BBC, *News at Ten*, 1 December 2007

10 He was born in 1918 in India, the son of a regimental sergeant major, but it was in 1931 in England when he discovered a taste for performance.
The Independent, 28 February 2002

11 In the beginning skating was used as a means of transportation, it wasn't until the last century when skating became viewed as recreational.
Notice in Stratford Museum, Stratford, Ontario, Canada. October 1999

12 It's here where we have the highest chance of frosts.
BBC TV weather forecast February 2002

We close this account of IT clefts with more structural peculiarities. Note first that prescriptive grammars of English would allow *It's he that cooked duck* and *It's I that cooked duck*. These examples look odd in writing and in spoken English the pronouns are always *him* and *me*: *It's him that cooked duck* and *It's me that cooked duck*. In the present tense a problem arises with person agreement across the clause boundary. *It's him that cooks duck* is straightforward, with third person singular *him* and third person singular *cooks*. But *it's me that cook duck* is straightforwardly unacceptable; it has to be *It's me that cooks duck*, with first person *me* but third person *cooks*. Reflexive pronouns increase the oddity. *It's him that's kicking himself for not paying the phone bill* is fine, with third person singular *him*, *'s* and *himself*. In contrast, *It's me that am kicking myself for not paying the phone bill* might fit prescriptive rules but the regular pattern, certainly in spoken English, is *It's me that's kicking himself...*, with first person *me* but third person *'s* and *himself*. (In the plural, *It's us that's driving to Istanbul* sounds more natural than *It's we that are driving to Istanbul*, but the patterns of usage have still to be properly investigated.)

We return to the example in (1), repeated as (13).

13 John cooked duck in our kitchen at Christmas.

(13) can be cleft in another way. The item to be put in focus is excised. Let us assume it is *duck*. The excised constituent is replaced by a wh word, here *what*, and the clause is converted to a free relative clause, here *what John cooked in our kitchen at Christmas*. The free relative clause

is followed by some form of *be*: *what John cooked in our kitchen at Christmas + was*. The excised constituent is then inserted into the structure as the complement of *was*: *what John cooked in our kitchen at Christmas + was + duck*.

There are limits on the formation of WH clefts. In (13) both *in our kitchen* and *at Christmas* can be put in focus, the free relative clauses being introduced by *where* and *when*: *Where John cooked duck at Christmas + was + in our kitchen* and *When John cooked duck in our kitchen + was + at Christmas*. The subject noun phrase *John* can also be put into focus, but not by means of a free relative clause: **Who cooked duck in our kitchen at Christmas + was + John* is not acceptable; the construction has to be *The person who cooked duck in our kitchen at Christmas + was + John*, but this is not a WH cleft. The first chunk consists of a noun phrase *the person*, with *person* modified by an ordinary relative clause; indeed it could be *the person that cooked duck in our kitchen at Christmas*. The third chunk in the construction is another noun phrase, here *John*, and the two noun phrases are linked by *was* (or some other form of *be*).

WH clefts can be used to put into focus a whole verb phrase or a whole clause, including the subject noun phrase. The classic construction, as described in reference grammars of English, is in (14).

14 a <u>What they do</u> is patrol the motorway.
   b <u>What they're doing</u> is patrolling the motorway.

The construction in (14a,b) consists of a free relative clause (underlined) plus a copula, here *is*, plus a bare verb stem as in (14a) or an *-ing* form as in (14b). (=> NON-FINITE CLAUSES: VERB STEM, NON-FINITE CLAUSES: GERUNDS (TYPE 1).) (14b) could equally well be *What they're doing is patrol the motorway*. Very frequent in spoken English is a construction in which the verb phrase is replaced by a complete clause, as in *What they do is <u>they patrol the motorway</u>* or *What they're doing is <u>they're patrolling the motorway</u>*. The free relative clause and the complete clause are linked by *be*, but also frequent in spoken English is a construction, or a combination of clauses, in which the free relative clause and the complete clause are simply juxtaposed, with no copula: *What they do – they patrol the motorway*, *What they're doing – they're patrolling the motorway*. These examples contain an em dash, but that is merely to show the boundary between the two clauses in writing. In speech there might be a short pause (but not necessarily) and each clause might have its own intonation.

In the examples of WH clefts formed from (13) the first chunk, the free relative clause, and the third chunk, the focused constituent, can be transposed. Thus, *What John cooked in our kitchen at Christmas + was + duck* yields

Duck + was + what John cooked in our kitchen at Christmas. Analogously we have *In our kitchen + was + where John cooked duck at Christmas* and *At Christmas + was + when John cooked duck in our kitchen,* and even *Patrol the motorway + is + what they do.* This construction is known as the reverse WH cleft.

The fourth cleft construction is the demonstrative cleft or TH cleft. We use the latter label here by analogy with the labels IT cleft and WH cleft; just as IT clefts begin with *it* and WH clefts with a wh word, so TH clefts begin with *that* or *this*. Examples are in (15)–(17), with the TH clefts underlined.

15 You see that villa? <u>That's what I'd like to buy</u>.

16 A: Follow that bit up vertically – right? – till it stops
    B: Uhuh
    C: <u>That's what I mean</u> [Task-related dialogue]

17 Oh. We're at the gates. <u>This is where we get off</u>.

The TH clefts are simple in structure: *this* or *that* (occasionally *these* or *those*) + *be* + free relative clause (*what I'd like to buy, what I mean, where we get off*).

Complement clauses

COMPLEMENT CLAUSES: COMPLEMENTISERS

Verb complement clauses can be introduced by *that*, or a wh word such as *who, what, when, how, whether/if.* These are known as complementisers. A complement clause may have no overt complementiser, as in (3), which is an example of a contact complement clause. The complement clause is directly in contact with the verb it is dependent on. The types are exemplified in (1)–(3).

    1 Philippa noticed <u>that</u> James had disappeared.
    2 Lucie confirmed <u>who</u> was on the committee.
    3 Rene thought [Ø] the plan was stupid.

As with relative clauses and adverbial clauses, non-standard English adds to the picture: varieties spoken in the south-east of England (but perhaps more widely) have verb complement clauses with the complementiser *as*, as in (4).

    4 a I heard <u>as</u> you were leaving us.
        b She knew <u>as</u> something wasn't right.

The choice of *that* versus a wh complementiser is controlled (or licensed) by the main verb of the clause containing a given complement clause. The verbs *inquire* and *choose*, for instance, allow wh complementisers but exclude *that*, as shown in (5) and (6).

    5 a The detective inquired <u>who</u> was present/<u>where</u> we had been/<u>how</u> we knew that.
        b *The detective inquired <u>that</u> the burglar escaped.

    6 a Pavel had to choose <u>whether</u> he would stay or leave.
        b *Rene chose <u>that</u> they would go by train.

Other verbs, such as *object*, allow *that* but not wh complements, as in (7).

7   a   The committee objected <u>that</u> the proposal had not been discussed.
    b   *The player objected <u>whether</u> he would take the penalty/<u>where</u> the foul happened.

The choice of complementiser may be determined not just by a given complement-taking verb but also by the construction of the clause containing that verb. For example, some verbs, such as *report*, only license *whether* if they are in a negative declarative clause, as in (8c), or an interrogative clause, as in (8d).

8   a   The chairman reported <u>that</u> the firm had made a large profit.
    b   *The chairman reported <u>whether</u> the firm had made a large profit.
    c   The chairman did not report <u>whether</u> the firm had made a large profit.
    d   Did the chairman report <u>whether</u> the firm had made a large profit?

Know in an affirmative (positive) clause licenses either *that* or *whether*, as in (9).

9   a   I know that there's a referendum coming up.
    b   I know perfectly well whether it's time to go. Don't bother me.

In negative declarative and in interrogative clauses *know* frequently, but not necessarily, licenses *whether*.

10 a   I know <u>that</u> the project has been approved.
    b   I don't know <u>whether</u>/<u>if</u> the project has been approved.
    c   Do you know <u>whether</u>/<u>if</u> the project has been approved?

Note the difference in meaning between *I don't know <u>whether</u>/<u>if</u> Freya's going to join the group* and *I don't know <u>that</u> Freya's going to join the group*. The former is a straightforward statement of fact about the speaker's knowledge; the latter is more likely in the context of someone assuming that Freya is going to join and another speaker expressing doubt.

To emphasise just how subtle the licensing patterns can be, consider *understand*. It licenses *that*, *why* and *how* but not *whether*, as shown in (11).

11 a   We understand that our plan is not viable.
    b   We understand why Katarina has made this decision.
    c   We don't understand how this could have happened.
    d   *We understand/don't understand whether Katarina has heard.

Importantly, there are more general patterns of licensing than the above. For instance, there is a group of verbs that might be labelled

THINKING. It includes *think, assume, believe* and *realise*. These verbs license *that* but not *whether* or the other wh complementisers.

Another group of verbs, which might be labelled AFFECT, includes *please, frighten, terrify, shock, scare, disgust*. They occur in different constructions from those in the above examples: either the complement clause is in subject position, as in *That she always gets things right frightens me*, or there is a dummy subject *it* and the complement clause is extraposed, as in *It frightens me that she always gets things right*. These verbs license *that* but no wh complementisers.

A third group of verbs, LIKE verbs, includes *like, hate, resent, dislike* and *loathe*. They occur in a construction in which their direct object is *it*, followed by a complement clause, as in *I like it that you're keeping the colour scheme*, *They hated it that he never replied to their e-mails*, *She resented it that she had to do all the back work*. These verbs likewise license *that* but no wh complementisers.

COMPLEMENT CLAUSES: EMBEDDED INTERROGATIVES

Yes-no wh interrogatives occur in an indirect form in verb complement clauses. Yes-no interrogatives are introduced by the complementisers *if* or *whether* and the word order is that of a declarative clause, as in (1b).

 1 a 'Have you seen my laptop?', he asked.
   b He asked if/whether we had seen his laptop.

(1a and b) draw attention to the important general phenomenon of indirect speech. (1a) relays the speaker's exact words: use of *you* for the listener and *my* referring to the speaker, and the use of the present tense form *have*. In writing, the direct question is enclosed in inverted commas, then separated from the verb of saying or asking by a comma. The verb of saying or asking may precede the direct question, as in *He asked, 'Have you seen my laptop?'* In (1a) the questioner is referred to by a pronoun, *he*, but could be referred to by a longer expression such as *the worried-looking student*. Such longer noun phrases are often, but not necessarily, accompanied by inversion; the verb of saying or asking immediately follows the direct question, followed in turn by the noun phrase, as in (2).

 2 'Have you seen my laptop?', asked the worried-looking student.

Note too the backshifting of tense: present-tense *have* is backshifted to past-tense *had* (*will* is backshifted to *would* – *'Will you help me'*, he asked → *He asked if we would help him*). The pronouns are changed as appropriate. The speaker is no longer presented as addressing the listener directly and *you* is replaced by *we, I, they* as required: *He asked if we/I/they would help him.* *Me* is replaced by *him* as the speaker is no longer presented as referring to him- or herself directly.

Embedded wh interrogatives also occur in verb complement clauses but follow a different pattern. They have the word order of declarative clauses but with the wh noun phrase at the front of the clause. Consider the direct questions in (3) and the corresponding embedded interrogatives (indirect questions) in (4).

3 a Who has a driving licence?
  b Which car are you driving?
  c Which drawer did you put the keys in?

4 a She asked <u>who</u> had a driving licence.
  b She asked <u>which car</u> I was driving.
  c She asked <u>which drawer</u> I put the keys in/in which drawer I put the keys.

(3a–c) show the normal word order for wh interrogatives, with the wh word at the front of the clause, followed by the verb, followed, where applicable, by the subject (*Which car <u>are you</u> driving?* (4a–c) show the normal word order for embedded wh interrogatives. Thus, in (4b) the wh noun phrase is at the front of the embedded clause – *which car I was driving*, but the rest of the clause has the usual word order of a declarative – *which car <u>I was driving</u>*.

Embedded wh interrogatives bring up two other issues. One is how far back wh words can reach. In (5) there is a single embedded clause and *who* 'reaches back' to the place where we would expect to find the direct object of *marry*. This place is marked with *t*. (*t* originally stood, in one generative model, for 'trace'. The idea was that *who* started out in the direct object position after *marry* but was moved to the front of the clause leaving a trace.)

5 I don't remember [<u>who</u> John wants to marry t]

Now consider (6), where the embedded wh interrogative is inside another embedded clause, *Mary thinks*.

6 I don't remember $_{\text{Comp Clause 1}}$[who Mary thinks $_{\text{Comp Clause 2}}$[John wants to marry t]]

In (6) *who* reaches back across the boundary between the complement clause 1 *Mary thinks* and the embedded interrogative (Complement Clause 2) *John wants to marry*. (6) is a correct structure of English, but only because in it Complement Clause 2 is a contact clause, with no complementiser. If the Complement Clause 2 is a *that* clause, the sentence is not acceptable.

6a *I don't remember _{Comp Clause 1}[who Mary thinks _{Comp Clause 2}[that John wants to marry t]]

As mentioned above, the problem of determining just how far and in what circumstances a *wh* word can reach back was first explored when analysts thought of wh words being moved from their original position. This was known as fronting, and the process illustrated in (6) by which a wh word moves across a clause boundary was known as, and is often still called, long-distance fronting. When analysts focus on dependency relations, that is, on wh words reaching back to slots or traces in structures, the term 'long-distance dependency' is used.

Fronted wh words may be oblique objects, that is, they may be the complements of prepositions. In simple clauses a preposition may be left ('stranded') at the end of a clause, as in *Who did you give your passport to?* This is the typical construction in every type of English except the most formal writing, where you can find the construction *To whom did you give your passport?* Here we have the object form of the pronoun, *whom*, and both pronoun and preposition have been fronted. Like the children following the pied piper in Robert Browning's poem *The Pied Piper of Hamelin*, the preposition (and any other constituents) follow the wh word to the front of the clause. The wh word is thought of as performing some pied-piping† and the preposition is said to be pied-piped. (=> RELATIVE CLAUSES: WH.)

Pied-piping is also found in embedded wh interrogatives, as in *It is now impossible to discover to whom the documents were issued*. This example sounds even more unnatural than *To whom did you give your passport?* but will probably survive thanks to the social capital associated with this very formal written English, and thanks to the gatekeepers who vet certain types of text before they appear in public print. The more natural version is *It is now impossible to discover who the documents were issued to*.

We close this discussion of embedded interrogatives/indirect questions with a construction that now occurs frequently in speech and in writing (but perhaps not in the most formal written texts). In spite of its frequency, and (as will be shown) its relatively long existence, the construction is ignored by reference grammars of English and is often declared to be incorrect.† Tensed verbs move to the front of direct question structures, as in *Are they filling in the forms?* versus *They are filling in the forms*. A general view is that such movement does not happen in embedded questions, that examples such as (7) are incorrect in standard

English and many dialects ('dialect' being used meretriciously). This view is particularly important in recent work in the minimalist framework, where it serves as evidence for a distinction between weak and strong features, which are then invoked in order to handle other constructions.

> 7 I asked are they filling in the forms.

The important feature of (7) is that the verb *asked* is complemented by the verb complement clause *are they filling in the forms*. This clause has the word order of a direct question, whereas manuals of 'correct' English prescribe *I asked if they were filling in the forms*. In the prescribed version the complement clause is introduced by the complementiser *if* (but *whether* is also permissible) and has the word order of a declarative clause.

The fact is that the construction exemplified in (7) is widespread and of relatively long standing. An example from the mid-19th century is given in (8).

> 8 I have <u>asked the orderlies why were these floors not cleaned</u>; and the answer was, and Dr McGregor told me so, that the wood was so rotten, that if it were properly washed it could not be got dry again.

March 1855 *Statement to the Select Committee of the House of Commons Enquiry into War in the Crimea. The Hon Sidney Godolphin Osborne*. Cited in Mugglestone (2006).
(9) is a contemporaneous example from Dickens.

> 9 I had thought beforehand that I knew its purport, and I did. It <u>asked me would I be the mistress of Bleak House</u>.
> Charles Dickens, *Bleak House*, part 14, chapter 44

(8) and (9) are from written texts, but not from representations of conversation. Examples from representations of conversation occur regularly in detective novels from the 1920s and 1930s, witness (10) from the author Freeman Wills Crofts.

> 10 You know him don't you? Well, find him and tell him this affair has developed into attempted murder and abduction, and <u>ask him can he give any information</u> to the Yard.
> Freeman Wills Crofts (1926), *The Cheyne Mystery*. [1953 Penguin Edition, p.157. Inspector French speaking.]

(11) is a modern example.

11 '... They say prisoners are sold as soon as a captain unloads them, and nobody <u>asks were these once free men and women</u>, who never ought to be in chains.'
Lindsey Davis (2004), *Scandal Takes a Holiday*. London: Century, p. 72

Direct questions turn up in other syntactic contexts where indirect questions are prescribed. Such contexts are *the question arises, find out, is sure, the biggest uncertainty is, know* as in (12a–e).

12 a But with just a few squadrons of Tornados on hand for the invasion, the question arises of <u>why did we have to rely on the Americans</u> to protect our troops.
New Zealand Herald, section B3, 8 February 2007. Citing the *Daily Telegraph*.
    b Log on at the BBC World Service Aids site to find out <u>how much do you know about condoms</u>.
[BBC webpage]
    c No one is sure <u>how long are the passages</u> leading off from this centre.
Scotland on Sunday, 13 November 1988. Article by Doreen Taylor
    d The biggest uncertainty hanging over the economy is <u>how red will things get</u>.
[Reference to map showing areas of house-price decreases in red]
The Economist, 10–16 May 2008, p. 97 'American housing. Map of misery'
    e I'd love to know *how much better a player is Tiger Woods* than Tom Morris.
The Herald (Scotland), 16 April 2008, Midweek Sport, p. 16

The sentence in (12d) was followed by a sentence with a classic indirect question: *Assessing <u>how much further house prices are likely to fall</u> gets even trickier.*

We close this discussion by drawing attention to an example in which direct and indirect questions combine, as in (13).

13 Karen McCarthy speaks to players and coaches about <u>why women play</u> and <u>how rough is it</u> out there on the paddock...
New Zealand Herald, 8 August 2005

Speaks about is modified by two conjoined complement clauses. The first is *why women play*, which has the word order of a declarative clause; the second is *how rough is it out there on the paddock* (= the pitch); it has the word order of a direct question. The example happens to come from a New Zealand newspaper but that is irrelevant. This pattern of two conjoined embedded interrogative complement clauses is widespread and not new. JM collected a number of examples from undergraduate examination scripts and dissertations in the 1980s. A final comment: some of the above examples are from spoken data but others are from written data. One or two spoken examples can be dismissed by doubters as performance errors, but not syntactic patterns occurring regularly in written texts.

COMPLEMENT CLAUSES: MOOD AND MODALITY

Complement clauses can modify what are called volitional verbs; that is, verbs expressing a wish or desire that some event happen or some state of affairs be brought about. The more common volitional verbs are *command, demand, insist, order, propose, recommend, suggest*. There is also a small set of volitional adjectives, such as *adamant, keen* and *insistent*. Complement clauses dependent on a volitional verb or adjective may contain a subjunctive verb form. The difference in meaning between the subjunctive and indicative is brought out by the following examples.

1 a Jennifer said that Jacob <u>had</u> been given a formal warning.
  b Jennifer demanded that Jacob <u>be</u> given a formal warning.

2 a The Chief Constable insists that the police <u>investigated</u> the report.
  b The Prime Minister insists that the police <u>investigate</u> the report.

3 a The doctor was adamant that the patient <u>had</u> missed his appointment.
  b The doctor was adamant that this medication <u>be</u> abandoned.

The complement clauses in the (a) examples contain indicative verbs, those in the (b) examples contain subjunctive verbs. Speakers use indicative verb forms to present some state of affairs as a fact: it is presented as a fact that Jacob was given a formal warning, that the police investigated the report and that the patient missed his appointment. In contrast, subjunctive verbs are used to present a situation as desirable and desired, one that the speaker wishes could be brought about (but which may not come about). Jennifer strongly wishes (*demanded*) the giving of a formal warning, the Prime Minister is obliging the police to carry out an investigation, and the doctor is not going to be swayed by any arguments from the patient: the particular medication is going to be replaced by another. Note that *insist* and *be adamant* can have a volitional interpretation, as in (2b) and (3b), or a non-volitional interpretation, as in (2a) and (3a).

It is generally assumed that the above examples relate to a difference between American and British English. The (b) examples above with the subjunctive are said to be typical of American English, while speakers of British English use *should* rather than the subjunctive, as in (3a–c).

3 a Jennifer demanded that Jacob should be given a formal warning.
  b The Prime Minister insists that the police should investigate the report.
  c The doctor was adamant that this medication should be abandoned.

We cannot say that all American speakers use one construction and all British speakers the other. It is a matter of preference, and KB and JM tend to use the subjunctive (especially in writing). It is also not always obvious whether a given verb requires the subjunctive or *should*, as shown by the following real example. University X has an ethics committee. The 2003 version of the Committee's regulations contained the following pieces of text.

4 It is expected that access to the Consent Forms be restricted to the researcher and/or the Principal Investigator. If you intend otherwise, please explain.
5 It is required that Consent Forms be stored separately from data and kept for six years.

On a first reading (4) seemed peculiar. A second reading pointed to the combination of *It is expected* and *be restricted* as the source of the peculiarity. Wondering whether his reaction was misguided, JM checked reference grammars of English and found the sets of volitional verbs and volitional adjectives listed above and the sorts of examples in (1)–(3).†
The list and the examples did not contain *expect* or *is expected*. In contrast, *is required* in (5) licenses the subjunctive in the complement clause *that Consent Forms be stored separately*, since *require* falls into the same semantic field as *demand* and *insist*.

What is the explanation for (4)? It could be a case of hypercorrection, the writer of the document being aware of the construction Verb + *that* + Clause with subjunctive verb form. Semantics and pragmatics might have led the writer to the construction. *Expect* in its basic meaning and in many contexts is not a volitional verb: *I expect they will arrive about six*, *We expect her to take at least the silver medal*. Where the speaker is in a position of authority, *expect* can be used to signal a very indirect command: *I expect you to be here at 6am* (spoken by police inspector to new constable) and in (4) *expect* is not just a statement of expectation but is part of an indirect command. Nonetheless, *expect* does not normally combine with a clause containing a verb in the subjunctive. Pinning down exactly what is grammatical and what is not can be very tricky, and even highly educated writers can go astray.

COMPLEMENT CLAUSES: GERUNDS, INFINITIVES AND MEANING

The section on verb complement clauses and complementisers looks at the licensing of *that* and the exclusion either of *whether* on its own or of all wh words, as well as the licensing of constructions with a dummy subject *it* and a complement clause (which might or might not be extraposed). The verbs controlling the licensing fall into groups that are labelled THINKING, AFFECT and LIKE. Here we look briefly at other patterns of finite and non-finite complement clauses that correlate with particular constructions.

We begin with the contrast between gerunds such as *writing letters* in *He hates writing letters* and infinitives such as *to visit Paris* in *I intend to visit Paris*. With certain verbs gerunds signal that some action has been carried out and some resulting state of affairs is a fact. With the same verbs infinitives signal that the action has still to be carried out and remains in the realm of intention.

1 a Michael will always remember climbing Mount Ararat.
 b Michael might remember to pay the telephone bill.

The climbing of Mount Ararat has been completed, the telephone bill is not yet paid. The difference in meaning is also clear from examples with *forget*.

2 a I forgot having given James the spare key.
 b I forgot to give James the spare key.

(2a) presents James as having the spare key, (2b) presents him as not having it. *Finish* and *complete* require gerund complements, as in *We finished/completed packing the china*. An action that is completed or finished is a fact. Actions that are presented as being started, begun or continued are not completed and there is no contrast between the infinitive and the gerund. *We started packing the china* is equivalent to *We started to pack the china*, and *They continued typing on their laptops* is equivalent to *They continued to type on their laptops*. A more subtle difference comes out with the lexical item *try*. Compare *I tried to take the medicine but it tasted vile and I spat it out* (taking the medicine was not completed) with *I tried taking the medicine but it doesn't seem to have helped* (taking the medicine was completed).

A number of verbs can only be used appropriately with respect to situations existing at the moment of speech or having existed in the past, that is, with respect to facts. Examples are in (3).

3 a We all regret her being ill.
 b Barnabas minded losing the match.
 c The children resented being left at home.
 d Philippa deplores their carrying guns.
 e The university took into account his being dyslexic.

The verbs *regret, mind, resent, deplore* and the phrase *take into account* can be complemented by gerunds, as above, and some can be complemented by *that* clauses. They cannot, however, take infinitive complements.

COMPLEMENT CLAUSES: NOUN COMPLEMENT CLAUSES

Relative clauses can modify (be dependent on) nouns, and any noun can have a relative clause (restrictive or non-restrictive) dependent on it. (=> RELATIVE CLAUSES: INTRODUCTION, RELATIVE CLAUSES: RESTRICTIVE AND NON-RESTRICTIVE.) A subset of nouns can be modified by complement clauses, as in (1).

1 We rejected the idea that the building would be demolished.

The direct object of *rejected* is the noun phrase *the idea that the building would be demolished*. The head of the noun phrase is *idea* and the chunk *that the building would be demolished* is a complement clause dependent on (modifying) *idea*. The label 'complement clause' is also applied to clauses modifying verbs, as in *Ishbel regretted that she had turned down the offer*. The clause *that she had turned down the offer* modifies *regretted*. It is a complement clause in that it is obligatory and completes the syntax of the main clause, where *regretted* requires a direct object, and it fills out the meaning of that verb. In (1) the clause *that the building would be demolished* is not obligatory (*We rejected the idea* is a complete clause by itself) but it does fill out the interpretation of *idea*, conveying the content of the latter.

We can usefully recognise three sorts of noun that can be modified by noun complement clauses. One set consists of nouns denoting entities such as proposals, ideas, offers, plans, theories, hypotheses, tales, guesses, and so on. Examples are in (2).

2 a Who approved the proposal that taxes should be increased?
 b There was a plan that we would visit Glasgow today but the weather is terrible.
 c Scientists have disproved the theory that the moon is made of green cheese.
 d His tale that he has a job in Turkey is just that, a tale.
 e My guess that they would change the law turned out to be wrong.

The complementiser *that* can be omitted, as in *There was a plan we would visit Glasgow today* and *Scientists have disproved the theory the moon is made of green cheese*, but the omission gives awkward results in *?His tale he has a job in Turkey* and *My guess they would change the law*.

Noun complement clauses look superficially like relative clauses. Both types modify (are dependent on) nouns and have the complementiser *that* or no complementiser, and both can be extraposed as in (3), showing a complement clause, and (4), showing a relative clause.

3 a The idea that the building would be demolished was rejected.
   b The idea was rejected that the building would be demolished.

4 a The idea that the chairman proposed was rejected.
   b The idea was rejected that the chairman proposed.

There are however major differences between the two types of clause, which is why the two types are retained. While noun complement clauses, like relative clauses, help to pick out one proposal or theory as opposed to others, the complement clauses always convey information about the content of a proposal, plan, theory or guess. Relative clauses can convey information about any aspect of an entity. With respect to the form of the clauses, relative clauses can also have the relativiser *which*: *the idea which the chairman proposed*, *the plan which they came up with*. Noun complement clauses exclude *which*: **Who approved the proposal which taxes should be increased?*, **My guess which they would change the law turned out to be wrong*.

A third difference is that relative clauses introduced by *that* may be incomplete. In (5) the relative clause *that my wife likes* is missing a direct object, although *like* requires one. In (6), in contrast, the complement clause introduced by *that* has a subject (*James*), a main verb (*buy*) and a direct object (*our house*). Its syntax is complete.

5 We're buying the house that my wife likes [...].
6 The idea that James should buy our house is not silly.

While noun complement clauses are never introduced by a complementiser *which*, there is a small set of nouns such as *question, reason* and *problem* that require or allow complement clauses introduced by a wh word, or by *which* in combination with a noun or with *one*. See (7).

7 a The reason why the house is to be demolished has not been properly discussed.
   b The question which one to choose is very tricky.
   c We haven't solved the problem where to store the books.

The second set of nouns that take noun complement clauses consists of abstract nouns derived from verbs or adjectives: *attraction* from *attract*, *assurance* from *assure*, *possibility* from *possible*, *likelihood* from *likely*.

8 a The theory has the attraction <u>that it is elegant</u>.
   b The chairman gave an assurance <u>that the firm would be kept going</u>.
   c I'm worried by the possibility <u>that there will be another banking crisis</u>.
   d The likelihood <u>that a tsunami will strike</u> is very low.

The underlined clauses in (8) describe the content of the attraction, the possibility and the likelihood, and cannot be introduced by *which*, as shown by (9).

9 a *The theory has the attraction <u>which it is elegant</u>.
   b *The chairman gave an assurance <u>which the firm would be kept going</u>.
   c *I'm worried by the possibility <u>which there will be another banking crisis</u>.
   d *The likelihood <u>which a tsunami will strike</u> is very low.

A final point: the removal of *that* from (8a–d) leaves three complete clauses: *it is elegant, the firm would be kept going, there will be another banking crisis* and *a tsunami will strike*.

The third set of items that allow noun complement clauses consists of semi-fixed and idiomatic phrases such as *have an idea, have a hunch, have a clue*. These idioms allow noun complement clauses introduced by *that* or by wh words as in (7).

10 I had an idea that things were going to go wrong.
They had no idea what was going to happen.

11 She didn't have a clue that she would be offered the job.
She didn't have a clue which post she would be offered.

Constructions

CONSTRUCTIONS: OVERVIEW

Grammars of English (and other languages) deal with combinations of items: morphemes combine to form words, words to form phrases, phrases to form clauses. Clauses combine to form clause-combinations (the concept and term used in analyses of spoken language) and sentences (the term and concept used in analyses of written language). The concept of construction has to do with smaller items being put together to build larger items. Many words are constructions, since they consist of one or more morphemes that are combined. The construction may be inflectional, as in *refuse* combining with *-s* to give *refuses*, or derivational, as in *re-*, *cycle-* and *-able* combining to give *recyclable*. (The quirks of English spelling can be ignored here.) Phrases are constructions: we distinguish different types of phrases by what the head word is, as in noun phrase, prepositional phrase, adjective phrase, verb phrase, adverb phrase. Clauses are constructions built up from phrases, and clause-combinations and sentences are also constructions – for a given example we can look at what types of clause occur, the order in which the clauses are combined, and the relationship between any two of the clauses.

When we analyse a construction, we are interested in the smaller blocks that have been combined to build up a bigger block. We look at what sort of smaller blocks have been used and the order in which they are set out: e.g., *field* + *ed* and not *ed* + *field*, *into the house* and not *the house into*. We can look at how the smaller blocks are linked: by order, as in the above examples, or by syntactic linkage such as agreement in number and person between subject noun and verb (*The girls were swimming*, not **The girls is swimming*). These structural properties – type of building block, order of blocks, linkage between blocks – are basic but once the structural properties of a construction have been determined, functional properties come into play. In phrases one word functions as the head, the others as modifiers. In clauses a given noun phrase may be a subject, direct object, second object or indirect object of the verb, and a further distinction is made between phrases that are complements of the verb and those that are adjuncts. (=> CLAUSE STRUCTURE: DEPENDENCY RELATIONS.)

This is not a book about formal models of syntax but a brief remark is in order on how the concept of construction has been applied in such models. At one point in the evolution of Chomskyan models of generative grammar it was thought more productive to focus on properties shared by many constructions, and individual constructions were viewed as accidental features of sequences of words, phrases and clauses. One current model, construction grammar, has restored constructions to a central place, and an extreme version, radical construction grammar, is based on the assumption that accounts of the overall grammar of a language are not justified, that analysis is only possible on the grammar of one construction at time. Which model survives is not relevant here but we do need to mention the traditional distinction between major and minor constructions. One reason that the Chomskyan notion of very general properties is not sufficient is that many sequences of items are minor constructions with their own peculiar properties. They range from relatively fixed to relatively flexible sequences and there is a larger number of them than used to be supposed.

Construction grammar is a new enterprise but constructions are a very old concept and remain central to most work on language. Reference and teaching grammars of languages have always relied on the concept; sociolinguists continued to employ it; and investigators working on the acquisition of language by children find the construction indispensable, as do linguists working on the typology of languages. Applying the concept of construction is not always straightforward. Faced with a set of data, say examples containing relative clauses, we need to ask whether it makes sense to talk of 'the relative clause' or 'the relative clause construction' or whether we should recognise many relative clause constructions and, if so, how many. The answers to these questions are important for, e.g., typology and theories of first language acquisition. (See the section on relative clauses.) Suppose we have a five-year-old child who can understand *The toy which she took* but not *The book in which we found that song*. If these are two different constructions – relative clause introduced by *which*, a direct object pronoun, as opposed to a relative clause introduced by a prepositional phrase – are we justified in saying, as investigators of child language acquisition have said, that the child 'has' the relative clause construction? Likewise if the child only uses relative clauses such as *the toy she took* or *the toy that she took*, but not wh relative clauses. (=> RELATIVE CLAUSES: INTRODUCTION, RELATIVE CLAUSES: WH.)

Fortunately this textbook does not require us to discuss the above question; the concept of construction is simply deployed as one of the traditional tools of syntactic analysis.

Non-finite clauses

NON-FINITE CLAUSES: INTRODUCTION

Syntactic theory recognises non-finite clauses, sequences of words that lack a finite verb but nonetheless are treated as subordinate clauses. Examples are given in (1), with the non-finite clauses underlined.

1 a James wanted <u>to visit the zoo on Saturday</u>.
   b Katarina regretted <u>leaving the party in a bad temper</u>.
   c <u>Having read the manifestos in the library</u>, Barnabas didn't vote.
   d Lucie remembered <u>to send Margaret a birthday card</u>.
   e Michael decided <u>to drive to Spain</u>.

Formerly such sequences were treated as phrases – for instance, *to visit the zoo* in (1a) was described as an 'infinitive phrase', *leaving the party* in (1b) as a 'gerund phrase', *Having read the manifestos* in (1c) as a participial phrase. Contemporary analysis treats them as clauses because finite and non-finite verbs take the same types of complements and adjuncts: *the zoo* in (1b), *the party* in (1b) and *the manifestos* in (1c) are direct objects; *to Spain* in (1e) is a directional complement (oblique object); *Margaret* in (1d) is an indirect object and a birthday card is, depending on your view of grammatical functions, a second object. *On Saturday* in (1a) is a time adjunct, *in a bad temper* in (1b) a manner adjunct and *in the library* in (1c) a place adjunct. It is even possible to find subjects, such as *Rene* in *Rene having taken the laptop, Jennifer couldn't e-mail her friend*.

Some non-finite clauses have aspect, as shown by (2a), which is perfect, and by (2b), which is progressive.

2 a I'd like to <u>have finished</u> the report by the time I go home.
   b Right now I would like <u>to be climbing</u> hills, not sitting at my computer.

Non-finite structures can be positive (see the above examples) or negative, as in (3), and active or passive, as in (4).

3   a   She decided <u>not</u> to leave the party.
    b   Having <u>not</u> read the report, we were at a disadvantage.
    c   I hate <u>not</u> knowing when guests are arriving.

4   a   She refused <u>to be swayed</u> by their arguments.
    b   <u>Being chased</u> by the dog, the cat leapt into the holly tree.
    c   He loves <u>being given</u> hardback books.

On the other hand, non-finite clauses allow a far more limited range of constructions than finite ones. Tense and modal verbs such as *can*, *may* and *must* are excluded. In spite of the subject-like *Rene* in the example above, *Rene having taken the laptop*, non-finite clauses, by their very nature, do not have nouns agreeing with verbs in number and person. They do allow constituents that correspond to subject nouns in finite clauses, as in the *Rene* example, in full gerunds with a possessive noun, such as <u>*Rene's having taken the laptop*</u> *doesn't surprise me*, and in *for to* clauses the noun enclosed by *for* and *to*, as in *For <u>Rene</u> to take the laptop was stupid*. (Like finite subordinate clauses they exclude interrogative and imperative constructions.) Gerunds exclude the Progressive, as in (5), and the verb stem construction excludes the Perfect, as in (6).

5   *I hate <u>being writing</u> when the sun is shining.
6   *All the coach has done is <u>have destroyed</u> their confidence.

Non-finite clauses cannot contain interrogative or imperative constructions, nor do they allow focusing and topicalising constructions such as negative fronting and adverb fronting. (=> SENTENCES AND CLAUSES: MAIN AND SUBORDINATE CLAUSES.)

Non-finite clauses do allow modality to be signalled, just not by means of modal verbs. Examples are in (7)–(9).

7   Katarina enjoyed having to review the work of the section.   [necessity]
8   The children asked to be allowed to watch the film.   [permission]
9   Freya's ambition was to be able to fly a glider.   [ability]

In a given sentence finite subordinate clauses have their own set of participants independent of the participants in the main clause. This is not true of most non-finite constructions. Consider (10), which brings us to the traditional concept of 'understood subject'.

10   James agreed to lend his car to Katarina.

The infinitive construction *to lend his car to Katarina* has no overt subject noun phrase but *James* is traditionally called the understood subject of *lend*. That is, it was recognised that (10) refers to two situations – James' agreeing, and someone lending his car to Katarina. James is the person doing the agreeing, so to speak, and also the person lending the car. The syntax is rather condensed relative to the semantic interpretation, since there is only one finite clause but two propositions, one for each situation. In contemporary terms, the notion of understood subject is translated into that of control. The subject of *agree* is said to control the subject of the verb in the dependent infinitive, here *lend*. The noun phrase *James* determines the interpretation of another, invisible, noun phrase, the subject of *lend*. The technical term for this relationship is 'control'; *James* is said to control the understood subject of *lend*.

A similar analysis applies to the underlined gerund in *Richard loves walking with dinosaurs*, where the understood subject of *walking* is *Richard*. In contemporary terms, the subject of *loves* controls the understood subject of the dependent gerund, *walking*. More complex structures are possible, as in (11).

11   Richard tried to persuade David to walk with dinosaurs.

The subject of *tried* controls the subject of the dependent infinitive, *to persuade*. *To persuade* in turn has the dependent infinitive *to walk*. The object of *persuade*, *David*, controls the understood subject of *to walk*.

To sum up, on the scale of clause-ness – the ability to take tense, aspect and modal verbs, the range of syntactic constructions allowed – main clauses outrank everything else, and subordinate finite clauses outrank non-finite subordinate clauses. Nonetheless, modern analysts see the non-finite sequences in (1) as clauses, though only as non-finite clauses, because they give priority to the fact that non-finite and finite sequences have the same set of complements and adjuncts. Verbs exercise the same control over the types and number of their complements in finite and non-finite constructions; e.g., *put* requires to its right a noun phrase and a directional phrase, in both *The child put the toy on the table* and *The child tried to put the toy on the table*. Meaning too is relevant. Finite clauses denote situations, and so do non-finite clauses, once the understood subject is supplied. (=> CLAUSE STRUCTURE: DEPENDENCY RELATIONS, CLAUSE STRUCTURE: LINEARITY AND GRAMMATICAL FUNCTIONS.)

We recognise eight types of non-finite clause but there is a major alternative analysis that offers only four types. (=> NON-FINITE CLAUSES: EIGHT TYPES OR FOUR?)

NON-FINITE CLAUSES: INFINITIVES

English has a number of non-finite clauses. They are distinguished from each other by their form, their function in a clause, and what they modify. In this they resemble the finite subordinate clauses. (=>

SENTENCES AND CLAUSES: MAIN AND SUBORDINATE CLAUSES, NON-FINITE CLAUSES.) They occur frequently, being used in both speech and writing. Infinitives modify verbs, functioning as subject, as in *To receive such praise* amazed her, or object, as in *The critics refused to praise her book*. The exception is the infinitive relative clause as in *a good place to eat, the best book to read on the topic.* (=> RELATIVE CLAUSES: INFINITIVAL.) It modifies nouns, here *place* and *book*. Infinitive non-finite clauses are marked by *to* or *for to* and are nominal, that is, they occur where ordinary noun phrases occur.

Note the two types of infinitive non-finite clause, one with *to*, the other with *for to*. The latter is used with 'emotive' words and phrases such as *idiotic, regrettable, a tragedy*, as in (1). (=> COMPLEMENT CLAUSES: GERUNDS, INFINITIVES AND MEANING.)

1 a It was idiotic for Leonora to resign.
  b For Leonora to resign was idiotic.

2 a It is regrettable for David to have these ideas.
    For David to have these ideas is regrettable.

3 a It will be a tragedy for the firm to go bankrupt.
    For the firm to go bankrupt will be a tragedy.

To is also used in constructions such as *All I want is to go home* and *All I needed was to borrow this book*. Infinitive non-finite clauses can express purpose: *I went there to borrow this book*. Some speakers of English use the non-standard *for to* construction to express purpose, as in *We rushed across for to see what had happened*, but this construction appears to be in decline. Not all instances of *for to* are non-standard. Examples like *I want for you to be happy* are on the border between standard and non-standard, at least in British English.

NON-FINITE CLAUSES: FREE PARTICIPLES

Free participle non-finite clauses contain verbs with the suffix *-ing* but, unlike gerunds, they modify whole clauses. In this respect they resemble finite adverbial clauses. (=> ADVERBIAL CLAUSES: INTRODUCTION.) A number of different structures and interpretations are possible, as illustrated by (1a–g).

1 a They were milling about in the foyer, flicking through a free booklet of his favourite recipes.
  b They say adult North Americans are addicted, each consuming 280 milligrams of caffeine daily.

c <u>Jumping up</u>, he dashed out of the room.
   d <u>Having locked the door</u>, he opened the parcel.
   e <u>Pleased with this thought</u>, he moved forward more confidently.
      Dorothy Sayers (2011), *Unnatural Death*. London: Folio Society, p. 191
   f My hake and hand-cut chips arrived, <u>the latter served in a metal pot</u>.
      Julian Barnes (2011), *The Sense of an Ending*. London: Vintage Books, p. 147
   g He arrived just as she was dishing up the pasta, <u>a whiff of carbolic still lingering around him</u> and <u>cans of beer clanking in a plastic bag</u>.
      Mark Billingham (2010), *From the Dead*. London: Little, Brown, p. 70

Free participles may denote events simultaneous with an event or state denoted by a main clause. In (1a), the event referred to by *flicking through a free booklet of his favourite recipes* is simultaneous with the event referred to by *They were milling about in the foyer*; in (1b), the events referred to by *each consuming 280 milligrams of caffeine daily* are simultaneous with the state referred to by *adult North Americans are addicted*. In (1c), however, *jumping up* refers to an event occurring just before the event referred to by *he dashed out of the room*. (1d) is another example of aspect occurring in a non-finite clause, and (1e and f) show that a free participle clause can have a passive participle at its centre, *pleased* in *Pleased with this thought* and *served* in *the latter served in a metal pot*. (1f) also shows that free participle clauses may contain a noun phrase corresponding to the subject in a finite clause, here <u>The latter</u> served in a metal pot = <u>The latter</u> were served in a metal pot. Finally, (1g) shows the same phenomenon as (1f) but each quasi-subject phrase is more complex and the two of them are conjoined: <u>*a whiff of carbolic*</u> still lingering around him and <u>*cans of beer*</u> *clanking in a plastic bag*.

Many, but not all, free participle clauses can be rephrased as subordinate adverbial clauses and many share another property of adverbial clauses: they can occur in different positions in a sentence. (1a) can be rearranged to give *flicking through a free booklet of his favourite recipes, they were milling about in the foyer*, (1d) as *He opened the parcel, having locked the door*, (1e) as *He moved forward more confidently, pleased with this thought*, (1g) as *A whiff of carbolic still lingering around him and cans of beer clanking in a plastic bag, he arrived just as she was dishing up the pasta*. Of course, in the texts from which these examples come, the rearranged versions might be unwelcome stylistically and from the perspective of information structure. (=> CLAUSE AND TEXT: THEME.)

The *-ing* form in (2a) poses an interesting problem.

   2 a <u>Knowing the country well</u>, he took a short cut.
      b <u>Slamming the door</u>, he ran down the steps.

The problem is this. Typically non-finite clauses can be correlated with finite clauses, say *since he was pleased with this thought* for (1e). (2a) contains *knowing* but *know* does not have *-ing* forms that combine with *be*, as shown by (3).

3 *He was knowing the country well.

Slamming the door in (2b) is also problematic. The free participle sequence cannot be related to *When/while he was slamming the door* but only to *When he had slammed the door*. That is, the path from the free participle to the time clause would involve the introduction of a different auxiliary, HAVE. In general, free participles are best treated as non-finite clauses having only an indirect connection with finite clauses.

We close this discussion with a final property of free participles, their frequent use as what are called hanging or dangling participles. In the examples in (1) the free participles all have an understood subject that is controlled by a noun phrase in the main clause: *they* in (1a) controls the understood subject of *flicking*, *adult North Americans* in (1b) controls the interpretation of *each*, *he* controls the understood subjects of *jumping up* in (1c), and *Having locked* in (1d). Consider now the example in (4).

4 "<u>Knowing the width of the rail tracks in the video is four feet, eight-and-a-half inches</u>, the animal photographed is clearly in excess of four feet." *The Herald* (Scotland), 4 February 2012, p.14 'Roger Tagholm on ... big cat sightings'

The underlined free participle has an uncontrolled or open understood subject. It is certainly not controlled by *the animal* in the main clause. Put another way, the free participle is not dependent on any constituent in the main clause. A possible paraphrase is 'Since we/you know that ...'. The construction is proscribed in manuals of good style but is extremely frequent in written texts of all kinds and has to be recognised as a regular construction of English. A more appropriate label would be 'absolute free participle'. (Whatever the label for the construction, there is no guarantee that the gatekeepers of 'correct' English will stop worrying about it.)

NON-FINITE CLAUSES: GERUNDS (TYPE 1)

The most frequent type of gerund non-finite clause is exemplified in (1).

1 a <u>Steeping grounds by filtering</u> extracts more caffeine.
   b Someone has reported <u>seeing a fox</u>.
   c They achieve this by <u>restricting their insurance cover</u>.

Gerunds contain a non-finite verb form with the suffix -*ing* and function as subject, as in (1a), as direct object, as in (1b), or as oblique object, as in (1c). (=> CLAUSE STRUCTURE: LINEARITY AND GRAMMATICAL FUNCTIONS.) That is, they occur in positions where nouns and noun phrases also occur, e.g., *Someone has reported <u>the accident</u>, <u>This method</u> extracts more caffeine, They achieve this by <u>hard work</u>*. There is a gerund structure in which a possessive noun corresponds to the subject of a finite clause, as in *<u>Phil's always being ill</u> is a nuisance* (= *It is a nuisance that Phil is always ill*). This 'full' gerund is very rare in informal speech and even in any but the most formal written texts. The preferred construction is *<u>Phil always being ill</u> is a nuisance* or *It is a nuisance <u>Phil always being ill</u>*. (The graduate students (mature teachers of English as an Additional Language) on one of JM's syntax courses thought at first that he was joking when he gave examples of the full gerund.)

NON-FINITE CLAUSES: GERUNDS (TYPE 2)

The underlined chunks in (1) look like participles but are analysed as gerunds. Why? One argument is historical. Earlier stages of English had, for (1a) *a-climbing in the window*, for (1b) *a-opening the safe* and for (1c) *a-sitting on the terrace*. The *a-* derives from *on*, which, being a preposition, indicates that *climbing* etc. in (1) were nouns.

1 a   I saw the burglar <u>climbing in the window</u>.
    b   I caught him <u>opening the safe</u>.
    c   I found Cordelia <u>sitting on the terrace</u>.
    d   It was there, at last, he saw her, <u>waiting for him</u>.
       Michael Dobbs (2012), *A Sentimental Traitor*. London and New York: Schuster, p. 357
    e   I could sense Mrs Ford <u>examining me while she made bacon and eggs</u>.
       Julian Barnes (2011), *The Sense of an Ending*. London: Vintage Books, p. 80
    f   I imagined him <u>taking his laptop to café terraces with Wi-Fi</u>.
       Julian Barnes (2011), *The Sense of an Ending*. London: Vintage Books, p. 80

The historical evidence is simple, attractive and suggestive, but does not carry much weight. After all, languages change considerably over 300 or 400 years. We need to construct an argument based on contemporary data. Consider the example in (2).

2   The police caught the burglar <u>climbing in the window</u>.

Is *climbing in the window* a gerund (Type 2) or a reduced relative clause/ participial phrase? If it were the latter, the whole chunk *the burglar climbing in the window* would be a noun phrase and it could become the subject of a passive clause, as in (3).

   3 The burglar climbing in the window was caught by the police.

(2) and (3) can be used in situations where there is more than one burglar, as in (4), which answers the question *Which burglar did the police catch?*

   4 The police caught the burglar climbing in the window; the burglar scrambling over the roof escaped.

There are restrictions on chunks such as *the burglar climbing in the window* where *climbing in the window* is a participle/reduced relative clause. (5a and b) are parallel to (2), but with a proper noun and a pronoun instead of *the burglar*.

   5 a The police caught Bill climbing in the window.
      b The police caught him climbing in the window.

In (5a,b) *climbing in the window* behaves differently from the way it does in (2). As (6a,b) show, they cannot be made passive, whereas (2) can be converted to (3).

   6 a *Bill climbing in the window was caught by the police.
      b *He climbing in the window was caught by the police.

Where *climbing in the window* is a participle/reduced relative clause it stays right next to the noun it modifies, as in (3). But look at (7a,b), and then (8).

   7 a <u>Bill</u> was caught by the police <u>climbing in the window</u>.
      b <u>He</u> was caught by the police <u>climbing in the window</u>.

   8 <u>The burglar</u> was caught by the police <u>climbing in the window</u>.

Bill, he and *the burglar* are at the front of the clause while *climbing in the window* is at the end. Moreover, (7b) and (8) do not answer the question *Which burglar did the police catch?* They answer a question along the lines of *What was Bill/he/the burglar doing when the police caught him?*

The difficulty is that the sequence of words in (2) represents two constructions – it is an example of grammatical ambiguity. Either *the burglar climbing in the window* consists of the noun phrase *the burglar* plus a participle/reduced relative clause *climbing in the window*, or it consists of the noun phrase *the burglar* plus something that is NOT a participle/relative clause. This something else we will call a Type II gerund. When *climbing in the window* is a participle/reduced relative clause, *the burglar* cannot be replaced by a proper noun or a pronoun. This is brought out by (6). Neither can *the burglar* be separated from *climbing in the window*. When *climbing in the window* is NOT a participle/reduced relative clause, *the burglar* CAN be replaced by a proper noun or a pronoun and *the burglar* CAN be at the front of the clause with the *-ing* phrase at the end, as in (8). When *climbing in the window* IS a participle/reduced relative clause, it answers one question; when it is NOT a participle or reduced relative clause it answers another question.

Note that the line of argument set out above supports the idea that (2) represents two constructions. Using the label 'Gerund Type 2' is a separate decision that is not based on the above evidence.

NON-FINITE CLAUSES: REDUCED ADVERBIALS

Reduced adverbial clauses are so called because they can be treated as the result of reducing full adverbial clauses. *While he was waiting for the train* can be reduced to *While waiting for the train* as in (1a); *When they were visiting Stirling* can be reduced to *When visiting Stirling* in (1b). What is cut out or ellipted is a pronoun and some form of *be*. Like full adverbial clauses and free participle non-finite clauses, reduced adverbial clauses modify other clauses and are always signalled by a subordinating conjunction such as *while*, *although* and *when*.

1 a   While waiting for the train, James lost his smartphone.
  b   When visiting Stirling, they always call in on Jennifer.
  c   Although in love with Prague, Lucie returned to Edinburgh.
  d   When ripe, these apples will be delicious.
  e   Once dismantled and repaired, the engine will be as good as new.

Like full adverbial clauses, reduced ones can precede or follow the clauses they modify. (1a) can be rearranged as *James lost his smartphone while waiting for the train*, (1d) as *These apples will be delicious when ripe*, and so on. Reduced adverbial clauses can be active or passive, as in (1e), and they are assigned tense according to the tense of the clause they modify: (1a) is interpreted as *While he was waiting*, (1b) as *When they are visiting*, (1e) as *Once it has been dismantled and repaired*. Like free participles, they can be analysed as having an understood subject controlled by a noun phrase in the clause they modify. In (1a) *James* controls the understood subject of *waiting*, in (1b) *they* controls the understood subject of *visiting*, in (1c) *Lucie* controls the understood subject of *(is) in love*, in (1d) the phrase *these apples* controls the understood subject of *(are) ripe*, and in (1e) *the engine* controls the understood subject of *(has been)*. Like free participles, reduced adverbial clauses can be 'dangling', that is, can have an understood subject not controlled by a noun phrase in the clause they modify. A (real) example is in (2).

2 When making an espresso, the water stays in contact with the coffee for only about 25 seconds.

The understood subject of *When making an espresso* is *you* or *one*: *when you are making an espresso, when one is making an espresso*. It is not controlled by *the water*. As with free participles, a more appropriate label would be 'absolute reduced adverbial'. As with absolute free participles, the analyst who is describing and analysing simply has to accept that the construction is frequent and a regular part of English grammar. (=> NON-FINITE CLAUSES: FREE PARTICIPLES.)

NON-FINITE CLAUSES: REDUCED RELATIVES

Like reduced adverbial clauses (=> NON-FINITE CLAUSES: REDUCED ADVERBIALS.), reduced relative clauses can be treated as the result of reducing full clauses, in this case full relative clauses. In (1a) the reduced relative clause *stolen from the art gallery* can be treated as a reduced version of *which/that had been stolen from the art gallery*. In (1b) the sequence *reading a* book can be treated as a reduced version of *who/that is reading the book*. In the heyday of transformational grammar reduced relative clauses were said to be produced by a process called whiz deletion. 'Whiz', because what was deleted from full relative clauses was a wh word (or *that* of course) and some form of *be* – very often *is*.

1 a The police found the picture <u>stolen from the art gallery</u>.
  b The woman <u>reading a book</u> is the person you're looking for.

Reduced relative clauses are assigned tense according to the tense of the clause they are embedded in. *Is* in (1b) imposes the interpretation *is reading a book*. If the clause had been *was the person you were looking for* the interpretation would have been *was reading a book*.

NON-FINITE CLAUSES: VERB STEM

This type of non-finite clause contains just the stem of a verb – no suffixes and no *to* or *for to*. The clause can of course also contain complements and adjuncts of a given verb. Verb stem non-finite clauses modify verbs: <u>lubricate the machinery</u> and <u>avoid the manager</u> are complements of *is* and *was* in (1c) and (1d); <u>sign this agreement</u> modifies *made* in (1b) and <u>glide up the tree</u> modifies *watched* in (1a).

1 a We watched the snake <u>glide up the tree</u>.
  b The firm made the employees <u>sign this agreement</u>.
  c All the mechanic does is <u>lubricate the machinery</u>.
  d What Rene did was <u>avoid the manager</u>.

Another possible example is *pass all the coursework* in *The students must pass all the coursework*. (=> CLAUSE STRUCTURE: DEPENDENCY RELATIONS.)

NON-FINITE CLAUSES: *WITH* + NP

This type of clause consists of *with* plus a noun phrase plus an *-ing* form of the verb – *loping* in (1a) – or a past participle – *transferred* in (1b). These *with* clauses modify other clauses and are most appropriately paraphrased by adverbial clauses: *while her setter loped along behind*, *As the funds have been safely transferred to our Swiss bank account* and *because Ian was playing*. We could analyse the construction more finely; for instance, *loping along behind* is probably a gerund (Type 2). What *transferred* ... might be is less obvious – not a reduced relative clause, for instance; analysing it as a *with* non-finite clause allows us to handle the construction without becoming bogged down.

1 a Jane strode up the hill <u>with her setter loping along behind</u>.
  b <u>With the funds safely transferred to our Swiss bank account</u>, we can retire.
  c the other thing was that I hadn't particularly been planning to take up golf <u>although with Ian playing it seemed like a good idea</u>.
     Wellington Corpus of Spoken New Zealand English: #DPC003:0060:FG

Non-finite constructions with infinitives and participles at least contain a verb form, even if it is non-finite. Some analysts even propose treating the underlined parts in (2) as clauses, although they have no verb form of any kind.

2 a <u>When ripe</u>, these apples will be delicious.
  b He left the train <u>with somebody else's wallet in his pocket</u>.
  c She walked up the hill, <u>her rucksack on her back</u>.

(2a) comes closest to a clause, since it contains the complementiser *when*. (2a) could be seen as resulting from ellipsis: *when they are ripe* à *when ripe*, that is, as a classic reduced adverbial. (2b and c) are unlikely candidates, on the grounds that they cannot be easily correlated with a main clause. It is impossible to convert (2b) to **He left the train with somebody else's wallet being in his pocket*. In fact, this *with* construction is only used preceding a main clause to present one situation as the cause of another: *With Emma* *having left Hartfield, Mr Woodhouse was unhappy,* and *With somebody else's wallet in his pocket, he was glad not to be stopped by any policemen.* It is nonetheless true that (2c), for instance, expresses several propositions: 'She walked up the hill' + 'She had her rucksack' + 'Her rucksack was on her back'. The moral is that while semantic facts should be taken into account, an analysis of syntax should never depend on semantic facts alone. (2c) expresses propositions but is not a non-finite clause. But the underlined chunk in (2a) can be analysed as a non-finite clause since it is related straightforwardly to *When they are ripe.*

The classic examples in (1a–c) have the sequence of constituents *with* + NP + participle (*loping, transferred, playing*). Two other constructions are found. In one the participle is replaced by an infinitive, as in <u>*With so many e-mails to answer Jacob got no work done at all.*</u> The second construction simply has *with* + gerund (Type 1), as in (3) and (4). This construction is not recognised by reference grammars of English but turns up in Scottish English and in New Zealand English (and very probably in spoken English in England and North America).

3 I reckon <u>with taking the people out</u> they've lost the community – no community spirit at all.
[Conversation recorded in Edinburgh, 1977]

4 and in the season um not this year because he missed the beginning of the season <u>with not being here</u>
Wellington Corpus of Spoken New Zealand English: #DPC003:0425:RW

The gerunds have understood subjects controlled by noun phrases in the main clauses, *they* in (3) and *he* in (4). Both *with* chunks can be paraphrased as adverbial clauses of reason: *because they took the people out* [= removed them from an inner-city area to new houses on the outskirts of the city] and *because he wasn't here.* (=> NON-FINITE CLAUSES: INTRODUCTION, NON-FINITE CLAUSES: GERUNDS (TYPE 1), NON-FINITE CLAUSES: INFINITIVES.)

NON-FINITE CLAUSES: EIGHT TYPES OR FOUR?

The eight types established here are infinitives, free participles, gerunds (Type 1), gerunds (Type 2), reduced adverbials, reduced relatives, verb stem and *with* + NP. The four-type analysis has *to*-infinitivals (= our infinitives), bare infinitivals (= our verb stem), past participle (= one of our reduced relative clauses, as in *the picture <u>stolen from the art gallery</u>*), and gerund-participials.† The gerund-participials correspond to our non-finite verb forms in *-ing*; that is, free participles, gerunds (Type 1), gerunds (Type 2) and one type of reduced relative clause, e.g., *the girl* *playing the piano*. (=> NON-FINITE CLAUSES: FREE PARTICIPLES, NON-FINITE CLAUSES: GERUNDS (TYPE 1), NON-FINITE CLAUSES: GERUNDS (TYPE 2), NON-FINITE CLAUSES: REDUCED RELATIVES.)

The verb forms all have the suffix -*ing* but differ in their other syntactic properties. What we are calling free participles modify whole clauses, occur in different positions in a sentence and correspond to adverbial clauses. (=> ADVERBIAL CLAUSES: INTRODUCTION.) The non-finite clauses that we call reduced relative clauses can be straightforwardly derived from a full relative clause by deleting a *wh* pronoun or *that* and any form of the verb *be*: *the girl who was playing the piano* → *the girl who was playing the piano* and *the picture that was stolen from the art gallery* → *the picture that was stolen from the art gallery*.

The gerunds differ from the -*ing* participials. The gerunds Type 1 are nominal, that is, they occur in the same positions as nouns and noun phrases and function as subjects, direct objects and oblique objects. The gerunds Type 2 derive historically from prepositional phrases and, to put it negatively, do not have the properties of reduced relative clauses, free participles or gerunds Type 1.

By recognising eight types of non-finite clause we respect the properties listed in the above two paragraphs. We also preserve the various types of non-finite clause that are employed in the teaching of English as an Additional Language,† in accounts of Englishes around the world and of non-standard varieties in the UK and elsewhere, and in typological comparisons of English and other languages.

Nouns and noun phrases

NOUNS AND NOUN PHRASES: INTRODUCTION

Consider the underlined phrases in (1a–e).

1 a <u>They</u> are arriving on Friday.
  b <u>The river</u> has broken its banks.
  c <u>This exciting film</u> attracted huge audiences.
  d <u>Gold</u> is heavy.
  e <u>Rabbits</u> dig <u>burrows</u>.

They are generally called noun phrases (NPs) and the head is taken to be the noun (N): *river* in (1b) and *film* in (1c). Of course *They* in (1a), *Gold* in (1d) and *rabbits* and *burrows* in (1e) are not phrases in the everyday sense of the term, namely consisting of two or more words. In syntactic analysis they are treated as phrases, since they occur in slots that can be filled by longer sequences of words: <u>*My favourite cousins from Madeley*</u> *are arriving on Friday*, <u>*Her expensive new luggage*</u> *is heavy*, *Rabbits dig* <u>*complex systems of tunnels*</u>. That is, in a clause such as __ *are arriving on Friday*, the slot marked by the underline can be filled by the single word *They* or the sequence of five words *My favourite cousins from Madeley* and for the purposes of syntactic analysis we say that a noun phrase (or any other kind of phrase) may consist of a single word, e.g. *they* or *gold*, or two words, e.g. *the river* or *this film*, or three words, e.g. *this exciting film*, and so on.

We immediately encounter a problem. The article *the* is obligatory in (1b) and the demonstrative *this* in (1c), as shown by the incorrect sequences **river has broken its banks* and **exciting film attracted huge audiences*. This property has led to an alternative view, that phrases such as *the river* and *this exciting film* have *the* and *this* as heads. A widely-used general term for articles such as *the* and *a* and demonstratives such as *this* and *that* is 'determiner' and analysts who treat *the* as the head of *the river* call such phrases 'determiner phrases' or DPs, not 'noun phrases' or NPs. Nonetheless, a majority of analysts and analyses of English grammar continue to talk of nouns as the heads of NPs, pointing out that determiners are not obligatory with mass nouns or plural count nouns, as in *Water is essential for life* and *Huge audiences were attracted*. Moreover it is the noun in an NP that has various important properties:

i allowing or disallowing (in some accounts 'licensing') a complement clause – *the idea that the bank would fail* versus **the description that the bank would fail*;
ii selecting particular prepositions – *the blame for the accident, her worry about the interview*;
iii participating in selectional and other restrictions with the verb in a clause – *The lawyer drew up a document* versus *The lawyer drew up a chair* versus *A car drew up in front of the shop, The engineer drew out his proposal* versus *The train drew out of the station*.

We follow the traditional and majority view and keep the concept and the term 'noun phrase'.

The underlined NPs in (1a–e), and the others – *Friday, its banks* and *huge audiences* – have a simple structure: a pronoun (*they*), a single noun (*gold, Friday*), an article + noun (*the river*), and adjective + noun (*huge audiences*), and demonstrative + adjective + noun (*this exciting film*). Such NPs are typical of spontaneous spoken English, especially in informal and relaxed contexts such as at home with close family. (Simple NPs are typical of the same text-type in other languages.) To them can be added NPs introduced by quantifiers such as *some, any, more*. There's *some milk in the fridge, Have you got any coffee?* Slightly more complex are NPs such as *Are any of your friends going?* and *Could you pass me some of that paper?* In them, the quantifier is followed by a prepositional phrase containing a definite NP: *of your friends, of that paper*. Also to be found regularly in all types of English text are NPs introduced by possessives: *Dad's laptop, my sister's flat, your stupid comments*.

Possessives, adjectives and quantifiers precede the head noun in an NP. Other modifiers of nouns follow the head noun. Prepositional phrases (henceforth PPs) are the most common, as in (2).

2 a I'm reading [a book about dogs].
  b [The house with the big garden] is for sale.
  c She accepted [the award for her latest book].

As mentioned above, the head noun controls the choice of preposition. (2a) can have with *a book on/about dogs* and *a book for dogs* (assuming there are literate canines somewhere). (2b) allows *the house in the big garden*, but the garden does not necessarily go with the house, whereas *the house with the big garden* signals that the garden is an appendage to the house and for sale along with it. (2c) only allows *award for*, just as *fear* requires *of* (*fear of the dark*), and *anxiety* only allows *about* (*his anxiety about the flight*).†

Relative clauses follow the noun they modify, as in (3).

3 a the car <u>she bought</u>
  b the book <u>that Freya wrote</u>
  c the sport <u>which Jennifer took up</u>

The contact relative clause in (3a) and the *that* relative clause in (3b) are very frequent in spontaneous spoken English. *Which* relative clauses, as in (3c), are typical of formal written English. (=> RELATIVE CLAUSES: CONTACT, RELATIVE CLAUSES: TH, RELATIVE CLAUSES: WH.)

Certain nouns can be modified by complement clauses, as in (4).

4 a George rejected [the proposal <u>that a currency union be set up</u>].
  b [The realisation <u>that they had been duped</u>] shocked everyone.
  c He paid no attention to [the threat <u>that the house would be demolished</u>].

(=> COMPLEMENT CLAUSES: NOUN COMPLEMENT CLAUSES.)

Participial phrases are very typical of formal written English but less frequent in informal spoken English. They follow the noun they modify, as shown in (5).

5 a the teams <u>taking part in the competition</u>
  b the novels <u>written by Trollope</u>
  c the present <u>sent to Jacob by his grandparents</u>

(=> NON-FINITE CLAUSES: REDUCED RELATIVES.)

Nouns can be modified by infinitive clauses, traditionally called 'infinitive phrases'. (=> NON-FINITE CLAUSES: INTRODUCTION, RELATIVE CLAUSES: INFINITIVAL.) Examples are in (6).

6 a I've found a place <u>to stay in for a day or two</u>.
  b There's a wonderful view <u>just to sit and contemplate</u>.
  c The place <u>to go for snow</u> is Glenshee.

These different types of modifiers can be combined with a head noun in various patterns. The simplest pattern is an NP with just a single constituent, which can be a personal pronoun, as in (7a), or a possessive pronoun, as in (7b), or a mass noun, as in (7c), or a plural common noun, as in (7d).

7 a <u>She</u> asked <u>them</u> to return her cheque.
  b Of the proposals, I preferred <u>hers</u> to <u>theirs</u>.

c   <u>Wine</u> is good for you in moderation.
   d   We've always had <u>dogs</u>.

The next most simple pattern is one in which a head noun has a single modifier. The latter can be an article, as in (8a), a demonstrative adjective, as in (8b), a quantifier, as in (8c), or a possessive adjective, as in (8d).

   8 a   <u>The</u> house smells musty.
      b   <u>Those</u> roses have no scent.
      c   <u>Many</u> people do not understand economics.
      d   <u>Her</u> proposal is bold and imaginative.

These simple patterns are frequent in spoken English, particularly in informal spoken English. NPs consisting of just a pronoun are very frequent, since speakers use pronouns to refer to things that are prominent in the context of conversations or to things that have already been mentioned. Of course longer NPs do occur in informal speech: NPs consisting of a determiner, adjective and noun (*some interfering nitwit, this long film*) occur regularly but not frequently. NPs containing relative clauses are relatively infrequent. (But such statements are based on the analysis of corpuses, which conceal differences between speakers. Some speakers produce complex NPs even in informal speech, others do not.)

Written English offers a wide range of NPs, from ones with the simple structures exemplified above to ones with a number of modifiers following the noun and with modifiers that are in themselves rather complex in structure. The number and complexity of such NPs depends on authorial style and text-type. A modern detective novel may contain one or two very complex NPs. For instance, Mark Billingham's *From the Dead* contains examples such as *Thorne's dislike of the typical English country pub*. The central, head noun is *dislike*. It has a possessive noun, *Thorne's*, as its determiner and a prepositional phrase as a modifier, *of the typical English country pub*. The prepositional phrase contains an NP in which *country pub* (treated here as a compound noun) is modified by two adjectives, *typical* and *English*. Of course, the novel also contains many simple noun phrases such as *they, the woman* and *politicians*. *The Oxford Companion to Philosophy* presents, in a limited number of words for each article, a large quantity of information about complex ideas. Complex NPs help to convey the information in the space available: one is *the need to reintroduce the excluded issues of experience, understanding and the place of language use in the context of a set of practical questions*. Another is *a situation which carries information used in interpreting the sentence*. *Situation* is modified by the relative clause *which ... sentence* and this clause in turn contains the participial clause/reduced relative clause *used in interpreting the sentence*, and it contains a prepositional phrase introduced by *in* complemented by the gerund *interpreting the sentence.*

In an NP the head noun and its modifiers are analysed as combining, not as a linear sequence of words, but as a hierarchical structure. This structure has to be quite intricate, even for the modifiers that precede the head noun. Consider the simple NPs in (9).

9 a the house
  b this house
  c my house

The structure for these NPs is shown in Figure 9. What that figure shows is a structure in which the NP consists of a DP, containing the determinative *the*, and the head noun *house.*† What we are calling 'determinatives' are items that precede the noun directly, such as the articles *the* and *a*, the demonstratives *this, that, these* and *those*, the possessive pronouns *my, your, his, her, our, their*, the interrogatives *which* and *what* (as in *Which car is she driving* and *What courses are you taking?*). As you can see, the term 'determinative' applies to a large class of items that divide into various sub-classes, mainly on the grounds of meaning. The large class is justified by the fact that its members can all occur immediately before the head noun in an NP. (As we will see shortly, other items can occur between all the determinatives and the head noun.) The determinative class also includes possessive nouns, as in *Freya's car.* Figure 10 shows the same high-level structure, but the DP contains the NP *Freya's* and the rightmost N is *car.* (The internal structure of *Freya's* is a matter for morphology and we simply treat *Freya's* as an indivisible word.)

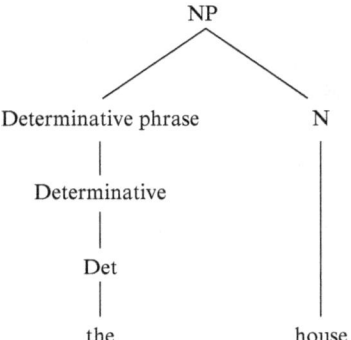

Figure 9

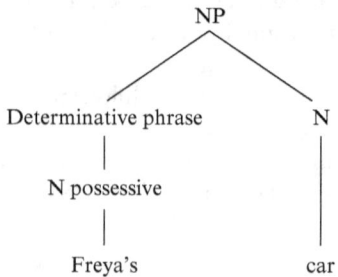

Figure 10

Cardinal numerals such as *one, three, fifty* are contained in Cardinality Phrases. Cardinal numerals occur before the head noun in an NP, as in *three houses*, and also combine with *the* and the demonstrative determinatives, as in *the three houses, these three houses*. A structure for these NPs is shown in Figure 11. Normally, adjectives come between numerals and nouns, as in *these three imposing houses*. Less frequent in occurrence, but not unusual or odd, are phrases such as *a good fifty protesters* (= 'at the very least fifty and quite possibly more'), *the odd two or three protesters*. We treat *good* and *odd* in these phrases as determining the cardinal numeral and as having the structure in Figure 12. Figure 13 shows the structure of *the odd two or three protesters*. The point to note here is that the Card2 phrase can contain two further Card2 phrases joined by *and* or *or*.

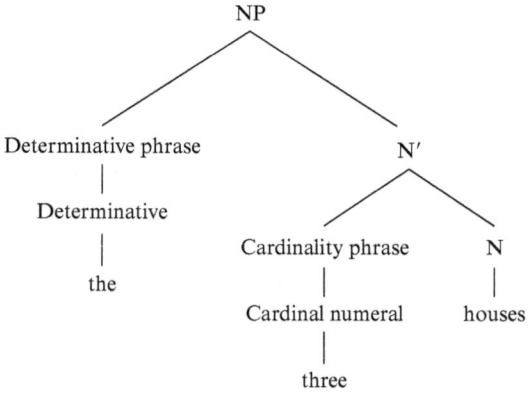

Figure 11

NOUNS AND NOUN PHRASES

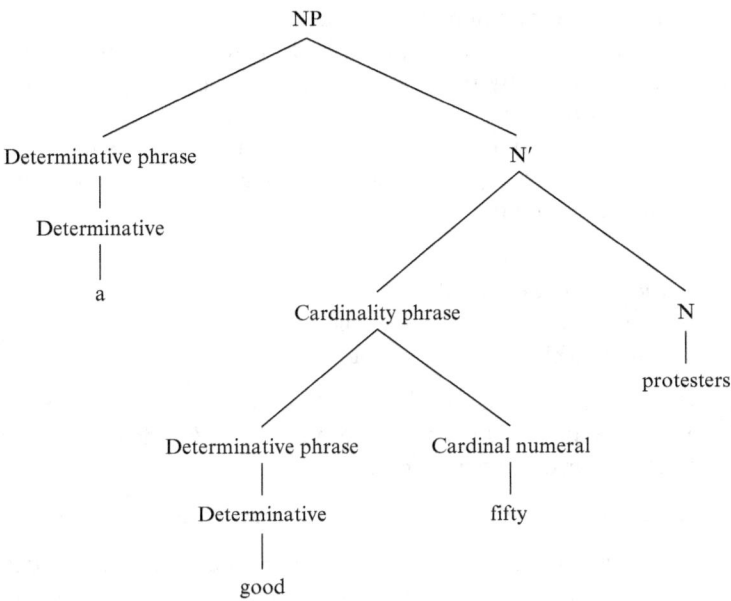

Figure 12

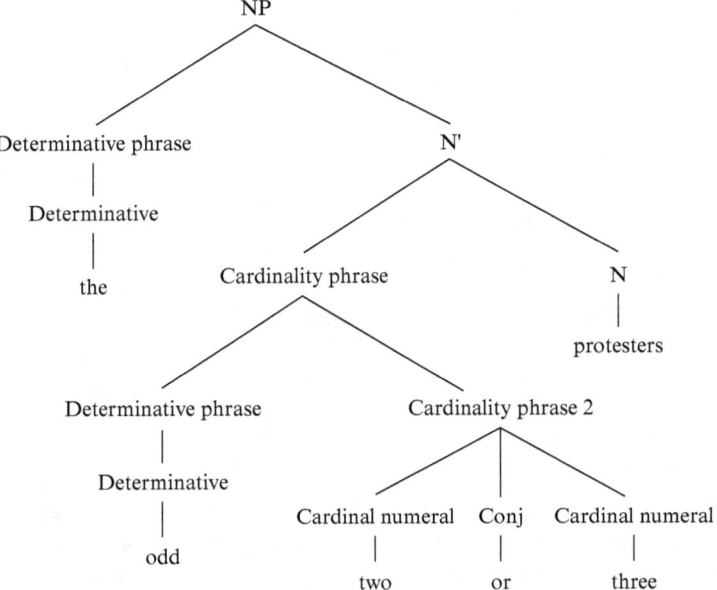

Figure 13

Inside NPs we also find items such as *all, both, some, several, few, no, every* and *each*. These are generally just called 'quantifiers', particularly in logic, since semantically they relate to quantity and are used in order to quantify sets of objects. From a syntactic point of view they can be treated as determinatives, on the grounds that they precede the head noun in an NP, occurring in the same slot as *the* and *this* but not combining with them, as shown in (10).

10 a the children; some children; any children; all children; both children each child; every child
 b *the some children; *the any children
 c *this each child; *the every child

The NP patterns with quantifying words are not confined to the one in (10). In (11) the quantifying determinatives *all* and *both* do combine with *the* and the demonstrative determinatives.

11 all the children; both the children; all these books; both these books

Fortunately we do not have to set up another type of quantifying determinative. All quantifying determiners license the combinations (and their structure) in (10a) but only *all* and *both* license the combinations in (11). An illustrative structure is in Figure 14.

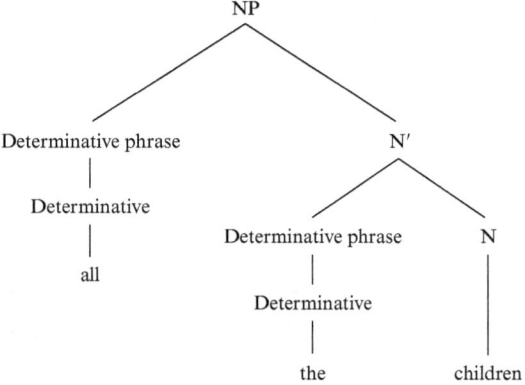

Figure 14

Another pattern is presented by phrases such as *all of the trees, some of the trees, each of the trees, several from that group, few in our street*, and so on, where the quantifying determinative is followed by a PP such as *of the trees, from that group* and *in our street*. Since PPs are preceded by NPs, we suggest the structure in Figure 15, in which *all, some, each, several* and *few* are nouns. By a happy chance the same structure applies to *a lot of books, lots of books, loads of money, heaps of books, piles of cash*, where *lots, loads, heaps* and *piles* are nouns.

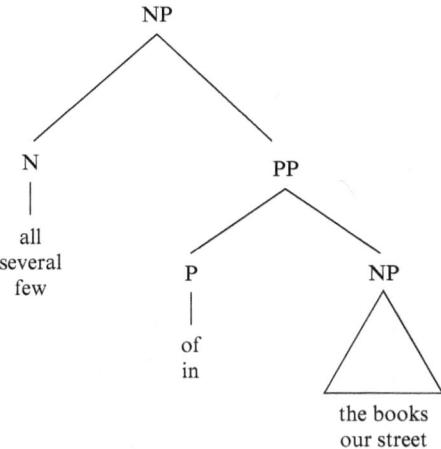

Figure 15

A final pattern (for this account) is exemplified by *the many failures* and *those few supporters*. The position between a determinative and a noun is occupied by adjectives and we treat *many* and *few* as adjectives, as shown in Figure 16.

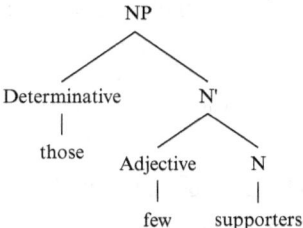

Figure 16

We return to modifiers that follow the noun in an NP, looking first at the structure for NPs containing relative clauses and complement clauses. Most work in formal syntax does not distinguish between sentence and clause and many analysts translated the further distinction between relative clause and complement clause into different arrangements of NP and S. Here we use the labels 'relative clause' (RC) and 'complement clause' (CC). As discussed in the section (=> CONSTRUCTIONS:

OVERVIEW.), the different functions of the two types of clause can be handled as part of the overall meaning of each construction. (A clause is a type of construction.) Figure 17 shows the structure for *the dog that didn't bark in the night*, in which the relative clause is *that didn't bark in the night*.

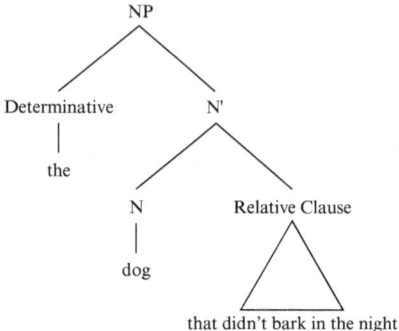

Figure 17

The definite article *the* (a determiner) is separate from the rest of the NP, with the noun *dog* and the RC *didn't bark in the night* gathered together under the lower NP. *The* picks out, or helps the hearer/reader to pick out, the entity being referred to. That might just be *dog* or *black dog* or *dog that didn't bark in the night*. The internal structure of the RC is not relevant here.

An NP containing a CC has the same structural arrangements as in Figure 17.

(5a and b), repeated below as (12), exemplify what are traditionally called 'participial phrases' – the underlined parts contain the verb participles *taking* and *written*.

12 a the teams <u>taking part in the competition</u>
   b the novels <u>written by Trollope</u>

As will be explained in the section on non-finite clauses, such participial phrases are analysed as RCs that have been reduced: (5a) derives from *that are taking part in the competition* or *which are taking part in the competition*, and (5b) derives from *that were written by Trollope* or *which were written by Trollope*. (=> NON-FINITE CLAUSES: REDUCED RELATIVES.) The process can be thought of as deleting a *wh* word or *that* plus some form of *be*. Ignoring the internal structure of reduced RCs, we can apply the structure in Figure 17 to (5a and b) and also to (6). In (6) *I've found a place <u>to stay in for a day or two</u>* the underlined chunk contains the infinitive *to stay in* and the construction is called an 'infinitival relative clause'. (=> RELATIVE CLAUSES: INFINITIVAL.)

We close this discussion of the structure of NPs with PPs, the final sort of modifier that follows the noun. Such NPs are exemplified in (2a–c), repeated below as (13).

13 a I'm reading [a book <u>about dogs</u>].
   b [The house <u>with the big garden</u>] is for sale.
   c She accepted [the award <u>for her latest book</u>].

NOUNS AND NOUN PHRASES: COMMON AND PROPER

Grammars of English traditionally distinguish between common and proper nouns, but the grammatical properties of the two sets can only be listed with the help of the adverb *typically*. Thus, proper nouns (in English) typically do not take plural endings – see (1a), typically do not combine with determiners – see (1b), and typically are not modified by restrictive relative clauses – see (1c).

1 a ?Katarinas were sitting round the table.
  b ?The Katarina wrote the introduction.
  c ?Katarina who was ill had to stay at home.

If you look long enough at such examples you can come round to the view that they are not too bad grammatically and that they can be interpreted. Common nouns do not require such efforts, witness (2a–c).

2 a Children were sitting round the table.
  b The assistant wrote the introduction.
  c Children who are ill have to stay at home.

The *typical* grammatical patterns of common and proper nouns differ, and the above characteristics of the two types of noun are supported by corpus data. The essential difference lies in their meaning. Common nouns have a denotation; that is, analysts can compare and contrast lexical items, examine the combinations in which lexical items occur and consider the contexts in which particular lexical items are used. By these means they account for the set of entities a given lexical item refers to. (This is a much easier task for concrete nouns than for abstract nouns.) The entries for lexical items in a dictionary constitute one type of account.

Proper nouns are typically just listed in dictionaries, sometimes with their etymology, if known. A common noun such as *dog* has as its denotation the set of properties of the prototypical dog, or, depending on your theory, the set of entities to which the noun *dog* can be applied. In everyday usage, proper nouns are applied, not to a set of properties or entities, but to an individual. Obviously there are in the English-speaking world many individuals called, say, *Hamish*, but a speaker or writer can refer to someone by means of *Hamish* precisely because in the very limited contexts surrounding the typical communication, there will be only one individual called *Hamish*. If there is more than one, the reference is made clear either by only one of the individuals being relevant to the communication or by the speaker making clear which individual they have in mind: *Hamish, the guy in HR*. (For a given speaker, a particular proper name in a particular context will evoke a set of properties: e.g., 'medium height', 'curly fair hair', particular qualities of voice and gait and so on. This is not the same as a common noun such as *dog* denoting the properties of the set of typical dogs: 'barking', 'tail wagging', 'average size', etc.)

Hamish is not just a proper noun but a (proper) name. Proper nouns function as the head constituent in a proper name. In *Welwyn Garden City* and *Livingston Village*, *Welwyn* and *Livingston* are proper nouns and the heads of the names. *Garden*, *City* and *Village* are written with initial capital letters and are part of the proper names but are themselves common nouns. Many proper names are introduced by *the* but some such proper names have lost the article. *The Royal Bank of Scotland* is now generally known as *Royal Bank* or *Royal Bank of Scotland*. In 2016, BBC radio broadcast a series of stories about forgotten events or participants in World War I. A preliminary announcement stated that the series was produced with the help of *Imperial War Museum*, not *The Imperial War Museum*. A large shopping centre on the outskirts of Edinburgh was known as *The Gyle*, which was the name of the piece of land it was built on. At some point advertisements for Marks and Spencer began referring to their shop at *Gyle*. The article seems to have been restored (speakers of Scottish English like definite articles), as their shop is again at *The Gyle*.

The discussion of count and mass nouns (=> NOUNS AND NOUN PHRASES: COUNT AND MASS.) gives examples of how count nouns can be used as mass nouns and vice versa. Similarly proper nouns can be used as common nouns, as shown in (3).

3 a There are four Michaels in this class.
   b There's no Judith in our family
   c I remember only too well the Edinburgh where everything was shut on Sundays.

(3a) and (3b) demonstrate the use of proper nouns to refer to sets of entities with particular properties: *Michaels* in (3a) refers to boys named 'Michael' and *Judith* in (3b) to the set of girls named 'Judith'. In (3c) the phrase *the Edinburgh where everything was shut on Sundays* refers to a mental representation. The use only makes sense if we assume that speakers have representations of entities in their minds and that NPs refer to these mental entities rather than directly to entities in the 'external' world.

NOUNS AND NOUN PHRASES: COUNT AND MASS

COUNTABILITY: INDIVIDUALS AND SUBSTANCES

Countability has to do with whether a noun denotes entities that are conceived and perceived as individuals that can be counted or an entity that is conceived and perceived as a substance, a mass. The former type of noun is called a count noun or countable noun and the latter is called a mass noun (or non-count noun or non-countable noun). The distinction is exemplified in (1).

1 a   How many biscuits did you put out?
  b   How much raspberry jam is left?

Biscuits are individual entities: the number of biscuits in a packet can be counted. Any kind of jam comes in a mass: the contents of a jar can be weighed but not counted. *Biscuit* is a count noun and *jam* (in this sense) is a mass noun. *Biscuit* occurs in the plural, as in (1a), and combines with determiners such as *many* and *few*. *Philippa eats few chocolate biscuits* versus *Philippa eats little jam*. (*Philippa eats little chocolate biscuits* reports the size of the biscuits; Philippa may eat quite a lot of them.) *Jam* does not occur in the plural (but see the following paragraph) and combines with determiners such as *much* and *less*. *A lot of* combines with both types of noun. Just as we can talk about one member of a set of countable entities – *one biscuit, three biscuits*, so we can talk about a sub-mass of a given mass – *jam* and *a spoonful of jam*, *bread* and *one piece/slice of bread*, *glue* and *a drop/blob of glue*, *sand* and *a grain of sand*. Both types of nouns combine with determiners such as *some, any*, and *more* – *some biscuits* and *some bread*, *more nails* and *more glue*.

The above account applies neatly to nouns that denote either countable entities or masses: typical count nouns are *chair, axe, student* and *cat*, while typical mass nouns are *sugar, water, mud* and *concrete*. But it has to be extended, because the concepts of count and mass play out in a more complex and interesting way. Most obvious is the fact that any mass noun can be used as a count noun if reference is to kinds of things. Thus, we can say *How many different cheeses do you sell?, The food was accompanied by six wines, Chemists recognize different sugars.* Count nouns can be used as mass nouns but this happens much less frequently. *Ball* is a count noun but rugby people talk of players 'not getting much ball'; that is, the ball is not being passed to them. Researchers apply for research *grants*, but may complain that the amount of *grant* they receive is too small. Some examples are highly marked (and uttered with (blackly) humorous intent), such as *There was dog all over the road* (after a traffic accident).

There are pairs of nouns such that one denotes a set of entities conceived as a mass while the other denotes the set conceived as a collection of countable entities. Examples (count nouns first) are *leaves* and *foliage, plates* (and *cups, saucers*, etc.) and *crockery, feathers* and *plumage, chairs, tables* etc, and *furniture*. Retailers require and invent collective mass terms such as *bakeware, beachwear, tableware*.

Some lexical items denoting concrete entities have both count and mass interpretations but the relationship between the interpretations varies, and the nouns can combine with different determiners depending upon the interpretation. *Chocolate* can denote a mass, as in *I like chocolate* (zero determiner), *Have some chocolate* and *Jennifer broke off a large piece of chocolate*. When denoting an individual sweet, *chocolate* functions as a count noun: *Lucie ate one chocolate, Barnabas took more chocolates, There aren't many chocolates left in the box. Coffee* and *tea* are basically mass nouns but can be used as count nouns in social contexts: *Who wants tea and who wants coffee? – OK, that's two teas and four coffees. Tea* and *coffee* in the first clause are mass nouns, *teas* and *coffees* in the second clause are count nouns. The plural nouns *coffees* and *teas* can also refer to kinds of coffee or tea.

In some pairs of lexical items one noun is concrete and the other abstract. Concrete nouns denote entities that can be touched, seen, heard, tasted, smelled and manipulated in some way. Abstract nouns denote entities that lack these properties. Many abstract nouns are also mass nouns, but not all. The nouns *idea* and *reason*, for instance, are abstract and count, having plural forms: *many ideas, several reasons*. A noun such as *difficulty* can function as a count noun with singular and plural forms and as a mass noun. It is a count noun in *the difficulties experienced by the climbers, The difficulty is that the document is lost, There will be more difficulties when the funding runs out*, and a mass noun in *They got into difficulty. Experience* is a mass noun in *Experience has to be gained the hard way* and a count noun in *They recounted their horrific experiences*. And *truth* is a mass noun in *Is there any truth in the rumour?* but a count noun in *She told him a few home truths*.

The distinction between count and mass applies to nouns denoting events and processes, particularly in clauses containing light verbs such as *do* and *give*, as in (3) and (4), and the existential-presentative construction, as in (2). (2a–c), (3) and (4) describe activities, (2d) describes achievements. (=> VERBS AND VERB PHRASES: SITUATION (LEXICAL) ASPECT.)

2 a There's some pheasant-shooting in winter.   **mass**
    b There will be no more pheasant-shooting till late autumn.   **mass**
    c Is there any/much/a lot of pheasant-shooting in this area?   **mass**
    d There were three/many/a lot of attacks on the convoy.   **count**

3 a Mike does some jogging every day.   **mass**
    b Does Mike do much/a lot of jogging?   **mass**
    c He goes for two jogs at the weekend   **count**
    d Mike does more jogging than Freya.   **mass**

4 a Jacob gave the problem much/a lot of thought.   **mass**
    b Jacob focused his thoughts on the new problem.   **count**
    c Jacob didn't give the problem any thought.   **mass**
    d Jacob needs to give the problem more thought.   **mass**

PARTITIVES

There are special nouns and patterns enabling speakers to talk of some members of a set of countable nouns or some portion of a mass. Quantifiers such as *any*, *some* and *more* combine with both count and mass nouns: *Any questions?*, *Any cake left?*; *some flowers*, *some bread*; *more refugees*, *more water*. There are special partitive nouns denoting length, volume, weight and area: *two metres/yards of cloth*, *a litre/pint of beer*, *a kilo of apples* (or, to turn the clock back, *a stone of potatoes*). Some very general partitive nouns denote a small bit of some mass, and the mass can be concrete or abstract. *A piece of meat*, *a bit of shortbread* and *an item of clothing* are concrete; *a piece of news*, *a bit of advice* and *an item of information* are abstract. Even more specialised partitive nouns denote bits of particular types of mass or individuals: *a grain of rice, a blade of grass, a drop of water, a flake of snow*.

NUMBER AND AGREEMENT

Typical count nouns can be singular or plural and are involved in number agreement with verbs and with certain determiners. In the simple present tense there is a contrast between singular and plural, as in *writes* versus *write*. The contrasts between *has* and *have*, *is* and *are*, *was* and *were* are particularly important, as *have* is both a main verb and the Perfect auxiliary and *be* is the copula and the Progressive auxiliary. These contrasts are illustrated in (5)–(8).

5 a His <u>sister has</u> many books
    b His <u>sisters have</u> many books

6 a His <u>sister is</u> older than him
    b His <u>sisters are</u> older than him

7 a <u>He has bought</u> a flat
    b <u>They have bought</u> a flat

8 a <u>He is buying</u> a flat
    b <u>They are buying</u> a flat

The determiners with singular and plural forms are *this* (*<u>this</u> idea*, *<u>these</u> ideas*) and *that* (*<u>that</u> idea*, *<u>those</u> ideas*). Numerals of course include *one*, which requires a singular noun, and *two* and upwards, which require plural nouns.

    The connection between count nouns and number is not straightforward. There are count nouns that have only plural forms and there are singular nouns that combine with either singular or plural verbs. We will refer to the former as plural-only nouns, though the very traditional Latin term is still in use, *pluralia tantum* ('plural only'). Some of the plural-only nouns have obvious motivation, such as *tweezers, tongs, scissors, shears*. These nouns denote instruments that have two moving parts that do the essential work. A noun such as *scales* denotes a device for weighing that consisted originally of two bowls hanging from chains attached to a moving bar. Weighing could not be done with only one bowl. The term *scales* is nowadays applied to all sorts of weighing machines: a nurse invites a patient: 'If you could just step on the scales.'

    A number of plural-only nouns denote items of clothing: *trousers, jeans, swimming trunks, pants* (in the American or British interpretation), *pyjamas*. These too have clear motivation: each garment has two connected sections into which wearers put their legs. (This is not to say that the above nouns represent the only way of conceiving the garments. French has the singular noun *pantalon* ('trousers'), which seems to represent a construal of trousers as a single garment.) It is important that the two sections of the garment be connected. People normally wear two socks at a time, one on each foot, but *sock* is not a plural-only noun: *one sock, two socks, five socks*.

    There is variation among speakers and text-types. For many speakers *compasses*, denoting a device for drawing circles, is plural-only, as in *With the compasses she drew two intersecting circles*. Some speakers allow it to be singular, *with a compass*. (The noun denoting a device for determining direction is singular, *With the compass she determined the direction of the route out of the forest*.) In most types of text *harm* is singular-only, but in medical texts it can be used in the plural, as in (9).

9 [The writer has mentioned the proven links between alcohol and heart disease, stroke, and many kinds of cancer.]
The <u>harm</u>s experienced as a result of alcohol do not just affect the Drinker ... in an effort to counter these <u>harms</u> ... the relationship between the price of a drink and the amount of health <u>harms</u> that occur ...
The Herald, 11 February 2014, article by a clinical lecturer in public health

Similarly, among non-specialists *behaviour* is singular-only but the plural *behaviours* occurs in texts from disciplines such as psychiatry and biology.

Collective nouns denote collections of individuals, especially animate ones. Examples are *committee, team, staff* (of a school, etc.). The denotations of collective nouns can be interpreted (construed) in two ways. Construed as denoting a single block, the nouns are treated as singular and combine with singular: *The team has lost five games in a row, The jury is still out*. Construed as denoting a set of several or many individuals, the nouns are treated as plural: *The jury are still out; The team are playing a cup-tie tomorrow*. Apart from variation caused by one and same speaker choosing different construals on different occasions of speech, there is variation among different speakers of British English. Some take the view that since, e.g., *committee* is a singular noun, the verb must also be singular. (This usage is often described as 'logical' in letters to newspapers.) The most frequent usage is singular collective noun with plural verb, perhaps because the typical context brings out the construal of a number of individuals engaged in joint activity. When the context brings out the construal of a collective as a single block or 'container' the verb is singular. Thus, *The team <u>is riven</u> by quarrels*, where <u>are riven</u> invites the interpretation that each member is riven; or *The board <u>has</u> only three women on <u>it</u>*, where <u>have</u> only three women on *it* is peculiar and <u>have</u> only three women on <u>them</u> invites an altogether different interpretation.

Usage varies from one community of speakers to another. The speakers of British English use both patterns described above, but speakers of New Zealand English favour the singular noun + singular verb. But

JM found it very strange to read sentences in NZ newspapers such as *Chelsea is playing Arsenal next Saturday,* where British newspapers would have *Chelsea are playing Arsenal next Saturday.*

There are special terms for a collection of individuals, such as *herd* (cattle, elephants), *flock* (sheep, goats, birds), *gaggle* (geese), *swarm* (of bees), and so on. It has been claimed that around 200 collective nouns are in common use in English, presumably excluding rare examples (possibly deliberately concocted and useful only to the compilers of quiz questions) such as *exaltation of larks, charm of nightingales* and *clowder of cats.*

The contrast between singular and plural and between count and mass is striking in the use of nouns denoting animals and birds. Nouns such as *duck* and *chicken* can combine with the definite and indefinite articles when referring to live birds: *The duck quacked loudly, We fed the chickens.* In the singular and without any article the nouns denote the meat of the birds, as in the report of what was on sale: *There's lots of duck, pheasant, woodcock, partridge and quail.* In this pattern *duck*, etc. are mass nouns. In hunting contexts the singular forms of these and other nouns are (or were) used, as in *They are hunting lion, We shot seven duck.* It is unclear how widespread the usage is; some shooters talk simply of *shooting pheasants* and *shooting partridges.*

The distinction between singular and plural was the basis of a long-held view among linguists that parts of speech cannot be defined or established in terms of meaning, and that there is no reliable connection at all between a given part of speech and meaning. The crucial example was *oats* and *wheat*: why should one be plural and the other singular when they both denoted types of grain? It is worthwhile pointing out that *oats* is the odd one out: *wheat, rye, barley* and *maize* are all singular. Perhaps the answer lies in how the grains are used and what the cereals look like when they are ready for use. For JM and KB, oats are used as readily-distinguishable grains or flakes to make porridge. The other grains are used in the form of flour for making bread. *Pease* was reinterpreted as a plural. We can surmise that this was partly because the form looks like a plural and partly because the individual peas in a peapod (or, nowadays, in tins) are very obvious and countable.

NOUNS AND NOUN PHRASES: DETERMINATIVES

In NPs such as *those books, the shelf* and *a novel* the first constituents, *those, the* and *a*, are in many accounts labelled 'determiners'. Here we follow the current usage among scholars of English Language and use the term 'determinative' for the set of words, applying 'determiner' to the function of determinatives. (=> NOUNS AND NOUN PHRASES: INTRODUCTION.) Determinatives play a different role from adjectives and occur in different positions in NPs, always preceding any adjective(s) (=> ADJECTIVES AND ADJECTIVE PHRASES: ADJECTIVE POSITIONS IN NOUN PHRASES.) and the head noun. In *the long book* and *a long book* the adjective *long* helps to pick out the sort of book the speaker is talking about, *long* not *short*, *interesting* not *boring*, and so on. The determinatives signal various sorts of information about what the speaker/writer is referring to but not about the type of entity. In semantic terms, adjectives have to do with the denotation of an NP, determiners do not. Questions to which determiners give an answer are:

i Is the speaker referring to a long book that has already been mentioned or not – *the* long book versus *a* long book?
ii Is the speaker referring to one or more long books – *one* long book versus *five* long books?
iii Is the speaker presenting a long book as near – *this* long book – or distant – *that* long book?
iv Is the speaker saying something about totality – *all* the long books, *half* the long books, *both* the long books, *double* the long books (recommended last year)?
v Is the speaker giving the number of items in a set – *five* long books – or estimating a set as being large or small – *many* long books, *few* long books, *much* whisky (is exported)?

We recognise various classes of determinatives, partly to account for their ordering in sequences and partly to account for their scope. What does the last statement mean? In an NP such as *half the students* or *all their belongings*, *half* applies to *the students* and *all* to *their belongings*. In a longer NP such as *all those twenty young politicians (went on to hold high office)*, *all* applies to *those twenty young politicians*. The speaker is referring to a set of politicians who were young and twenty in number, and presenting that set as distant (*those*). Every member of that set went on to hold high office. *Young* applies to N; *twenty* applies to NP4; *those* applies to NP3; *all* applies to NP2. We show these relationships by means of the structure in Figure 18.

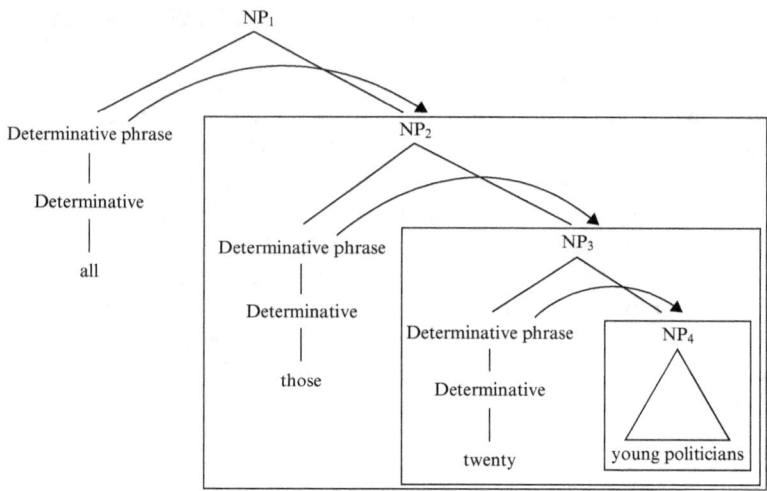

Figure 18

We need to recognise two major subsets of determinatives: central determinatives and post-determinatives.

Central determinatives: *the, a/an, this, these, that, those*
Post-determinatives: *many, few, much, five*

A central determinative can be followed by a post-determinative, as shown in (1).

   1 a the three committees [were disbanded]
      b those fifty sheep [have all produced twin lambs]
      c the many/the few objectors [failed to block the proposal]

There are restrictions on the possible combinations of central and post-determiners. *A* combines with *few*, as in *A few comments were offensive*, but not with any other post-determiner. *These*, *those* and *the* combine with *many, few* and numerals – these ten *abstentions (were decisive)*, those few *days (turned out to be very exciting)*, the many *supporters* – but not with *much* – *these much money. *Much* can combine with *this* and *that* – that much *money (is unnecessary)*, *(I can give you)* this much *fuel*.

If we think in terms of using the major classes of determiners to construct NPs, various choices are open.

i   Choose no determinative: *Mambas (are to be avoided)*.
ii Choose a quantifying determinative: *all mambas (are dangerous), both cars (were damaged)*.

iii Choose a central determinative: *the mamba, those cars.*
iv Choose a post-determinative: *many/few students (choose this course), (Do you drink) much coffee?, Nine climbers (were missing).*
v Choose any combination, one from each set of determinatives, as allowed by the restrictions and following the patterns of order: *mambas, all mambas, all the mambas, all the many mambas (make life difficult).*

The set of central determinatives includes possessive pronouns – *my, your, his, her, its, our, their* – and possessive noun phrases, such as *Freya's* and *Katarina's.* These determinatives combine with quantifying determinatives and post-determinatives: *all Freya's many friends, half Katarina's few mistakes.* They do not combine with the other central determinatives: **these Freya's books.*

The above sketch deals with most of the major structures with determinatives but an important pattern has still to be introduced. This is the pattern, in fact patterns, with *which, what* and *how.* *Which* and *what* can be straightforwardly analysed as central determinatives. They combine with quantifying determinatives, as shown in (2).

2 a [You sold] <u>all what</u>/<u>all which</u> books?
  b <u>half which</u> faction [is defecting]?
  c [You'll pay] <u>double what</u> amount of money?

Which and *what* combine with numeral post-determinatives, as in (3).

3 <u>Which ten</u>/<u>what ten</u> candidates [have failed]?

They do not combine (or at least do not combine easily) with *many, few* or *much.* Crucially, they do not combine with the central determinatives – **what this, *what those,* and they only combine with the central determinatives *a* and *the* in fixed phrases such as *What a shame!, What a mess!, What the hell!,* or even just *What the!*

How does not combine with the quantifying determinatives nor, like *which* and *what,* with the central determinatives, except in fixed phrases such as *How the hell did you do that?* It does combine with post-determinatives, as in *How many, how much,* and *how few.* It too can be treated as a central determinative.

There are two items that follow different patterns from the ones set out above. They are *other* and *same. Other* combines with the quantifying determinatives *both* and *all* – <u>All other</u> *applications (will be rejected),* <u>Both other</u> *candidates (failed). Other* and *same* both combine with central determinatives, the order being [central determinative + *other/same*] – <u>an other</u> *idea,* <u>the other</u> *woman,* <u>those other</u> *teams,* <u>the same</u> *mistake,* <u>those same</u> *criminals.*

Other and *same* both combine with the numeral post-determinatives and *few* – the *other two* doctors, the *same three* writers, the *same few* volunteers. The obligatory presence of *the*, and *this*, etc., and the exclusion of *a/an* are to be explained by the speaker referring to an entity that has already been mentioned and is therefore given; indeed, *same* can only be used for given entities. When mentioning an entity for the first time speakers cannot say **(Can you get me) a same jacket?* but utter something along the lines of *Can you get me a jacket of the same kind?* or *Can you get me a similar jacket?*

We return to the NP *the other two doctors*. *Other* precedes *two*, but in *two other doctors* the numeral *two* precedes *other*. The obvious difference between the two NPs is that *the other two doctors* contains *the* and is used to refer to doctors who are given, that is, who have already been mentioned or are salient in a given context, as in (4a). The NP *Two other doctors* does not contain *the* and is used to mention 'new' doctors for the first time in a conversation, as in (4b).

4 a There was a group of five doctors. Three went away but the other two doctors stayed to talk to the patients.
  b I was talking to Doctor Dickson when two other doctors came in who I didn't know.

How to account for the different word orders? What we propose here is that there are not just different determinatives, *a* versus *the*, *that*, etc., but different determinative constructions. One construction is for referring to specific ('given') entities; the other is for referring to 'new' entities. The given construction requires sequences such as *the other two doctors*, *these other ten applications*; the new construction requires *two other doctors*, *ten other applications*. The new construction allows *more*, as in *two more volunteers*, but excludes *same*, as in **a same e-mail* (cf. *an identical e-mail*); the given construction excludes *more* – **the more volunteers* – but allows *same* – *the same e-mail*.

Some, *many*, *few*, *much*, *all* and *both* were treated above as determinatives, as in *some friends*, etc. They also occur in examples such as (5), where there is no overt noun for them to determine. Are they determinatives, or a kind of pronoun, or what?

5 a I have discussed the proposals with my colleagues. Some will accept them.
  b We invited the whole staff but many couldn't come.
  c Her sisters phoned immediately. Both were very pleased.

One solution is to treat the examples as involving ellipsis: *some* in (5a) results from the ellipsis of *colleagues* or *of my colleagues*: *some (of my) colleagues* ➔ *some* ~~*(of my)*~~ *colleagues*. Similarly *many (of the) staff* ➔ *many (of ~~the) staff~~* and *both (of her) sisters* ➔ *both* ~~*(of her)*~~ *sisters*. A second solution is to treat *some*, etc. as some kind of deictic pronoun whose deictic target is made clear by the preceding text or by the context. (=> NOUN PHRASES: PRONOUNS.) Thus in *I know you think the rules are inadequate. Many would disagree with you*, *many* can be interpreted as 'many people' or 'many colleagues' or 'many scholars', depending on the topic of conversation and what rules are under discussion. Suppose that someone is holding a bowl of crisps and asks a child *Would you like some?* The child will understand 'some crisps', but ellipsis is not the only road to that understanding. It is equally possible to think of the child enriching the utterance by means of the context: *some* points to something salient in this context; what is it? – aha, crisps! This is the type of solution proposed by a theory of semantic/pragmatic interpretation called Relevance Theory, and 'enrichment' is one of its technical terms.

The enrichment analysis works well for examples such as (6).

6 a [Speaker points to a copy of a newspaper] This is very poor print.
  b [Speaker points to a copy of a newspaper] This has come out in favour of immigration.

The listener has to construct an interpretation. In (6a) *this* has as its deictic target the physical qualities of the ink used to produce the text on paper. In (6b) its deictic target is the editors and owners of the newspaper.

The above discussion focuses on determinative patterns typical of formal written English, though they do occur in speech too. However, different determinatives and different patterns are typical of informal spoken English, such as *the both of you* as opposed to *both of you*. In this structure *both*, preceded by *the* and followed by the prepositional phrase *of you*, looks like a noun. *Many* and *much* are not frequent in informal speech. Instead we find *a lot of, loads of, heaps of* (a favourite with New Zealanders), *tons of: a lot of problems, a lot of fruit, loads of friends, heaps of ideas*. The use of these alternative phrases is restricted. You can have sequences such as *all his many friends* but not **all his loads of friends*.

We finish this section by noting that it is worthwhile scrutinising English texts for unusual NP structures. The magazine *Alpaca World* (Winter 13/14, p.44) contained the sentence in (7).

7 We've now got getting on for five year's worth [of fleece] still waiting.

The determiner is *five year's worth* and it is modified by *getting on for*. Possible alternatives are *approaching five year's worth* and *approximately five year's worth*.

NOUNS AND NOUN PHRASES: PRONOUNS

Number, gender and case are still very visible in the pronouns of English. The category of person is central to the personal pronouns: in the prototypical usage *I* refers to the speaker or writer, who is at the centre of any act of communication, taking first place and being the 'first person'. *We* refers to the speaker plus one or more other participants. If that set includes the listener, *we* is said to be inclusive – *You and me, we'll show them!* (or *you and I*, if grammatically 'correct' but unrealistic dialogue is required); if it does not include the listener, *we* is said to be exclusive –*Freya and me, we're leaving now; you stay and keep an eye on the house.* *You* refers to the addressee (hopefully also the listener), who is regarded as the second person in a communication and in this case has been excluded from the referents of *we*. Speaker/writer and listener/reader are central to typical acts of communication and may discuss other people or things that are not at the centre of the acts but are 'third persons'. The latter are referred to by means of third person pronouns, *he, she, it, they*.

The personal pronouns show distinctions of number: *I* and *he, she, it* are described as singular personal pronouns since they are used to refer to one individual and *we* and *they* are described as plural personal pronouns, since they are used to refer to more than one individual. *You* can be treated as vague with respect to number, the number of addressees only being made clear by context.

The personal pronouns are deictics, having to do with deixis. (*Deixis* derives from the Classical Greek verb *deiknumi* 'to show, point out'. The root *deik-* is connected with *dig-*in *digit* (= finger), the body part that is used for pointing.) The speaker points to himself or herself with *I* and to the addressee with *you*. 'Speaker' and 'addressee' are roles in a dialogue and the participants in a dialogue take it in turn to play each role. This means that what *I* and *you* (and indeed the other personal pronouns) refer to changes constantly during a conversation; their reference is said to shift, but at any given point in a conversation the reference is anchored to the speaker. Consider the dialogue in (1), based on a real conversation.

1 I_1 said to Mr Surname 'Can I_2 ask you$_1$ a question? Is there any faint possibility of me$_3$ getting an A in my maths exam?' and he looked at me and he said 'You$_2$'d have to work awfully hard Firstname, very very hard. I_4 doubt it very much.'

I_1, I_2 and me_3 point to Firstname but I_4 points to Mr Surname; you_1 points to Mr Surname but you_2 points to Firstname.

Case is signalled by all the personal pronouns except *it* and *you*: the subject forms are *I, we, he, she,* and *they*, while the non-subject forms are *me, us, him, her* and *them*: thus, *She admires them* versus *They admire her*. We use the term 'non-subject' because *me*, etc. do not function just as objects. Manuals of good usage still recommend patterns such as *It is I, It was they who alerted the fire service* but speakers have long used *It's me* and *It was them that alerted the fire service*. Spoken English also offers focusing constructions such as *Him, he's just an idiot* and *Me, I don't like the idea*, and certain non-standard varieties have the construction *He's some runner, him*, with the non-subject form of the pronoun at the end of the construction. And note the classic pieces of dialogue in (2) and (3).

2   A: Who's going to help me?
    B: Me!

3   A: Who broke the window?
    B: Him!

A construction that has disturbed many an arbiter of good grammar is exemplified in *I can run faster than her*. For such arbiters, the correct version is *I can run faster than she*, with *can run* understood: *I can run faster than she can run*. The trouble is that the 'correct' version is used by nobody in speech and by very few people in writing. KB and JM might avoid *than her* in formal writing but get round the peculiarity of *than she* by using *than she can*. What, anyway, is the structure of *than she can*? Is it derived by ellipsis from *than she can run*? *Than she can* certainly is, but how to account for the peculiarity of *than she*? An alternative analysis is to treat *than* as a preposition. Since prepositions assign objective case to their object nouns, the occurrence of *than her* is explained.

Case is implicated in a construction that is widely used but found objectionable by some speakers. Examples are *He said he'd help Jane and I to move house* and *Between you and I, he's pretty useless at the job*. What is found unacceptable is the use of *I* as opposed to *me*; the standard argument against the construction is that *help I* is incorrect (in standard English), as is *between I* (ignoring the fact the *between* requires a plural noun or conjoined NPs). The difficulty for analysts of English is that the construction has been in use since at least the time of Shakespeare; *The Merchant of Venice* contains the clause *All debts are cleerd between you and I*. That is, the construction is not going to vanish and has to be included in descriptions of the language. Perhaps the standard argument is wrong and we should treat *help Jane and I* not as deriving from *help Jane + help I* but as a separate construction in which the final pronoun receives 'subject' case. (See the discussion of pronoun exchange below.)

A final comment on case in pronouns. There is, or was, in the varieties spoken in south-west England and in Essex (and possibly elsewhere in the south-east) a phenomenon known as 'pronoun exchange'.† What are subject and object forms in standard English occur as object and subject forms, as shown in (4).

4 I'll give *he* what-for some day, that I will ...
   From Charles Benham (1890), *Essex Ballads*

5 Well, if I didn't know *they*, they knowed *I*.
   Freiburg English Dialect Corpus

It has been suggested that the subject pronouns occur as objects when the pronoun is emphasised and object pronouns as subjects when the pronoun is not emphasised. Whatever the explanation, the usage is probably in decline, though a British pop song in the late 1970s did contain the line *Don't tell I, tell ee* (= *he*). The object pronouns *I* and *ee* are indeed emphasised, being in contrast with each other.

The personal pronouns also signal gender via the contrast between the third person pronouns *he* and *she*, while animacy is relevant to the contrast between *it* and *he/she*. Usage of the third person pronouns is rather more complex. Consider first how speakers of standard English use these pronouns when referring to children or animals. Adults with close links to a baby or child use *he* or *she*. Adults without a close link to a baby might use *it* (*Does it sleep through the night?*) at the risk of gravely offending the parents. (The colour-coding of babies in pink or blue can be useful.) The use of proper names indicates knowledge of a baby's gender and requires *he* or *she* as appropriate: *How is Katarina? Is she sleeping well?* (But not **Is it sleeping well?*). Animals, though animate, are generally referred to by means of *it*, but not when there is a close link between human speaker and animal. Pet dogs, cats and horses (not to mention rabbits, budgies and hamsters) are referred to by *he* or *she* by members of the family they belong to and by speakers who know them and have a positive attitude towards them. *What's wrong with your dog? She's been barking all day* and *What's wrong with your dog? It's been barking all day* convey different social signals, the latter putting a metaphorical distance between the speaker and the dog and conveying a less tolerant attitude.

In standard British English, countries conceived of as political units are talked of as though they were feminine: *France is sending her top civil servants to the conference.* When thought of as geographical units countries are treated as inanimate: *France is big but it has good motorways and high-speed rail links.* Reference grammars report that some speakers (of standard and non-standard British English) apply *she* and *her* to cars and boats, especially ones with which they have a close relationship. This usage may be typical of male speakers and may be in retreat. In her novel *The Nine Tailors*, published in 1934, Dorothy Sayers comments that, at least in East Anglia, the large bells rung in church towers were referred to by *she*.

In various non-standard varieties of English both *he* and *she* are applied to inanimate entities. The use of *he* and *him* for, inter alia, plants, tools and vehicles appears to be widespread in Devon, Cornwall and Somerset: *He 'ave been a good watch, I bet thee cansn' climb he* [= a tree]. It is reported for Australian vernacular English that speakers treat, e.g., plants as masculine and, e.g., vehicles, buildings and geographical features as feminine: *That one there, e's a wild cherry, ... that river, she is dangerous with all them crocodiles, ... we was building a garage. She was an excavation job.*†

To complete this sketch of gender in English we look at the use of *he* and *him* as supposedly gender-neutral, the use of *he or she, his or her* and *him or her* in the interests of gender-inclusiveness and the use of *they* to refer to individual persons. In (6) the neutral noun *chairperson* is followed by *his* and in (7) the gender-neutral *child* is followed by *his*.

6 The chairperson, whoever that is, will cast his vote last if necessary.
7 The child observes the patterns in his environment.

(6) and (7) represent traditional usage, which is now avoided by many speakers as being male-oriented. A good number of academic papers in the past thirty years have offered a version of, e.g., (7) in which *his* is replaced by *her*. *The child observes the patterns in her environment.* This usage is just as far from gender neutrality as (7). A genuinely gender-neutral construction has been available since at least the 16th century: *The child observes patterns in their environment* and *The chairperson, whoever that is, will cast their vote last if necessary*, and, with *they, I'll keep people informed once the new manager tells me how they want to organise the office.*

This construction is the regular one in spoken English, standard and non-standard, though not yet regular on BBC news broadcasts. It also occurs frequently in informal writing. For users who approach grammatical correctness from a logical point of view, it has the drawback that *their* and *they* are plural pronouns employed to refer to single individuals, but they have the advantage, shared by *we*, that the English plural pronouns do not signal gender. And of course we should note the long-established uses of plural pronouns in reference to a single person in constructions such as the editorial *we* and the royal *we*, as in *We intend to abdicate when the time is right*. This extension of usage is no more peculiar than the extension of masculine *he*, *him* and *his* to male and female humans collectively. It is, furthermore, a natural usage, not driven by the arbiters of 'good English', very conscious of grammar and meaning. (=> GRAMMATICALITY: GRAMMATICALITY AND POWER, GRAMMATICALITY: GRAMMATICALITY: DESCRIPTIVE AND PRESCRIPTIVE GRAMMAR.)

This, *that*, *these* and *those* can be used as demonstrative pronouns, as in (8) or as demonstrative determinatives, as in (9). We deal with both the pronoun and the determinative uses here as they are both deictic and subject to the same interpretations.

8 a <u>That</u> was delicious.
  b <u>These</u> are too dear.

9 a <u>That</u> programme was absolute rubbish.
  b <u>These</u> trainers are too dear.

The basic interpretation of *this* and *that* depends on where the speaker and addressee are in a given location and where things or people are relative to them. *This* is used for things that are relatively near the speaker or the speaker and the addressee, as in (10).

10 a I'll give you <u>this</u>/<u>this book</u> as soon as I've finished it.
     [Speaker indicates a book on the desk beside her]

   b Can you guess what's in <u>this</u>/<u>this parcel</u>?
     [Speaker has come in holding a parcel]

That is used to refer to things that are relatively far from the speaker or the speaker and the addressee, as in (11).

11 Could you pass me <u>that</u> please?
   [Speaker points to a dictionary on the other side of the table, next to the addressee]

Some, possibly many, speakers of Scottish English and other northern English varieties have a three-way system of demonstratives: *this* for an entity near the speaker, *that* for an entity near the addressee, and *yon* for an entity far from both speaker and addressee. (12) is based on a real example.

12 Do you see <u>yon</u> houses on the other side of the square?

Literary, especially poetic, texts offer examples of *yonder*, now archaic: *Who dwells in yonder castle?* Distance may be related to the speaker's perception or presentation of an entity.

The relative pronouns are *who*, *whom*, *which*, and *whose*. (=> RELATIVE CLAUSES: INTRODUCTION, RELATIVE CLAUSES: WH.) *Who* is the subject form and *whom* the non-subject form but *whom* is rarely found outside formal written texts and (very) formal speech. (There are various relative clause constructions and the one with the *wh* pronouns is quite rare in informal spoken English.) *Which* is used to refer to inanimate entities and *who* to inanimate entities. *Whose* is a possessive pronoun. It was formerly held (by arbiters of 'good' grammar) to apply only to animate entities, as in *the boy whose mobile phone was stolen*, but it is now regularly used for inanimate entities too, as in *the roof whose slates were ripped off by the storm*, as opposed to *the roof the slates of which were ripped off by the storm*. (*Whose* is now quite rare in informal spoken English. Possessive relative clauses can either be avoided or constructed with *that* and a shadow pronoun: *the roof that its slates were ripped off by the storm*. The latter construction occurs regularly in spoken English but not in writing.) The relativiser *that* is not a pronoun. (=> RELATIVE CLAUSES: INTRODUCTION, RELATIVE CLAUSES: TH.)

The *wh* pronouns also function as interrogatives, and the same comments apply to *who* versus *whom* and *whose*, with the extra comment that in interrogative clauses *whose* still cannot be used in reference to inanimate entities: *Whose slates are those?* is a request to identify the human owner of the slates, not the house or roof they have come from. There is also another *wh* interrogative pronoun, *what*. For some speakers *what* is an indefinite pronoun, suited for questions such as *What did you see at the Museum?*, whereas *which* is a definite pronoun, suitable for contexts in which somebody has to choose one out of a number of things, as illustrated in (13).

13 A: I looked at a silver brooch and a pair of gold earrings.
   B: Which did you go for?
   A: I went for the brooch

For another set of speakers *what* would be perfectly appropriate in (13). The entity pointed at by means of a deictic is known as the deictic target. The deictic target of *we* is not always the speaker and another. The 'royal' *we* and the 'editorial' *we* point to a single person (but the editorial *we* is used less and less these days). *You* is vague as to number, which is usually made clear by context. Speakers do have the choice of combining *you* with *both* and *all*, as in *I'm asking you both to leave* or *I want you all to be here by noon*. As clause subject, *you* is separated from *both* and *all*, as in *You're both leaving* and *You've all to be here by noon*. *You* and *all* have coalesced to give the plural second person form *y'all* in certain varieties of American English, especially in the south-east of the USA. Speakers of certain non-standard varieties of British English use the plural form *yous*.

Prepositions and prepositional phrases

PREPOSITIONS AND PREPOSITIONAL PHRASES: INTRODUCTION

Prepositional phrases (PPs) are phrases with a preposition as their head. Examples, with the prepositions underlined, are (*She was standing*) *beside the tree*, (*The plane descended*) *towards the landing strip*, (*The dog pushed her ball*) *under the sofa*, (*The children were sitting*) *at the table*, (*She received a legacy*) *from her aunt*. Without the preposition the phrases are noun phrases (NPs) and the examples have incorrect syntax: **She was standing the tree*, **The dog pushed her ball the sofa* and so on.

Prepositions can be split into three subsets. The first contains 'core' prepositions whose historical source cannot be determined. Some members of this subset are *in, on, from, with, to, for, off* and *out*. (*Out* as in *The child scampered out the door*, as opposed to *The child scampered out of the door*, is in reference grammars labelled 'especially American English'. *Out* as opposed to *out of* is however widely used in spoken British English, both standard and non-standard. Commentators who take a restrictive and solipsistic view of what counts as standard English would probably disagree that phrases such as *out the door* count as standard English.)

The second subset consists of (mainly bisyllabic) prepositions that have their historical source in the core prepositions *on* (reduced to *a*) and *by* combined with another preposition or a noun. Examples are *atop, amid, beside, beneath* and *but* (from *by* + *out*) and, with *out* and *in*, *outside* and *inside*.

The third subset consists of what many analysts treat as complex prepositions. There are two-word sequences such as *ahead of, along with, apart from, due to, thanks to,* and *instead of*. There are also many three-word sequences such as *by virtue of* (*The mayor was re-elected by virtue of his hard work and honesty*) and *by way of* (*We went by way of the bookshop*), *in view of* (*In view of his admission of guilt, the magistrate simply imposed a fine*), *in case of* (*In case of fire, leave by the fire exit*), *in front of* and (definitely American English) *in back of* (= *behind*). From a syntactic point of view these do not have to be analysed as complex prepositions, that is, as a single preposition that has two or three components. They can be analysed as what they look like – sequences of two or three words. We can say that *view* and *case* require the preposition *of*, that *along* requires *with*, *thanks* requires *to*, and so on.

The class of prepositions is small compared with the classes of verbs, nouns, adjectives and adverbs and does not readily acquire new members. Nonetheless a small number of new members have appeared relatively recently: *bar* (*He's not seeing anybody bar his clients* = *except his clients*), *plus* (*She's published three articles plus a book*), *regarding* (*Regarding his request, the manager has turned it down*). *Plus* and *minus* occur in arithmetical formulae such as *two plus two* and *ten minus six*, although the formulae currently in favour in primary schools in Britain are *two add two* and *ten takeaway six*. Are *add* and *takeaway* imperative verbs or prepositions?

PREPOSITIONS AND PREPOSITIONAL PHRASES: PREPOSITIONS AND PARTICLES

Many of the words that are classed as prepositions combine with verbs and are known as particles. The label 'prepositional verb' (=> PREPOSITIONS AND PREPOSITIONAL PHRASES: PREPOSITIONAL VERBS.) and the label 'preposition' are not appropriate, as the verb + particle combinations have different syntactic properties from prepositional verbs and from sequences of preposition + NP. (=> PREPOSITIONS AND PREPOSITIONAL PHRASES: PREPOSITIONS AND PARTICLES.) The differences are illustrated by the examples in (1).

1 a The sweep called up the chimney.
    b *The sweep called the chimney up.

2 a The general called up reinforcements.
    b The general called reinforcements up.

3 a The sweep looked up the chimney.
    b *The sweep looked the chimney up.

4 a The student looked up the word.
    b The student looked the word up.

The prepositions in (1a) and (3a) cannot be moved to the end of the clause. (1b) and (3b) are incorrect. In contrast, the particles in (2a) and (4a) can be moved to the end of the clause. (2b) and (4b) are correct structures of English. In the above examples the prepositions have concrete spatial meanings while the particles have abstract spatial meanings (though *up* in (2) is less abstract than *up* in (4)). This is an accident of these particular examples, as shown by the preposition and particle *down* in (5a–c), all three instances of *down* denoting movement from a higher to a lower position.

- 5 a The girl ran <u>down</u> the hill.
-   b The girl put <u>down</u> her book.
-   c The girl put her book <u>down</u>.

The close link between preposition and complement NP is demonstrated by the fact that such sequences can be moved to the front of a clause, as in (6), although (6b) is not entirely felicitous. The important syntactic point is that the preposition cannot be left behind nor can it be moved to the front of the clause leaving its complement NP behind. (6c) and (6d) are both incorrect.

- 6 a <u>Down</u> the hill ran the girl.
-   b <u>Up</u> the chimney looked the sweep.
-   c *The hill ran the girl <u>down</u>.
-   d *Down ran the girl the hill.†

(7) demonstrates the looser connection between particle and NP; they do not form a sequence that moves en bloc to the front of the clause.

- 7 *<u>Down</u> her book put the girl.

The verb-particle combinations differ from prepositional verbs; in the latter, the verb and preposition must be adjacent, as in (8), with the prepositional verb *call on*. (9) shows that *switch on* is a combination of verb and particle, as *on* can move to the end of the clause, as in (9b).

- 8 a They <u>called on</u> their grandparents.
-   b *They called their grandparents on.

- 9 a They switched <u>on</u> the floodlights.
-   b They switched the floodlights <u>on</u>.

Since we have been keen to use labels that capture parallels and similarities among apparently different sets of words, we could replace 'particle' with 'prepositional particle'. This label reflects the fact that most of the forms in the set of prepositions (with some exceptions, such as *from* and *with*) are also in the set of particles, and the label also points at the relationship between prepositions, particles and prepositional verbs. As we will see, it is not just similarity of form that the label captures but similarity in meaning, since all these sets of forms have basic spatial meanings from which other, more abstract and metaphorical, meanings are derived.

Morphology lies outside the scope of this book but this section would be incomplete if we failed to mention that some forms that function as prepositions and particles also function as components of compound verbs, participles and nouns. Thus, an *outcast* is someone who is cast or thrown outside of their community; someone who is *downcast* has, figuratively at least, been thrown down by some event. An *intake* is the cohort of children accepted into a given school at the beginning of the school year, or that part of a piece of equipment that allows gases or liquids to flow into it. A play on the relationship between particles and verb prefixes is exploited in a line of the song that Bugs Bunny sings in the 1959 cartoon *Backwoods Bunny*. The line is reproduced in (10).

10   I'm looking over a four leaf clover that I overlooked before.

To *look over something* is to examine it. *Over* here is a prepositional particle, as it can occur either immediately after the verb or after the direct object: *I looked over the document before signing it* and *I looked the document over before signing it*. To *overlook something* is to fail to see it. This failure can be accidental or deliberate, as in the extended meaning 'not to take account of some fault': *We decided to overlook his unexplained absence*.

PREPOSITIONS AND PREPOSITIONAL PHRASES: PREPOSITIONS, TRANSITIVE AND INTRANSITIVE

The concepts of transitive and intransitive prepositions are unusual in contemporary analyses of English syntax but are not new, being first proposed in the early 1970s.† How can we justify the concept of intransitive preposition? After all, the traditional definitions of preposition all say that they are relational items that connect nouns, adjectives or verbs with NPs. That is, traditionally prepositions are regarded as transitive, and indeed prototypical prepositions are transitive. The concept 'intransitive preposition' has arisen in connection with examples such as those in (1)–(7); the underlined words in the (b) examples are intransitive prepositions.

1   a   The light switch is inside the cupboard.
    b   The light switch is inside.

2   a   Everybody ran outside the lecture room.
    b   Everybody ran outside.

3   a   Our friends came across the road to have a chat.
    b   Our friends came across to have a chat.

4 a We are close <u>behind</u> the fastest group of walkers.
  b We are close <u>behind</u>.

5 a All <u>around</u> the house were beech woods and fields.
  b All <u>around</u> were beech woods and fields.

6 a The manager is not in his office just now.
  b The manager is not <u>in</u>.

7 a The cat leapt <u>out (of)</u> the window.
  b The manager is <u>out</u> at the moment.

The (a) examples show the prototypical distribution of prepositions, preceding an NP. In the (b) examples the same 'prepositions' have no complement NPs. There is a sound pragmatic explanation for the (b) examples: in context there may be no need to mention the cupboard, the lecture room, the road or the fastest group of walkers.

Some prepositions, such as *with* and *from*, require a complement NP: **She arrived with* and **She has driven from* are incorrect structures. Some analysts give the label 'prepositional adverb', or just 'adverb', to items such as *ahead*, *away*, *back* and *overseas* because they exclude a complement NP: **ahead the convoy*, etc. These two labels are unsatisfactory.

- They extend the label 'adverb', which the authors would prefer to restrict to forms with the suffix *-ly* that derive from adjectives, such as *skilfully* and *badly*.
- The label 'adverb' is applied to forms that have a very different distribution from the *-ly* forms. For example, *overseas* occurs after NPs – *our factories overseas*, and as the complement of *be* – *Our biggest factories are overseas*. That is, words such as *overseas* do not have the same syntactic properties as words such as *skilfully*, and sequences such as *our factories <u>overseas</u>* can be seen as parallel to *our factories <u>in China</u>*.
- The label 'adverb' splits off words such as *overseas* and *back*, with spatial meanings, from words such as *in* and *round*, also with spatial meanings, as in *I'll come round this evening* and *The bell rang and the children went in*.

For the above reasons, we prefer the term 'intransitive preposition'.

PREPOSITIONS AND PREPOSITIONAL PHRASES: PREPOSITIONAL PHRASES, THEIR DISTRIBUTION

PPs function most frequently as the complements of verbs and nouns but also as the complements of adjectives and (more rarely) of prepositions.

COMPLEMENTS OF VERBS

PPs are required by a number of verbs, as shown in (1).

1. a Sabrina placed the vase <u>on the hall table</u>.
   b *Sabrina placed the vase.
2. a The boys plunged <u>into the lake</u>.
   b ?The boys plunged.
3. a The grandfather clock stands <u>in the library</u>.
   b *The grandfather clock stands.
4. a The wombat burrowed <u>under my lawn</u>.
   b ?The wombat burrowed.
5. a The lawnmower is <u>in the garden shed</u>.
   b *The lawnmower is.

COMPLEMENTS (OR POSTMODIFIERS) OF NOUNS

PPs occur freely as the complements of nouns.

6. books <u>about architecture</u>
7. the wall <u>round the garden</u>
8. a present <u>for James</u>
9. their policy <u>on road-building</u>

COMPLEMENTS (OR POSTMODIFIERS) OF ADJECTIVES

10. rich <u>in shale gas</u>
11. resistant <u>to change</u>
12. eligible <u>for promotion</u>
13. angry <u>at her colleagues</u>

COMPLEMENTS OF PREPOSITIONS

14. in <u>behind the sofa</u>
15. from <u>outside the house</u>
16. in <u>under the caravan</u>
17. out <u>through the window</u>
18. up <u>over the wall</u>
19. until <u>after Easter</u>

Complements, as opposed to adjuncts, have two properties. One is that a head word may require or exclude a particular type of phrase. The other is that a head word may require a particular lexical item as the head of a dependent phrase. Thus only one or two prepositions can be followed by PPs; most prepositions exclude them. The typical sequences consist of *in, from, out, down,* or *up* followed by *outside, inside, under* or *above*. Many individual adjectives and nouns require particular prepositions: *the blame <u>for</u> something, resistant <u>to</u> something*. Some allow a choice, as in *a report on/ about crime*, and some noun-preposition sequences have been affected by change: KB and JM prefer *a debate <u>about</u> health policies* but many speakers now use *a debate <u>around</u> health policies*. Verbs such as *stand* in (3) require a PP; verbs such as *place* in (1) require both a PP and an NP. No verb excludes a PP, since PPs of place (as opposed to direction) and time are adjuncts and all verbs allow such PPs: *The baby is still sleeping <u>in a cot</u>*, He snoozed <u>during the lecture</u>. In contrast, PPs denoting direction are excluded by many verbs and allowed (or licensed) by verbs denoting movement: **She sat into the garden* versus *She went into the garden*.

PREPOSITIONS AND PREPOSITIONAL PHRASES: PREPOSITIONS AND MEANING

Accounts of word classes/parts of speech typically distinguish between full lexical items or content words and form words, grammatical words or grammatical markers. Full lexical items are lexical items that have a denotation. Prototypical members of the set are nouns, verbs, adjectives and adverbs: *dog* denotes the subset of animals categorised as dogs; *write* denotes the set of actions producing marks on some material such as paper or digitally on a screen; *tall* denotes a property of persons or things; *quickly* denotes a property of actions. (We pass over the problem of entities that do not fall neatly into one category, such as containers that resemble both a cup and a mug, and over the problem of deciding what counts as 'being tall' in a particular context.)

Typical form words/grammatical words in English are the articles, *the* and *a*, and auxiliary verbs such as *will, do, shall*. They do not have a denotation. Where do prepositions fit into this scheme? Many accounts treat them as form words but examples such as (1) show that this analysis is not adequate.

1 a Could you bring me the dictionary <u>on</u> the bureau?
    b Could you bring me the dictionary <u>in</u> the bureau?
    c Could you bring me the dictionary <u>beside</u> the bureau?
    d Could you bring me the dictionary <u>under</u> the bureau?

The action that is carried out in response to such a request differs depending on whether the speaker uses *on, in, beside* or *under* (and whether the addressee hears the prepositions correctly). *On* denotes the surface of an object, and the addressee will look for a dictionary sitting on top of the bureau. *In* denotes an interior space and the addressee will look for the dictionary inside the bureau, opening the lid if necessary. *Beside* denotes a space at the side of an object and the addressee will look for a dictionary at either side of the bureau, perhaps lying on a table or even on the floor, but not in front of or behind it. *Under* denotes a space underneath an object and the addressee, perhaps finding the request unusual because books are not usually stored underneath bureaus, will look underneath the bureau.

Since this is a book on syntax and not semantics we will not go into detail on the spatial meanings of prepositions, but it is worthwhile pointing out that some spatial meanings are quite complex; for instance the analysis of *along* as in *Fiona strolled along the path* requires the concept of an axis that has a length with Fiona moving on the length of the axis. The interpretation of a preposition can vary from context to context; the interpretation of 'being beside' varies depending on whether we are dealing with a book beside a bureau or a person standing beside a river, and the interpretation of 'being in' varies depending on whether we are talking of a crack in a cup or a picture hook in a wall. A further complication is that prepositions with spatial meanings have metaphorical extensions, witness *in the bureau* versus *in a bad mood*, *on the bureau* versus *on this topic (he has nothing to offer)*, *beside the bureau* versus *beside himself with rage*, *under the bureau* versus *under the weather* (= not well, ill), *under this heading (we will deal with discourse particles)*.

Many prepositions have temporal meanings, as in *after six o'clock*, *until Christmas*, *during the holidays*, *before the New Year*, and so on.

There are two key points in the above discussion. The examples involve contrasts between prepositions: *in* versus *on* versus *beside* versus *under* with the same complement NP, *the bureau*. And the interpretation of the prepositions applies to locations in space (or locations in time). We now turn to the question whether any prepositions can be regarded as grammaticalised in any of their uses; that is, whether they have lost whatever concrete (typically spatial) meaning they might have had and become mere markers of a particular structure. Obvious examples are combinations of verbs, nouns and adjectives with particular prepositions. For instance, in *She's not very keen on the idea*, can *on* be treated as having any residue of the denotation 'surface of an entity'? Probably not. In *They headed for home*, does *for* carry any spatial meaning? Again, probably not. It is difficult to see any spatial meaning attaching to *for* in *The police blamed him for the accident*.

Other cases are not so easily decided. Consider *to* in *The bank transferred the money to them.* This has been proposed as a grammaticalised use, but the example can be straightforwardly interpreted as denoting the movement of money from one location (the bank) to another location (the recipients), and *to* does contrast with *from*, as in *The bank transferred the money from them.* The alternation between *to* and *from* matches the alternation with verbs denoting the movement of animate beings: *We went to Newcastle* and *We came from Newcastle. By* is trickier. It has obvious spatial (directional) uses in examples such as *Go by the cathedral. It's quicker* and *Freya drove by James' house but didn't go in to see him.* In these examples *by* can be replaced by *via* or *past* and contrasts with, e.g., *round, to* and *from. By* also occurs in the long passive (=> VERBS AND VERB PHRASES: PASSIVE VOICE.), as in *The money was transferred by the bank.* Is this a grammaticalised use that has no connection with spatial meanings of *by?* In standard written English it may well be, and this is the view presented in some grammars of English. In non-standard varieties of English, however, other prepositions occur in the passive: *with, from, off, off of.* (Whether any of these is used in spoken standard English is not clear: *with* is one candidate.) Depending on what data are covered by a particular grammar of English, *by* in the passive could be treated as a grammaticalised use or not.

The status of *by* in the long passive can also be considered from a typological perspective. One function of the full passive is to mention an agent but at the same time downgrading the agent in status. In a number of languages the passive construction presents the agent as a Path, that is, not as a prototypical Agent exercising its volition and energy but as a less active participant in a given situation. If we were trying to place English in a typology of passive constructions, we might well treat *by* as denoting movement along a path.

To sum up, the question as to the status of *by* in the full passive allows different answers. Is it grammaticalised? Analysts focusing on standard (written) English will decide it is; analysts working on non-standard English or taking a typological perspective may decide it is not. The essential point in the above discussion, however, is that the typical preposition has a denotation and is a lexical word class, even if it is a very small word class to which new items are rarely added.

PREPOSITIONS AND PREPOSITIONAL PHRASES: PREPOSITIONAL VERBS

Some analysts recognise a category of prepositional verbs, verbs requiring a particular preposition in a following prepositional phrase. Such verb-prepositional phrase combinations can be handled as pieces of syntax or as complex lexical items. Consider the verb *supply* in (1).

1 a This firm supplies our army with weapons.
   b This firm supplies weapons to our army.

(1a) entails (1b) and vice versa. There is a difference in meaning, in that (1a) denotes an action carried out on an army while (1b) denotes an action carried out on weapons. The *Oxford English Dictionary*, for example, deals with this by having a single entry for *supply* and listing various sub-meanings. One sub-meaning requires the construction in (1a), the other the construction in (1b). The same treatment is given to *consist of* as in *The committee consists of six elected members and three officials* and *consist in* as in *The country's strength consists in its mineral reserves*. That is, the prepositions are taken to be a component of the syntactic construction and not part of complex lexical items.

Come across and *come by* are analysed in a different fashion, with separate entries, or at least sub-entries, for *come across* and *come by*, as in (2) and (3).

2 We came across some very peculiar people on our holiday.
3 How did she come by such a large sum of money?

Come across and *come by* are prepositional verbs, but *supply with*, *supply to*, *consist of* and *consist in* are not. As a final example, consider the verb *abide* and the sentences in (4) and (5).

4 Jennifer can't abide that teacher.
   [= strongly dislikes her and cannot bear to be in her presence]

5 Jennifer promised to abide by the rules
   [= to follow the rules]

The interpretation of (4) is possible only with the bare verb *abide*, the interpretation of (5) only with the combination *abide by*. *Abide* can be entered as one entry in a dictionary and *abide by* as another entry, a prepositional verb.

Relative clauses

RELATIVE CLAUSES: INTRODUCTION

Relative clauses provide an excellent illustration of the range of structures available for what many analysts count as one construction. Prima facie there are three types of relative clause in English, exemplified in (1)–(3).

1. a The girl <u>that phoned</u> is Jennifer.
   b The bridge <u>that collapsed</u> is being rebuilt.
   c I've already seen the film <u>that's on tonight</u>.
   d Have you heard about the guy <u>that they've arrested</u>?

2. a The girl <u>who phoned</u> is Jennifer.
   b The bridge <u>which collapsed</u> is being rebuilt.
   c I've already seen the film <u>which is on tonight</u>.
   d Have you heard about the guy <u>whom/who they've arrested</u>?

3. a *The girl [Ø] <u>phoned</u> is Jennifer. [The girl that/who phoned]
   b *The bridge [Ø] <u>collapsed</u> is being rebuilt. [The bridge that collapsed]
   c *I've already seen the film [Ø] <u>is on tonight</u>. [The film that is on tonight]
   d Have you heard about the guy [Ø] <u>they've arrested</u>.

(1a–d) are examples of relative clauses introduced by *that* and known as th relative clauses or *that* relative clauses. (2a–d) are examples of relative clauses introduced by *wh* words such as *who*, *whom* and *which* and known as wh relative clauses. *That* and the *wh* words are called 'relativisers'; the term relates to their function in signalling the presence of a relative clause. (3d) is an example of what is called a contact relative clause, that is, a relative clause without an overt relativiser. We can think of *the guy that/whom they've arrested* as equivalent to *the guy [they've arrested the guy]*, and *the girl phoned* as equivalent to *the girl [the girl phoned]*. The words in the square brackets are converted to surface relative clauses by substituting *whom* for *the guy* and *who* for *the girl*, or by deleting *the guy* and *the girl* inside the square brackets. But the latter deletion gives an incorrect relative clause, as shown by (3a). The problem is that in *the girl* [*the girl phoned*] *is Jennifer*, *the girl* is the subject of the relative clause. In standard written English such subject noun phrases (NPs) can be replaced by a wh word or can be deleted, but only if the relativiser *that* is present.

One approach to the wh, th and contact relative clauses, especially in models that derive surface constructions from abstract underlying structures, is to have a single structure underlying the various surface constructions. This approach allows analysts to say that there is only one relative clause construction in English. Here we are going to say that there are at least three relative clause constructions in English, the ones in (1)–(3). (The number will increase.) Our reasons are:

i   The different constructions are used in different types of text. Wh relatives are particularly common in formal writing, contact relatives are typical of spoken English and th relatives are found in both spoken and written texts.
ii Many users of English do not produce wh relatives in speech and infrequently in writing.
iii There are particularly complex wh relative clauses that occur only in formal writing, but formal written English is practised by a minority of the English-speaking population.
iv Other relative clause constructions in spoken English (both standard and non-standard) indicate that the th and contact relatives are more different in structure from wh relatives than many accounts suppose.

In the light of the above points we take the view that there are different relative clause constructions, all sharing the function of modifying nouns (but => RELATIVE CLAUSES: WH, RELATIVE CLAUSES: PROPOSITIONAL.) and ranging from the typically simple structures of spontaneous speech to the very complex structures found only in formal written language. The different constructions have long been appealed to by sociolinguists, educational linguists, typologists, investigators of spoken and written language and specialists in first language acquisition.

The three major relative clause constructions exemplified in (1)–(3) differ in their syntax. The obvious difference is that as relativiser they have zero, that, or wh. The relative pronouns *which* in (1c) and *who* in (1d) are the direct objects of their relative clauses. In (1b) the relativiser that is not a pronoun. It is invariable, in contrast with the oppositions between *who* and *whom* and between *who/whom* and *which*, and it cannot be preceded by a preposition – *the house *in that* we live* versus *the house that we live in*. *Who* and *which* also allow prepositions to be at the end of the relative clause, as in *the house which we live in*, but they can also be preceded by a preposition, as in *the house in which we live*. We assume that the structure of *that* relative clauses is, e.g., the house $_{\text{Rel Cl}}$[that we live in [Ø]], i.e., that [Ø] represents a gap corresponding to the NP modified by the relative clause.

The view that *that* is not a pronoun but a conjunction is indirectly supported by the constructions discussed in the section on non-standard English, in which relative clauses can be introduced by *as*, also an invariable word. Like *that* in standard and non-standard English, in non-standard English *as* can introduce both relative clauses and complement clauses. (=> COMPLEMENT CLAUSES: COMPLEMENTISERS.)

The examples in (1)–(3) do not exhaust the range of structures. There are more wh structures (=> RELATIVE CLAUSES: WH.) and relative clauses with no relativiser. (=> RELATIVE CLAUSES: CONTACT.) Contact relative clauses are surprisingly extensive. A structure that generally goes unmentioned in reference grammars of English involves what is called a shadow or resumptive pronoun, exemplified by the underlined *them* in *the spikes that you stick in the ground and throw rings over them*. (=> RELATIVE CLAUSES: SHADOW PRONOUNS.)

Also typical of formal written English are non-restrictive relative clauses, that is, relative clauses that are used to provide extra, incidental information but not to help the listener pick out what the speaker is referring to, as in (4). (=> RELATIVE CLAUSES: RESTRICTIVE AND NON-RESTRICTIVE.)

4 My sister, who's a lawyer, helped me sort out the problem.

RELATIVE CLAUSES: CONTACT

According to the conventions of formal written English *who*, being the subject of the relative clause *who likes his beer*, cannot be omitted from (1), and *that* cannot be omitted from (2). (3) is incorrect, i.e., not acceptable in standard (written) English).

1 He's a man who likes his beer.
2 He's a man that likes his beer.
3 *He's a man likes his beer.

But (3) is a regular structure in some varieties of non-standard English and subject wh pronouns and *that* are regularly omitted in existential-presentative constructions as in (4).

4 There's a man in this pub [Ø] likes his beer.

Other existential-presentative constructions are exemplified in (5)–(7). The relative clauses are underlined.

5 We had this French girl [Ø] came to stay.
(Cf. We had this French girl that/who came to stay)
6 My friend's got a brother [Ø] used to be in the school.
7 I know a guy [Ø] can repair your laptop.

A written example is in (8).

8 There is a porch of solid construction which has been rendered, under a pitched slate roof. There is a sash and case window in the porch [Ø] requires repainting.

The construction has been recorded in spoken Australian and New Zealand English, and in Newfoundland English. (9a–c) were recorded by Anna Shnukal in Cessnock, New South Wales, (10) is a spoken communication reported in writing and (11a and b) were reported by Sandra Clarke.

9 a Then I have my youngest son [Ø] lives in Cessnock.
  b Edwards was the only one [Ø] used to be out there.
  c I think it was only about one out of ten of us [Ø] did the finals.

10 "We had a lot of very big old mahogany trees [Ø] have fallen – one on top of a house, one into the local supermarket..." Fregon told ABC radio. *New Zealand Herald*, 15 March 2005

11 a There's no one [Ø] pays any attention to that.
   b Couple o' fellas [Ø] got their boats wrecked up in Cow Head is here.
   (A couple of fellows that got their boats wrecked... are here.)

RELATIVE CLAUSES: FREE

In this section we investigate wh clauses like those in (1)–(3).

1 a Tell me what you need?
  b What frightens me is the cost.

2 a Who we saw was the Cardinal.
  b Who didn't come to the meeting was Charles.

3 a The children just went where their parents took them.
  b Where we met was in Stirling.

Sequences such as *what you need*, *what we saw* and *where their parents took them* are called relative clauses because they have a wh word in initial position, *what*, *who* and *where*. As in relative clauses, the wh word can be the subject or object of the verb in the clause: *what* is the object of *need* in (1a) and the subject of *frightens* in (1b); *who* is the object of *saw* in (2a) and the subject of *didn't (come)* in (2b). *Where* in (3a) and (3b) is the oblique object of *took* and *met*.

What do these 'relative clauses' modify? There is no overt head noun that they modify, hence the label 'headless relative' or 'free relative' – free in that the clause is not dependent on a noun. One current analysis treats *what* as derived from *that which*. *Tell me what you need* is derived from *Tell me that which you need*. The object of *tell* is *that* and *which* is the relativiser of the relative clause *which you need*. *That* and *which* are said to fuse together into *what*, and *what* is called a fused relative.†

One disadvantage of the 'fused relative' analysis is that the wh pronouns are not just equivalent to that which. In (2) *who* is equivalent to 'the one who' or 'he/she who' and in (3) *where* is equivalent to 'there where' or 'the place where'. In (4) *how* is equivalent to 'the way/manner in which'; in (5) *when* is equivalent to 'the time at which' or 'the time during which'. And in (6) *why* is equivalent to 'the reason for which'.

4   How she avoided the photographers puzzles me.
5   When the event will begin has not been decided.
6   And yet even as a novice, it's not overly difficult to appreciate why that should be so. They are, after all, both Porsche 911s.
    Chris Horton 'Defenders of the faith', *911 & Porsche World*, July 2009, p.84

A second disadvantage of the 'fused relative' approach, as currently applied, is that the headless relatives introduced by what are NPs but those based on where and when are prepositional phrases (PPs). The view taken here (and by many analysts) is that being able to paraphrase *where* by 'the place in which' or *when* as 'the time at/during which' is not a good reason for assigning different syntactic structures.

The analysis we do adopt treats *what*, *who*, *how*, *when*, *where* and *why* as pronouns, moreover as deictic pronouns. (=> RELATIVE CLAUSES: WH WORDS AS DEICTICS, CLEFTS: CLAUSES: CLEFTS.) The structures we assign to the examples in (1)–(6) are set out below.

7   a   Tell me what [you need (it)]?
    b   What [(it) frightens me] is the cost.
8   a   Who [we saw him] was the Cardinal.
    b   Who [(he) didn't come to the meeting] was Charles.

9 a The children just went where [their parents took them (there)].
   b Where [we met(there)] was in Stirling.
10 How [she avoided the photographers (thus)] puzzles me.
11 When [the event will begin (then)] has not been decided.
12 And yet even as a novice, it's not overly difficult to appreciate why [that should be so (there-for)]. [*There* in *there-for* pronounced as in *over there*]

In this analysis† the wh words are no longer part of the chunk labelled 'headless relative'. In (7a) *what* is the direct object of *tell* and the relative clause has a missing direct object, represented by *it*. In (7b) *what* is the subject of *is (the cost)* and the relative clause has a missing subject. In (9a) *where* is the oblique object of *went* and the relative clause has a missing oblique object, represented by *there*. In (9b) *where* is the subject of *was (in Stirling)*. Note that we no longer need the labels 'headless relative' and 'free relative' as the relative clause chunks are no longer headless or free. In (7a) *you need (it)* modifies *what*, and in (10) *she avoided the photographers thus* modifies *how*.

RELATIVE CLAUSES: INFINITIVAL

Grammars of English list infinitival relatives such as *a house in which to live*. Such relative clauses, with wh relativisers, are found in formal writing but are quite untypical of informal spoken English. What do turn up are infinitival relatives as in (1), with no wh relativisers.

1 Have you brought a book to read?
2 He's got something to tell you.

Wh relativisers cannot occur in (1) and (2) anyway. *Have you brought a book which to read* and *He's got something which to tell you* are incorrect. Even where there could be a wh pronoun, the spoken English structure has none, as in the examples from recorded conversation.

3 There's vandals and it's a horrible place to live.
4 It's not the ideal place to go.

(3) in written English could be *it's a horrible place in which to live* and (4), in speech and writing, could be *It's not the ideal place to go to*. But the wh relativisers typically do not occur in (informal) spoken English and the clause-final prepositions are regularly omitted too.

RELATIVE CLAUSES: NON-STANDARD

Non-standard varieties of English, whether in Britain, Ireland, North America, Australia or New Zealand, offer a range of other relative clause constructions. The most common relativisers are *what*, *as* and *at* – specialists consider the latter not to be a shortened form of *that*. Examples are in (1).†

1. a He's a man <u>what</u> likes his beer.
   b He's a man <u>as</u> likes his beer.
   c He's a man <u>at</u> likes his beer.
   d He's a man [ ] likes his beer.
   e He's a man [ ] <u>he</u> likes his beer.

What occurs throughout the UK and in various parts of North America but *as* is reported only for the south-east of England. The problem for sociolinguists investigating usage is that the syntax of most non-standard Englishes has not been studied in detail and, being stigmatised and re-stigmatised in the school systems of the English-speaking world, is difficult to record by means of questionnaires. (Respondents to questionnaires tend to stick very closely to intuitions inculcated in the classroom.) For our purposes what is important is that we know what constructions are in use and can give a broad picture of relative clause structures in English as opposed to the structures approved in style guides and grammars of English as a second language.

The significance of the constructions in (1a–e) is this. *What* in (1a) is a wh pronoun but invariable. It combines both with inanimate nouns and animate nouns and is never preceded by a preposition – *the letter <u>what</u> you said that <u>in</u>* but not **the letter <u>in what</u> you said that*. *What* looks very like *that*, namely a pronoun that has become a conjunction. *As* in (1b) is definitely a subordinating conjunction and the *as* version of the previous example can only be *the letter as you said that in*. The author Mark Billingham, who seems to have an ear for the spoken English of south-east England, provides the example in (2).

2. He bought me an orthopaedic bed ... one of those <u>as goes up and down</u>.
   Mark Billingham (2010), *From the Dead*. London: Little, Brown, p.166

What this means is that English overall has three relative clause constructions with the structure assigned to *the house that we live in*, namely

_{NP}[the house _{Rel Cl}[that we live in [Ø]_{Rel Cl}]_{NP}

where **[Ø]** represents a gap corresponding to the NP *the house* modified by the relative clause. (=> RELATIVE CLAUSES: INTRODUCTION.) *That* can be replaced by *what* or *as* and all three are conjunctions, not relative pronouns. (1d) is parallel to *the man that likes his beer, the man what likes his beer* and *the man as likes his beer*, the only difference being that (1d) is a contact relative with no relativiser. The structure of (1d) is

He's a man _{Rel Cl}[[**Ø**] likes his beer]_{Rel Cl}

with a missing subject NP. Normally missing NPs inside relative clauses are objects, as in *the book [you recommended [ ]]*, where one analysis assumes that the bold square brackets enclosed either the pronoun *it* or the full NP *the book*, which have been deleted. In spoken English, the subjects of relative clauses can be omitted in various existential-presentative constructions. We can imagine that, in context, (1d) could come close to functioning as such a construction.

In (1e) the clause *he likes his beer* has the structure of a main clause but modifies the noun *man* and functions as a relative clause. We can treat this as a very basic type of relative clause. This construction occurs regularly in spoken English generally, not just in non-standard English. (=> CLAUSE STRUCTURE: INTEGRATED AND UNINTEGRATED SYNTAX.)

RELATIVE CLAUSES: PROPOSITIONAL

Relative clauses typically modify nouns, that is, they supply further information about the referent of some noun. Relative clauses can also supply information about events or propositions, as in (1)–(3).

1 Brian offered to cook the meal, <u>which everyone thought was a great idea</u>.
2 She helped us with the computer, <u>which we were very grateful for</u>.
3 He declared that the snow would last for weeks, <u>which we refused to believe</u>.

In (1) the event of Brian cooking the meal is 'modified' by the relative clause *which everyone thought was a great idea*. In (2) the relative clause *which we were very grateful for* 'modifies' the event of her helping with the computer. In (3) the relative clause *which we refused to believe* 'modifies' the proposition 'The snow will last for weeks'.

Relative clauses 'modifying' events or propositions always have the relativiser *which*. If (1b) were *She helped us with the computer, that we were very grateful for*, the relative clause could only be interpreted as modifying *computer*. Of course, relative clauses 'modifying' events and propositions are typically non-restrictive, and non-restrictive relative clauses are always introduced by *which*.

RELATIVE CLAUSES: RESTRICTIVE AND NON-RESTRICTIVE

Relative clauses can be split into two types according to their function in a given text. Consider the example in (1).

    1 We bought the car <u>that John recommended</u>, not the others.

In (1) the relative clause *that John recommended* helps the listener to scan the set of relevant cars and pick out the one that the speaker is referring to. That is, it restricts the set of relevant cars, hence the label 'restrictive relative clause'.†

Non-restrictive (non-defining or non-identifying) relative clauses are used merely to add incidental information and are not intended to help the listener or reader pick out the correct referent. (Some analysts use the term 'supplementary', meaning that the information conveyed by such clauses supplements, but is not an integral part of, the information signalled by the larger message of which they are a part.†) An example is in (2).

    2 A: Do you like driving your new car?
         B: No, I hate driving our new car, <u>which I wasn't consulted about in the first place</u>.

In the presumed context the referent is salient, the new car. B does not utter the underlined relative clause to help A identify the car but as additional information and as an indication of why B hates driving it. In speech non-restrictive relative clauses have their own intonation and may be separated from the preceding clause by a pause. In informal conversation non-restrictive relative clauses are not frequent, speakers preferring main clauses. The latter may be conjoined – *I hate driving our new car and I wasn't consulted about it in the first place*, or simply juxtaposed – *I hate driving our new car. I wasn't consulted about it in the first place.* Note that the sequence *and I wasn't consulted about it in the first place* is not a relative clause but a main clause; *and* is not a relativiser but a conjunction.

Non-restrictive relative clauses typically have a wh relativiser (but not all, see (7) below). Some style guides and publishers' manuals suggest that writers use *that* for restrictive relative clauses and *who*, *which*, etc. for non-restrictive relative clauses but there is no basis for this suggestion apart from a fashion among, in particular, American publishers. British writers use both *that* and wh words in restrictive relative clauses and even American writers follow the same practice.

In writing, a non-restrictive relative clause is usually separated from the preceding clause by some punctuation symbol, often a comma, as in (3).

3 We spent a week in Istanbul, which is an enthralling city.

The comma may give the impression that the non-restrictive relative clause is an integral part of the structure of the sentence, but other common formatting practices highlight the independence of such clauses. They may be separated from the preceding clause by an em-dash, as in (4), or enclosed in parentheses, as in (5) and (6).

4 Those with advanced degrees are especially likely to leave...This is regrettable...But it is also an opportunity – <u>which the country is squandering</u>.
The Economist, 9–15 August 2014, 'The British diaspora', p. 26.

5 While the 63-year-old legend of telly cookery is having a stiffener in the pub next door, 100 of his faithful are milling about in the foyer of the Pocklington Arts Centre in North Yorkshire, flicking through a free booklet of his favourite recipes (<u>some of which are printed on these pages</u>).
The Independent, 11 October 2007, *Extra*, pp. 2–3

6 In her 3rd year she did an ERASMUS placement in Barcelona (<u>which was amazing</u>) and is bilingually fluent in English/French and can also speak Spanish.
http://langsoc.eusa.ed.ac.uk/blog/?page_id=277 (accessed on 1 September 2011)

We pass over theories about the constituent structure of (3)–(6), merely pointing out that this question received no satisfactory answer in the heyday of transformational grammar and constituent structure and is not much discussed nowadays. We finish this section with two examples from a recent detective novel in which a noun is modified by two relative clauses, the second following directly the first. Consider (7).

7 The breeze made reading the newspaper tricky, so he reached for a paperback <u>that had been sitting beside his bed for several months</u>, <u>that he had picked up at the airport on his last trip across to North Africa</u>.
Mark Billingham (2010), *From The Dead*. London: Little, Brown, p. 157

The first clause looks like a restrictive relative clause (although strictly speaking the reader does not need the information it conveys nor to use the information to pick out the referent from a number of candidate referents). But it has the relativiser *that* and is not separated from *paperback* by any punctuation mark. The second relative clause, *that he had picked up* . . ., could be non-restrictive (although it too has the relativiser *that*). In contrast, the relative clauses in the second text sentence in (8) both look restrictive, in that they both help to identify the father. The interesting syntactic property is that the second clause, *who became obsessed* . . ., is not embedded in the first clause, *whose young son* . . ., but simply placed next to it. The relative clause ***who** became obsessed with finding the football his son had had with him at the time* modifies the whole NP A *father **whose** young son had been the innocent victim of a drive-by shooting.*

> 8 He remembered a woman who had taken a carving knife to her husband and would not stop talking about how bad she felt for ruining his best shirt. *A father* **whose** young son had been the innocent victim of a drive-by shooting **who** became obsessed with finding the football his son had had with him at the time.
> Mark Billingham (2010), *From The Dead.* London: Little, Brown, p. 165

RELATIVE CLAUSES: SHADOW PRONOUNS

In this section we consider a construction that is controversial because it is excluded from written texts by editors but does occur regularly in informal speech. It is tempting to dismiss as a performance error a phenomenon found only in informal speech but two important points can be made in response. One is that if we were investigating a language that was spoken-only, that was not used in written texts, we would record everything that was uttered in conversations, ceremonies, formal discussions and so on and analyse all the structures that occurred regularly. One difficulty in investigating spoken English is that English has been used in written texts for hundreds of years, the language of such texts has been recorded and described in grammars and it is this written language that has prestige and is considered systematic and correct. Anything that does not meet the norms that have been established by the users and protectors of formal written English is 'written off'.† It becomes harder to write off these structures when they appear in writing; at least, the idea that they are performance errors is more difficult to defend, although they can still be dismissed as incorrect in written English.

The second point does apply to the analysis of all syntax: when is a structure to be treated as a proper construction to be included in the grammar of a given language and when is it to be treated as a 'hapax legomenon' (a one-off, Greek 'once spoken')? A sequence that is produced by only one speaker in recordings of data can be confidently classed as a one-off. A sequence that is produced by five speakers can be classed as 'more evidence required'. A sequence produced by ten out of ten speakers, even if just once by each one, can be classed as a construction and given a suitable label.

The above paragraphs relate to sequences that could be called 'resumptive pronoun relative clauses' or 'shadow pronoun relative clauses'. Examples are in (1).

1 a spikes that you stick in the ground and throw rings over <u>them</u>
    b an address which I hadn't stayed <u>there</u> for several years
    c a diversion on the A80 where there's roadworks <u>there</u>
    d He and his father ran a racing team that these three drivers were all involved in <u>it</u>
      BBC Radio Scotland, *Good Morning Scotland*, 14 April 2008

The examples in (1) were recorded informally by JM; that is, there is no audio recording that other analysts might listen to. Fortunately the other examples in this section either occurred in writing or in transcripts of audio recordings made as part of publicly funded research projects. In (1a) *them* is in a relative clause conjoined to the first relative clause. We can show the clauses more clearly by inserting the missing relativiser *that*: *[that] you stick in the ground and [that] you thrown rings over them*. The resumptive/shadow pronoun is *them*.

In (1b) the resumptive/shadow pronoun is *there*. 'Resumptive' reflects the idea that the pronoun resumes (takes up again) the reference of *which* and *an address*. 'Shadow' is based on the metaphor of the relative pronoun *which* casting a shadow that hits the ground somewhere in the relative clause. If you like your academic writing to contain weighty words, then 'resumptive' is for you. If you like unusual metaphors, you will probably prefer 'shadow'. Note that shadow pronouns can be a demonstrative pronoun such as *there* or a personal pronoun such as *she, them* and *it*.

In (1c) the relative clause is *where there's roadworks there*. This example was picked up from traffic news on the BBC. The shadow pronoun is again *there*. In (1d) the relative clause is *that these three drivers were all involved in it*.

Further examples from writing or recorded and transcribed speech are in (2)–(3). The relative clauses are in bold square brackets and the shadow pronouns are underlined.

2 They only put books in [that they think people will be wanting to grab the chance to get <u>one</u>].
   [E-mail from a colleague. (The books are prizes in a competition.)]

3 A: I would like to know these days how much support the police really have out there

B: There's a lot of people [who <u>they</u> expect the police to come and help them] and there was actually a um a couple of years ago two policemen beaten up on James Smith's corner one Friday night
Wellington Corpus of Spoken New Zealand English. Recorded radio discussion: DGB041:0020 Z1-0025 Z1. (The formatting has been changed to make the example easier to read.)

Shadow/resumptive pronouns are frequent where the syntax of relative clauses is more complex than in, e.g., (1b). A good example is (5).

4 they're keeping the memory of a child [that they don't know where <u>she</u> is]
BBC Radio 4 presenter, August 2002

The relative clause *that they don't know where <u>she</u> is* contains the complement clause *where she is*, and it is in the latter clause that the shadow pronoun occurs. An example with *who* as the relativiser is in (6).

5 We are taking proactive steps to contact individuals [who records show <u>they</u> have no valid right to be in the UK], some of which date back to December 2008. We believe it is right to enforce the immigration rules.
The Herald (Scotland), 19 October 2013, p. 7, Home Office spokesman

The relative clause is *who records show they have no valid right to be in the UK*. Like the relative clause in (5), it contains a complement clause *they have no valid right to be in the UK*. A careful written version would be *who records show have no valid right to be in the UK*, with no resumptive pronoun *they* following *show*. A written version of (5) requires rather more rephrasing. Simply omitting the resumptive pronoun will not do (**a child that they don't know where is*); neither will the introduction of *who* (**a child who they don't know where is* or, even worse, **a child that they don't know where who is*). An acceptable version calls for a possessive relative, as in *a child whose whereabouts they don't know*.

For whatever reason, possessive relatives are very rare in spoken English; possibly they are difficult to produce and process in spontaneous speech. The structure in (5) is very common, possibly because it is easy to produce and process: the relativiser *that* plus a straightforward main clause with a complete set of subject and object NPs. In this case the term 'relativiser' does not mean that the upcoming clause has the structure of a classic relative clause but simply that it modifies the noun preceding *that*. With respect to (6), it is reasonable to speculate that *who* may be better analysed as a conjunction and not a relative pronoun. That is, *who* in (6) may function like the discourse connective *which*. (=> RELATIVE CLAUSES: *WHICH* AS DISCOURSE CONNECTIVE.)

The construction in (4) is not new. A pleasing example comes from Trollope's 1858 novel *Doctor Thorne*. In the example, Arabella is the countess' sister and the 'it' in the first line is a relationship between Arabella's son and the doctor's niece.

> 6 'Stop it at once, Arabella: stop it at once,' the countess said. 'That, indeed, will be ruin. If he does not marry money, he is lost. Good Heavens! The doctor's niece! A girl <u>that nobody knows where she comes from</u>!'
> Anthony Trollope (1858), *Dr Thorne*. Oxford World Classics 2014. Oxford: Oxford University Press, p.144

The relative clause in (6) is *that nobody knows where she comes from*, which has the same structure as the relative clause in (4), with a complement clause *where she comes from*. To produce a classic relative clause construction the countess would have had to go for something along the lines of *whose origins nobody knows* or *whose parentage nobody knows*, that is, a possessive relative. (See the comments above.)

Our final shadow/resumptive pronoun is in (7), a genuine written example – i.e., not speech represented in writing. (7) also illustrates that the syntax of relative clauses is not made complex just by the presence of a complement clause.

> 7 Despite these occasional blips the car handles reasonably well and there is tons of grip on cornering. It is a vehicle [that the more you are in <u>its</u> company the better you get to know <u>it</u>].
> *The Herald*, 6 December 2013, Drive section, p.1 Andrew Mackay 'All the key ingredients for success'

The relative clause, as before, is introduced by *that*. The body of the relative clause consists of a special comparative construction *the more... the better*. A wh relative clause can be created, but only by a complete rephrasing: *It is a vehicle which you get to know better the more you are in its company*. This version, however, loses the snappiness of the original sentence because it loses the parallelism *the more... the better* and puts the result, *which you get to know better*, before the cause, *the more you are in its company*.

RELATIVE CLAUSES: TH

1. a The girl <u>that phoned</u> is Jennifer.
   b The bridge <u>that collapsed</u> is being rebuilt.
   c I've already seen the film <u>that's on tonight</u>.
   d Have you heard about the guy <u>that they've arrested</u>?

The relative clauses in (1a–d) are introduced by the relativiser *that*. *That* is invariable, having the same form whether interpreted as a direct object as in (1d) – *the guy* [*they've arrested **the guy***] – or as a subject as in (1a) – *the girl* [***the girl** phoned*]. The invariability of *that* contrasts with the oppositions between *who* and *whom* and between *who/whom* and *which*. These parallel the oppositions between, e.g., *she* and *her*, *he* and *him* and between *she/he* and *it*. That is, the wh forms are certainly pronouns and *that* looks more like a conjunction.

Another piece of evidence supporting the view that the relativiser *that* is a conjunction comes from relative clauses containing prepositions. In wh relatives a preposition can either be 'stranded' at the end of the clause, as in *the house which we live in*, or can precede *which*, as in *the house in which we live*. *In which*, at the front of the clause, is parallel to *To him* (*his father bequeathed the house*) or *To James* (*we gave our books*), where the first phrase in the clause consists of a preposition followed by a pronoun or noun. In relatives with the relativiser *that*, prepositions must be stranded: *the house that we live in* is correct but **the house in that we live* is not. This makes the relativiser *that* very unlike a pronoun but very like a conjunction.†

We pick up the traditional idea that such clauses can be analysed with reference to main clauses. Thus, *The girl that phoned* can be analysed with reference to *the girl* [*the girl phoned*]. The chunk in the square brackets is a main clause; it can be turned into a relative clause by inserting the relativiser *that* (a 'subordinating conjunction' in traditional terminology) and deleting the noun phrase that is repeated, to give *the girl* [*that Ø phoned*], where Ø represents the empty slot previously occupied by *the girl*.

To get a wh relative clause *the girl* is replaced by the relative pronoun *who* and *who* is put at the front of the clause where it functions both as the subject of *phoned* and as a relativiser. The structure can be thought of as *the girl* [*who Ø phoned*]. Ø represents the original slot occupied by the subject *who*. The relative clause has all its constituents, but one of them, *who*, has moved from its original slot into the relativiser slot. The movement is more obvious when the wh pronoun is the object of the verb in a relative clause. Thus, *the guests* [*you invited*] can be related to *the guests* [*you invited the guests*]. *Who* [or *whom*] replaces *the guests* in the relative clause, giving *the guests* [*you invited who*], and *who* moves to the front of the relative clause to the relativiser slot *the guests* [*who you invited*]. Th relative clauses are different: they lose one of their constituents and acquire a relativiser. The corresponding structure for *the house that we live in* is *the house* (*that we live in Ø*) and for (1d) the structure is *the guy* (*that they've arrested Ø*).

(We're not suggesting that the above has anything to do with how speakers of English might produce relative clauses or even that it is the best linguistic account of relative clauses. It is simply a way of bringing out the difference between th and wh relative clauses.)

RELATIVE CLAUSES: UNATTACHED

Relative clauses typically modify nouns in an immediately preceding clause, as in *I read the report which you sent*. The relative clause *which you sent* modifies the noun *report*. In written texts, clauses occur that are introduced by a wh word and modify a noun or proposition. They look like normal relative clauses apart from the fact that they occur in a different sentence from the one containing the modified noun or the expression of the proposition. Examples can be found in texts ranging from the 19th century to the present day. (1) is from Dickens.

> 1 '... I shall be offended if you don't take it [a half-crown], as a mark of my good- will. Good night, Robin.'
> 'Good night, ma'am,' said Rob, 'and thank you!'
> <u>Who ran sniggering off to get change</u>, and tossed it away with a pieman.
> Charles Dickens (1848), *Dombey and Son.* Folio Society 1984, p. 504, chapter XXXVIII

Who in the final sentence picks up the referent of *Rob* in the preceding one.
The examples in (2) and (3) are from a different novel by Dickens and offer different relative clause structures.

> 2 Since then she has been, as I began by saying, hovering – Hovering sir,' Mr Snagsby repeats the word with pathetic emphasis 'in the court. <u>The effects of which movement</u> it is impossible to calculate ...'
> Charles Dickens (1853), *Bleak House.* Penguin 1996, p. 663
>
> 3 We had next to find out the number. 'Or Mr Vholes's office will do,' I recollected, 'For Mr Vholes's office is next door.' <u>Upon which</u> Ada said, perhaps that was Mr Vholes's office in the corner there. And it really was.
> Charles Dickens (1853), *Bleak House.* Penguin 1996, p. 783

In (2) the phrase *which movement* picks up the referent of *hovering* in the first sentence. In (3) *which* picks up a rather abstract referent, along the lines of 'the writer's recollecting and uttering the propositions 'Mr Vholes' office will do' and 'Mr Vholes' office is next door'.

(4) is from a modern newspaper text. (5) is from a newsletter to

people who buy a certain kind of wine from a firm called 'Laithwaites'. In (4) *which* refers back to the previous piece of discourse and in (5) *which* refers to the proposition 'The address is wrong'.

> 4 ... anyone would think that I was too bored with politics to bother about it, perish the thought. Which brings me to the question of what my thought about bendy buses should be.
> *The Independent*, 12 October 2007, p. 46, Terence Blacker

> 5 The hills are the same, the soil is the same, the exposure is the same. Just the address is wrong. Which means property owners in Saint-Emilion can snap up vineyards at a fraction of the price that the same surface would cost on their home patch.
> *Laithwaite's Private Cellars.* Spring 2013

The final example is from a contemporary novel. *Which* in the final sentence picks up the referent of the noun phrase *Clifton Suspension Bridge* in the previous sentence.

> 6 And finally I remembered the postcard I'd sent Adrian as a holding response to his letter ... The card was of the Clifton Suspension Bridge. From which a number of people every year jump to their deaths.
> Julian Barnes (2011), *The Sense of an Ending.* London: Vintage Books, p. 98

The authors have chosen to have a sentence break between the clause containing the wh word and the sentence containing the noun or the expression of the proposition modified by that clause. There are stylistic reasons for doing so, such as isolating a particular statement and making it prominent for the reader. For the analysis of the syntax the important point is that the relationship, say between *Clifton Suspension Bridge* and *which* in (6), cannot be handled by sentence grammar, which deals with one sentence at a time. Instead, the relationship has to be handled by discourse models designed to explain relationships that cross sentence boundaries. The relationship can be treated as deictic; the wh words point back to an entity or entities, as in (5) and (6), or an act of uttering a proposition, as in (3). (=> Nouns and noun phrases: pronouns, Relative clauses: wh words as deictics.)

We conclude the section with an unusual example of wh relativisers detached from the nouns they modify, the nouns not even being part of a sentence and, on the page, not even linearly connected with the relativisers. The example is from the list of chapters and contents at the beginning of Thackeray's novel *Pendennis*.

CHAPTER III

In which Pendennis appears as a very young Man indeed   24

CHAPTER XVII

Which concludes the First Part of this History   171

CHAPTER XXXVII

Where Pen appears in Town and Country   401

The first line in each entry in the list contains the word 'chapter', all in capitals, followed by the number of a given chapter in Roman numerals. On the next line is a clause. It has the structure of a standard relative clause, being introduced by a wh word, *which* or *where*, and modifies the Chapter + Number sequence on the preceding line. It is definitely a relative clause. As with the unattached relative pronouns in (1)–(6), the relationship between the wh word and what it modifies – not to be handled by sentence grammar, and possibly not even by discourse models – supports the idea of the wh words as deictics.

RELATIVE CLAUSES: UNINTEGRATED

In written English texts (certainly in formal texts) relative clauses are integrated with the clauses containing the nouns they modify. Consider (1).

1. We went to the restaurant <u>(that) you recommended</u>.
2. We went to the restaurant you recommended.
3. We went to the restaurant <u>which you recommended</u>.

In (1) the integration is reflected in the relative clause having no direct object noun *it*. The degree of integration is increased in (2) by the absence of a relativiser. In (3) there is no direct object noun following *recommended* in the relative clause but the relativiser *which* is a relative pronoun that can be interpreted as the direct object. (4) has been invented to show a greater lack of integration.

4. We went to the restaurant that you recommended it.

The link with *restaurant* is signalled by *that*, but *that* is followed by a complete clause, with subject and object pronouns. In other words, the relative clause is not reduced in any way. Unintegrated relative clauses occur regularly in informal speech; relative clauses with shadow pronouns are all unintegrated. (=> RELATIVE CLAUSES: SHADOW PRONOUNS.) Another example of an unintegrated relative clause in a written text is in (5).

5 There is an added twist to the fixture as it is being held in Manaus and there has already been enough made about England playing in a city surrounded by a jungle <u>you almost needed a machete to get through it</u>.
The Herald, 7 December 2013, Sport section, p. 7 Gianni Russo 'The first signposts appear on Road to Rio'

Completely unintegrated relative clauses do not even have a shadow pronoun picking up the referent of the modified noun. Examples are in (6) and (7). (6) is from domestic conversation and picked up on the hoof but (7) is from the transcriptions of the Wellington Corpus of Spoken New Zealand English.

6 We have a filing cabinet <u>that you can only open one drawer at a time</u>
7 even if we have any meetings over here it's still just as long as those <u>that we go somewhere else</u>
Wellington Corpus of Spoken New Zealand English: #DPC004:0385:IB

(7) can be more closely integrated with *We have a filing cabinet* by changing it to a wh relative clause, say *only one of whose drawers can be opened at a time*, and (8) could be changed to ... *as long as those for which we go somewhere else*.

RELATIVE CLAUSES: WH

Wh relative clauses are introduced by wh words such as *who* and *which*. They are relatively rare in informal conversation but frequent in formal written English. The simplest wh relative clause structures are exemplified in (1) and (2).

1 The woman <u>who bought our house</u> was very taken with the kitchen.
2 The alpacas <u>which arrived last week</u> seem to be contented.

Who and *which* are the subjects of the above relative clauses but can also function as the direct object, as in (3) and (4). Style manuals recommend the use of *whom* as direct object, as in (5). *Whom* is typical of formal written English but is very infrequent in informal conversation and not at all frequent in informal written texts. Its demise has often been predicted over the past fifty years but it will probably survive through the efforts of teachers, editors and authors of style guides.

3 The candidate <u>who James recommended</u> was appointed.
4 Freya studied the recipe <u>which Jennifer liked</u>.
5 The candidate <u>whom James recommended</u> was appointed.

Whom and *which* occur after prepositions, as in (6).

RELATIVE CLAUSES

6 a the account <u>into which</u> the payment was transferred
  b the lawyer <u>from whom</u> we received advice

(6a and b) are typical of formal written English. In informal writing and conversation (but wh forms are infrequent in conversation) the structures in (7) are far more common (not to mention that th and contact relatives are favoured in these types of text).

7 a the account which the payment was transferred into
  b the lawyer who we received advice from

Note *who* and not *whom* in (7b), since *who* does not complement a preposition. Note too that the pronoun/relativisers *which* and *who* are at the front of the clause while the prepositions are at the end. This is not an unusual structure. PPs can be split up that way for emphasis; for example, in *We got good advice from this lawyer but we got bad advice from that one*, *this lawyer* and *that one* can be moved to the front of the clauses, leaving *from* stranded at the end: *This lawyer we got good advice from, that one we got bad advice from*. ('Stranded' is a technical term.)

The possessive relative pronoun *whose* is even rarer than *whom* in speech. There was a fashion, still followed by some older users of English, to use *whose* for animate nouns only, especially nouns denoting humans, and to use *of which* for inanimate nouns. This gave rise to the contrast in (8).

8 a the tourist <u>whose wallet</u> was stolen
  b the house <u>the roof of which</u> was destroyed by the tornado

The fashion has changed; most users write, e.g., *the house whose roof was destroyed by the tornado*.

Relative clauses can be introduced by *where* and *when*, though in formal writing these can be replaced by *(the house) in which*, *(the day) on which*, and so on. Examples are in (9).

9 a We visited the house where she was brought up.
  b I remember quite clearly the day when he was born.

Certainly in speech, informal and not so informal, time nouns are not usually followed by a wh relativiser. Thus we have *the day he was born*, *the year they were elected*, *the month the battle took place*.

The examples of wh relative clauses in (9) are straightforward in structure but more complex constructions are possible.

10 We received hundreds of applications, <u>all of which</u> were processed within a week.

The relative pronoun *which* is inside a prepositional phrase, *of which*. This phrase modifies the head pronoun *all*. This complete structure might in turn be part of another PP, as in (11). *All of which* complements the preposition *in*.

11 We received hundreds of applications, <u>in all of which</u> crucial information was missing.

Analogous relativiser phrases are, e.g., *both of whom, many of which, from each of whom*. A slightly archaic construction, but one that is still found in formal writing, is exemplified in (12).

12 They transferred their business to Leeds, <u>in which city</u> they prospered.

In (12) the wh relativiser *which* is inside the PP *in which city*. It is not a pronoun but a determiner, modifying *city*. The construction allows even more complexities, as in (13).

13 David has read the book, <u>by the conclusions in the final chapter of which</u> he was greatly alarmed.

(13) scores zero points for style but its syntax is correct. Here the relativiser *which* is a pronoun, the complement of the preposition *of*. But the PP *of which* complements the noun *chapter*. This noun is inside the PP *in the final chapter*, which complements *conclusions* and is inside the NP *the conclusions in the final chapter of which*. The relativiser is buried deep, which makes the relative clause difficult to process. Not surprisingly, such relative clauses do not occur in informal speech and are very rare even in formal writing. Like the pied piper in Robert Browning's poem *The Pied Piper of Hamelin*, the wh word moves to the front and takes the rest of the *by* phrase with it. The wh word is thought of as indulging in some pied-piping and the preposition is said to be pied-piped.

Examples (1)–(13) contain relative clauses that modify nouns, are constituents of complex sentences and are restrictive. There is much more to say: wh relative clauses can modify propositions, they can occur in a different sentence from the noun they modify, and they can be non-restrictive. A further type of wh relative clause is the headless or free relative clause. This construction poses problems of analysis and also bears on the question of what wh pronouns are. (=> Relative clauses: restrictive and non-restrictive, Relative clauses: propositional, Relative clauses: unattached, Relative clauses: free, Relative clauses: wh words as deictics.)

RELATIVE CLAUSES: WH WORDS AS DEICTICS

Wh relative clauses and the nouns they modify can occur in different sentences. (=> RELATIVE CLAUSES: UNATTACHED.) That is, wh pronoun-relativisers have the capacity to point back across sentence boundaries. In old-fashioned lists of contents, wh pronouns are able to point back to a phrase right outside the relative clause and on a different line on the page, with no sentences in sight. (=> RELATIVE CLAUSES: WH.) And finally *which* has developed into a discourse connective with the capacity to point back to previous sections of discourse. (=> RELATIVE CLAUSES: *WHICH* AS DISCOURSE CONNECTIVE.) Since this usage is found only in spoken English, and since analysts of spoken English typically work with clauses and clause combinations and not with sentences, it is best analysed, not in terms of relations inside sentences and not in terms of relations across sentence boundaries.

Wh pronouns can be analysed as deictics. In the examples mentioned above the wh relativisers are definite deictics in that they point back to specific nouns (or to the referents of specific nouns) or to specific chunks of discourse. Thus, in *the house which she bought*, *which* points back to the referent of *house*; in *He laughed. Which turned out to be a mistake*, *which* points back to an event, the referent of *He laughed*. In *take your coats which that's the rain on now in fact*, *which* points back to the chunk of discourse *take your coats*.

There are two constructions and another usage that support the idea that wh pronouns are deictics. The first construction is the WH cleft (=> CLEFTS: CLAUSES: CLEFTS.), as in (1).

1 What she did was write under a pseudonym.

In (1) *what* points forward to an upcoming piece discourse and the information it encodes. That is, *what* is definite for the speaker, who knows what is about to be said, but not for the hearer, who is waiting to be enlightened.

The second construction is the reverse WH cleft as in (2).

2 Write under a pseudonym is what she did.

In (2) *what* is definite for both speaker and hearer as it refers back to *Write under a pseudonym*. It is worth noting that any plausible paraphrases are based on definite NPs: *the thing she did was . . ., . . . is the choice she made/ decision she took*.

The usage is exemplified in (3)–(6).

3 Tell you what: you stay here and I'll bring the car round.

4 Can you tell me what the children like to eat?
5 Take the carpets home and let me know which you prefer.
6 The region that has captured the crown for 'rising star' status is Castillon ... It's easy to see why ...
   Laithwaite's Private Cellars. Spring 2013. Citing Oz Clarke.

What in (3) is definite since it points forward to a proposition expressed by a clause that the speaker is planning to utter. In (4), *what* is definite; the speaker assumes that the listener knows the children's preferences. This instance of *what* can be paraphrased as *that which* or, better, *the food* or *the things*. In (5), *which* points to the carpet that the listener will prefer, even if that is as yet unknown. A suitable paraphrase is *the one* – *Let me know the one you prefer*. *Why* in (6) is equivalent to *the reason*.

The final example, in (7), is from the Wellington Corpus of Spoken New Zealand English.

7 <u>what</u> IS important is that you understand um <u>how</u> things
   WORK and <u>WHERE</u> YOU CAN FIND out <u>what</u> you want to know
   <u>when</u> you want to know it
   Wellington Corpus of Spoken New Zealand English: #MUS002:0080:TT

What is equivalent to *the thing*, *how* to *the way*, *where* to *the place in which*, and *when* to *the time at which*. In (8), from an advertising leaflet sent out by a housebuilding firm (no relation to JM), *where* is equivalent to *the place which/that*.

8 Make a Miller Difference to where you call home.

RELATIVE CLAUSES: WHICH AS DISCOURSE CONNECTIVE

Spoken English has a *which* construction that has been in use at least since the 1840s. It appears in dialogue in the novels of Charles Dickens, in the humorous magazine *Punch* throughout the 19th century and into the 20th, in the novels of Dorothy Sayers from the 1920s and 1930s, and numerous examples have been found in recent recordings of BBC Radio 5 football and cricket programmes. In this construction *which* functions not as a relativiser but as a discourse connective. We begin with an example where the *which* sequence does look like a relative clause.

1 You have a little keypad down here <u>which</u> you can use your mouse to click on the keys.
   Presentation on Financial Information Systems, Old College, University of Edinburgh, 1 May 1996]

Note that *which* is followed by a complete clause, *you can use your mouse to click on the keys*, unlike standard relative clauses such as *a keypad which you can click on [ ]* or *a keypad that you can click on [ ]*. The brackets in bold show where there could be a pronoun such as *it* or an NP such as *the keypad*. (=> RELATIVE CLAUSES: WH.) In spite of the unusual syntax (that is, unusual for relative clauses in written English) the *which* sequence can be interpreted as pointing back to the noun *keypad* and inviting the listener to assign to the referent of *a little keypad* the property of allowing the mouse to be used. We can analyse the *which* sequence as an example of the sort of unintegrated relative clause that turns up regularly in informal speech. (=> RELATIVE CLAUSES: UNINTEGRATED.)

Now consider (2).†

2 He pitched the ball high, which I'm always saying if you're gonna bowl a bouncer, bowl it at shoulder height
Geoff Boycott, BBC Radio 5 *Sports Extra*

In (2), the sequence beginning with *which* does not modify any particular noun but the chunk *I'm always saying if you're gonna bowl a bouncer, bowl it at shoulder height* does relate to the initial clause *He pitched the ball high* – the bowler's action accords with the advice dispensed by the commentator, a retired Yorkshire and England batsman. In (2), *which* can be analysed as simply a connective linking two chunks of discourse.

Examples of such *which* structures do not always lend themselves unambiguously to one analysis or the other. In (3), for instance, the *which* sequence can be interpreted as modifying the noun *Gerrard*, that is, we take *which* to be a relativiser. Alternatively, we can interpret the sequence *I think he needs to bounce back* as relating to the entire first clause *One of the potential keys could be Gerrard*, that is, we take *which* to be a discourse connective.

3 One of the potential keys could be Gerrard, **which** I think he needs to bounce back
Gabriel Marcotti, BBC Radio 5

We note at this point that a number of analysts have applied the term 'gapless relative clause' to *which* sequences such as those in (1)–(3). The label is appropriate for (1), where the *which* sequence can be interpreted as an unintegrated relative clause modifying *keypad*. Relative clauses have gaps, in the sense that a constituent is missing. Thus, in *a keypad (that) you can click on*, there is a gap after *on* where in a main clause there would be an object NP: *you can click on it*. Similarly for *the book which you destroyed*: *which* is interpreted as the direct object of *destroyed* and the usual analysis assumes that there is a gap after *destroyed* were a direct object could go, as in *you destroyed which*. Even *the actor who won the Oscar* is analysed as having a gap where the subject would go. *Who* is interpreted as the subject but is treated as being in a different slot, where it functions as the relativiser: *the actor [who [Ø won the Oscar]*. In contrast, the unintegrated relative clause in (1) is gapless in that it has no empty slots in its structure: *you can use your mouse to click on the keys* has a complete set of subject and direct object NPs. The term 'gapless' is inappropriate for the *which* sequence in (2), where we are interpreting *which* as merely connecting two pieces of discourse. Whether we consider the label appropriate for (3) depends on which interpretation we favour.

The structure is of long standing – the written evidence is valuable as it makes it very difficult to treat the structure as a mere performance phenomenon or performance error. (4) dates from 1853.

> 4 'About a year and a half ago,' says Mr Snagsby strengthened, 'he came into our place one morning after breakfast, and, finding my little woman (which I name Mrs Snagsby when I use that appellation) in our shop, produced a specimen of his handwriting and gave her to understand that he was in wants of copying work to do . . .'
> Charles Dickens (1853), *Bleak House*. Penguin 1996, p. 170

(5) and (6) are from *Punch* and the *Daily Chronicle*.

> 5 Bin took for a nob, and no error this time; which my tailor's A1.
> (= I've been taken for an upper-class chap . . . which my tailor's first class.)
> J. A. Hammerton (ed.) (1906), *Punch Library. Cockney Humour*. London: The Educational Book Co. Ltd., p. 96

> 6 If anything 'appens to you – which God be between you and 'arm – I'll look after the kids
> *Daily Chronicle*, 1905

The *which* sequences in (4)–(6) are not relative clauses. *Which* is best treated as a discourse connective introducing supplementary information relating to a previously expressed proposition. The *Oxford English Dictionary* recorded this usage of *which*, describing it as 'in vulgar use, as a mere connective or introductory particle'. Whether the construction was just in vulgar use or in general use in spontaneous speech among all classes of speakers, it is now widespread. But it is certainly the case that authors such as Dorothy Sayers put the usage in the mouths of her working-class characters, as in (7). (7) is interesting in that the discourse connective *which* is used by one character, Mrs Ruddle, to connect what she says with the utterance of another character, the baker.†

7 'Since you are so good', replied Mr Bunter, 'the dispatch of the grocer's assistant with streaky rashers and eggs would enable us to augment the deficiencies of the breakfast menu.' 'Say, boy,' said the baker, 'that's okay by me. I'll tell Willis to send his Jimmy along.'
'Which', observed Mrs Ruddle, suddenly appearing from the sitting-room in a blue- checked apron and with her sleeves rolled up, 'there's no call to let George Willis think 'e's to 'ave all me lord's custom, seeing the 'Ome & Colonial is a 'apenny (= a halfpenny) cheaper per pound not to say better and leaner...'
Dorothy Sayers (1937), *Busman's Honeymoon*. Folio edition 2011, p. 63

A final example, from contemporary Scottish English, is in (8). (The original formatting has been changed in the interest of readability.)

8 A: this was what I wondered, if it was basically these families that were still in the Dumbiedykes [an area of Edinburgh]
   B: No. Well, actually there're one or two that went back in [= returned in to the city centre] – <u>which so happens that I'm a member of the kirk</u> [=church] <u>just locally here</u> – the Kirk o'Field church, which is the parish of Dumbiedykes area (uh huh)
   [recorded by Karen Currie for Brown et al., 1980]

In B's contribution to the excerpt in (8) the discourse connective is the *which* in the underlined sequence. The connective function of the *which* comes from the fact that the speaker's membership of the local church explains how he comes to know about the return of previous residents to the area. The second *which* is a relativiser, introducing the relative clause modifying *Kirk o'Field church*.

Sentences and clauses

SENTENCES AND CLAUSES: INTRODUCTION

Both clause and sentence are very traditional units of grammatical description and analysis and both are very difficult to define. (By a rough reckoning more than two hundred definitions of 'sentence' have been proposed.) Many analysts take sentences as basic and define them as the largest unit subject to rules of grammar. A clause is then said to be a unit that can be seen as like a sentence in structure, or as resulting from some sentence structure being reduced. Other analysts take the concept of construction as basic, define clauses as a grammatical units incorporating some construction, say agent-patient as in *The dog barked* or *The python attacked the crocodile*, and then define the sentence as the largest grammatical unit.

Here we take the concept of construction as basic.† Constructions are arrangements of smaller bits and pieces into bigger chunks: which sort of units combine, how many, and in what order. Word forms are constructions consisting of stems and roots, prefixes and suffixes, as in *deselections – de + select + ion + s*. The internal structure of words is not part of syntactic analysis; we are concerned rather with how whole words combine to make phrases, how phrases combine to make clauses and how clauses combine to make sentences.

Our central syntactic unit or construction is the clause. Our reasons for this decision are these. Dependency relations between words and the distributional properties of words and phrases are densest inside single clauses. Dependency relations occasionally cross from one clause to another or even, in written texts, from one sentence to another but these long-distance connections are quite a minor phenomenon. The classic criteria for distribution – substitution and transposition – apply inside single clauses. In books on formal syntax, discussions of constituent structure and distribution almost always offer examples consisting of a single clause. (=> CLAUSE STRUCTURE: DEPENDENCY RELATIONS.)

There are various types of clause. At this point in the account we focus on the most frequent kind of clause in spoken and written English texts and the kind that allows us to handle the minor and, in some cases, potentially awkward clause types. The prototypical clause is one with a finite verb as its head and central constituent. This head is accompanied by one or more modifiers – in many languages a finite verb on its own counts as a good prototypical clause. The head verb controls how many modifiers it requires and excludes: *collapse* requires a subject (*The runner collapsed*) but excludes a direct object (*The heat collapsed the runner*); *affect* requires a subject and a direct object – **The heat affected* but *The heat affected the runners*; *place* requires a subject, a direct object and a prepositional phrase – *The woman placed the keys on the hall table.*

The verb in a clause also controls the type of nouns that occur with it: various types of subject noun, various types of direct object noun, and so on. Some verbs allow complement clauses, others exclude them: *propose* allows them – *The party proposed that the scheme be cancelled*, *create* does not – **We created that new regulations be applied.*

The above paragraph mentions the syntactic reasons for taking as the central syntactic construction a single clause headed by a finite verb. There are semantic and pragmatic reasons that run parallel to the syntactic ones, and the semantic and pragmatic factors affect the choice of syntactic patterns. Single clauses are central to the analysis of situations: the verb is the nucleus, denoting an event, process or state; the core consists of the verb and the constituents denoting the principal participants in a situation; the periphery consists of the constituents denoting such properties of a situation as location, time and manner. The status of the principal participants is reflected in the corresponding constituents typically being obligatory and placed closer to the verb than the constituents denoting location, time and so on. The clause and its syntax signal whether a speaker is making a statement, asking a question or issuing a command and is the typical locus in which information is presented as given or new or is made salient (focused). Finally, the clause is the locus in which speakers and writers signal what they are going to talk about or refer to (the topic or theme) and what they are going to say about the topic (the comment or predicate). (=> CLAUSE AND TEXT: THEME.)

The clause is a good basis for dealing with sentences. Sentences are constructed out of clauses, the minimum required being one main clause. They are often referred to as the largest units of syntax, although the situation is not so straightforward. (=> SENTENCES AND CLAUSES: SYSTEM SENTENCE AND TEXT SENTENCE.) Within sentences consisting of more than one clause, particularly where there are subordinate clauses, the question of distribution arises as several clauses can be arranged in different orders, as in *When we understood the problem, we began to collect evidence, We began to collect evidence when we understood the problem, We began, when we understood the problem, to collect evidence.* Dependency relations can reach from one clause to another (though this is not typical); when they do, they too are relevant in the analysis of sentences. Thus, in the English wh relative clause construction, the noun modified by the relative clause determines whether the wh relativiser in the relative clause itself is *who* or *which*. *The woman [who chaired the meeting]* versus *[The table which we sat round]*. The relative clauses are inside the bold square brackets. A dependency relation reaches from *woman* to *who* and from *table* to *which*.

To close this section, we note one more advantage offered by clauses. Clauses (at least of the prototypical sort referred to above) contain a finite verb and whatever constituents modify it. This means that clauses can be identified in both written and spoken texts and, although not important for this account of English syntax, is of great value to analysts working on and presenting descriptions of spoken English. Sentences are difficult to identify in spoken English, indeed in the spoken varieties of any language, because there are no constant patterns of pausing and rhythm marking sentence boundaries. They are identifiable in written language because the authors of written texts usually signal the beginning of sentences with capital letters and the end of sentences with a full stop, and leave a space between the end of one sentence and the beginning of the next.

These facts suggest that the sentence, although of interest for syntactic analysis, is a low-level discourse unit resulting from writers combining clauses, not with a completely free hand but with a good measure of freedom. Many children are introduced to sentences through listening to stories and beginning to recognise patterns in written text before they go to school. Many children do not have this experience and learn about sentences at school. All children are shown at school (with varying results) how to produce written sentences with more than one clause. Of course speakers put clauses into sequences even in informal speech but they do so in a much looser fashion. Analysts of spoken language prefer to talk of clause combining and clause combinations rather than sentences.

SENTENCES AND CLAUSES: CLAUSES

Prototypical clauses consist of a finite verb and its dependents (modifiers), whether complements or adjuncts. (=> CLAUSE STRUCTURE: DEPENDENCY RELATIONS.) In many languages a clause can consist of just a finite verb but English prototypical clauses require at least one complement, the subject noun phrase. The word 'prototypical' must be emphasised. Particularly in informal speech such as domestic conversation, clauses are used that have no subject: *Found it yet?*, *Where's John? – Gone to look for Jennifer*, and so on. We see in the section on non-finite clauses that the set of clauses now includes chunks of syntax consisting of non-finite verbs and their modifiers – but the finite clause is still the basic yardstick, and the starting point, for any account of clause structure.

What are the major properties of finite clauses?

i   Each clause contains a finite verb; that is, a verb marked for tense. Finite verbs are traditionally said to be marked for tense, person and number. A given verb denotes a type of event (or process or state). In order to refer to a specific event speakers and writers place it at a specific time (not necessarily to the nearest second!) and assign it to some actor. Past tense verbs place an event in past time (*They were visiting Jean last week*) and present tense verbs place an event in present time (*They are visiting Jean right now*). Person has to do with whether an action is assigned to the speaker (*I am listening*, first person), the hearer (*You are listening*, second person) or someone other than the speaker and hearer (*He/she is listening*, third person). Number has to do with whether the speaker or writer refers to one person (*She is listening*, singular) or more than one (*They are listening*, plural).

Because inflectional suffixes are in short supply in English – for verbs other than *be*, just the third person singular *-s* – deciding whether a given verb is finite or non-finite requires a game of substitution. Thus, is the verb form *destroyed* in a given clause a finite or non-finite form? You have to see if the form can be replaced by a progressive, *am/is/are destroying* (ignoring changes of interpretation). If it can, the verb form is finite; if it cannot, the form is non-finite, *destroyed* also being a passive participle and a perfect participle, as in *was destroyed (by the tsunami)* and *has destroyed*. (Other languages have a richer system of person and number contrasts, as in the Russian *pishu* 'I am writing', *pishem* 'we are writing', etc. Such richer sets of contrasts make it possible for a single verb to function as a perfectly good finite clause by itself.)

ii   In each prototypical clause the finite verb is accompanied by its complements and possibly by one or more adjuncts: <u>The cat</u> [C] *caught <u>the mouse</u>* [C] <u>*in the kitchen*</u> [A], <u>*We*</u> [C] *set off <u>at 8 o'clock</u>* [A]. (=> CLAUSE STRUCTURE: DEPENDENCY RELATIONS.)

iii Finite clauses have aspect: *The children were playing in the garden* versus *The children played in the garden until it was dark*; *Magnus is visiting his parents* versus *Magnus visits his parents every Sunday*. (=> VERBS AND VERB PHRASES: TENSE AND ASPECT: INTRODUCTION.)
iv Each clause has a modality. Modality has to do with two sets of distinctions. One set marks the difference between making statements (*The guests have gone*), asking questions (*Have the guests gone?*) and issuing commands or directions (*Go away!*) The other set has to do with whether the speaker or writer presents an event as possible (*She may have forgotten to take a key*) or as necessary (*She must have forgotten to take a key*) or as a fact (*She has forgotten to take a key*). (=> VERBS AND VERB PHRASES: MOOD AND MODALITY.)
v Clauses describe situations, the participants in them, such as agents carrying out actions on patients, as in *The staff* [Agent] *welcomed the new students* [Patient], and the circumstances in which they take place, as in *Donald worked in Glasgow* [Place] *last year* [Time]. (=> CLAUSE STRUCTURE: LINEARITY AND PREDICATE-ARGUMENT STRUCTURE.)

The clause is a fundamental unit in the analysis of syntactic structure. It is particularly important because we can recognise clauses in any type of text by examining which phrases depend on (modify) which verb. This enables us to establish clauses in real texts such as novels, newspapers, poems, academic textbooks and even the transcripts of informal conversation. We are not claiming that the entire transcript of a given conversation can be split into clauses; a portion of any such transcript will consist of phrases that are not part of a clause and of fragments that are not even complete phrases. (=> SENTENCES AND CLAUSES: SENTENCE FRAGMENTS.) Interestingly, if a clause fragment does not have the minimum number of complements required by a particular verb, we do not treat it as a clause but label it a text clause by analogy with text sentences. (=> SENTENCES AND CLAUSES: SYSTEM SENTENCE AND TEXT SENTENCE.) What we are doing here is introducing the clause as part of our analysis, and it will be useful to have different labels for the two sorts of clause. Clauses in real texts we will call 'text clauses'; clauses in our analysis we will call 'system clauses', capturing the fact that in our analysis we try to establish a system of grammar and 'ideal' clauses are part of the system.

SENTENCES AND CLAUSES: COMPLEX SENTENCES

Prototypical complex sentences consist of a main clause and one or more subordinate clauses. Examples are in (1).

1 a We're off on holiday tomorrow, <u>though the weather is going to be awful</u>.
   b Angus has an old van <u>that always has something wrong with it</u>.
   c She did tell him <u>that he was taking the wrong road</u>.
   d I have a feeling <u>that things are going too smoothly</u>.

The subordinate clauses are underlined: an adverbial clause of concession in (1a), a relative clause in (1b), a (verb) complement clause (traditionally called a noun clause) in (1c), and a noun complement clause, modifying *feeling*, in (1d). In written, especially formal, texts sentences can be more complicated, not just one main clause together with more than one subordinate clause but both compound and complex, as in (2). *But* coordinates the two parts of the compound sentence, and each part of the compound sentence is complex. Again, the subordinate clauses are underlined.

2 <u>Although snow is forecast</u>, Juliet insists <u>she will drive to Skye this afternoon</u> **but** Lucie, <u>who is cautious</u>, says <u>she will wait till Friday</u>.

SENTENCES AND CLAUSES: COMPOUND SENTENCES

System sentences (and text sentences) may consist of two or more main clauses. These may be connected by one of the coordinating conjunctions *and*, *but* and *or*, as in (1). The coordinated clauses are underlined.

1 a <u>Susan went to London</u> and <u>Kate went to York</u>.
   b <u>Susan went to London</u> but <u>Kate went to York</u>.
   c <u>Susan will go to London</u> or <u>Kate will go to York</u>.

The protypical case of coordination is (1a), in which the clauses can occur in the alternative order: *<u>Kate went to York</u> and <u>Susan went to London</u>*. The sentence in (2) is also compound but the clauses cannot change position, because *and* here is equivalent to *and then*.

2 She whistled and the dog came to heel.

The sentence *The dog came to heel and she whistled* describes a different sequence of events; that is, the order of clauses cannot be reversed without changing the interpretation. From a syntactic point of view the sentence is compound, but not prototypically so. The clauses in a compound sentence need not be linked by an overt coordinating conjunction but may simply be juxtaposed, as in (3).

3 The chairman made a proposal, the committee rejected it, the meeting broke up in acrimony.

In a compound sentence three or more clauses in a sequence need not all be connected by *and* or *or* but only the penultimate and the last, as in (4).†

4 The driver sounded the horn, the car skidded and both vehicles ended up in the ditch.

SENTENCES AND CLAUSES: MAIN AND SUBORDINATE CLAUSES

In the discussion of finite clauses the examples presented are all main clauses but the major distinction between main and subordinate clauses is passed over in silence. (=> SENTENCES AND CLAUSES: CLAUSES.) This section focuses on that distinction, which is essential for an understanding of how, in written English, clauses are combined into sentences. Examples of main clauses are given in (1).

1 a We went camping last weekend.
   b From her front door Fiona Callander could see the police car approaching.
   c You haven't seen my mobile anywhere, have you?

(1a–c) are prototypical finite clauses and prototypical main clauses. A major property is that by themselves they can be the first contribution to a discourse, whether spoken or written. The speaker or writer of (1a) expects the addressee to know who 'we' refers to. (1b) is a common type of beginning in a novel and the reader expects the author to make clear as the story progresses who Fiona Callander is and why a police car is approaching her house. (1c) is a very typical contribution to a conversation in a domestic setting. Being able to function as the first contribution to a discourse might not seem like a syntactic property but it reflects the fact that main clauses do not depend on (modify) other clauses or words. In contrast, subordinate clauses typically modify other constituents. Adverbial clauses modify other clauses, complement clauses modify verbs or nouns and relative clauses (typically) modify nouns (but => RELATIVE CLAUSES: PROPOSITIONAL).

A caveat is needed at this point: all prototypical main clauses (with finite verbs) can function as the opening contribution to a discourse but not all opening contributions to a discourse are prototypical main clauses. This is demonstrated by the extracts in (2) and (3), one from Dickens (as an example of classical English literature) and one from Lee Child (as an example of contemporary 'light' novels).

2 London. Michaelmas Term lately over ... Implacable November weather. Fog everywhere. Fog up the river ... Fog down the river.

Charles Dickens (1853), *Bleak House.* Penguin 1996, p. 1

3   Friday. Five o'clock in the afternoon.... [The man with the rifle drove north.] Not fast, not slow. Not drawing attention.
Lee Child (2005), *One Shot.* Bantam Press, chapter 1

Prototypical main clauses contain, as a minimum, a finite verb† and a subject noun phrase. Depending on the verb, they may also contain a direct object noun phrase and/or a second object noun phrase, and/or a directional phrase. (=> CLAUSE STRUCTURE: CONSTITUENTS, CLAUSE STRUCTURE: DEPENDENCY RELATIONS.) A central syntactic property of main clauses is that they allow four major constructions creating different clause-types: declarative, interrogative, imperative and exclamative, as in (4a–f).

4   a   Shirley wrote a letter to Caroline [Declarative]
    b   Did Shirley write a letter to Caroline? [Interrogative, yes-no]
    c   Who wrote a letter to Caroline? [Interrogative, wh]
    d   Shirley wrote a letter to Caroline, didn't she? [Interrogative, tag]
    e   Write a letter to Caroline! [Imperative]
    f   What a letter Shirley wrote! [Exclamative]

Three major types of subordinate clause are recognised: adverbial clauses, relative clauses and complement clauses. Here these labels are applied to clauses containing finite verbs (but => RELATIVE CLAUSES: INFINITIVAL). A fourth set of subordinate clauses contain non-finite verbs and are discussed separately. (=> NON-FINITE CLAUSES: INTRODUCTION.) The different types of subordinate clause (finite and non-finite) are distinguished not so much by their form as by the type of constituents they modify. Consider the examples in (5a–c).

5   a   We asked when the test would take place.
    b   When we asked questions, the lecturer got flustered.
    c   We remember the occasion when the lecturer got flustered.

(5a–c) all contain subordinate clauses introduced by *when*. But *when* introduces a complement clause in (5a), an adverbial clause in (5b) and a relative clause in (5c). The complement clause modifies the verb *asked*, the adverbial clause modifies the whole clause *the lecturer got flustered* and the relative clause modifies the noun *occasion*. The form of subordinate clauses is not entirely irrelevant. Complement clauses modify nouns as well as verbs. Relative clauses also modify nouns and we need some property that distinguishes relative from complement clauses. The property is that, apart from a handful of exceptions, complement clauses are not introduced by wh words, as shown by (6).

6 a We approved the proposal <u>that</u> a new hospital be built.
 b *We approved the proposal <u>which</u> a new hospital be built.

The exceptions to the above property are examples such as those in (7).

7 a the question <u>why</u> they rejected the grant, the reason <u>why</u> she resigned
     the problem <u>where</u> to park the car

The central chunks, *the question why*, etc., can be treated as fixed phrases, since a very small number of nouns allow wh complements. Alternatively, the structure can be seen as required by the denotation of the same small number of nouns, which all denote problems to be solved or explanations of the problems.†

Finite subordinate clauses are distinguished from main clauses by a number of characteristics. They must have declarative syntax, as shown in (8). (The situation is actually more subtle and complex. (=> ADVERBIAL CLAUSES: SUBORDINATE CLAUSE OR MAIN CLAUSE?, COMPLEMENT CLAUSES: EMBEDDED INTERROGATIVES.))

8 a *<u>Because did Shirley write a letter to Caroline</u>, she felt pleased.
     [Adverbial clause: cf. <u>Because Shirley wrote a letter to Caroline</u>, she felt pleased]
 b *The letter <u>which did Shirley write to Caroline</u> was very persuasive.
     [Relative clause: cf. The letter <u>which Shirley wrote to Caroline</u> . . .]
 c *Shirley wondered <u>if would Caroline read the letter</u>.
     [Complement clause: cf. Shirley wondered <u>if Caroline would read the letter</u>]

Similarly all types of subordinate clause exclude the imperative construction (e.g., *I can deliver the letter <u>which write to Caroline</u>!) and the exclamative construction is excluded by relative and adverbial clauses. However, complement clauses such as *We were astonished <u>how quickly she wrote the book</u>* do allow the same structure as exclamative main clauses, as in *How quickly she wrote the book!*

Various other syntactic constructions occur freely in main clauses but not in relative clauses or adverbial clauses, as shown in (9)–(11).

9 *Prepositional phrase fronting*
 a <u>Into the room</u> came the dog. [cf. The dog came into the room]
 b She said that <u>into the room came the dog</u>. [Complement clause]
 c *The dog that <u>into the room came</u> was a Border Collie. [Relative clause]
 d *Because <u>into the room came the dog</u>, the guests became agitated. [Adverbial clause]

Clauses with prepositional phrase fronting have a prepositional phrase in first position; e.g., (*into the room*) followed by the main verb (*came*) followed by the subject noun phrase, (*the dog*).

10 *Negative fronting*
   a <u>Never</u> had he been so worried. [He had never been so worried.]
   b They realised that <u>never</u> had he been so worried. [Complement clause]
   c *The person <u>who never had he been so worried</u> was her brother. [Relative clause]
   d *Because <u>never</u> had he been so worried, he contacted his lawyer. [Adverbial clause]

In (10a) *never* is at the front of the clause, followed by the finite verb *had* and the subject noun phrase *he*.

The next construction, the tag question, is excluded by all types of subordinate clause.

11 *Tag questions*
   a He was very worried, <u>wasn't he</u>?
   b *We realised <u>that he was very worried, wasn't he</u>? [Complement clause]
   c *The person <u>who was very worried wasn't he,</u> was her brother. [Relative clause]
   d *Because <u>he was very worried wasn't he</u>, he contacted his lawyer. [Adverbial clause]

Wasn't he in (11a) is a tag question, so named because the structure consists of a declarative clause, *He was very worried*, with a question tagged on at the end, *wasn't he*. Tag questions consist of verbs such as *did, might, can* and so on plus a pronoun and possibly an optional negation marker *n't* or *not*. The examples in (11) are intended to be taken as written language; if interpreted as spoken utterances, they must be supposed to carry a single intonation pattern and to have no breaks. The latter stipulation is necessary, because speakers do produce utterances such as, *because he was very worried*, break off the utterance and ask the tag question, and then, having received an answer, go back to the main clause. That type of interrupted syntax is not relevant for present purposes. The data in (8)–(11) suggest that there is a hierarchy of subordination. The least subordinate are complement clauses, which allow preposition fronting, negative fronting and, depending on the head verb, interrogative structures. Most subordinate are relative clauses and adverbial clauses, which exclude all the constructions in (8)–(11), together with interrogative and imperative structures. (=> ADVERBIAL CLAUSES:

INTRODUCTION, COMPLEMENT CLAUSES: COMPLEMENTISERS, RELATIVE CLAUSES: INTRODUCTION.)

SENTENCES AND CLAUSES: SENTENCE FRAGMENTS

Consider the examples of sentence fragments in (1) and (2).

1 Even worse, in our conscientious way, we'd stripped leaves off the vines to expose the grapes to more sunshine. <u>Usually a good idea; this year, bad</u>. Some of the berries suffered severe sunburn from strong evening sunshine – reduced to shrivelled raisins. <u>Heartbreaking</u>. Still, it wasn't too many.
Laithwaite's Private Cellars. Spring 2013, p.1

2 We were ready as soon as there was a dot of rot. <u>Snip</u>. <u>Gone</u>. And it didn't spread.
Laithwaite's Private Cellars. Spring 2013, p.1

Usually a good idea and *this year, bad* are clause fragments and the two together make up a sentence fragment. The chunk preceding the semi-colon has no subject and no finite verb – cf. *This is usually a good idea, It is usually a good idea*; the chunk following the semi-colon has no subject, no finite verb and no noun modified by *bad* – *This year it was a bad idea*, or even *This year it turned out to be a bad idea*. (3) is another example of a real clause/sentence fragment, from spoken English.

3 A: What's he going to do anyway that boy?
   B: <u>Play golf</u>
   C: <u>Be a professional golfer</u>
   B: <u>If he could he would</u>. I think he's applied for a sports scholarship
   A: <u>In this country?</u>

(3) is an excerpt from the transcript of a conversation with three participants. (The original transcript had no punctuation or capital letters and has been altered to make it easier to read.) It contains various clause/sentence fragments: *play golf, be a professional golfer, If he could he would* and *In this country*. The fragments can be converted to complete clauses by copying the appropriate sequences from the preceding text: thus, [*He's going to*] *play golf,* [*He's going to*] *be a professional golfer, If he could* [*be a professional golfer*]*, he would* [*be a professional golfer*]*,* [*has he applied for a sports scholarship*] *in this country?* This type of ellipsis is called by some analysts 'anaphoric ellipsis'. What is missing is reconstructed by going back over

the text, just as the reference of a pronoun may be determined by going back over a given text. Since text plays a central role, the term 'textual ellipsis' is also used.

Where clause/sentence fragments can be converted in the above way to complete clauses, we talk of ellipsis and of bits of clause being ellipted. The idea is that a complete clause, say *He's going to be a professional golfer*, is compared with the preceding text and a sequence of words identical with or highly similar to a sequence in the preceding text can be deleted (ellipted). The phrase 'highly similar' is necessary because sequences occur in natural conversation such as *Have you cleared the table?– I am. I am* can be expanded to *I am clearing the table*. The original question and the reply contain the same lexical items, *clear* and *table*, but the syntax is different, *Have you cleared/you have cleared* but *I am clearing*.

The fragments in (1) and (2) can also be treated as ellipsis, but not anaphoric or textual ellipsis, as there is nothing in the preceding text that might have led to the deletion of *this is* or *it was*. This type of ellipsis can be labelled 'structural', since correct interpretation depends on the listener being familiar with the construction and knowing that the pronouns *it* and *this* and forms of *be* are regularly unstressed and omitted (in speech). Other idioms that are frequently used in speech (and nowadays also on social media) are [*It's a*] *Good thing you brought the spare key*, [*It's a*] *Pity you didn't say that earlier* and [*It's*] *Just as well she didn't go*.

Other items that are regularly omitted in speech are *there* and *there's*, as in *Oops, [there's] too much water in the kettle* and *[There] should be a box of screws here somewhere*. Examples such as *Find what you were looking for?* and *Told you it would be tricky* also require knowledge of the construction and the fact that the subject pronouns *you*, *I* and *we* can be omitted. In *Find what you were looking for?* (*Did*) *you* has been omitted but whether it is to be taken as singular or plural depends on the situation. In the *told you* example the missing pronoun could be *I* or *we*, again the correct interpretation requires knowledge of the situation. This type of ellipsis can be called 'situational ellipsis'.

Many sequences that look like fragments are best handled as special constructions. Some are exclamatory noun phrases, such as *Good Heavens!*, *What the hell!*; others are fixed expressions with unusual syntax, such as *No pain – no gain, better late than never, first things first, the more the merrier*. A third set look more clause-like: *To think that we nearly cancelled our booking!*, *She went on holiday and him lying in hospital!* but there is no obvious full-clause paraphrase for *to think* and *and him lying in hospital*.

A final set of fragments are those that appear in newspaper headlines – *School destroyed by inferno*, notices of various sorts – *Last one out switch off lights, Elderly crossing, Police aware, Wash hands after use*, diaries, postcards, etc. – *Here today, gone tomorrow, Weather atrocious, Improving suntan*, and other light-hearted comments.

SENTENCES AND CLAUSES: SIMPLE SENTENCES

System sentences are treated here as low-level discourse units constructed out of one or more clauses containing finite verbs; text sentences regularly consist of clauses containing non-finite verbs or phrases with no verb at all. (=> SENTENCES AND CLAUSES: SYSTEM SENTENCE AND TEXT SENTENCE.) The simplest type of system sentence consists of one clause, as in (1), and is known as a simple sentence.

1 a The dog barked.
  b The dog jumped into her basket.
  c The dog gnawed the bone.
  d The dog is very fierce.

The traditional concept does not include sentences consisting of a single clause which normally functions as a subordinate clause in a complex sentence, as in (2), or as a conjoined clause in a compound sentence, as in (3). That is, it applies to 'ideal' system sentences but not to all text sentences.

  2 She refused his offer. <u>Which surprised nobody</u>.
  3 He walked out of his office. <u>And did not have a single regret</u>.

SENTENCES AND CLAUSES: SUBORDINATE CLAUSES: PREPOSITION OR COMPLEMENTISER?

In traditional grammar the underlined words in (1) were analysed as subordinating conjunctions introducing subordinate clauses.

  1 a <u>When</u> the dog growled, we quickly retreated.
    b <u>After</u> the old bridge collapsed, they built a new one.
    c Fiona heard <u>that</u> the holiday had been cancelled.
    d The person <u>who</u> phoned was your bank manager.

A more recent usage, particularly in formal models of syntax, has been to call the words complementisers, extending that term from words such as *that*, introducing complement clauses, to all subordinating conjunctions. This is the term used here.

A very recent proposal is that the words introducing adverbial clauses are to be analysed as prepositions and that only *if, that* and *whether* are markers of subordination.† One argument for this analysis is that words such as *before, after, since* and *until* are prepositions that have developed into constituents preceding adverbial clauses. But they have not become part of adverbial clauses; rather they stand outside them and the clauses function as their complements. That is, *before*, etc. are the head of whatever constituent contains one of them and an adverbial clause. Since prepositions are the heads of prepositional phrases, presumably this constituent is also a prepositional phrase.

Words such as *although, because, unless,* and *provided* have their own independent meaning and are also treated, by extension from *before*, etc., as heads. That is, in *Although I worked hard, I failed the test, although* is the head of *Although I worked hard.*

A third argument is that prepositions such as *before* can (and should) be treated as analogous to verbs such as *know. Know* can precede a noun phrase (*She knows that city*), a complement clause (*We know that the task is difficult*) or zero (*Who knows?*). In spite of the different frames, *know* and *knows* are treated as verbs. Similarly, so it is argued, *before* can precede a noun phrase (*before the accident*), a clause (*before she leaves*) and zero (*I knew that before*). This indicates that instead of analysing *before* as a preposition, a subordinating conjunction, and an intransitive 'adverb', the simplest analysis is just to treat all three instances as prepositions.

This analysis is presented as simpler than the traditional one, but it brings problems. One is that *although, though, unless, provided, lest* and so on never have been prepositions and cannot take a noun phrase as their complement. That does not prevent, e.g., *provided*, being regarded as the head of *Provided you repay the loan on time*, but it does stand in the way of its being classed as a preposition.

That (*We know that this idea is wrong*), *if* (*I'll ask if they accepted us*) and *whether* (*I inquired whether they made copies of the document*) function as complementisers of complement clauses (underlined). This raises two problems. One is that a distinction can be drawn between syntactic heads and syntactico-semantic heads. A syntactic head word both requires a particular type of phrase and, once a phrase is in place, signals that the phrasal constituent of head word + phrase is indeed of that type. On this distinction rests the widely-adopted view (at least within formal syntax) that determiners are the heads of noun phrases and that auxiliary and modal verbs are the heads of verb phrases. Main verbs in clauses are syntactico-semantic heads as they control the number and types of nouns that can occur as their complements and can be treated as controlling person and number agreement. (=> CLAUSE STRUCTURE: DEPENDENCY RELATIONS.) The distinction also raises the possibility that in *that this idea is wrong, that* is the syntactic head; that *if* is the syntactic head of *if they accepted us*, and *whether* is the syntactic head of *whether they had copies of the document.* That is, they are more than mere markers of subordination. Of course, *is, accepted* and *made* are the syntactico-semantic heads of the core clauses.

The second problem is whether word class labels such as noun, verb, preposition and so on have to do with lexical classes and their denotations or with the syntactic slot or slots occupied by a given word.† Relative clauses have not been mentioned in this section but it is worth pointing out that relative pronouns are treated as complementisers in many models of formal syntax.† That is, a word can be both a pronoun and function as a complementiser. Following this line of analysis, we keep the label 'complementiser' and allow that all types of subordinate clause have a complementiser. The complementiser slot in adverbial clauses may be filled by items that were originally prepositions or passive participles (*provided*) or discourse markers (*though, although*); once attached to an adverbial clause they are simply labelled 'complementiser'.

SENTENCES AND CLAUSES: SYSTEM SENTENCE AND TEXT SENTENCE

We draw an important distinction between system sentences and text sentences. System sentences are abstract units traditionally employed by analysts of syntax to handle distribution and dependency relations (types of constituent, order of constituents, subcategorisation, selection). Here we employ the clause for these purposes. (=> SENTENCES AND CLAUSES: INTRODUCTION, CLAUSE STRUCTURE: DEPENDENCY RELATIONS.) Text sentences are the sentences found in texts. For the purposes of their analyses, syntacticians assume that the prototypical system sentence is a construction containing a finite verb and one or more modifiers such as subject and object. This assumption does not constitute a claim that all text sentences must have this structure but simply reflects the observation that many text sentences do have this structure. The structure offers a solid analytical basis for dealing with other types of text sentence and with phenomena such as sentence fragments and ellipsis. (=> SENTENCES AND CLAUSES: SENTENCE FRAGMENTS, CLAUSE AND TEXT: ELLIPSIS.)

Two misunderstandings about sentences and written language must be cleared up. One is the belief, held by many educated users of English, that a 'correct sentence' must have the structure of the prototypical system sentence. To discuss this belief thoroughly we would have to explore the notion of correctness and who determines it. Since space does not allow this, we merely point out that other types of text sentence occur regularly in published material, and illustrate the point below. Readers should also note that what counts as a good text sentence varies over time. The text sentences in the novels of Jane Austen and Charlotte Brontë are rather different from the text sentences in those of Penelope Lively, Margaret Forster and Kate Atkinson.

The second misunderstanding is the idea that written language is closer to the 'ideal' grammar speakers have in their heads (according to some theories), whereas spoken language is 'externalised' and subject to performance factors, such as slips of the tongue, stammering, coughs, losing the thread of one's topic or one's syntax, selecting the wrong lexical item, and so on. Suppose there is an ideal grammar in speakers' heads. The fact is that written language is just as much an externalisation of that putative ideal grammar as spoken language. In the days when people wrote with pens and pencils, a written text might display the effect of many changes – scoring out, insertions signalled by carets, text in the page margins and so on. Making a clean copy hides all the editing, just as a text produced on computer typically does not show the pre-final versions and all the changes made by the author. And written text, like speech, is affected by performance errors. In the days of pen and pencil, ink pens could make blots on the page, letters might be mis-formed or missed out, spelling might go awry. In the days of word processing on computer, letters can still be omitted and words misspelled, though some misspellings can be passed off as 'typos'. Slippages in syntax and poor choice of lexical items are common to both periods of time.

The flexible nature of text sentences could be illustrated from e-mails and texts from the social media but we present examples from the work of very respectable authors. These examples show that the authors manipulate text sentences for discourse purposes, to build up tension, for emphasis, to contrast description of background with narration of events. The fact that authors can manipulate the structure of text sentences in this way is another fact supporting the idea that sentences are low-level discourse units. The text sentences are easy to understand; authors who rearrange the syntax of clauses, as say the American poet E. E. Cummings, fashionable in the 1960s, create text that is very difficult to interpret.

The text sentence in (1) is from Charles Dickens. No finite verbs, but the series of noun phrases creates the impression of immense speed (for 1848) and noise.

1 <u>A trembling of the ground</u>, and <u>a quick vibration in his ears</u>; <u>a distant shriek</u>; <u>a dull light advancing</u>, quickly changed to two red eyes, and <u>a</u>

fierce fire, dropping glowing coals; and irresistible bearing on of a great roaring and dilating mass; a high wind, and a rattle – another come and gone, and he holding to a gate, as if to save himself.
Charles Dickens (1848), *Dombey and Son*, chapter LV

The example in (2) shows Dickens using verbless text sentences to build up the confusion of impressions and thoughts as Carker's carriage thunders over long, long French roads. Note that the dependency relation between *vision* and *of* not only reaches across sentence boundaries but across two paragraph boundaries.

2 It was a vision of long roads; that stretched away to an horizon, always receding and never gained; of ill-paved towns, up hill and down, [4 lines]; of bridges, crosses, churches, postyards, ... Of morning, noon, and sunset; night, and the rising of an early moon. Of long roads temporarily left behind, and a rough pavement reached; of battering and clattering over it, and looking up, among house-roofs, at a great church-tower; of getting out and eating hastily, ... [9 lines omitted]
Of never sleeping, but sometimes dozing with unclosed eyes, and springing up with a start, and a reply aloud to an imaginary voice. Of cursing himself for being there, for having fled, ... [3 lines omitted].
Charles Dickens (1848), *Dombey and Son*, chapter LV

A text sentence may consist of a subordinate clause such as the second text sentences in (3) and (4). The separate text sentence in (3) highlights an essential point in the advertisement and the one in (4) highlights the important components of the author's thinking about his ex-wife.

3 People trust you to invest for them.
Because you are not the average investor.
You are a professional investor.
The Economist, 30 March–5 April 2013, Advert for MFS, p. 7

4 Next I thought about her. Not about how she might have felt on first reading the letter – I would come back to this – but why she had handed it over. Julian Barnes (2011), *The Sense of an Ending*. London: Vintage Books, p. 98

The last two examples are from a news report circulated to clients by a wine merchant. (Commercial people are very careful about the language of such documents.) In (5) the verbless text sentences, underlined, emphasise the comments and reactions and reinforce the impression that the wine merchant is having a conversation with his customers, while in (6) they create the impression of the speed with which rot was dealt with.

5   Even worse, in our conscientious way, we'd stripped leaves off the vines to expose the grapes to more sunshine. <u>Usually a good idea; this year, bad</u>. Some of the berries suffered severe sunburn from strong evening sunshine – reduced to shrivelled raisins.
    <u>Heartbreaking</u>. Still, it wasn't too many.
    Laithwaite's Private Cellars. Spring 2013, p. 1

6   We were ready as soon as there was a dot of rot. <u>Snip</u>. <u>Gone</u>. And it didn't spread.
    Laithwaite's Private Cellars. Spring 2013, p. 1

Verbs and verb phrases

VERBS AND VERB PHRASES: TENSE AND ASPECT: INTRODUCTION

The topics of tense and aspect play a central role in the organisation of texts and could be handled under the rubric of clause and text. Here we follow tradition in discussing tense and aspect in relation to verbs, for the simple reason that in clauses it is the verb that carries the distinctions in morphology and syntax that signal differences in tense and aspect. The contrast between *Freya took a photograph* and *Freya was taking a photograph* is one of aspect. Speakers use the former clause to present a single event as completed and the latter clause to present a single event as ongoing/ in progress. Events that follow one after the other at the centre of a narrative are typically presented as completed, as in (1); events that provide a background for other events are typically presented as stretched out in time, as in (2). (You will not be surprised to hear that the analysis is more complex; at the very least we need to allow for habitual and repeated events. Replace *a photograph* with *photographs* and a clause with the verb form *took* can be interpreted as denoting a habitual or repeated event: *Freya took photographs (every weekend)*.)

1 Freya composed the picture, steadied the camera, took a photograph and walked on.
2 Freya was taking a photograph when the storm broke and she had to run for shelter.

The contrast between *Freya was taking a photograph* and *Freya is taking a photograph* is one of tense. Tense allows events to be located in past or present time and to be located relative to other events. There are constructions that allow speakers to present events as located in future time but these involve modality. Speakers talk with relative confidence about events that happened in the past and events that are happening in the present (but of course a given speaker may be mistaken about a supposed event). They talk with less confidence about events that they locate in the future, the future being uncertain. There is some controversy as to whether English constructions with *will* and *shall* (*She will take up her post tomorrow, I shall / will contact you next week*) should be analysed as a future tense or as a modal construction.

A very important distinction is drawn between two types of aspect. In many grammars of different languages the two types are still labelled lexical aspect and grammatical aspect. 'Lexical' captures the fact that the choice of grammatical aspect depends to a certain extent on the lexical aspect class of a given verb. 'Grammatical' relates to the signalling of distinctions such as that between *took* and *was taking* via morphology or syntax. Newer labels are 'situation aspect' (for lexical aspect) and 'viewpoint aspect' (for grammatical aspect). 'Situation' reflects the idea that what is important is not just the types of event or state denoted by given verbs but whole situations, and situations are denoted by clauses. That is, situation aspect is a property of clauses, not just of the verbs in clauses. 'Viewpoint' reflects the idea that in choosing grammatical aspect speakers signal what view of a given situation they want to present. (=> VERBS AND VERB PHRASES: TENSE AND ASPECT IN ENGLISH, VERBS AND VERB PHRASES: SITUATION (LEXICAL) ASPECT.)

Tense (from the Latin *tempus* 'time', via French) has to do with the location of a situation in time. Like person, it is a deictic category, since it points at times relative to the speaker's location in time. Three central concepts are deployed in the analysis of tense: the moment of speech, event time and reference time. (A fourth concept is presented below, topic time.) The moment of speech is self-explanatory. Present time includes the moment of speech. Past time is time preceding the moment of speech and future time is time that follows the moment of speech. Event time is the time of an event. If event time includes or coincides with the moment of speech, present tense is used. If event time precedes the moment of speech, past tense is used. (=> VERBS AND VERB PHRASES: PRESENT PERFECT AND ADVERBS, VERBS AND VERB PHRASES: PRESENT PERFECT AND RESULTATIVE, VERBS AND VERB PHRASES: PRESENT PERFECT AND SIMPLE PAST.) If event time follows the moment of speech, future tense is used (or whatever constructions are available for reference to future time). (VERBS AND VERB PHRASES: FUTURE TENSE.)

The concept of reference time is required for the analysis of the past perfect (also called the pluperfect) and the future perfect. Consider the example *Freya phoned but Katarina had left*. The event of Freya phoning precedes the moment of speech, so past tense is used: *phoned*. The event of Katarina leaving took place before the event of Freya phoning. The time of Freya's phoning is the reference time for Katarina's leaving, which is further back in past time. This is signalled by the past perfect: *had left.* Consider now *Freya will phone but Katarina will have left.* The event of Freya phoning follows the moment of speech so future tense is used: *will phone.* Katarina's leaving precedes Freya's phoning; that is, the time of Freya's phoning acts as a reference time for Katarina's leaving, as with the past perfect. But now the order of the events is reversed and the future perfect is used: *will have left.*

The concept of topic time is invoked to handle examples such as (3).

3 I noticed a car parked at the gate. It was dark blue with tinted windows.

The car may well still exist at the moment of speaking and still be dark blue with tinted windows but the speaker uses the past tense *was.* The use of the past tense is typical in narratives about past situations. Speakers sometimes try to resolve possible misunderstandings as follows: *The house was cold and damp – in fact still is cold and damp* or *David was – is – the managing director.* If the topic of conversation is some series of past events, past tense is used, even where present tense would be more accurate.

We have given a brief introduction to aspect and tense. It has been convenient to put the topics into separate pigeonholes, but as with the other concepts in this book, these grammatical categories cannot be kept neatly apart from each other or from the category of mood. Tense and aspect are closely connected in every language which has both and in English and other languages tense and mood interact. The difference between *Fiona may be here by 5 o'clock* and *Fiona might be here by 5 o'clock* involves what looks like present tense – *may* – versus past tense – *might.* In fact the past tense form *might* does not relate to past time but is used to present Fiona's being 'here' as remote from reality. *May* presents the situation as much closer to reality. There is a connection with time: past time is remote from the time at which a speaker says something, while present time includes the moment of speech. Degree of probability also rests on a more basic notion of a situation being located nearer to or more remote from the speaker.

With regard to the connection between the concept of past time and situations remote from current reality, note that the construction in (4a) presents the situation of Fiona getting a job as something that should have happened some time ago. This construction serves only to present situations as remote; as the unacceptability of (4b) shows, present tense is not possible, because it serves to present situations as close to the speaker in time.

4 a It's high time Fiona got a job.
   b *It's high time Fiona gets a job.

VERBS AND VERB PHRASES: TENSE AND ASPECT IN ENGLISH

The core of the English tense-aspect system is the contrast between the simple and progressive forms and between past and present tense, as illustrated in (1). Apart from the simple present, the examples in (1), denoting single events, can be called episodic clauses. They denote single episodes rather than habitual or repeated events.

1		Simple		Progressive
Past	a	James felled a tree.	b	James was felling a tree.
Present	c	James fells a tree.	d	James is felling a tree (in our garden).

In addition there is the perfect, as in (2), and the two constructions by which speakers can refer to future time, as in (3). (=> VERBS AND VERB PHRASES: FUTURE TENSE.)

2 James has felled the dangerous ash tree.

3 a James will fell the dangerous ash tree.
  b James is going to fell the dangerous ash tree.

The traditional analysis is that both the simple and the progressive forms can denote single events or habitual/repeated events, and that the simple present can also denote generic events.

Prima facie the core examples in (1) lend themselves to an analysis in terms of binary oppositions, simple (or non-progressive) versus progressive and present (or non-past) versus past. The difficulty is that the simple present is out of kilter with the rest of the core network. Episodic clauses in which simple present verbs denote a single event are limited to certain text-types: narratives (including jokes) and sports commentaries, as in *Federer serves, Murray returns to Federer's backhand, Federer lobs the ball, Murray volleys.* (=> VERBS AND VERB PHRASES: SIMPLE PRESENT.) Outside these text-types, simple present verbs are used to denote habitual events, as in *James fells a tree every weekend*. The habitual interpretation is even more dominant with plural object noun phrases, as in *James fells trees every weekend/for a living*.

Simple present verbs are also used to denote generic events, as in (4a–c).

4 a White phosphorus ignites instantaneously.
  b Over time frost shatters rocks.
  c Small snakes eat rodents.

Clauses denoting habitual events can be called habitual clauses. They assign properties to particular individuals, as in *James fells trees (for a living)*. Clauses denoting generic properties apply to whole sets of individuals (such as *small snakes*) or all the instances of some stuff (such as *white phosphorus*) or all occurrences of some phenomenon (such as *frost*). They can be labelled 'generic clauses', although the label 'gnomic clause' has also been used. (From the Greek *gnome* 'a judgement, an opinion, a proposition'). Generic clauses such as (4a–c) have what is called a contingency interpretation. Alternatively, they permit certain entailments: if some stuff is white phosphorus, then it will ignite instantaneously; if frost occurs over a long time, it will shatter rocks; if a creature is a small snake, it will eat rodents. Summing up the above, the opposition between the simple present and the progressive present looks neat if the analysis is confined to forms set out on the page but when we examine actual usage the relationships turn out to be much more complex and the simple present becomes the odd one out. (=> Verbs and verb phrases: simple present.)

Progressive present verbs are used to denote single events and present them as taking place, as being in progress. They are not typically used to denote habitual events, although occasional examples are found: *James is felling a tree in our garden* (single event) versus *James is felling a tree (every weekend just now)*.

Simple past verbs are typically used to denote single events, as in *James felled a tree*, and clauses containing simple past verbs are typically interpreted first as denoting single completed events. *James felled a tree* could be interpreted as habitual, as in *James felled a tree every weekend*, but the habitual interpretation is not the favourite. The default interpretation (demonstrated by years of classroom exercises with students) is the episodic one (single completed event). The habitual interpretation is not even the default one for clauses with plural object noun phrases, as in *James felled trees*, but is brought to the fore by additional time phrases such as *every weekend, on Fridays, at weekends*.

A focus on forms as opposed to usage allows the simple and progressive past tenses to be seen as participating in a binary opposition between past (or non-perfect) and perfect, as in (5).

5

Non-Perfect

	Simple past	*Progressive past*
	James felled a tree	James was felling a tree
Perfect		
	('Simple') Present perfect	*Progressive present perfect*
	James has felled a tree	James has been felling a tree

When usage is taken into account, the binary oppositions turn out to be illusory. They are least illusory in formal written English, especially in texts inspected by editors and other gatekeepers, but they do not match the usages to be found in spoken English and in informal written texts or in written texts not subject to inspection by editors. The perfect is unstable. There are users who combine it with definite past-time adverbs, using it as if it were a simple past. Other users prefer the simple past to the perfect, with the possible exception of the result perfect. (=> VERBS AND VERB PHRASES: PRESENT PERFECT AND SIMPLE PAST, VERBS AND VERB PHRASES: PRESENT PERFECT AND RESULTATIVE.) And accounts of tense and aspect in English usually do not include the resultative constructions that occur regularly in spoken English but also in written English.

VERBS AND VERB PHRASES: FUTURE TENSE

Traditional grammars of English talk of past, present and future tense. Past tense and present tense are at the heart of the tense system of English but the concept of future tense (in English) is controversial. There are obvious differences between past tense and present tense on the one hand and so-called future tense on the other. Apart from irregular verbs such as *swim – swam – swum*, past tense and present tense verbs consist of stem plus suffix, *-s* and *-ed*. (For convenience we use written forms.) That is, these tenses are realised by inflectional morphology. Future tense is realised by a syntactic construction, an auxiliary verb, *shall* or *will*, plus a main verb. Following our guideline that differences in grammatical structure indicate differences in meaning, we must scrutinise the traditional future tense more closely.

A preliminary comment is required on *will* and *shall* in the phrases *I will* and *I shall*. For the past 100 years linguists (such as the renowned Danish scholar of English Otto Jespersen) have noted that *I will* is far more frequent in spoken English, not just in Scottish, Irish and American English, as Jespersen stated, but throughout Britain and the English-speaking world. Schools and universities have ensured the survival of *shall* at least in formal writing but even in formal written texts *will* is gaining ground. Of course there are speakers, particularly in southern England, who use *I shall* and *we shall* but *you will, he/she/they will*. Some speakers use *I will* in declarative clauses but *Shall I* in interrogative clauses. *Shall* does survive in legal and quasi-legal notices, such as the one spotted in a shop window in Edinburgh: *This shop shall be closed on Tuesdays*.

The most conservative style and grammar guides still recommend the use of *I/we shall*. The rationale is that, since *will* has to do with intention and volition while *shall* has to do with obligation, the loss of *shall* would make English less precise. More observant and relaxed grammar guides simply state that *shall* is very infrequent and that the general use of *will* began at least by Shakespeare's time. In speech the *will-shall* distinction is typically obscured anyway by the use of *I'll*.

What is important for this discussion is that *will* does not just refer to future time but carries modal meanings, whether volition, intention or prediction. The volitional-intentional component is particularly strong with first person singular, as in (1a and b).

1 a I will/I'll return the book tomorrow.
    b I will/I'll drive you to the station.

Both (1a) and (1b) refer to future time but they also, and more importantly, convey the speaker's intention. The speaker who utters the third person example in (2) may be talking about the third person's intentions but may just be making a prediction about a future event.

2 He'll hand in the essay on Friday.

(3) is simply a prediction.

3 The snow will arrive tomorrow.

With *you* as subject, particularly in declarative clauses, the volitional-intentional component is usually absent; the speaker simply makes a prediction, as in (4).

4 You will enjoy this novel.

The volitional-intentional component is much stronger in interrogative clauses such as (5a and b).

5 a Will you lend me a fiver?
    b Will you supervise the work yourself?

The main component of meaning in past and present tense verb forms is reference to past or present time. (See below for the use of present tense verbs to refer to future time.) The traditional future tense with *will* or *shall* does refer to future time but the principal component of meaning is modal. Because of these differences in meaning, combined with the differences in construction, we abandon the traditional label of 'future tense'. The label 'future-modal' is more accurate.

Will can be used to convey predictions about situations in past and present time, as shown by (6) and (7).

6 Fiona will have left a message with Donald. (Past time)
7 Fiona will be on her way to work. (Present time)

Present tense verbs are regularly used to refer to events that we might think of as set in the future, as in (8).

8 a Bayern Munich play Real next week.
  b Jennifer is leaving for York tomorrow afternoon.

The essential characteristic of the situations denoted by (8a and b) is that the events are under human control and are arranged and scheduled. Picking up a point made in the section on participants (=> CLAUSE STRUCTURE: LINEARITY AND PREDICATE-ARGUMENT STRUCTURE.), speakers choose particular constructions in order to present situations in a particular way. Clauses and sentences in English (in any language) do not relate directly to the external world. Instead they relate to mental representations of the external world. Continuing the theme of grammatical choices being meaningful, we assume that the use of the present tense in (8a and b) is not accidental. Rather, because the events are under control and scheduled, we can explain its use in terms of the speakers conceiving the events as being in their (the speakers') present time. (Cf. the comments below on the 'historic present'.) None of the above points preclude controlled and scheduled events from being disrupted by unforeseen circumstances.

It has been suggested that the label 'present' could be replaced by 'non-past' on the grounds that past tense verbs only refer to past time and that present tense verbs can refer to either present time or future time, but not to past time. This relabelling would only be appropriate on the view that language refers directly to the external world, but even on that view would not be accurate. The historic present is used in narratives to convey past events as though they are happening at the time of speaking, as in the opening line of a joke: *A man goes into a bar with his pet crocodile on a leash.* (=> VERBS AND VERB PHRASES: SIMPLE PRESENT.)

In contrast, (9) is bizarre because it can only be interpreted in a scenario where the eruption of the volcano is under human control and can be scheduled. It is acceptable in a work of science-fiction but not in relation to the world as it is in 2015.

9 *The volcano erupts on Tuesday.

There are other constructions by which speakers refer to future time. *Be going to* is the progressive form of *go*. When speakers use the present tense, *am/is/are going to*, we can assume that, as in (8a,b), they place an event in their present time because they conceive of it as unavoidable or imminent. Thus, (10a) conveys a prediction, possibly not based on strong evidence, whereas (10b) is more a statement of something obvious.

10 a   Just wait. It'll snow. Happens quite often in January.
   b   We should turn round and go home. It's going to snow. Look at the sky.

In contrast, *It'll snow. Look at the sky* is peculiar. *She's going to sack the manager* is not a prediction but a statement of a decision already taken and about to be put into effect. *She'll sack the manager* is a prediction that could be proved wrong.

Finally, two more constructions for referring to future time are *be about to* and *be on the point of*. Both are used to refer to imminent events and the level of imminence can be increased by the use of *just*. *We were (just) about to give up (when the mist cleared and we saw the summit), I was (just) on the point of buying the house when I heard about the industrial development.*

VERBS AND VERB PHRASES: MIDDLE CONSTRUCTION

In addition to the active and passive constructions English has a third major construction, the middle. Typical middles listed in grammars of English are given in (1). Such typical middles are said to denote situations that are habitual or generic because of permanent properties of some participant (usually inanimate). Middles were held to allow mainly simple present tense verbs, but only the simple present, and to require adverbs of manner such as *well, quickly, impressively*.

1 a   This sweater washes well.
  b   Her latest novel reads well.
  c   My children photograph well.

Some accounts of the English middle use the label 'mediopassive'. This label is a mistake in relation to English. It is justifiably used in some grammars of Classical Greek, in which many of the middle and passive forms of verbs are identical (but not all). Some analysts see the English middle construction as having a strong resemblance to the passive, but this view is not supported by the evidence. The obvious point to make is that English middle clauses and English passive clauses share no syntactic properties. Middle clauses contain active verbs that are basically transitive and only one noun phrase, denoting a participant that is definitely not an agent but not a patient either. (Note that (1c) does not relate to the skill with which the speaker's children use cameras but to their being photogenic.). Passive clauses can contain a subject noun phrase and a second noun phrase preceded by *by*. (=> VERBS AND VERB PHRASES: PASSIVE VOICE.) Middle clauses require no auxiliary verb, whereas passive clauses require the auxiliary verbs *be* or *get* (and occasionally *become*). (The name 'middle', which corresponds to the ancient name given to the equivalent construction in Classical Greek, captures the idea that this construction is neither active nor passive but in the middle.)

Contrary to the received view, many middles do have an 'episodic' interpretation, that is, they denote a single episode or event as in (2a and d). Other middles denote a situation that will occupy some time but that is not habitual or generic, as in (2b and c), and allow verbs in the progressive, as in (2c).

2 a These cars sold very quickly last week.
  b It will take years for the Mersey to clean.
    [Water engineer interviewed on BBC TV News]
  c The course is jumping well.
    [Participant in equestrian competition interviewed on BBC News]
  d One bomb didn't guide and crashed.
    [American Army spokesman]

(2a) refers to a single event of selling; (2b) refers to a single, albeit lengthy, cleaning event; (2c) referred to a property of a particular course at a particular period of time; and (2d) referred to a single event of a bomb failing to guide and crashing. (2c) contains a verb in the progressive and (2b and d) have no adverb of manner.

It has been suggested that examples such as (2a–d) represent a different construction, the passival as opposed to the middle. Passivals are non-generic, do not involve inherent properties and allow the progressive. The distinction is a semantic one and is not easy to apply. KB and JM take the view that there is a single middle construction with clear semantic (see below) and discourse properties (=> CLAUSE AND TEXT: COHESION – ACTIVE, PASSIVE, MIDDLE.), that it is reclaiming (so to speak) grammatical properties that it had previously and that it is used with an increasing number of lexical verbs.†

What type of participant is denoted by the subject noun phrase in middle clauses? In passive clauses the subject noun phrase refers to an entity undergoing some process, i.e., to a patient. *The vase was/got broken* and *This candidate was elected* are answers to questions such as *What happened to the vase?* and *What happened to this candidate?* Does the subject noun phrase in a middle clause denote a patient? The sentence *His novels sell very well* is not an answer to questions such as *What is happening to his novels?* but rather presents the books as 'selling themselves'. There is no contradiction between two examples referring to the same novel such as *This novel reads very well* and *It is a pity that nobody reads this novel nowadays*. *This novel reads very well* denotes an inherent property of the novel. The property may be unknown to the current generation of readers but may be rediscovered by a future generation. It is quite possible to say *These cars sold very quickly last week* and then add *in spite of the inept performance of our new sales staff*. The expert knitter or tailor who declares *This wool knitted up without any trouble* and *The cloth was cutting beautifully* is not taking credit but giving it to the wool and the cloth. (=> CLAUSE AND TEXT: COHESION – ACTIVE, PASSIVE, MIDDLE.)

A solution adopted by a number of analysts is to assign the subject noun in the middle construction the role of 'neutral'; that is, they regard the subject noun as neutral between agent and patient but as controlling the situations. To take the examples at the end of the preceding paragraph, the cars, by their qualities, determine the rate at which people buy them and the wool and the cloth determine how easily and how well a human can work with them. The River Mersey, with the powers of cleansing and rejuvenation inherent in clean, flowing water, determines how long it will be before the pollutants are removed altogether. The utterance comes from a television documentary dealing with the River Mersey. The interviewer had been talking about the enforcement of legislation to stop factories discharging noxious materials into the river. Once the discharges stopped, the river had to be left to, as it were, get on with the task of removing the poisons already in the water. The spokesman uttering (2d) was apparently attributing blame to the bomb, which refused to respond to the guiding signals and crashed, killing civilians. (2c) conveyed the message that the course permitted accurate jumping of the obstacles and good times for the circuits of the course.

The middle construction occurs regularly in 18th-century novels. Jane Austen has examples such as *The story told well*, while (3) and (4) are middles with (depending on the reader) unexpected verbs.

3 It is like a man who has a sword that <u>will not draw</u>. (I.e., will not allow itself to be drawn from its scabbard.)
James Boswell, *Life of Samuel Johnson*, chapter 24. Quoted in David Crystal (2004), *The Stories of English*. London: Allen Lane

4 ... the language will gradually <u>polish and refine</u>.
First Statistical Account of Scotland (1790s) Kilmadock or Doune. Cited in Millar and Horsbroch (2000)

Middles with unexpected verbs occur in 20th-century novels, as in (5).

5 'Oh, yes. He likes the ones that <u>illustrate well</u>.' (I.e., the advertising slogans that allow the illustrators to produce interesting illustrations.)
Dorothy Sayers (1933), *Murder Must Advertise*. London: Victor Gollancz Ltd

A recent example from a syntax textbook is in (6). Note the use of the passive and the middle.

6 ... the features won't match, and the uninterpretable [$u$past] feature won't be Checked ... However, if the features are privative and require no value, then they <u>simply check</u> in the way that we have already seen: ...
David Adger (2003), *Core* Syntax. Oxford: Oxford University Press, p. 168

(7) is from a magazine (not text produced by a journalists but by a specialist contributor).

7 'Sunset' is ready to pick by late September and <u>will store</u> until the end of the year. *The Independent Magazine*, 20 October 2007, p. 99, Anna Pavord 'Be amazed'

Advertising texts find the middle construction very useful since it allows the advertisers to present the properties of some product as controlling situations. See (8) and (9).

8 It <u>won't crush</u> in your sports bag.
[Advertisement in New Zealand for cotton-polyester sweatshirts]

9 TKA micro-fleece ... <u>launders</u> well and <u>packs</u> easily.
[Leaflet on hillwalking gear from Graeme Tiso, Edinburgh, Autumn 2009]

(10) is from a telephone conversation between JM and an employee of Scottish Gas. The speaker is the employee, who was referring to a new invoice being prepared on computer as a result of a meter reading supplied by JM.

10 That'<u>s processing</u> for us now.

IT is a fruitful source of middles, from software installing easily and characters displaying on screen to faxes not sending.

We close this section by noting what might be called a quasi-middle construction. Consider (11) and (12).

11 A modest colony of fur seals <u>has established</u> ... at secluded Waterfall Bay. *New Zealand Geographical* 81, September–October 2006

12 Beef had remained strong because of the artificial trading conditions caused by the bans, a situation that was always going <u>to correct</u>.
Dorothy Sayers (1933), *Murder Must Advertise*. London: Victor Gollancz Ltd

(11) and (12) are like middles in that they contain verbs that are normally transitive. Unlike the previous examples, they can be paraphrased as *has established itself* and *was always going to correct itself*. What is not clear at the time of writing is whether (11) and (12) are to be analysed as involving the deletion of the reflexive pronoun or whether *establish* and *correct* are to be regarded as extending their range of occurrence to the middle construction by analogy with the many other verbs that occur in that construction.

The final example in this section is another one that looks on the surface like a middle in that a transitive verb occurs with no overt direct object and no covert direct object that could be treated as having been deleted. Furthermore, the subject noun phrase, *which = Wynns Coonawara Estate Cabernet Sauvignon*, is not presented as controlling the situation, and anyway such an interpretation would not be sustainable. Is there a more general tendency for basically transitive verbs to be used intransitively?

13 The winery is lacking 1963 and 1964 Wynns Coonawara Estate Cabernet Sauvignon, which <u>bottled</u> as Wynns Claret

VERBS AND VERB PHRASES: MOOD AND MODALITY

Modality is a general concept relating directly to language use because it has to do with the speaker's attitude. Speakers (and writers) have a range of attitudes to adopt depending on the context. They can choose to treat some situation as factual or non-factual: *Philippa has gone to collect the children* presents an event as factual. The speaker signals that they 'know for a fact' that Philippa has gone off to pick up the children. (The speaker, of course, might be mistaken or lying. What is at issue is how the speaker wishes to present some situation, not whether the situation actually exists in the real world.) The choice of non-factual imposes other choices: is the situation to be presented as possible or probable or as necessary? Thus, *Philippa might have gone to collect the children* presents the event as a possibility. *Philippa must have gone to collect the children* presents the event as necessary. The speaker declares that, given what they know about Philippa's daily schedule and what they know about the immediate situation (it is 3 o'clock and the car is not at the front door), they are forced to the conclusion that Philippa is off to the school.

One set of attitudes is expressed by different clause constructions. (=> SENTENCES AND CLAUSES: MAIN AND SUBORDINATE CLAUSES.) Having decided to treat a situation as factual, the speaker can declare that it is factual – *Philippa is going to collect the children*, can ask if it is factual – *Is Philippa going to collect the children?*, or demand/suggest that it become factual – *Philippa, go and collect the children.* (In the real world polite speakers tend to avoid direct commands like the preceding example.)

In various languages further attitudes are expressed by the choice of indicative or subjunctive mood, which is regarded as a verbal category because across languages it is typically realised by affixes on verbs. In English the choice of indicative or subjunctive is extremely limited compared with languages such as French. The subjunctive used to occur regularly in conditional clauses such as *If I were to press this button, an alarm would go off.* (=> ADVERBIAL CLAUSES: TIME, CONDITION, REASON, CONCESSION.) Many speakers of English do still use that pattern, but many use the pattern *If I was to press this button, ...* There is an alternative pattern, typical of formal writing but not of speech, in which the old subjunctive form is obligatory: *Were I to press this button, an alarm would go off.* **Was I to press this button, ...* is not attested. We might expect to find it in non-standard varieties of English but since these are typically spoken and not written, our expectations are doomed to disappointment.

It is often asserted that the subjunctive is dead in modern English but, as the preceding example of a conditional clause shows, it has not disappeared completely. Contrasts between indicative and subjunctive are possible, as in *Fiona insisted that her secretary handed over the report.* (Fiona presents the handing over as a fact) versus *Fiona insisted that her secretary hand over the report.* (Fiona wants the handing over to become a fact, i.e., issues a command.) The contrast is still alive, but only for a small number of speakers and only with a small set of verbs such as *insist*. For most speakers the sentence *Fiona insisted that her secretary handed over the report* is ambiguous between command and statement of fact. (=> GRAMMATICALITY: GRAMMATICALITY AND POWER.)

In the remainder of this section we give an account of modal verbs, which serve to express possibility, necessity (including obligation) and volition. The central modal verbs are *will, shall, can, must* and *may* with their originally past-tense forms *would, should, can, must* and *might*. These modal verbs share a set of formal properties that used to be known by the convenient label of NICE properties. They also all express the modalities of possibility (*can, could, may, might*), necessity (*must*) and volition (*will, would*). The NICE properties are these.

N is for 'negative'. The central modal verbs combine directly with the negative word *not* and the suffix *-n't* without the help of *do*. Compare *couldn't*, **wroten't* and *didn't write*.

I is for 'interrogative'. The central modal verbs occur at the front of yes-no interrogatives without the help of *do*. Compare *Could you see the mountains yesterday?*, **Wrote you these poems?* and *Did you write these poems?*

C is for 'code', a now-disused technical term for the use of *so* in ellipsis. Compare *Kirsty can swim a kilometre and so can Shona* (where *so* substitutes for *swim a kilometre*) with **Kirsty writes poems and so writes Shona* and *Kirsty writes poems and so does Shona*.

E is for 'emphasis'. The central modal verbs can carry emphatic stress, say in answer to a negative statement: *Kirsty can't swim a kilometre* versus *Kirsty CAN swim a kilometre*. Main verbs require the support of *do*: *Kirsty didn't swim a kilometre* versus *Kirsty SWAM a kilometre* (only possible if swimming is contrasted with running or walking, etc.) versus *Kirsty DIDN'T swim a kilometre*.

The central modal verbs share other formal properties: they do not take the third person singular suffix *-s*, they cannot be preceded by the infinitive marker *to*, they do not take the suffix *-ing* and they combine directly with verb stems (*can swim* but not **can to swim*).

The verbs *need*, *ought*, *dare* and *used to* are known as 'semi-modal' because they have some of the formal properties of the central modal verbs and some properties of main verbs.† None of them take the *-s* suffix, not surprising in the case of *used to*, which originated as a past tense form and can still be analysed as one. There is no present tense **I use to read detective novels*. *Ought* also originated as a past tense form but is used just as a present tense form in modern English. (It was the past tense of *owe*. It is pleasing to see *owe* also being used to express obligation: *She owes it to her readers to explain this point*, *I owe it to my friend to support him*. In this pattern the current past tense *owed* also occurs: *He owed it to his friend to help*.) *Ought* and *used* combine with *to*-infinitives: *You ought to visit your sister*, *We used to visit her a lot*. *Dare* and *need* also combine with the *to*-infinitive – *I didn't dare to contradict her*, *We need to keep the garden in order* – but also combine directly with verb stems – *She didn't dare leave her room*, *You needn't invite them to the house*.

Need and *dare* combine directly with verb stems when they are negative: *She dared leave her room* and *You need invite them round* sound distinctly peculiar, although there is the fixed phrase *I dare say* and the fixed phrase *How dare you (accuse him of fraud)!* The semi-modals combine directly with the negative suffix *-n't*. *Needn't* occurs above, but note also

She daren't tell him and *She didn't dare leave her room, He oughtn't to be so rude. Usedn't* is rare; the common patterns are *never used to* and *didn't use to*, as in *He didn't use to be so rude. Oughtn't* occurs infrequently and *dare* is not a common verb in modern English. Non-standard varieties of English have *didn't ought to* (and the interrogative *Did he/she ought to?*) but whether that negative pattern is exclusively non-standard is uncertain. JM recalls committee meetings chaired by an eminent professor who regularly uttered *didn't ought to*. The common verb in spoken and written English is *should*.

In standard English none of the semi-modals occurs in the progressive but *need* and *dare* do have -*ing* forms that occur as free participles: *Needing to consult a book, she went to the library very early, Not daring to pass the dog, she stayed in her room*. (=> NON-FINITE CLAUSES: FREE PARTICIPLES.)

In negative or interrogative clauses *need* in the present tense can be used either as a modal verb or a main verb: *She needn't worry about that, Need she worry about that?, She doesn't need to worry about that, Does she need to worry about that?* In the past tense it behaves like a main verb: *She needed to buy a car* versus **She needed buy a car, She didn't need to buy a car* versus **She neededn't/needed not buy a car*. In positive declarative clauses *need* follows the pattern of main verbs: *She needs to learn Russian* versus **She needs learn Russian*. In informal speech *need* takes the progressive: *You're needing to fix that spot of rust*.

Analyses of modal verbs employ a widely accepted distinction between epistemic and deontic modality. Epistemic modality (from the Greek *epistēmē* 'knowledge') is concerned with the speaker's assessment of factuality: is a situation to be presented as a fact, as a possibility or as a certainty? (The term 'evaluative modality' is occasionally used.) Deontic modality (from the Greek *deō* 'I bind') is concerned with necessity; directly when an obligation is imposed and indirectly when permission is granted, since being permitted not to do something is equivalent to not being obliged to do something.

Root or dynamic modality is a third type. It has to do particularly with the use of modal verbs such as *will* and *can* to refer to the volition and capacities of animate beings (but also of machines, as in *This crane can lift a railway locomotive*).

Clauses expressing epistemic modality with *can/may* (possibility) and *must* (necessity) can be seen as indicating the speaker's growing strength of conviction that a proposition is true. Clauses with *will* often express a prediction that a proposition will become true. In *That may be the postman, The postman could have left the gate open*, propositions are presented as possible or likely. Speakers who utter *That must be the postman* signal a strong presumption that what they say is true, while recognising that it is open to challenge. Of course, straightforward declarations are also open to challenge: A: *That's the postman* – B: *No it's not. It's just Dad. That will be the postman* expresses a prediction.

The contrast between epistemic *may* and *might* is worth mentioning, because it involves a recent change in English usage. *Might* expresses a weaker possibility than *may*. *They may e-mail us this evening (let's wait and see before we contact them)* versus *They might e-mail us this evening (but I wouldn't bet on it)*. When they were small, JM's children came to understand an utterance such as *We might go there* as expressing such a weak possibility that it was equivalent to *We're not going there*.

Might occurs in indirect speech, as in (1) and in conditional constructions denoting situations that were possible at some time in the past but are no longer so, as in (2).

1 He shouted that the building might collapse.
2 If he had taken my advice, he might have passed the exam.

Consider now (3) and (4).

3 A St John medical adviser acknowledged that Mr Boonen may have lived had he not waited for an ambulance.
New Zealand Herald, 28 February 2007
4 If the style had matched the content, it may have had more success in crossing the sectarian divide.
Norman Davies (1999), *The Isles. A History*. London: Macmillan, pp. 512–513

(3) and (4) are both from written texts, indeed (4) is from a book by an eminent historian and published by a very respectable publisher. KB and JM would write *acknowledged that Mr Boonen might have lived* and *If the style had matched the content, it might have had more success* ... KB and JM first noticed this usage in the mid-1980s but it spread rapidly, so much so that by 1996 a member of a department at the University of Edinburgh devoted a page of a departmental style guide to the iniquities of examples such as (3) and (4). As always, in vain. One side-effect of the change is that it reintroduced *may* to Scottish English. By the late 1970s *may*, whether denoting possibility or permission, was very rare. By the mid-1990s epistemic *may* was in constant use and epistemic *might*, in the above contexts, had retreated except in the usage of older speakers.

There is an indirect link between epistemic possibility and epistemic necessity that emerges when we consider the uses of *can, could* and *might*. The latter two can both express epistemic possibility.

5   A: Let's phone Jennifer. She <u>might</u> be at home.
    B: OK. She <u>could</u> be at home, but remember she has to collect John from the airport.

In (5), both *might* and *could* are used to state that a particular situation is possible. *Can* is not used in this sense. *Jennifer can be at home* is only used to convey permission for Jennifer to stay at home. To say that it is possible that Jennifer is not at home requires a sentence with the pattern in (6).

6   Jennifer <u>might not</u>/<u>mightn't</u> be at home.

The pattern in *Jennifer can't be at home* exists but is used to convey the interpretation 'It is not possible that Jennifer is at home.' Similarly, *Jennifer couldn't have been at home* conveys the interpretation 'It is not possible that Jennifer was at home.' The link between possibility and necessity lies in an entailment. Using a quasi-logical layout, *NOT POSSIBLE (P)*, or *NOT POSSIBLE (S)* – P stands for 'proposition' and S for 'situation' – entail *NECESSARY (NOT P)* or *NECESSARY (NOT S)*, i.e., it is necessarily the case that proposition P is not true or it is necessarily the case that situation S does not exist. *It isn't possible for Jennifer to have been at home* entails *Jennifer of necessity was not at home* (or related wording).

Deontic clauses with *can/may* (permission) and *must* (obligation) indicate speakers' growing strength of a sense of obligation, either for themselves or their hearers. In saying *You can go to the party* or *You may go to the party* the speaker grants permission or enables a possible event. With *you must go to the party* the speaker lays an obligation on an addressee and expresses the idea that going to the party will necessarily happen.

Must contrasts with *have to* and *have got to*, which also express obligation. The contrast is particularly interesting with first person subjects, as in (7).

7   a   I must go to Edinburgh. I would like to visit the bookshops.
    b   I have to go to Edinburgh. I would like to visit the bookshops/The police have summoned me to be interviewed.
    c   I've got to go to Edinburgh. The police have summoned me to be interviewed.

(7a) shows the pattern whose favourite interpretation is that the speaker puts the obligation on himself or herself. (7c) shows the pattern with the interpretation that someone else, or just circumstances, make it necessary for the speaker to do something. The speaker can easily cancel a proposed visit to bookshops but a summons by the police is regarded as irresistible. Failure to comply has unpleasant consequences. (7b) is a neutral pattern, very frequent in informal speech. In legal and quasi-legal texts the contrast in meaning does not apply, because the verb that is used is *must*. The statement *Passengers must have a valid ticket and must show it to the conductor when requested to do so* puts a very strong obligation on each passenger. As with the situation described in (7c), the obligation is irresistible because failure to comply has consequences.

Deontic necessity and negation combine in two ways, or in two ways that affect choice of syntactic construction. A speaker can tell an addressee that it is <u>not necessary</u> to do something. That is, some proposition will not necessarily be true or some situation will not necessarily hold. Examples are in (8).

8 a Juliet doesn't need to walk the dog.
  b Jennifer doesn't have to tidy her room.

With (8a) the speaker does not absolutely forbid Juliet to walk the dog, but merely says that, if she likes, it is possible for her not to take the dog out. Similarly for (8b). That is, there is an entailment between 'It is not necessary that P be true' or 'It is not necessary that S hold' – P and S stand for 'proposition' and 'situation' as above – and 'It is possible that P will not be true' or 'It is possible that S will not hold', where P and S stand for 'Juliet walk the dog'.

In contrast, a speaker can tell an addressee that it is <u>necessary not</u> to do something. The constructions available for this message are in (9).

9 a Juliet mustn't/must not walk the dog.
  b Juliet is not to walk the dog.

In (8) the negated auxiliary verb *doesn't* precedes the semi-modals *need to* and *have to*. In (9) the negatives follow *must* and *is*. That is, the syntactic order parallels the semantic order, as in the quasi-logical paraphrases of the meaning: *not necessary to* and *doesn't have to*, *necessary not to* and *must not* and *is not to*.

Dynamic or root modality has to do with capacity or volition, either the speakers' observations about inherent abilities (*He <u>can</u> sing treble*), or their own and other people's willingness (*I <u>can</u> sing, if you like*) or general characteristics (*He <u>can</u> be very silly* = *He is capable of being very silly*). Volition is referred to in examples such as *She <u>will</u> wear those stupid shoes* and *We remonstrated with him but he <u>would</u> make insulting remarks to our guest*. (=> VERBS AND VERB PHRASES: FUTURE TENSE.) There is no direct entailment connection between dynamic modality and deontic necessity but inferences can be invited. For instance, a notice on the edge of a bush reserve in New Zealand reads *Dogs can kill kiwis*. Intelligent readers are expected to apply their pragmatic knowledge and skills to rule out the interpretation 'Dogs are hereby given permission to kill kiwis' and to arrive at the interpretation 'Dogs have the capacity to kill kiwis'. (Using their sense of smell they can find kiwi burrows and dig out and kill any resident kiwis.) Intelligent readers are further expected to make the inference 'It is necessary to keep dogs on the lead'. That is, readers of the notice are expected to make an inference from a statement about dynamic modality to a proposition about deontic necessity.

Modality is pervasive in language and can be expressed by modal verbs but also by a number of other constructions. Thus, for epistemic modality: *She's probably on holiday* (adverb); *It's possible she's on holiday* (adjective); *there's a possibility she's on holiday* (noun); *It seems she's on holiday* (verb of appearances); *I'm told she's on holiday* (evidential verb), *I hear she's on holiday* (another evidential verb) and *Apparently/evidently she's on holiday* (speaker does not want to make a commitment to a definite statement). For deontic modality: *You may not smoke* (modal auxiliary); *It is impermissible to smoke* (adjective); *I insist that you do not smoke, You are required not to smoke* (main verbs), *It is not permitted to smoke*.

VERBS AND VERB PHRASES: PASSIVE VOICE

The category of voice has to do with the different constructions available for taking an event or state and presenting it from different perspectives.† Suppose we take a situation in which someone attacked someone else. We can to choose to keep all the participants out of our report by using the existential construction exemplified in (1).

  1 There was an attack yesterday.

We can choose to mention the person(s) attacked, the patient(s), but to leave out the attacker(s). This is done by using the passive construction, in which the patient noun is the subject, as in (2).

  2 Bill and Ben were attacked yesterday.

If we want to convey all the details, we mention both the agent and the patient(s), and we have a choice of construction, as in (3).

  3 a Emma and Harriet were attacked by those ruffians.   PASSIVE
     b Those ruffians attacked Emma and Harriet.   ACTIVE

(2) shows the main use of the passive: to mention only the patient and to omit the agent. The construction is known as the short passive and is the most frequent type of passive in spoken English and in many written text-types. From passives such as (2) listeners can infer that some agent carried out the attack, and adverbs can be inserted – e.g. *Bill and Ben were*

viciously attacked, *The vase was smashed deliberately* – which bring the agent very close but still without specifying who played that role. (=> CLAUSE AND TEXT: COHESION – ACTIVE, PASSIVE, MIDDLE.)

The construction in (3a) is known as the long passive. The agent is specified but is presented as peripheral, the 'agent' phrase being at the end of the clause, inside a prepositional phrase, and optional. Many analyses treat the preposition *by* in the long passive as a mere grammatical marker, with no denotation. One argument for this view is that there is no contrast between *by* and other prepositions; that is, there is no contrast in meaning. This argument does not hold up. Even in standard English the preposition *with* is found in long passives, and in informal spoken English (and in non-standard varieties too) the prepositions *off* and *off of* are also found. From a typological perspective what is interesting is that *by* occurs in path expressions: *We went by Zeebrugge*, *We strolled by their house*, *There's a good picnic spot by the river*. This is interesting because across languages a common way of presenting an event with the agent mentioned but, so to speak, demoted is to present the agent as a path. That is, the agent is presented as merely the path or conduit by which some event happens.

English has another passive construction with the auxiliary verb *get*, as shown in (4).

4 a The sheep got infected with scrapie.
  b The coach got blown over.

The *get* passive is dynamic. An example such as *The vase was broken* can describe an event or the state of the vase: *She noticed that the vase was broken and picked up the pieces* (state) and *The vase was broken (while the children were rampaging)* (event). *The vase got broken* denotes an event. The dynamic meaning of the *get* passive may come from *get* being a verb of movement, as in *We got to St Andrews in an hour*. The concept of movement has been extended to changes in state, as in *The sky got dark*, *We got cold*, and *get* passives denote changes of state.

There has been controversy over the *get* passive. Some analysts see a contrast in meaning between (5) with *were*, and (6) with *got*, and treat (7) as unacceptable.

5 The fans were deliberately provoked by a rival group.
   [The rival group acted deliberately]
6 The fans got deliberately provoked by a rival group.
   [The fans acted deliberately]
7 Six students got shot accidentally.

(7) is stated to be unacceptable because of a mismatch between the use of *got* and the use of *accidentally*. *Got* can supposedly be used only if the

students acted deliberately. There is no support for this analysis in any British corpus. If the students acted deliberately, the required construction is *The students got themselves shot*, with a reflexive pronoun. The *get* passive is simply a major passive in spontaneous spoken English. One sample of conversation recorded in Edinburgh had eighteen *be* passives and eleven *get* passives; another had fifty-seven *get* passives and three *be* passives.

Examples of *get* passives from written English show clearly that there is no question of the patient acting deliberately to cause an action.

 8 He gets the bad reports from clients but the good ones never get written.
    Graeme Green (1951), *The End of the Affair*. Heinemann
 9 We haven't had a man catch the midday [train] since young Simpkins got sent home with chickenpox last summer.
    Dick Francis (1964), *Nerve*, chapter 10

Occasional passives have *become* as the auxiliary verb: *The cable had become severed* (BBC news broadcast).

VERBS AND VERB PHRASES: PRESENT PERFECT AND ADVERBS

The perfect is usually described as excluding past-time adverbs referring to specific times, as in (1).

 1 *I have discussed this yesterday/last year/five minutes ago.

Such a description needs to be nuanced, even for standard written English. Consider the (invented) text in (2).

 2 At 1 o'clock on the afternoon of 29th May 2009 a passenger is sitting in the departure lounge. He has checked in around 12.30, has gone through security around 12.45, and is waiting for his colleague.

Why is the text in (2) acceptable in spite of the combination of the perfect with definite past-time adverbs? The answer lies in the concept of secondary deixis. Tense is a deictic category, that is, any tense is interpreted in relation to the moment of speech (or writing). This moment is the primary deictic centre. The deictic centre for (2) is not the time at which the text was written or spoken but a time specified in the narrative. It is a secondary deictic centre and the definite past-time adverbs are past time with respect to that centre. The constraint on the perfect and such adverbs only applies with respect to the primary deictic centre. (=> VERBS AND VERB PHRASES: TENSE AND ASPECT IN ENGLISH, VERBS AND VERB PHRASES: PRESENT PERFECT AND SIMPLE PAST.)

The concept of deictic centre, or the lack of one, allows us to explain why definite past-time adverbs can combine with the perfect in (3) and the perfect infinitive in (4).

- 3 It's annoying to arrive at the station at 10.30 only to find that the train <u>has left at 10.15 and not 10.50</u>
- 4 <u>To have arrived at 2 pm on Tuesday</u> was a miracle [is a miracle/will be a miracle]

The only tense in (3) that is anchored to the moment of speech is *'s* in *It's annoying*. This is a generic statement that includes the moment of speech but denotes the whole set of such occasions. As a consequence, the adverbial phrase *at 10.15 and not 10.50* does not relate to any deictic centre. Similarly, the perfect infinitive in (4), being non-finite, is not anchored to a fixed moment of speech.

Even where there is a primary deictic centre the constraint on the combination of perfect and definite past-time adverb is not universally observed. Examples from written texts are in (5) and (6).

- 5 The invoice <u>has been sent off</u> to Finance for payment <u>before I went off on holiday</u>
   [Letter from staff in university finance department]
- 6 BEI's success is all the more welcome as Britain <u>has lost ground 10 years ago</u> with the Saudis' decision to opt for American frequencies of 60 hertz rather than the British 50 hertz – giving the American manufacturers a head start.
   The Times

Examples from spontaneous speech are in (7) and (8).

- 7 <u>I've talked</u> to the player <u>this morning</u> and he isn't leaving the club
   [TV interview]
- 8 Some of us <u>have been to New York years ago</u> to see how they do it
   BBC *News at Ten* interview, January 2002: Simon Hughes, former Liberal Democrat MP

The perfect is the required construction in formal written English for reference to recent past time (possibly in combination with *just*). Very common in spontaneous spoken British English (standard and non-standard) is the simple past. Examples are in (9)–(11).

- 9 Er, as Charlie <u>just pointed out</u>, it is of great concern
   [Discussion at Trades Union Congress, recorded in the British National Corpus]
- 10 Sorry, Jane's not in. She <u>just went out</u> [= has just gone out]
   [Informally noted in conversation]

11 Hey! You just stepped on my foot! [You've just stepped on my foot!]
  [Informally noted in conversation]

(12) is an example of a simple past verb without *just*. KB and JM would say *you've forgotten the boy* and *I haven't forgotten the boy*.†

12 my father bought a round of drinks after the meal there wasnae one for me you see and one of the men happened to comment he says "Bob" he says "you *forgot* the boy" "No" he says "I *didnae forget* the boy"

The combination of the simple past with *just* is widespread. It is the norm in North American English. The Australian component of ICE in the Macquarie Corpus (S1A, private dialogue) revealed an equal number of simple pasts and perfects combining with *just*. A suggestive New Zealand example, *Did you hear what just happened?*, comes from an advertisement seen on a bus in Auckland in 2007, suggestive because dialogue in advertisements usually reflects up-to-date spoken usage.

The experiential meaning is regularly expressed by means of the simple past combined with *ever*, as in (13)–(16). KB and JM would use *have you ever heard*, *have you ever tried* and *have you ever been interested in football*.

13 Did you ever hear the joke about the Glasgow man who goes into a bar with his pet crocodile?
  [Informally recorded in conversation]
14 Did you ever try to give up smoking?
  [Advert on ITV in 2003]
15 You said you enjoyed fishing. Were you ever interested in football?
  [Conversation]

The construction is not new. (16) is from Dickens, *Bleak House*, chapter 4. A reading of 19th-century novels will provide other examples.

16 'May I ask you a question?' said I, when we had sat before the fire a little while.
  'Five hundred', said Ada.
  'Your cousin, Mr Jarndyce. . . . Would you mind describing him to me?'
  'Esther!' she cried . . . 'You want a description of my cousin Jarndyce?'
  'My dear, I never saw him'. [= I've never seen him]
  'And I never saw him!' returned Ada.

Certain semelfactive verbs do not occur easily in the perfect. (=> VERBS AND VERB PHRASES: SITUATION (LEXICAL) ASPECT.)

17 a ?He has knocked on the door.
   b ?She has blinked.

c ?The baby has hiccoughed.
   d ?James has winked at Freya.

(17a–d) can be made acceptable via special contexts, hence the above phrasing 'do not occur easily'. If the verbs did occur straightforwardly in the perfect, special contexts would not be necessary. There are two interesting facts. One is that the addition of *yet, ever* and *just* makes the examples entirely acceptable, as shown by (18). The other is that the examples are far less peculiar in interrogative and negative constructions, as shown by (19)–(20).

18 a He has just knocked on the door.
    b She has just blinked. [Possible as a signal to someone]
    c The baby has just hiccoughed.
    d James has just winked at Freya.

19 a Has he knocked on the door (yet)?
    b Has she blinked (yet)? [As in a contest to find out who blinks first]
    c Has the baby hiccoughed (yet)?
    d Has James winked at Freya (yet)? [As part of a children's party game]

20 a Has he ever knocked on the door? [cf. He has never knocked on the door]
    b Has she ever blinked? [She has never blinked]
    c Has the baby ever hiccoughed? [The baby has never hiccoughed]
    d Has James ever winked at Freya? [James has never winked at Freya]

We close this section with a comment on combinations of the perfect and adverbs such as *ever, yet* and *just* in conversation and in dialogue from business meetings (admittedly, in one variety of English, Scottish English). Twenty five out of 145 instances of the result perfect were combined with an adverb. Twenty six out of forty experiential perfects combined with *ever*, seven out of thirteen recent-past perfects and twenty-two out of twenty-eight persistent-situation perfects combined with *just*. The result perfects (as in *I have paid the invoice – here's the receipt*) differ from the experiential and recent-past perfects. They were much more frequent in the data but only a tiny proportion had an adverb. The experiential, recent-past and persistent-situation perfects were far less frequent but a large proportion of each had an adverb. The results suggest that what are currently described as various meanings or interpretations of the perfect are moving apart, to be expressed by different constructions.

VERBS AND VERB PHRASES: PRESENT PERFECT AND RESULTATIVE

It is generally accepted by scholars of English that the present perfect developed from a resultative construction. (1b), for instance, is held to derive historically from (1a).

1 a Angus <u>has</u> all the food for the party <u>bought</u>.
  b Angus <u>has bought</u> all the food for the party.

The resultative construction in (1a) conveys two propositions, one to do with Angus and possession – Angus has the food in his possession – and one to do with the food and a result – the food has the property of being 'bought', a property resulting from a previous action. The perfect construction in (1b) expresses a proposition about Angus: he has carried out a buying action on the food.†

Resultative constructions appear to be important; that is, it is important that speakers have ways of talking about the results of previous actions. This importance is reflected in what is called the 'persistence' of the resultative. The construction in (1a) gave rise to the perfect but has itself 'persisted' and is still in regular use. Not only has it persisted, it has itself developed an alternative version, exemplified in (2), that differentiates it clearly from the perfect.

2 Angus <u>has got</u> all the food <u>bought</u>.

Has got occurs in possessives, as in *Angus has got a Persian cat*, but never in the perfect construction. A central role in the resultative constructions in (1a) and (2) is played by the passive participle *bought*. Other examples are in (3).

3 You have access to a vein <u>gained</u> and cardiac analysis <u>done</u> within one minute.
   [BBC Radio. A consultant in Accident and Emergency discussing a new technique]
4 and he does <u>have a car parked not far away</u>.
   Wellington Corpus of Spoken New Zealand English: #DPC003:1045:FG

(4) is ambiguous in that *parked not far away* could be interpreted as a reduced relative clause equivalent to *a car that is parked not far away*. (=> NON-FINITE CLAUSES: REDUCED RELATIVES.) The ambiguity is removed if the example is changed to the resultative *I've got my car parked not far away*. This is not equivalent to *I've got my car parked that is not far away*, which does not make sense. (5) is another example from the same corpus. The speaker is referring to a bottle of pills.

5 I said they've got those well labelled for this.
Wellington Corpus of Spoken New Zealand English: #DPC002:0710:MK

(2)–(5) are examples of the possessive-resultative construction but *get* and passive participles also occur in a causative-resultative construction. (6) is a question regularly put by host to guest at gatherings in city-centre flats.

6 Host: Did you get your car parked not far away?
   Guest: In fact I got it parked right outside.

The guest who replies *I've got it parked right outside* is using the possessive-resultative, not the causative-resultative.

Other examples of the causative-resultative are in (7).†

7 We used our jackets to get him carried to the pithead.
[The speaker is narrating a mining accident]
8 As long as she gets her work done.
[Mother talking about daughter]
9 It might take you a week to get an alert concurred.
[Businessman talking about sending out alerts about production problems]

Passive participles are a central component in a number of resultative constructions that do not involve *get*, *have* or *have got*. (10a–c) are examples of an existential-presentative construction that is also resultative. The construction is used to introduce a situation treated as new information about the result of a previous event. (=> CLAUSE AND TEXT: GIVEN AND NEW.)

10 a   There's something fallen down the sink.
    b   There's a cat trapped up the tree.
    c   There's one person injured in the explosion.

In the existential-presentative construction there's is pronounced with the reduced vowel. The Wellington Corpus of Spoken New Zealand English contains at least one example of an existential-presentative with the full deictic and a passive/resultative participle. See (11), from a sports commentary.

11 there's the ball won by the Australians
Wellington Corpus of Spoken New Zealand English: #MUC002:0005:JM

(11) contains a definite NP, *the ball*, whereas typical existential-presentatives contain indefinite noun phrases. What is being presented is not the ball, which has been mentioned many times in the course of the match, but the situation 'the ball having been won by the Australians'.

Consider now the construction in (12).

12 a That's the letters <u>written and posted</u>.
     b That's him <u>consulted</u>.
        [BBC TV comedy show *Harry Enfield and Chums*]
     c <u>Here's</u> the tyre <u>repaired</u> and good as new.
        [Conversation in garage]

(12a–c) are instances of a copula construction: *that* is connected by the copula *'s* with noun phrases containing a resultative participle, *the letters written and posted, him consulted* and *the tyre repaired*. In this respect they are parallel in structure to reverse WH clefts such as *That's what you need to do* and are a type of TH cleft. (=> CLEFTS: CLAUSES: CLEFTS.)

(12a–c) could in principle be replaced by the basic perfect construction – *I've written and posted the letters, I've consulted him* and *The tyre has been repaired and is as good as new*. The replacements, however, introduce an explicit or implicit agent in a non-cleft construction, thereby changing what is highlighted and reducing the salience of the current result. The construction is used throughout the UK. (12a) is from Scottish English dialogue in a novel, (12b) is from a television comedy programme from southern England.

In (12a–c) the passive-resultative participles modify patient, or at least non-agent, nouns – *letters, him, tyre*. There is another resultative construction, exemplified in (13)–(17), in which the passive-resultative participle modifies the subject noun. (The examples below have been collected from Scottish English, in which the construction is frequent, but it occurs in another varieties too.) The subject noun may refer to an agent, as in (13b and c) – and in (13a), depending on the analysis of *see*. The participle also modifies an agent subject noun in (14)–(16).

13 a but that's me <u>seen</u> it [= I've seen it now]
     b that's you <u>finished</u> [= 'You have finished (the task)]
     c that's Ian <u>arrived</u>
        [Informally recorded in conversation]

14 and ... the farmer came out and he says '<u>That you left the school now Andrew?</u>' Says I '<u>It is</u>'. He says 'You'll be looking for a job'

15 A: Where does she go after that?
     B: <u>That's her finished</u> ... She goes to college again for a few weeks

16 Sally is the kind of person that will say '<u>that's me done it</u>' and then stop and she'll go off ...

That's her finished in (15) is a TH cleft and the interpretation is not that she has been finished off but that she has finished her period of training on hospital wards. In (14) *That you left the school* is a reduced interrogative TH cleft. The full structure is *Is that you left the school*, as shown by the reply *It is*. The quote in (16) likewise is a TH cleft.

The final example, in (17), shows the resultative construction with past tense, the equivalent of a past perfect.

17 He just lay down on the settee and turned over and that was him gone [= he had gone, i.e., died]

VERBS AND VERB PHRASES: PRESENT PERFECT AND SIMPLE PAST

Another syntactic construction central to the tense-aspect system of English is the present perfect (or simply the perfect) exemplified in (1).

1 The snow has blocked the track.

Analysts have found it difficult to classify the perfect as an aspect or a tense. It has two constituents, *has* or *have* and a past participle, here *blocked*. (The label 'participle' is not helpful; its Latin source means 'participate' and it reflects the fact that in, e.g., *the blocked track*, *blocked* is related to the verb *block* but is itself a sort of adjective.) The participle indicates an action that is completed, and this is why the perfect looks like an aspect, but *has* signals present time, and this makes the perfect look like a tense. We make no attempt here to solve the problem; the perfect is a syntactic construction, unlike the morphological constructions *blocks* and *blocked*, and may be indeterminate with respect to tense and aspect.

The perfect has been defined as focusing upon the presently accessible consequences of a past event, rather than upon the past event per se; this is summed up in the traditional formula that the perfect has current relevance. *The snow has blocked the track* so the track is blocked (and the speaker cannot leave). These definitions make good sense with respect to the comments in the preceding paragraph. The result or consequences of a past event are denoted by the past participle and the current relevance of the consequences is signalled by the use of present tense forms of *have*.

The perfect in standard written English has four major uses, exemplified in (2).

2	a	I have written up my thesis.	Resultative
	b	The Minister has (just) arrived.	Hot-news/recent past
	c	I've been at work for six hours.	Extended now/persistent situation
	d	Have you (ever) visited Doubtful Sound? Yes, I have been there.	Experiential/indefinite anterior

(2a–d) go from the most accessible to the least accessible consequences. The speaker who utters (2a) has the finished thesis to show. If (2b) is uttered, the listeners know that the Minister is there with them. The speaker who utters (2c) is saying 'I started work six hours ago and as you can see I am still at it.' The consequences of (2d) are not so obvious. The question is about a possible visit at an unspecified time in the past, hence the term 'indefinite anterior'. The answer, *Yes, I have been there*, does not specify a time but merely contains an assertion that a visit to Doubtful Sound took place. One consequence might be that the speaker can provide information about how to get to Doubtful Sound, can describe Doubtful Sound and can say whether the journey is worthwhile.

The English perfect has been the subject of much debate and analysis and we can do no more than indicate the main points. Three aspects of the English perfect are in need of investigation. Insufficient attention has been given to the role of *just* in (2b) and of *ever* in (2d), as demarcating the hot-news (recent past) perfect and the experiential perfect from the other interpretations. Research has shown that the simple past with *just* for recent events and *ever* for experiential meaning is the majority use in American English but this is also the regular pattern in the speech of many speakers of British English (not to mention Australian and New Zealand English). There are grounds for thinking that (2b) and (2d) should be treated as separate constructions, not just separate interpretations. (=> VERBS AND VERB PHRASES: PRESENT PERFECT AND ADVERBS.)

In written English the perfect excludes definite time adverbs – **The snow has blocked the track last Monday evening.* This appears to be because speakers using the perfect focus on the consequences of an action, not on when it happened in the past. In spoken English, and informal written English, this exclusion of definite past-time adverbs is breaking down. The development is not mentioned in the standard reference grammars of English but has been noted by several analysts. The same development has been observed in New Zealand and Australia, where police regularly use perfects in their reports to the media, even with definite time adverbs: *An accident has occurred last night.* The view taken here is that the classic perfect unmodified by adverbs exists only in a very restrictive variety of standard English and that in spoken English the different perfect constructions distinguished by adverbs have long been the typical pattern. The construction has a long history. In Middle English the present perfect and the simple past were used interchangeably with definite past-time adverbs and examples have been found in writers such as Shakespeare, Pepys and Galsworthy.†

Finally we should note that past participles were originally resultative, that is, they expressed the result of a completed action. The participles survive in a number of resultative constructions, not just in the resultative perfect. Examples, all from spontaneous speech, are given in (3). (=> VERBS AND VERB PHRASES: PRESENT PERFECT AND RESULTATIVE.)

   3 a   You have access to a vein <u>gained</u> and a cardiac analysis <u>done</u> within one minute. [Radio discussion]
       b   That's you <u>finished</u>.
           [Task-related dialogue]
       c   There's something <u>fallen</u> down the sink.
           [Conversation]

There appears to have been a complex pattern of grammaticalisation: the possessive-resultative construction with relatively specific meaning evolves into the perfect with a more general and more abstract interpretation; the perfect in turn splits into different constructions, each with a more specific meaning than the general perfect and marked by an appropriate adverb; the original possessive-resultative construction not only persists but itself undergoes change that increases the morpho-syntactic distance between it and the perfect; and various other resultative constructions develop.

VERBS AND VERB PHRASES: PROGRESSIVE ASPECT

Standard analyses of the English verb have the simple and the progressive in opposition. For single events, simple past forms of verbs present actions as completed whereas progressive past forms present actions as in progress/ongoing (in the past). The relationship between the simple present and the progressive present forms is much weaker. Usage shows splits just within the set of simple forms, with the simple present and the simple past also moving apart, and it also shows changes in the progressive. (=> VERBS AND VERB PHRASES: SIMPLE PRESENT.)

The classic progressive is used to present single actions or processes as ongoing and has long been treated as excluded by stative verbs. It is certainly true that the prototypical stative verb, *know*, does exclude the progressive, but verbs such as *like, believe* and *understand* do allow it, as shown by examples (1)–(9). These also show that the progressive appears to be spreading into habitual clauses and into gnomic clauses. From a typological-historical perspective these uses of the progressive are not surprising, since the change of progressives into imperfectives is common and since imperfective verbs are used to refer to single ongoing events, to habitual events and to generic events. (Russian is a classic Indo-European language with a perfective-imperfective system of aspect. The terms 'perfective' and 'imperfective' turn up in accounts of aspect in English. Even where they are applied to a viewpoint (=> VERBS AND VERB PHRASES: TENSE AND ASPECT: INTRODUCTION.) and not to the actual verb forms, these terms are best left to analysts of languages such as Russian and to typology.) Of course the classic pattern of use of the English progressive will survive for some time yet, particularly in formal written texts scrutinised by editors, but the new pattern is visible in speech and in informal writing.

Early English originally had a simple present and a simple past. Appearing in the 14th century, the progressive came into regular use in subordinate clauses by the 18th century and by the late 20th century, in British English, had become very frequent in main clauses, especially in speech. Digital databases show the progressive becoming generally more frequent but also spreading into new parts of the verb system such as the passive. The same development has been observed in Australian English and New Zealand English. Here we focus on main clauses and the spread of the progressive to all lexical or situation aspects.

We return to the question of stative verbs occurring in the progressive. It is not yet the case that stative verbs in general regularly take the progressive (although *like* does occur quite frequently in the progressive). However, stative verbs do turn up in the progressive, including examples such as (1) that reference grammars of English declare unacceptable. In contrast, (2), (3) and (4) offer three classic stative verbs in the progressive, *understand, see* and *believe*. (5)–(8) are examples of stative constructions, even if the verbs are not classically stative. It is worthwhile emphasising that (2) was part of a formal e-mail written by an academic senior in status and age and that (6) is from an academic text. Academic texts are scrutinised by referees and performance errors are unlikely.

1 *I am understanding that the offer has been accepted.
   Quirk and Greenbaum (1985), *Comprehensive Grammar*. London: Longman, p. 203
2 I am sorry to have to worry you again with . . . X's resubmission. However

Department Y <u>is still not really understanding</u> what it is that X needs to do.
[University of Auckland, 2004, e-mail from a committee convener]
3 And there is an older generation who <u>are seeing</u> NCEA as lowering the standards.
New Zealand Listener, 9–15 June 2007, p. 23
4 And people weren't even believing the true stories.
Australian ICE, S1A-026(B):64
5 She lives in a house which <u>is dating back 200 years</u>.
[BBC photography programme, Sunday 17 June 2007, 9–9.30 pm]
6 it may be that internal linguistic factors ... are governing the choice between <u>have to</u> and <u>have got to</u> ...
Tagliamonte (2004), *Have To, Gotta, Must*. In Lindquist and Mair (eds) *Corpus Approaches to Grammaticalization in English*. Amsterdam: John Benjamin, p. 43

(7) and (8) occurred in final degree examination scripts. In examinations students have little time for planning and editing and produce constructions typical of speech or informal writing but unusual in formal writing. (7) and (8) are generic (the set of utterances of *complaints*, the set of children) but have stative verbs in the progressive, *precede* and *depend*. (7) and (8) may reflect a choice of perspective. In examinations students discuss examples given in the question paper and write down their analysis as it proceeds. They may use the progressive to metaphorically put their readers in the middle of ongoing events. If correct, this explanation does not contradict the comments on the increasing frequency of the progressive but provides one of its causes.

7 The first vowel in [complaints] is short as it <u>is preceding</u> the nasal bilabial /m/.
[Honours examination script, June 2002]
8 Naturally a child <u>is depending</u> on his parents, or other adults to provide an environment where he can learn new words.
[Honours examination script, June 1983]

(9) has a progressive in a clause denoting a repeated event: the students repeatedly forget the new numbers.

9 The code is often changed and students **are forgetting** the new number.
[Minutes of Staff-Student Committee Meeting University of Edinburgh, February
1998. Written by a 4th-year student]

VERBS AND VERB PHRASES: SIMPLE PRESENT

The simple present and the simple past appear to share the property of not being progressive, that is, of not denoting a single event presented as ongoing. The default interpretation of a simple past verb is that it denotes a single completed event, but that is not the default interpretation of a simple present verb. Simple present verbs can certainly denote a single completed event in present time, or one that includes the moment of speech, but only in a restricted number of text-types: stage directions, sports commentaries or in a special narrative style. Their default interpretation – their interpretation in clauses taken out of context and containing no adverbs of time – is as denoting a habitual or repeated event: *Jacob sends a Christmas card (every year)*. Simple present verbs can also denote generic events, that is, events and behaviour typical of a class of entities or a whole type of stuff. This is a major distinction in interpretation that keeps simple present verbs apart from simple past verbs: the default interpretation of simple past verbs is as denoting single completed events. Of course, simple past verbs can also have habitual, or generic interpretations, but their default interpretation is episodic.

KB and JM's attention was first drawn to differences in the use of the simple present and simple past while working on a corpus of Scottish English conversations. The idea that they had different default interpretations was supported by intuitions collected from many classes of students. For instance, students might be given a list of sentences such as We visited London and We visit London and asked to add an adverbial phrase or clause. The first example always elicited additions such as last year or when we were on holiday last summer and the second elicited additions such as every summer or whenever we go to see our cousins.

Further support comes from two 2,000-word extracts from the Wellington Corpus of Spoken New Zealand English and two 2,000-word extracts from the corpus of spoken Scottish English. The Wellington Corpus extracts are from a radio phone-in discussion programme and a rugby commentary; one Scottish English extract is a narrative, the other a discussion. The tokens of simple present and simple past verb forms were coded so that all the tokens could be collected by computer and sorted into those denoting states and those denoting events. Examples of tokens denoting states are in (1).

1 a Now I know of a person who's got two teenagers plus herself.
   b I just feel that he is actually doing it just for his for his uh client.
   c I'm glad you share a sense of outrage.

d That's what I want to hear.
e How does that knee look?

The simple forms denoting events were then split into those occurring in main clauses and those occurring in subordinate clauses, as in (2).

2 I would like to you to ask them if you can if you ever get on to them.

The forms occurring in main clauses were divided into those that occurred in the actual dialogue or monologue and those that occurred in the Wellington Corpus meta-commentary, where the coding includes 'paralinguistic anthropophonics', e.g., 'laughs', 'drawls', 'inhales', 'snuffles'. Finally the former were sorted with respect to whether they denoted single (possibly instantaneous) completed events or repeated/habitual events, or were examples of narrative use, or discourse organisers, sequences such as you see, you know, I mean, as I say. The results of the analysis and sorting are presented in (3).

3		*State*	*Hab/rep*	*Single*	*Narr*	*Discourse*
NZspc	SPr	11	0	78	0	2
	SPst	6	0	21	0	2
NZrp	SPr	8	21	0	1	7
	SPst	3	0	26	0	0
SCnarr	SPr	9	13	0	0	1
	SPst	10	6	74	0	0
SCdisc	SPr	27	16	0	0	28
	SPst	3	0	4	0	0

(NZspc = 'New Zealand sports commentary', NZrp = 'New Zealand radio phone-in programme', SCnarr = 'Scottish English narrative', SCdisc = 'Scottish English discussion'. Hab/rep = 'habitual/repeated', Single = 'single completed event', Narr = 'narrative', Discourse = 'discourse organisers'.)

The figures support the view that sports commentaries are different from the other three text-types. None of the simple present forms in the sports commentary denotes habitual or repeated actions but 78 denote single completed events of the sort in (4). Importantly, the present tense verbs are used to describe events happening at the moment of speech, i.e., in present time.

4 a Lynagh gives it on to Horan
      Wellington Corpus of Spoken New Zealand English:#MUC002:0095:JM

b   Innes gets it kicks away
    Wellington Corpus of Spoken New Zealand English:#MUC002:0120:JM

In the other text-types the simple present forms do not denote single completed events. Instead they all denote repeated or habitual events, with the exception of (5), which looks more generic than habitual. (Can inanimate entities have habits?) It is uttered in response to the question What's Galliano?

5   It comes in a long bottle with a twig in the centre of it
    [Scottish English narrative]

It refers to Galliano, a proper name when referring to the company that makes the liqueur but a mass noun when referring to the type of liqueur, as in (5). That is, (5) has a contingency interpretation, which is a central property of generic propositions: if some liquid is Galliano, it comes in a long bottle with a twig in the centre of it. (=> VERBS AND VERB PHRASES: TENSE AND ASPECT IN ENGLISH.)

In the New Zealand radio phone-in programme and the Scottish English narrative and discussion most of the simple present verbs refer to habitual or repeated actions. In the discussion, however, a large number of simple present verbs refer to states: e.g., I wonder, I recognise the building, I think, I regret, I reckon that . . ., ( ) so happens that (I'm a member of the kirk just locally here), I suppose, I remember, I still maintain . . .(lots of cinemas would have still been open).

There are 156 tokens of simple past verbs. One hundred and twenty-five, or 86%, refer to single completed events. Twenty-two refer to states and six refer to habitual or repeated actions. If the sports commentary is put on one side, we find that no simple present forms refer to single completed events and only six simple past forms refer to habitual/repeated events. It is not helpful to view the simple present and the simple past as constituting one member of an opposition whose other member is the progressive.

How is the simple present to be analysed? Following the principle that patterns of syntax and morphology are meaningful, we must accept that these present tense forms are used because speakers want to present an event as taking place, a state as existing or a proposition as being valid at the time of speaking. This is most obvious in the use of what has traditionally been called the historic present, as in (6).

6   I'm sitting enjoying the sunshine and silence when suddenly there's this horrible screaming from the next-door garden.

The person telling the story presents the events as happening as they speak. This heightens the drama and puts the listener (or reader, in the case of a written text) in the place of someone actually witnessing the events as they happen. This usage is the norm in the telling of jokes. As an example from literature, consider the extract from *Bleak House* in (7).

> 7 Mr Tulkinghorn <u>takes</u> out his papers, <u>asks</u> permission to place them on a golden talisman of a table at my Lady's elbow, <u>puts</u> on his spectacles, and <u>begins</u> to read by the light of a shaded lamp.
> Charles Dickens (1853), *Bleak House.* Penguin 1996, p. 26

Bleak House is instructive with respect to the simple present. The events are narrated by two people. One is Dickens, the omniscient narrator. That role enables him to present the events as though they were being witnessed by readers, and this effect is a clue that the historic present can be related to present time. Both have to do with events being described as they happen, and both involve a mixture of simple present and progressive. The other narrator is one of the leading characters, Esther Summerson. Her portion of the narrative purports to be from her diary and is written in the past tense, with lots of simple pasts. Being a character in the novel and writing up the events from her perspective, Esther Summerson cannot pretend to omniscience and cannot use the simple present.

The habitual and gnomic uses of the simple present are also described as 'timeless statements' and 'timeless presents'. They are certainly timeless in the sense that a habitual or gnomic/generic clause does not present a particular event taking place at a specific time but they do invite the listener or reader to infer that they relate to long stretches of time that, crucially, include the moment of speech or writing. Because such clauses do not refer to a particular event or state, they can be regarded as a type of irrealis. To refer to a particular instance of some type of event happening at the moment of speech, the progressive is required, as in (8) and (9).

> 8 They go to Brussels twice a year, in fact they're driving there at the moment.
> 9 Water boils at 100 °C. The water in this kettle is boiling so it must have reached 100 °C.

An assertion of a habitual or gnomic proposition may be followed by a denial that the proposition is about to be translated into an action or process.

> 10 They go to Brussels twice a year, but they might not go there this autumn.

The validity of the proposition that they go to Brussels twice a year is not affected by the lack of an autumn visit; this is possible because of the irrealis nature of habitual clauses.

There are two special types of generic clause, both typical of instructions. One type is in (11).

> 11 You <u>take</u> the first turning on the left then you <u>cross</u> a bridge and <u>bear</u> right.

(11) has a contingency interpretation: 'If you are going to X, then you proceed thus.' It does not specify any particular time but it will relate to the present time of whoever reads the instructions. Demonstrations often involve the pattern in (12).

> 12 I <u>pick</u> up the fruit with a skewer, <u>dip</u> it into the batter, and <u>lower</u> it into the hot fat.

I can be replaced by *you* or *one* and they have a contingency reading: 'If you want to make this dish, you carry out the following steps' or 'If one wants to make this dish ...'

Finally, there is the use of the simple present in speech acts, as in (13) and (14).

> 13 I apologise for the delay in replying.
> 14 We thank you for your recent inquiry.

(13) and (14) are examples of archaic usages that are now highly formulaic (and may be falling into disuse) and not relevant to the core of the English verb system. But even they can be related to present time, not the writer's present time but the reader's present time. If JM opens a letter written a week previously, he might report the contents to his wife using the present progressive: *He's apologising for the delay.* As he reads the letter, the apology is in JM's present time, the moment of reading.

VERBS AND VERB PHRASES: SITUATION (LEXICAL) ASPECT

There is a connection between specific lexical items and particular constructions. (=> CLAUSE STRUCTURE: DEPENDENCY RELATIONS, CLAUSE STRUCTURE: LINEARITY AND PREDICATE-ARGUMENT STRUCTURE.) Similarly, connections exist between specific lexical verbs and situation aspect, though we will also see that the situation aspect of a given clause may be determined by the verb together with its modifiers (subject, direct object, directional phrases) and not just by the lexical properties of a given verb. (=> VERB PHRASES: TENSE AND ASPECT, INTRODUCTION.)

Verbs are divided into two major lexical classes by the major distinction between stative and non-stative (or dynamic) verbs. Stative verbs denote situations in which no energy or will-power is expended and which do not change over time. The classic English stative verb is *know*. Its stative nature is established by three central properties.

i The clause *Katarina knew all the answers* cannot be used in reply to the question *What happened?* A suitable reply would be, e.g., *Katarina wrote down all the answers*.
ii It cannot be used in WH clefts – **What Katarina did was know all the answers*. But *What Katarina did was write down all the answers* is perfectly acceptable. (=> CLEFTS: CLAUSES: CLEFTS.)
iii It cannot be made progressive – **Katarina was knowing all the answers*. But *Katarina was writing down all the answers* is acceptable. (=> VERBS AND VERB PHRASES: PROGRESSIVE ASPECT.)
iv A minor property is that stative verbs typically exclude adverbs such as *enthusiastically* and *quickly*. **They quickly knew his parents* is not acceptable and **They were quickly very cold* has the interpretation 'they quickly became cold'.

Know is the prototypical stative verb. Other common but not quite so prototypical stative verbs are *believe, understand, love* and *own*. They are less prototypical because they occur, though not frequently, in the progressive, as in (1).

1 a You'll soon be owning all the land round here.
   b They're believing everything he writes.
   c She isn't understanding a single word we're saying.

On the other hand, the verbs in (1a–c) do not occur in WH clefts or in clauses answering *What happened?* (2) demonstrates this for *own*.

2 a *What she did was own all the land.
   b *What happened?
      She owned all the land.

The fact is that excluding the progressive is a weak criterion for stative verbs, but occurring in WH clefts and in clauses answering the question *What happened?* are strong criteria.

The non-stative or dynamic verbs divide into three types: activities, accomplishments and achievements. (These labels were devised by the philosopher Zeno Vendler, who in the 1960s proposed what he called lexical classes of verbs. Alternative labels have been proposed from time to time but Vendler's are the most widely used.)

Examples of activity verbs (or activity clauses) are in (3).

3 a The dog chased the cat (for hours).
  b James talked to his grandfather (for hours).

Activities have three important properties.

i They are (relatively) homogeneous; a given activity can be conceived of as continuing without any change in the participants or any result. If the cat starts chasing the dog, the previous activity has ended and a new one has begun.
ii Activities can be conceived of as lasting over an indefinite stretch of time. In real life dogs tire themselves out and cats climb onto high places that dogs cannot reach. But some activities can go on for a very long time, such as fasting or sitting reading.
iii Activities do not involve a culmination or some anticipated result. They are not conceived of as having a 'built-in' boundary, hence the suitability of adverbial phrases such as *for hours* but not *in five minutes*. *The dog chased the cat in five minutes* does not have any obvious interpretation.

Examples of accomplishment verbs (or accomplishment clauses) are in (4).

4 a James told the whole story to his grandfather.
  b Jennifer played the tune on the piano.

Accomplishments have intrinsic duration. They can be conceived of as having an activity phase and a culmination phase. Thus, James takes time to tell the story and doesn't stop until the culmination phase is reached. This is a set point, namely when the last part of the story has been told. There is no set point at which chasing or talking come to an end, just when exhaustion sets in. Playing a tune has a built-in end-point: the event is completed when the end of the tune is reached. If Jennifer decides to play the tune again, she initiates a new event. Accomplishment verbs combine easily with adverbial phrases such as *in ten minutes*. *James told the whole story to his grandfather in ten minutes*. Accomplishment verbs/clauses exclude *for* time adverbial phrases: **James told the whole story to his grandfather for twenty minutes*. Note that *Jennifer played the tune on the piano for twenty minutes* is interpreted as referring to at least two events of playing the tune but probably many more.

Achievement verbs capture the inception or end-point of an act but are conceived as not occupying a stretch of time. Examples are in (5).

5 a The climbers reached the summit late in the day.
  b The injured driver died at 4 am.

    c Our daughter was born at 2.45 in the afternoon.
    d We arrived at the airport in plenty of time.

The best examples of achievements are what might be called 'border-crossings'. The climbers spend a long time climbing towards the summit; a border is crossed when they arrive at the summit. *Die* has two interpretations. In the progressive, as in *The injured driver was dying*, the verb denotes a process occupying an indeterminate length of time. The end-point of the process is the border-crossing, *The injured driver died*. The actual arrival of a baby is preceded by a process. Arrival at some place is preceded by travel. (Note the aphorism *It is better to travel hopefully than to arrive*.)

    In (4a), *James told the whole story to his grandfather*, the process or activity phase and the culmination or achievement phase are wrapped up in one verb and one clause. In contrast, there are some pairs of verbs in which one verb denotes the activity phase and another verb denotes the achievement phase. Thus, *The dog chased the cat* refers to an activity and *The dog caught the cat* refers to the culmination of that activity (assuming the speaker is referring to the same event of chasing and the same participants). Similarly *The mountain rescue team searched/looked for the climbers* refers to the activity phase of an event and *The mountain rescue team found the climbers* refers to the achievement phase. (Assuming the activity phase is successful.)

    The original class of achievement verbs included *knock, stab, kick, wink, blink*. These denote actions that are conceived as not occupying a stretch of time, as instantaneous, but they do not denote the inception or culmination of some activity. Some analysts put them in a separate set of semelfactive verbs. ('Semelfactive' derives from Latin *semel* 'once' and *factum* 'done'.) Achievement verbs, as in (5), do not combine easily with the progressive but *knock*, etc., do. Of course, activity and accomplishment verbs also occur in the progressive but there is a difference of interpretation. *I knocked on the door* may refer to a single event, the speaker knocking once; *I was knocking on the door* refers to a series of events, the speaker knocking again and again. In contrast, *Katarina was reading* (activity) and *Katarina was writing a letter* (accomplishment – the built-in end-point is the conclusion of the letter) refer to single events, not repetitions of the reading or the letter-writing.

    Some languages, such as Russian, have a special suffix for semelfactive verbs denoting a single instantaneous action. English verbs such as *knock* and *stab* can in theory denote repeated actions but the favourite interpretation of *She knocked at the door* is one knock. In newspaper reports of assaults in the street verbs such as *stab, kick* and *punch* are typically accompanied by adverbs such as *repeatedly* if more than one action took place. If speakers want to emphasise the occurrence of a single instantaneous action they can use a construction with *give*. *His assailant gave him a kick*, *She gave a knock on the door*, *I gave him a punch*, *She gave a blink*, *He gave his daughter a wink*.

Sentences such as *The dog chased the cat for five minutes* and *James talked to his grandfather for hours* are staple fare in discussions of situation aspect but are not the only, or even the most common, way of associating periods of time with events. One is *take n hours/minutes etc. to do something*. This construction focuses on the end-point of an accomplishment or achievement: *She took two hours to find the missing document* has the interpretation that the search lasted two hours before the border-crossing was reached between not having the documents and having them, that is, finding them. *Barnabas took two hours to write the report* has the interpretation that the writing process lasted two hours before the border-crossing was reached of concluding the report and stopping writing.

Another construction is *spend n hours/minutes doing something*. This focuses on the extent of the event, the length of time occupied by the whole event. Thus, *Barnabas spent two hours writing the report* is perfectly acceptable, since writing a report is a type of event that has extent in time. *She spent two hours finding the missing document* is at best peculiar (but unacceptable for KB and JM), since *find* refers to the end-point of the process, not to the search. *She spent two hours searching/looking for the missing document* is quite in order. And note *She spent two hours pottering in the garden*. The 'spend time' construction is compatible with both accomplishments and activities, but not with achievements.

A final construction emphasising extent of time involves a main clause with a verb of position – *sat, stood, lay* – and a Type 2 gerund. (=> NON-FINITE CLAUSES: GERUNDS (TYPE 2).) *Jacob lay on his bed for hours thinking about the proposal*, *Barnabas sat for two hours writing the report*, *Jennifer stood for an hour and more buying a new top*. Note that these examples refer to single actions whereas *Jennifer stood for five minutes knocking at the door* refers to a sequence of repeated actions of knocking on the door.

It is nowadays accepted that the type of situation aspect may depend on an entire clause, not just on the choice of lexical verb. Consider the examples in (6).

  6 a Jane was out walking.
      b Jane was walking to the park [when we saw her].
      c Jane was walking round the park.

The lack of a prepositional phrase in (6a) gives an activity, with no built-in end-point. Jane will get tired at some point but that is not relevant. *To the park* in (6b) gives an accomplishment; when Jane reaches the park the event is completed. *Round the park* in (6c) gives another activity. There is no end-point; Jane could keep walking round the park for hours. What these examples show is that the presence or absence of a prepositional phrase affects situation aspect and so does the choice of preposition. In (7) *the Fat Boy* refers to a character in *The Pickwick Papers*.

7 a   The Fat Boy was eating a packet of biscuits.
  b   The Fat Boy was eating biscuits.
  c   The Fat Boy took twenty minutes to eat the packet of biscuits.
  d   ?The Fat Boy took twenty minutes to eat biscuits.
  e   The Fat Boy ate biscuits for twenty minutes.
  f   *The Fat Boy ate biscuits in twenty minutes.

The type of direct object affects situation aspect. *A packet of biscuits* provides a built-in end-point for the eating, hence (7c) with the 'take-time' construction is acceptable, since it focuses on the end-point. *Biscuits* on its own does not provide an end-point for the eating, hence (7d) is peculiar – it can only have the interpretation that the Fat Boy set aside twenty minutes from his normal duties to eat biscuits. (7e) is acceptable because *ate biscuits* has no built-in end-point and combines happily with the adverbial phrase *for twenty minutes* that focuses on extent of time. (7f) is not acceptable because *in twenty minutes* requires an end-point but there is no end-point.

The type of subject noun phrase can affect situation aspect, though examples are much rarer. But consider (8a–c)

8 a   The gallon of brandy evaporated through the oak barrel for fifty years.
  b   The gallon of brandy evaporated through the oak barrel in fifty years.
  c   Brandy evaporated through the oak barrel for fifty years.
  d   *Brandy evaporated through the oak barrel in fifty years.

The bare noun *brandy* provides no end-point and excludes *in fifty years*. It allows an extent-of-time interpretation and *for fifty years* in (8c) is acceptable. Interestingly, the phrase *a gallon of brandy* allows both adverbial phrases.

We close this account of situation/lexical aspect with remarks on what was known as 'The Imperfective Paradox'. (NB The use of 'Imperfective' in that label was misguided. (=> VERBS AND VERB PHRASES: PROGRESSIVE ASPECT.)) The paradox begins with the observation that a sentence such as (9a) entails (9b) and a sentence such as (10a) entails (10b).

9	a	Harriet was talking to Emma	b	Harriet talked to Emma
10	a	The dog was chasing the cat	b	The dog chased the cat

That entailment is not paradoxical. What is puzzling is that (11a) does not entail (11b) and (12a) does not entail (12b).

11	a	Jane was crossing the street	b	Jane crossed the street
12	a	The beaver was building a dam	b	The beaver built a dam

The reason for the difference in entailment is clear from the above discussion. *Talking to Emma* does not have a built-in boundary, and the interpretation of *talked to Emma* does not contain the idea of a boundary being reached. In (10a) *chasing the cat* likewise does not denote an event with a built-in boundary and neither does *chased the cat*. In contrast, *crossing the street* does have a boundary; the event is completed when the pedestrian reaches the other side. (11a) merely conveys the information that the crossing event was in progress at some point in the past but leaves it open as to whether the event was completed. Jane might have turned back or been knocked down by a vehicle. *Jane crossed the street* does state that the event was completed, hence the lack of an entailment. Similar considerations apply to (12a) and (12b). The event is completed when the dam is completed but (12a) says nothing about a boundary being reached. The beaver might have given up or the incomplete dam might have been washed away by a flood. On the other hand (12b) does assert that the boundary was reached and the event completed. (12a) cannot entail (12b).

Word classes

WORD CLASSES: INTRODUCTION

Labels such as 'noun', 'verb' and 'adjective' are very familiar but their familiarity disguises what a complex task it is to establish classes of words. Following the principles set out in the Introduction, we maintain that there is a semantic rationale behind the division of words into different word classes but follow the line that analysts cannot establish a reliable system of word classes on the basis of meaning. Rather, we adopt the only linguistically sensible approach: first establish word classes on formal grounds (what classes of words combine, the kinds of affixes that can be attached to words (stems) of a given class, their syntactic function), then look for semantic correlations with the formal classes.

A brief reminder: the term 'word' is ambiguous. It is applied to word forms, say *sink, sinks, sinking, sank* and *sunk*. It is also applied to lexical items or lexemes: the forms *sink*, etc. are said to realise the lexeme SINK. If you are asked to write an essay of not more than 2,000 words, 'word' refers to word forms. The number of lexical items will be much smaller. Some analysts recognise a third type of 'word', the morpho-syntactic word. This has to do with the combination of a lexeme and particular grammatical categories, such as singular and plural number or past and present tense. *Sunk* realises two morpho-syntactic words: SINK plus past participle as in *The battleship had sunk* but also SINK plus past tense, as in *The battleship sunk*. (The latter usage is now old-fashioned.)

WORD CLASSES: MAJOR AND MINOR

A distinction is generally recognised between major and minor word classes. The major word classes are also called content words or lexical words and the minor classes are also called form words or grammatical words. Another pair of terms is open class and closed class. The distinction rests on the fact that some classes of words have obvious denotations or lexical meaning (=> WORD CLASSES: SEMANTICS.), are very large and constantly acquire new members. The traditional major word classes in grammars of English are noun, verb, adjective and adverb. (=> NOUNS AND NOUN PHRASES: INTRODUCTION, CLAUSE STRUCTURE: VERB PHRASES, ADJECTIVES AND ADJECTIVE PHRASES: INTRODUCTION, ADVERBS AND ADVERB PHRASES: INTRODUCTION.)

The traditional minor classes are prepositions, determinatives and conjunctions. Determinatives (=> NOUNS AND NOUN PHRASES: DETERMINATIVES.) and conjunctions are clear candidates for the class of form words/grammatical words. They constitute small classes of items, the classes are almost closed and they are not usually considered as having denotations. Words with a denotation apply to people, places, things (in the broadest sense), actions, states and properties. In English they include nouns (e.g., *villa, baby, idea*), verbs (e.g., *buy, destroy, think*), adjectives (e.g., *wooden, strong, abstract*), and adverbs (e.g., *rapidly, hopefully*). English word classes that are generally recognised as grammatical are the definite and indefinite articles, *the* and *a*, the demonstrative adjectives *this, these, that* and *those*, the auxiliary verbs *is, has*, etc. (as in *is reading a book, has read this book*).†

Also classed as grammatical words in many accounts of English word classes are modal verbs such as *may, could* and *must* and prepositions such as *with, from* and *by*, but this treatment is doubtful. It is certainly possible to keep text messages short by omitting articles, auxiliary verbs and prepositions. Instead of typing in *We are arriving on Tuesday at 5 pm* a texter might enter *Arriving Tuesday 5 pm* or even *Arrive Tuesday 5 pm.* The problem is that, in spite of the texting practices, the distinction between *Press the button above the green light* and *Press the button below the green light* is rather important; the prepositions *above* and *below* cannot be left out, because a wrong interpretation might lead to just as regrettable consequences as the difference between *Press the red button* and *Press the green button.* All texting practices show is that in some contexts some missing words can be easily guessed while others cannot. Prepositions such as *on* and *at* in time phrases have no competitors – the sender of the text might have meant *after 5 pm*, but we would expect *after* or *before* to be stated explicitly in the message. Recent analyses of prepositions have shown that many have major meanings and can only be described as words with denotations. Equally we must concede that the meaning of prepositions such as *of* and *at* are hard to establish, but for most prepositions a clear basic meaning can be established. We regard prepositions (along with modal verbs such as *can* and *must*) as a major word class. In the general class of all lexical items they are not as central as nouns but neither are they grammatical items such as *the* and *a*. (=> PREPOSITIONS AND PREPOSITIONAL PHRASES: INTRODUCTION.)

The class of conjunctions is traditionally treated as containing two types, coordinating conjunctions and subordinating conjunctions. Coordinating conjunctions are words such as *and* and *or* that coordinate, or conjoin, two or more words of the same class: *small and beautiful, quickly and efficiently, wind and rain, dug and weeded (the garden), up and down*. The nouns, verbs, prepositions and so on are said to be coordinated or conjoined, and the coordinated items are all of the same status as heads or dependents. In *The children ran and jumped and shouted*, the coordinated verbs are all heads. (=> CLAUSE STRUCTURE: DEPENDENCY RELATIONS.) In *We invited the aunts and uncles and grandparents to the party*, the coordinated nouns are all dependents, being the direct objects of *invited*. Subordinating conjunctions signal that one clause is subordinate to another. In *I stay at home when it snows*, the clause *when it snows* is dependent on/modifies the main clause *I stay at home*. Its subordinate status is signalled by *when*.

Here we do not discuss conjunctions further apart from two comments. If we were dealing with conjunctions in detail we would recognise two separate word classes of coordinating conjunctions and subordinating conjunctions rather than a single class containing two sub-types.† Their syntactic properties such as the status of the coordinated words and where they occur in clauses is strong evidence for such an analysis. The second comment is that we do not agree with the proposal, also by Huddleston and Pullum but with older antecedents, to treat the words that introduce adverbial clauses as prepositions. We discuss this elsewhere. (=> SENTENCES AND CLAUSES: SUBORDINATE CLAUSES: PREPOSITION OR COMPLEMENTISER?)

A major question that we do discuss elsewhere is the status of verb phrases; whether the unit called 'verb phrase' is justified, and whether verbs are heads of verb phrases or of clauses. (=> CLAUSE STRUCTURE: VERB PHRASES, CLAUSE STRUCTURE: DEPENDENCY RELATIONS, CLAUSE STRUCTURE: HIERARCHICAL STRUCTURE.) Finally, the class of determinatives is discussed in some detail in view of their important role in the structure of noun phrases. (=> NOUNS AND NOUN PHRASES: DETERMINATIVES.)

WORD CLASSES: GRADIENCE

Setting up classes of words on the basis of formal criteria is not straightforward. Word classes can indeed be set up, but within the classes there are central members, less central members and peripheral members.

The central members are words that meet all or most of the criteria for a given class: they are prototypical members or prototypes. Peripheral members may meet only one of the criteria but none of the criteria for other classes. Less central members meet some but not all of the criteria. A recent term for this property of classes of words is 'subsective gradience'. 'Gradience' (cf. *gradient = slope* or *cline*) has to do with the metaphor of members of a given class of words being on a gradient; the members with the most properties pertaining to a given class are at the top, while the members with the fewest properties are at the bottom. The members of the class are said to be graded, placed at different points on the gradient. Progression from the top to the bottom of the gradient is graded in the sense that there is no definite borderline between central members, less central members and peripheral members.

The assignment of word forms to word classes is bedevilled by another type of gradience known as 'intersective gradience'. A relatively clear example is offered by the traditional word class of participles, as in *a frightening attack, the frightened townspeople, a working model, a worked example* (as in a mathematics textbook).† *Frightening*, for example, is derived from the verb *frighten*, denotes an action but occurs in a slot typically occupied by adjectives in a noun phrase, as in *a [fierce] attack* and *a [frightening] attack*. The term 'intersective gradience' applies to the relationship between the set of participles (though on syntactic grounds we could just say 'a certain subset of adjectives') and two sets of properties, one the properties of adjectives, the other the properties of verbs. *Frightened* can be preceded by adverbs such as *very* or *extremely, frightening* by *unexpectedly: the extremely frightened townspeople, an unexpectedly frightening attack*. In contrast, *working* typically does not take any adverbs and neither does *worked*. The intersection between *frightening* and the two sets of properties, of adjectives and verbs, produces a word that is equally adjective and verb. That is, it is on the mid-point of the gradient going from adjective to verb. The intersection between *working* and the two sets of properties produces a word that is less adjective-like, that is, closer to the verb end of the gradient.

The approach to word classes adopted in this book is that syntactic criteria outweigh morpho-syntactic and derivational criteria. The fact that in the phrases *a very convincing hypothesis* and *the most convincing hypothesis* the word *convincing* occurs in an adjective slot outweighs the fact it derives from the verb *convince*. In contrast, while you can have the phrase *a working hypothesis*, the phrases **a very working hypothesis* and **the most working hypothesis* are not possible. Within the set of syntactic criteria a distinction is drawn between major and minor ones. Occurring in the frame Det ___ Noun is more significant than occurring in the frames *very* ___ or *more* ___. Occurring in the frame *be* ___, *become* ___ or *seem* ___ is likewise more significant. That is, in *a convincing hypothesis* and *a working hypothesis*, *convincing* and *working* are both adjectives, though *convincing* is a more central member and *working* is a peripheral member. Note that the statement '*convincing* is a more central member of the class of adjectives than *working*' does not entail different positions on a gradience from verb to adjective. Both words are adjectives, just as *major* is an adjective but a peripheral member of the class. (But less peripheral than it was forty years ago, when JM and KB were not aware, in British English, of examples such as *This incident is major.* Such examples now occur regularly.)

Many instances of intersective gradience are tricky to analyse, such as *near* in (1a–d).

1 a Don't go near the logstack.
  b The farm is the one nearest the village.
  c Pull the sofa nearer the window.
  d You're too near the edge. Come back here.

2 a Don't go close to the logstack.
    The farm is the one closest to the village.
    Pull the sofa closer to the window.
    You're too close to the edge. Come back here.

In *near the logstack*, *near* occupies a frame that is otherwise occupied by prepositions, as in *on the logstack, behind the logstack*. Taking this syntactic frame as a major criterion, we have to treat *near* in (1a) as a preposition. The difficulty for some analysts is that occupying the putative prepositional slot in examples (1b–d) are *nearer, nearest* and *too near*; that is, word forms with comparative and superlative suffixes that still carry comparative and superlative meanings. '*Bigger*' is interpreted as 'exceeding some other entity in size'; '*nearer*' is interpreted as 'exceeding some other entity in nearness to something'. (1d) contains *too*, which typically modifies adjectives.

What we have in (1a–d) are the results of grammaticalisation; in this case the process of a word belonging to a major lexical category splitting into two categories, one of which is an adjective, as before, the other of which is a preposition. (1b–d) illustrate what is called 'persistence'; in spite of the change, certain properties persist. The view taken here is that *near*, *nearer* and *nearest* are prepositions, although unusual ones. The construction has developed from an earlier construction in which *near* was followed by *to*: *near to the village*. This is still the construction required by *close*, as in (2a–d).

Even more issues are raised by clauses such as *We had a fun time*. Is *fun* a noun or an adjective? Examples from dictionaries and corpuses include *someone fun* (cf. *someone energetic*), *It may not be as fun to watch it close up* (cf. *as interesting*), *the funnest language*. Questions that arise (which may have perfectly adequate answers) are: Is *fun time* a fixed phrase or does *fun* combine with other nouns? Are *as fun* and *funnest* used by many speakers of English or are these idiosyncratic? (KB and JM's usage is '*It may not be as much fun to watch it close up*, in which *fun* is a noun, and *the language that gives you the most fun*.) If the above examples turn out to be representative of structures in wide use, then we have to say that *fun* in *a fun time* is in an adjective slot (or adjective phrase slot) and is an adjective. And we would also have to say that another subset of speakers (possibly old) still use *fun* only as a noun.

Finally (at least as far as this discussion is concerned) there are examples such as *She congratulated him on his almost success*. Is this example acceptable? Not to some analysts, so how widespread is it? Is *almost* in an adjective slot or is *almost success* a compound noun? The latter seems very likely given that the Internet offers written examples in which the writers have put *almost-success* or *almost-victory*. The presence of a hyphen is a clear signal that the writer of a given example is treating *almost-success* as a compound noun.

WORD CLASSES: CRITERIA

Five types of criteria are employed to set up word classes – syntactic, morphological, morpho-syntactic, functional and semantic/pragmatic. We begin with a brief explanation of morphological and morpho-syntactic criteria, which have to do with inflectional morphology. Consider the English examples *The tiger is smiling* and *The tigers are smiling*. The contrast between *tiger* and *tigers* shows that *tigers* can be split into *tiger* and *-s*. *Tiger* is the stem and *-s* is the suffix added to the end of the stem. The stem *tiger* is a noun and the addition of *-s* does not affect this property. The addition of the derivational suffix *-ish* does affect it; *tiger* is a noun but *tigerish* is an adjective. In dictionaries of English *tigerish* and *tigers* are treated differently. *Tigerish* is listed as a separate lexical item, that is, it might be listed in the same entry as *tiger* but appear in bold and with a short explanation of its meaning; *tigers* has no entry at all, since the makers of dictionaries assume that users will know how to convert the singular form of a given noun to a regular plural form.

The morphological criterion has to do with whether a given word can take inflectional affixes, or indeed be affected by any kind of morphological change. For instance, *sheep* and *deer* are invariable: *one sheep*, *five sheep. Ape* is a typical noun that takes the plural affix: *one ape, five apes*. And there is the set of nouns that signal plural in some other way, whether by an unusual affix as in *ox – oxen* or a change inside the stem, as in *mouse – mice*.

Morpho-syntactic criteria have to do with inflectional suffixes and the information signalled by them. English nouns take suffixes expressing number (*cat* and *cats*, *child* and *children*, etc.) and English verbs take suffixes expressing tense: *pull* and *pulls* versus *pulled*. Person and number are expressed only by the *-s* suffix added to verbs in the present tense – *pulls*, *writes*, and so on. Of course English verbs cannot occur on their own in clauses but require at least one noun phrase, which could consist of just a personal pronoun – *I, you, he, she, it, we, they*. We can regard person as a category intrinsic to the verb in English. (Non-personal pronouns and nouns are by definition third person.)

English adjectives are not associated with number or case but many of them do signal grade, that is a greater quantity of some property (e.g., *bigger, more interesting*) or the greatest quantity of some property (e.g., *biggest, most interesting*).

The syntactic criteria for word classes are based on what words a given word occurs with and the types of phrase in which a given word occurs. Syntactic criteria are the most important. They are important for English with its relative poverty of morpho-syntactic criteria and they are crucial for the analysis of word classes in general because there are languages, such as Mandarin Chinese, which have practically no inflectional suffixes (such as plural endings); in contrast, all languages have syntax. Simple examples in English are that prepositions precede noun phrases, as in *with little enthusiasm*, but even here all is not straightforward. As the section on syntactic criteria shows, what should preferably be a good, solid, single class of words, such as verbs or nouns, turns out to split into sub-classes. (=> WORD CLASSES: SYNTACTIC CRITERIA AND SUB-CLASSES, WORD CLASSES: GRADIENCE.)

A second syntactic criterion, with a semantic component, is the syntactic function of a given word. With respect to grammatical functions, can a given word function as subject or object? With respect to dependency relations, can a given word function as head of a phrase or as a modifier? If the latter, can it function as a complement or adjunct? And with respect to predicate-argument structure, does a given word function as an argument or a predicate, or as head of a phrase that is an argument or a predicate?

Semantic criteria on their own do not enable us to decide whether any given word is a noun, adjective, verb, adverb or preposition. Meaning cannot be exploited in this way. As examples of the problems to be solved, consider the failure of the traditional definition of nouns – words denoting people, places or things – to explain why words such as *anger*, *idea* or *death* are classified as nouns. *Race* the noun and *race* the verb both denote an event, as do the verb *transmit* in *They transmitted the concert live* and the noun *transmission* in *The live transmission of the concert*.

On the other hand grammar plays an essential role in the communication of coherent messages of all sorts. It has been demonstrated many times that humans cannot (easily) remember meaningless symbols such as random sequences of words or numbers, like telephone numbers and personal identification numbers (PINs). Psycholinguists know that children cannot learn sequences of symbols without meaning and it would be surprising were there no parallels at all between patterns of grammar and semantic patterns. Having abandoned the idea that classes of words can be established on the basis of what words denote, we nonetheless accept that careful analysis brings out semantic patterns. We can talk sensibly about the denotation of words, but just as importantly we can also pin down what speakers and writers do with words. (=> WORD CLASSES: SEMANTICS.)

WORD CLASSES: SEMANTICS

For a long time it was accepted that there was no reliable connection at all between a given word class and meaning.† Consider, for example, *oats* and *wheat*: why should one be plural and the other singular when they both denote types of grain? (Perhaps the answer lies in how the grains are used and what the cereals look like when they are ready for use. Wheat comes in a mass of flour, whereas oats come in readily-distinguishable grains or flakes. *Pease* was reinterpreted as a plural, probably because the individual peas in a peapod are very obvious and countable. The peas that nowadays come out of deep-frozen packets are very obvious individual units.) Bloomfield's extreme view was influential until the 1970s but nowadays better and more subtle theories of prototypes, denotation and speech acts have brought about more subtle treatments of word classes in which meaning does play a part, though word classes for a given language first have to be established on formal criteria. (=> WORD CLASSES: CRITERIA.)

Three concepts are essential for a coherent account of word classes and meaning: first-, second- and third-order entities, prototypes, and speech acts. First-order entities are physical objects. They have relatively constant perceptual properties, are located in 3D space (or are perceived as so located, as when small children look at pictures) and are publicly observable and describable. Prototypical nouns, that is, noun forms that meet all the distributional criteria for nounhood, denote first-order entities such as tables, books, teddies, dolls, baths, water, nappies, different kinds of food, milk, juice apples, dogs, trees and so on. These are the sorts of entities that parents talk about with small children and that small children talk about in the early stages of language acquisition. The connection between nouns, distributional properties and concrete entities is straightforward and quickly established.

Second-order entities are events, processes and states-of-affairs. They are located in time and may have perceptible (and even significant) duration in time. Events and processes are denoted by verbs. A key property is the fact that a single event or process is typically of short duration. Adjectives denote states, which are typically, if not permanent, at least of longer duration than events and processes. And events and processes are dynamic, involving change over time and the expenditure of energy (in the broadest sense), while states are homogeneous and do not involve the expenditure of energy.

Third-order entities are abstract objects such as propositions, which are outside space and time. First-order entities are said to exist or to be (as in *There exists a peculiar fish* and *There is a mixer in the kitchen*) and second-order entities are said to happen or take place (as in *The collision happened around 1 am* and *The wedding took place last month*). Propositions do not exist or occur but are held or entertained by humans.

Adjectives are traditionally said to denote the properties of things, while adverbs denote the properties of events, processes and states-of-affairs. But if things are thought of as bundles of properties, what is the distinction between a property and a thing? The idea of different orders of entities can only be made to work if we assume that a notion of 'permanent object' is fundamental to human perception, that the object comes first and properties are sorted out later. The perceptual 'mechanism' is able to differentiate an object from the background against which it appears. What is at one moment a perceptual figure may become part of the background the next, but people assume that it continues to exist in a stable form even when they are not looking at it. The simplest perception of a concrete object seems to depend on a prior concept of object permanence which enables humans to recognise an object they have seen before under different conditions, such as from different angles, in different lights, partly hidden, in the half-dark, by touch. That is, the distinction between entities and properties is not just naïve folk philosophy but is an essential part of theories of perception. We can sensibly ask (expecting the answer 'no') if it is accidental that humans distinguish between things and properties in their everyday talk of people, things and events.

The key move in the investigation of word classes is to accept that word classes must be defined on the basis of formal criteria – their morphological properties, their morpho-syntactic properties and their syntactic properties. Only when these formal patterns have been established can we move on to investigate the connection between meaning and word classes. The majority of protypical nouns, and certainly the nouns used by young children, denote first-order entities and for them the traditional definition of nouns as referring to persons, places and things is perfectly adequate. Nouns such as *girl*, *town* and *car* combine with *the* and *a*, take the plural suffix -*s*, are modified by adjectives and occur to the left or the right of the verb in active, declarative clauses. They also denote observable entities such as people, places and things. What is significant is the combination of syntactic and morpho-syntactic properties with the semantic property of referring to people, places or things.

In contrast, it is generally held that nouns such as *anger*, *idea* and *event* do not denote things. However these nouns do possess all or many of the syntactic and morpho-syntactic properties possessed by *girl*, *town* and *car*: *an idea, the ideas, an interesting idea, to develop an idea, This idea surprised us* and so on. *Anger* meets some of the major criteria – *The anger frightened him* [subject, and combination with *the*] but not all. The combination **an anger* is very peculiar, but the occurrence of the indefinite article is quite acceptable in examples such as *an uncontrollable anger*. The fact that the major formal criteria for prototypical nouns apply to words such as *property* and *anger* is what justifies the latter being classed as nouns.

How can we explain the fact that abstract nouns such as *anger* and *event* share the major formal criteria that apply to prototypical concrete nouns? On the assumption that these formal properties are not accidental, it also suggests that 'ordinary speakers' of English treat, e.g., *anger* as though it denoted an entity. There is a theory that these patterns of grammar enable children to break into meaning via the most concrete objects and relations, moving out from that platform into more abstract and complex relations. The relations between concrete objects are transferred to abstract domains and the ways of talking about concrete objects and their relations are also transferred. Much of language, as has been emphasised over the past thirty years, involves metaphor, and much metaphor is so familiar that it is not recognised as such.

Perhaps even more important than denotation are the speech acts that speakers and writers perform with language. Discussions of speech acts usually start with the basic acts of making statements, asking questions and issuing commands (in the broadest sense). Other acts, not so prominent but central to human communication and relating directly to word classes, are referring to entities and predicating properties of them. In English the class of nouns, established on formal criteria, contains words denoting entities, and nouns enter into noun phrases, the units that speakers use when referring to objects. This is not to say that every occurrence of a noun phrase is used by a speaker to refer to something; nor is the difference between nouns and other word classes connected solely with referring; nonetheless speakers require noun phrases in order to refer and noun phrases can be used to refer only because they contain nouns.

The notion of predication as a speech act is prevalent in traditional grammar and is expressed in the formula of 'someone saying something about a person or thing'. Predication has been largely ignored in discussions of speech acts, perhaps because it is always part of a larger act such as making a statement or asking a question or issuing a command. It is important, however, because in English (and all languages) verbs, including *be*, signal the performance of a predication.

Whether adjectives and adverbs are associated with a speech act is not a question that has received much discussion, but in traditional grammar adjectives are also labelled 'modifiers', a label which reflects the function of these words in clauses. Speakers and writers use verbs to make an assertion about something and the assertion involves assigning a property to that something. They do not use adjectives to make an assertion but merely to add to whatever information is carried by the head noun in a given noun phrase. That is, they use adjectives to modify nouns and adverbs to modify verbs and adjectives.

Explaining the different word classes or parts of speech in terms of speech acts removes a difficulty with the traditional definitions; the class of things is so wide that it can be treated as including events; even properties, which are said to be referred to by adjectives, can be thought of as things. In contrast, different speech acts correspond to different word classes. Although this book is about English syntax, it is worthwhile remarking that the comparison of two or more languages brings out clearly the need for both formal and semantic criteria. For example, an analyst might discuss nouns in English and Russian, but the English and Russian word classes have completely different formal criteria. In spite of this, analysts find no difficulty in talking of nouns in English and nouns in Russian and in equating the two. The basis for this behaviour must be partly semantic and partly to do with speech acts: central nouns in Russian (according to the Russian formal criteria) denote persons, places and things (as do central nouns in English) and speakers of Russian use nouns to refer (as do speakers of English). Verbs in Russian enable speakers to make predications, as do verbs in English.

We end this chapter with a comment on terminology. Linguists nowadays use the term 'word classes' and not the traditional term 'parts of speech'. 'Word classes' is neat and self-explanatory but is associated with the idea of words pinned down on the page or in the transcript of speech. 'Parts of speech' is not self-explanatory but it does have the merit of reminding us that we are dealing not with dead text but with speakers and writers doing things with language.

WORD CLASSES: SYNTACTIC CRITERIA AND SUB-CLASSES

The recognition of syntactic criteria as central is a major step forward but their application is not straightforward. Consider the English words that are called nouns. They all have several properties in common, namely they can occur in various positions relative to the verb in a clause. (1a–c) are examples of the active declarative non-copula construction (that is, containing verbs other than a copula verb such as *be* or *become*).

1 a The dog stole the turkey.
   b The children chased the dog.
   c The cook saved no scraps for the dog.

Dog occurs to the left of *stole* in (1a), to its right in (1b) and to its right but with the intervening word *for* in (1c). *Dog* also occurs in a noun phrase and can be modified by a word such as *the* – *The dog stole the turkey* – or by an adjective – *Hungry dogs stole the turkey* – or by *the* and an adjective together – *The hungry dog stole the turkey*.

All other nouns in English can occur to the left of the verb in an active declarative clause, but not all nouns combine with an article, or combine with articles in the same way as *dog* does. (=> CLAUSE STRUCTURE: DEPENDENCY RELATIONS.) *Dog stole the turkey* is unacceptable (assuming *Dog* is not a proper name), whereas *Ethel cooked the turkey* is fine. The difficulty is that the class of English nouns is a very large class of words that do not all keep the same company (or, to use another metaphor, do not all behave in the same way). All nouns meet the criteria of occurring to the right or the left of a verb in an active declarative clause and of being preceded by a preposition. These are major criteria, but there are the minor criteria mentioned above, such as combining with an article, or being able to occur without an article, or typically not allowing a plural suffix (**Ethels*). These split the class of nouns into sub-classes. (=> NOUNS AND NOUN PHRASES: COUNT AND MASS.)

A sufficiently detailed examination of the company kept by individual nouns would probably reveal that each noun has its own pattern of occurrence. Thanks to very large electronic bodies of data and the search power of computers, analysts are carrying out such examinations and finding such individual patterns. For the purposes of analysing syntax, however, it is not helpful to gather information about individual nouns and it is impossible to produce a useable analysis of English syntax (or the syntax of any other language) with, say, 20,000 word classes. To analyse and discuss the general syntactic structure of clauses and sentences we need fairly general classes and analysts try to keep to major criteria plus those minor criteria that lead to relatively large classes of words. For other purposes, such as building a dictionary, smaller classes are required, down to information about individual words.

A concept that is central to discussion of word classes, and indeed to any class of items, linguistic or non-linguistic, is that of the central and peripheral members of a class. Consider the adjective *tall* in the examples in (2).

 2 a a tall building
   b This building is tall
   c a very tall building
   d1 a taller building
   d2 a more beautiful building

There are two criteria labelled 'd' because some adjectives take the comparative suffix *-er* while others do not allow that suffix but require *more*. Some adjectives, like *tall*, meet all the criteria in (2) and are central or prototypical members of the class. Some adjectives fail to meet all the criteria. *Unique* satisfies (2a–c), as in *a unique building*, *This building is unique* and *a very unique building*. (Publishers' copy-editors might object to *very unique* but the combination occurs regularly in speech and in informal writing and even in newspapers.) *Unique* does not combine with *-er* or *more*: *a uniquer building*, *a more unique building*. In the class of adjectives *unique* is slightly less central than *tall*. *Woollen* meets even fewer criteria. *A woollen cloak* and *This cloak is woollen* are acceptable but *a woollener cloak*, *a more woollen cloak* and *a very woollen cloak* are not. *Woollen* is less central than *unique*, which in turn is less central than *tall*. Right at the edge of the class is *asleep*, which meets only one of the criteria in (2), namely (2b). *The child is asleep* is acceptable but not *the asleep child*, *the very asleep child*, *the more asleep child*. On the other hand, *asleep* meets none of the criteria for nouns, verbs, prepositions or adverbs; it is a peripheral adjective.

Notes

Introduction: why study the grammar of English?

Page 3, A good account of English as a Lingua Franca is provided by Seidlhofer (2011).

Introduction: what counts as the grammar of English?

Page 5, The structure of indirect questions: e.g., Adger (2003: 357).

Grammaticality: grammaticality and intuition

Page 11, *It's unfair what they're doing to the union.* This construction is deemed incorrect in Huddleston and Pullum (2002).

Page 11, Indirect questions: Both Swan (2005: 276–277) and Carter et al. (2011: 314) exclude examples such as *He asked were we leaving.* Given the debate about what should be included in the grammar of English worldwide for courses in English as an Additional Language, it might help if the debaters paused to look at spoken English and the structures that are used even by educated speakers of 'standard' English.

Page 12, *Was sat* and *was stood*: The handbook of usage for the BBC, Burchfield (1981), was written by an eminent lexicologist and scholar of English.

Page 12, The dictionary of linguistics is Trask (2001).

Grammaticality: grammaticality and power

Page 14, Volitional verbs and adjectives: Quirk et al. (1985: 155–157).

Grammaticality: descriptive and prescriptive grammar

Page 16, The recent prescriptive grammar is Heffer (2011). He says (p. 111), '*That* defines; *which* is parenthetic, or non-defining.' He is out of step with Carter et al. (2011), Swan (2005) and even with Gwynne (2013), a compendium of exceedingly conservative views on what counts as grammatical.

Grammaticality: grammaticality and language change

Page 18, *Whatever* and language change: The argument that the new uses of *whatever* do not count as language change is made in Sampson (2007).

Adjectives and adjective phrases: introduction

Page 20, Adjectives as predicative adjuncts: The regular term in formal models of syntax is 'small clause'. This could be argued for on the grounds that the semantic interpretation of examples such (1a–c) contains a separate proposition corresponding to the adjective. The question is how much semantic interpretation is to be included in the representation of syntactic structures. The view taken in this book is that syntactic structures should focus as far as possible on syntax, with semantic structures being separate and constructed from different building blocks. This idea goes back to the 1960s; a recent coherent exposition is Culicover (2009).

Page 20, Predicative complement: Quirk et al. (1985) apply the label 'supplementive adjective clause' to the adjectives in (1a–c) and the label 'contingent adjective clause' to the adjectives in (2a–d) and (3a–c). Following the syntax, which offers no strictly syntactic reasons for deploying the concept of an adjective clause, we keep to 'predicative adjunct' for the adjectives in (1a–c) and predicative object complement for the adjectives in (2) and (3).

Adjectives and adjective phrases: adjectives as heads of noun phrases

Page 26, Donald Rumsfeld: Secretary for Defense in the United States when George W. Bush was President (2000–2008).

Adjectives and adjective phrases: adjective positions in noun phrases

Page 28, *Younger than me*: We treat *than* as a preposition. The object form of the pronoun follows it, as with other prepositions: *to me, around me*, etc. A derivation from *younger than I am* is very unlikely, given the forced and peculiar character of *younger than I* and the fact that a derivation would require a change from *I* to *me* for no good reason (if *than* is treated as a conjunction rather than a preposition).

Page 29, Order of adjectives: See Quirk et al. (1985: 437, 1337–1344).

Page 30, Noun phrases in British newspapers: See Jucker (1992).

Adverbs and adverb phrases: adverbs and adjectives

Page 35, Use of the adverb for the adjective form: See Quirk et al. (1985: 405–408).

Clause and text: focus: special syntactic constructions

Page 66, NP Clause: Some of the speakers are highly educated professionals and Iain Stewart is not only a professor of geology but a regular presenter of television programmes. That is, they are users of standard English and accustomed to public speaking.

Clause and text: theme

Page 79, *The Duke gave this teapot to my aunt*: The Duke and teapot examples are from Halliday (1985).

Page 80, *Personally, strictly speaking*, etc.: These are called 'disjuncts' in Quirk et al. (1985).

Clause structure: constituents

Page 85, Radical construction grammar: This approach was developed by William Croft. At the time of writing (January 2016) googling 'William Croft' brings up a concise, undated (but after 2011) overview on CiteSeerX.

Page 85, Hierarchy of constructions: A very brief account, not quite devoid of detail, is in Miller (2008: 29–40).

Clause structure: dependency relations

Page 86, Heads and modifiers: Many analysts use 'dependents' for items other than the head of a phrase or clause. The use of 'modifiers' in this sense goes back to a debate that took place in the late 1960s between the Chomskyans, who saw constituent structure as primary, and opponents who saw dependency relations as primary. There is a move nowadays to restrict 'modifier' to adjectives in noun phrases. It is however a useful general term because it reflects the view that dependents do not just depend passively on some head but have an important role in bringing additional information and in applying to particular types of head. (=>NON-FINITE CLAUSES: INTRODUCTION, NON-FINITE CLAUSES: EIGHT TYPES OR FOUR?)

Clefts

Page 108, Annex clause: The term was introduced by Quirk et al. (1985: 1386–1387, 1407).

Complement clauses: embedded interrogatives

Page 116, Pied-piping: the term was introduced by John Ross in his classic 1967 doctoral thesis *Constraints on Variables in Syntax*.

Page 116, I asked are they filling in the forms: Carter et al. (2011: 466) give as an incorrect example *She asked us what were we doing* (with the score out) and Swan (2005: 249) gives *I asked **where Alice was*** (not . . . *where was Alice*). As remarked elsewhere, EAL teachers looking for ways to simplify the grammar that is taught to students who need English for practical purposes but not for university degree programmes would be well-advised to look at the structures actually in use in spontaneous spoken English.

Complement clauses: mood and modality

Page 120, Volitional verbs and volitional adjectives: (3a and b) are from Quirk et al. (1985).

Non-finite clauses: eight types or four?

Page 120, The analysis with four types is set out in Huddleston and Pullum (2005: 204–224). A more detailed account is provided in Rodney Huddleston and Geoffrey K. Pullum (2002).

Page 140, For information about English as an Additional Language, have a look at Swan (2005). It is the Bible of EAL teachers.

Nouns and noun phrases: introduction

Page 143, *His anxiety about the flight.* Over the past fifteen years (perhaps longer) the preposition *around* has come to be used instead of prepositions such as *about* or *of.* Thus, *anxiety around the flight, issues of health and safety* => *issues around health and safety.*

Page 145, (9a–c) Determiner phrase: In the recent major grammars of English, Quirk et al. (1985) and Huddleston and Pullum (2002), the term 'determinative' is applied to the class of words containing *the, my, which* and so on. The term 'determiner' is applied to the function that these words have in clauses. In formal syntax (the various models of Chomskyan generative grammar (from Transformational Grammar to Minimalism), Head-Driven Phrase Structure Grammar, Lexical Functional Grammar, Construction Grammar, Cognitive Linguistics etc.) the word class is called determiner and no particular label is reserved for their function in clauses. We go with the English Language flow and use 'determinative' for the word class.

Nouns and noun phrases: pronouns

Page 166, Pronoun exchange: There is a good discussion of pronoun exchange in Wagner (2008).

Page 167, *he* and *she* are applied to inanimate entities: See Wagner (2008) for examples from south-west England. For a discussion of the Australian data see Pawley (2008).

Prepositions and prepositional phrases: prepositions, transitive and intransitive

Page 173, Intransitive prepositions: The term was introduced into formal syntax by Jackendoff in the early 1970s but the idea goes back to Jespersen and beyond. Jespersen (1924: 87) proposes 'to revert to the old terminology' whereby adverbs (including intransitive prepositions), prepositions and conjunctions (and interjections) are treated as one class called 'particles'. Clearly this is rather different from our use of the term 'particle'.

Page 172, *Down ran the girl the hill*: The asterisk reflects the non-operation of pied-piping, which is obligatory. For pied-piping (=> RELATIVE CLAUSES: WH.).

Relative clauses: free

Page 184, Fused relatives: The current analysis as a fused construction is presented in Huddleston and Pullum (2005: 191–192) and earlier in Huddleston (1984). In essence this analysis was proposed by scholars of the late 19th and early 20th centuries such as Henry Sweet and Otto Jespersen.

Page 185, *Tell me what [you need (it)]?*: The analysis was proposed by Bresnan and Grimshaw (1978).

Relative clauses: non-standard

Page 186, (1): The non-standard constructions were listed in Trudgill (1983).

Relative clauses: restrictive and non-restrictive

Page 188, 'it restricts the set of relevant cars, hence the label "restrictive relative clause"': Alternative labels, widely used in the world of English as a Second Language (ESOL), are 'defining relative clause', as used in Carter et al. (2011: 450–452) and 'identifying relative clause', as used in Swan (2005: 479–480) 'Identifying' is more informative than 'defining', since it captures the idea that, the set of referents having been restricted, the listener can identify the referent. Corresponding to 'non-restrictive' are 'non-defining' and 'non-identifying'.

Page 188, Instead of 'restrictive relative' Huddleston and Pullum (2005: 187–191) use the term 'integrated relative', meaning that the information expressed by the relative clause is an integral part of a larger message. 'Integral' also signals that the clauses are an integral part of the constituent structure of a larger chunk of syntax and are not separated by pause or intonation from the remainder of the sentence. Corresponding to 'non-restrictive' they use 'supplementary relative'. The label reflects the fact that such relative clauses convey additional, supplementary information that is not an integral part of the main message.

Relative clauses: shadow pronouns

Page 190, Carter et al. (2011: 254) condemn as typical errors the examples *That's the school that it does lots of music and drama, They went to the same restaurant that Mark had been to it.* Swan (2005: 486) comments that (real) examples such as the following are sometimes heard in informal speech: *There's a control at the back that I don't understand how it works, I was driving a car that I didn't know how fast it could go.*

Relative clauses: th

Page 194, This makes the relativiser *that* very unlike a pronoun. Swan (2005: 477–478) treats the wh forms as pronouns but does not label *that*. Carter et al. (2011: 459) incorrectly call the relativiser *that* a pronoun.

Relative clauses: *which* as discourse connective

Page 203, Examples (2) and (3): These examples come from an unpublished paper by Andrew Radford.

Page 204, Example (7) from Dorothy Sayers: It is worthwhile noting that Dorothy Sayers was the daughter of an East Anglian vicar and was brought up in the kind of village where many of her novels are set. She had a good ear for East Anglian speech.

Sentences and clauses: introduction

Page 206, Construction: The concept of a construction is very old, long predating its deployment in Construction Grammar in the 1980s.

Sentences and clauses: compound sentences

Page 212, Punctuation: In written text the punctuation of such sequences is governed by two conventions. The punctuation in (4) is possibly the most widespread pattern but there is a second pattern in which there is a comma between the end of the penultimate clause and the *and* (known as 'the Oxford comma').

Sentences and clauses: main and subordinate clauses

Page 213, Finite verb: Finite verbs are traditionally said to be marked for tense, person and number. This definition applies neatly to languages such as Latin or Italian in which verbs have suffixes signalling tense, person and number but it does not apply so neatly to English. For example, past tense verb forms such as *played* and *climbed* are only marked for past tense, though they do combine with personal pronouns: *We played, they played*, and so on. A residue of verb forms do show contrasts of tense and person and number; for example, *I was reading* versus *I am reading* (tense), *I was reading* versus *We were reading* (number) and *I am reading* versus *He is reading* (person).

Page 214, *The question why*. Note examples such as *the question of why they rejected the grant* and *the problem around where to park the car*. In examples such as these the wh complement clause modifies the prepositions *of* and *around*.

Subordinate clauses: preposition or complementiser?

Page 218, 'the words introducing adverbial clauses are to be analysed as prepositions': This analysis is argued for by Huddleston and Pullum (2005: 129–130). Their argument is essentially the one set out in Jespersen (1924: 87–90). Jespersen (1924: 90) uses the term 'sentence preposition' instead of 'conjunction'.

Page 220, The idea that word classes or parts of speech labels relate to syntactic slots rather than lexical classes was first stated explicitly by an eminent American linguist of a previous generation, Zellig Harris.

Page 220, Relative pronouns as complementisers: there are variations. As an example of a formal model of syntax, Haegeman (2006: 344–346) has relative pronouns as complementisers. Swan (2005: 500), a traditional non-formal grammar, explicitly declares relative pronouns to be complementisers. Böjars and Burridge (2001) and Givon (1993) are silent about relative pronouns as complementisers.

Verbs and verb phrases: middle construction

Page 233, A single middle construction: Hundt (2007) offers a detailed discussion of middles (her term is 'mediopassive') and passivals. To be dipped into. There is a recent, interesting discussion in Hundt (2014).

NOTES 289

Verbs and verb phrases: mood and modality

Page 238, The analysis of modals as main verbs was proposed in Pullum and Wilson (1977) and deployed in the model known as Generalised Phrase Structure Grammar, later overtaken by Head-Driven Phrase Structure Grammar.

Verbs and verb phrases: passive voice

Page 243, The category of voice: The term 'voice' derives from the Latin word *vox*, with the accusative form *vocem*. *Vox* was used both for voice in its phonetic sense and for the form of a word. From the latter use came the third use for active and passive constructions, justified by the fact that Latin verbs had different active and passive forms.

Verbs and verb phrases: present perfect and adverbs

Page 247, *'You forgot the boy*': (12) is from a narrative by an Ayrshire miner. The example is cited in Macaulay (1991).

Verbs and verb phrases: present perfect and resultative

Page 249, (1a) and (1b): This change from a possessive-resultative construction to a perfect is an example of grammaticalisation: a construction with a relatively concrete meaning develops into one with a relatively abstract meaning. This particular change has taken place in a number of Indo-European languages, Romance, Germanic and Slavic.

Page 250, (7)–(17): (7), (14) and (17) are from Macaulay (1991). (12a) is from A. L. Kennedy's 1994 novel, *Looking for the Possible Dance* (London: Minerva).

Verbs and verb phrases: present perfect and simple past

Page 254, 'examples have been found in writers such as Shakespeare, Pepys and Galsworthy': See Elsness (1997).

Word classes: major and minor

Page 269, Auxiliary verbs: The term 'auxiliary' reflects the fact that these verbs do not refer to actions or states but 'help' main verbs such as *read* to build a construction.

Page 270, 'two separate classes of coordinating conjunctions': This analysis is proposed in Huddleston and Pullum (2005: 21).

Word classes: gradience

Page 271, Participle: The term 'participle' comes from the Latin translation of a Greek verb *metexo* meaning 'to share', the underlying metaphor being that the word forms at issue share properties of both verbs and adjectives.

Word classes: semantics

Page 275, 'no reliable connection at all between a given word class and meaning': In his book *Language*, published in Britain in 1933, Leonard Bloomfield argued that not only is it impossible to define or establish word classes in terms of meaning, but there was no connection at all between word classes and particular meanings.

Bibliography

Adger, David (2003) *Core Syntax. A Minimalist Approach.* Oxford: Oxford University Press.
Böjars, Kersti and Kate Burridge (2001) *English Grammar.* London: Arnold.
Bresnan, Joan and Jane Grimshaw (1978) 'The syntax of free relatives in English'. *Linguistic Inquiry* 9, 331–391.
Brown, Gillian, Karen Currie and Joanne Kenworthy (1980) *Questions of Intonation.* London: Croom Helm. Republished as Brown, Gillian and Karen Currie (2015) *Questions of Intonation.* (Routledge Library Edition: The English Language.) London: Routledge.
Burchfield, R. W. (1981) *The Spoken Word: A BBC Guide.* London: BBC Publications.
Burridge, Kate and Bernd Kortmann (eds) (2008) *Varieties of English. The Pacific and Australasia.* Berlin: Mouton de Gruyter.
Carter, Ronald, Michael McCarthy, Geraldine Mark and Anne O'Keeffe (2011) *English Grammar Today. An A–Z of Spoken and Written Grammar.* Cambridge: Cambridge University Press.
Culicover, Peter W. (2009) *Natural Language Syntax.* Oxford: Oxford University Press.
Elsness, J. (1997) *The Perfect and the Preterit in Contemporary and Earlier English.* Berlin/New York: Mouton de Gruyter.
Givon, Talmy (1993) *English Grammar. A Function-Based Introduction.* Amsterdam: John Benjamin.
Gwynne, N. M. (2013) *Gwynne's Grammar.* London: Ebury Press.
Haegeman, Liliane (2006) *Thinking Syntactically. A Guide to Argumentation and Analysis.* Oxford: Blackwell Publishing.
Halliday, Michael A. K. (1985) *An Introduction to Functional Grammar.* London: Edward Arnold.
Heffer, Simon (2011) *Strictly English. The Correct Way to Write and Why it Matters.* London: Windmill Books.
Huddleston, Rodney D. (1984) *Introduction to the Grammar of English.* Cambridge: Cambridge University Press.
Huddleston, Rodney D. and Geoffrey K. Pullum (2002) *The Cambridge Grammar of the English Language.* Cambridge: Cambridge University Press.

Huddleston, Rodney D. and Geoffrey K. Pullum (eds) (2005) *A Student's Introduction to English Grammar*. Cambridge: Cambridge University Press.

Hundt, Marianne (2007) *English Mediopassive Constructions. A Cognitive, Corpus-Based Study of Their Origin, Spread and Current Status*. Amsterdam: Rodopi.

Hundt, Marianne (2014) '"Books that sell" – mediopassives and the modification constraint'. In Hundt, Marianne (ed.) *Late Modern English in Context*. Cambridge: Cambridge University Press, pp. 90–109.

Jespersen, Otto (1909–1949) *Modern English Grammar on Historical Principles*. London: Allen & Unwin.

Jespersen, Otto (1924) *The Philosophy of Grammar*. London: Allen & Unwin Ltd.

Jucker, Andreas H. (1992) *Social Stylistics: Syntactic Variation in British Newspapers*. Berlin: Mouton de Gruyter.

Kortmann, Bernd and Clive Upton (eds) (2008) *Varieties of English. The British Isles*. Berlin: Mouton de Gruyter.

Leech, Geoffrey, Marianne Hundt, Christian Mair and Nicholas Smith (2009) *Change in Contemporary English. A Grammatical Study*. Cambridge: Cambridge University Press.

Macaulay, R. K. S. (1991) *Locating Dialect in Discourse*. Oxford: Oxford University Press.

Millar, Robin McColl and Dauvit Horsbroch (2000) 'Covert and overt attitudes to the Scots tongue expressed in the *Statistical Accounts of Scotland*'. In Dieter Kastovsky and Arthur Mettinger (eds) *The History of English in a Social Context*. Berlin: Mouton de Gruyter, pp. 169–198.

Miller, Jim (2008) *Introduction to English Syntax*. 2nd edition. Edinburgh: Edinburgh University Press.

Mugglestone, Linda (ed.) (2006) *The Oxford History of English*. Oxford: Oxford University Press, pp. 274–304.

Pawley, Andrew (2008) 'Australian Vernacular English: some grammatical characteristics'. In Kate Burridge and Bernd Kortmann (eds) *Varieties of English. The Pacific and Australasia*. Berlin: Mouton de Gruyter, pp. 362–397.

Pullum, Geoffrey and Deirdre Wilson (1977) 'Autonomous syntax and the analysis of auxiliaries'. *Language* 53, 741–788.

Quirk, Randolph, Geoffrey N. Leech, Sidney Greenbaum and Jan Svartvik (1985) *A Comprehensive Grammar of the English Language*. London: Longman.

Sampson, Geoffrey (2007) 'Grammar without grammaticality'. *Corpus Linguistics and Linguistic Theory* 3/1, 1–32.

Seidlhofer, Barbara (2011) *Understanding English as a Lingua Franca: A Complete Introduction to the Theoretical Nature and Practical Implications of English Used as a Lingua Franca*. (Oxford Applied Linguistics.) Oxford: Oxford University Press.

Swan, Michael (2005) *Practical English Usage*. 3rd Edition. Oxford: Oxford University Press.

Tagliamonte, Sali A. (2013) *Roots of English. Exploring the History of Dialects*. Cambridge: Cambridge University Press.

Trask, R. L. (2001) *Mind the Gaffe. The Penguin Guide to Common Errors in English.* London: Penguin Books.
Trudgill, Peter (1983) *Sociolinguistics.* Harmondsworth: Penguin Books.
Wagner, Susanne (2008) 'English dialects in the Southwest: morphology and syntax'. In Bernd Kortmann and Clive Upton (eds) *Varieties of English. The British Isles.* Berlin: Mouton de Gruyter, pp. 417–439.
Wales, Katie (2006) *Northern English. A Social and Cultural History.* Cambridge: Cambridge University Press.

Index

adjective phrase, 19–31
adjectives, 19–31
  as heads, 23
  criteria for, 26–7
  denotation, 21
  gradability, 22
  object complement, 23, 36, 43
  order, 28–30
  position, 28
  reduplication, 30
  subject complement, 23, 36, 43
adverbial, 32–3
adverbial clauses, 38–47
  in spoken English, 44
  position, 40–3
  reduced, 136
  types of, 39–40
adverb phrase, 32–7
  structure of, 36–7
adverbs, 32–47
  and adjectives, 34–5
  criteria, 32
agreement, 88
aspect, 224–8
  grammatical, 225
  lexical, 225, 261
  perfect, 245–53
  progressive, 254
  resultative, 249–51
  situation, 225, 261
  viewpoint, 225

case, 164
clause, 48–102
  adverbial, 38
  complement, 112–24
  finite, 207

  non-finite, 128–40
  relative, 180–205
clause and text, 48–80
  and non-finite clauses, 71
  and spoken and written text, 72–4
  clefts, 107–11
  discourse markers, 61
  ellipsis, 62
  focus, 63–69
  theme, 75–80
Clause-NP, 66–7
clause structure, 81–106
  constituents, 81–5
  dependency relations, 85–91
  hierarchical structure, 92–4
  integrated and unintegrated syntax, 103–6
  linearity, 95–100
  predicate-argument structure, 95–6
  verb phrases, 101–2
clefts, 50–4
  IT cleft, 50–1, 107–9
  reverse WH cleft, 53, 110–11
  TH cleft, 54, 111
  WH cleft, 42, 109–10
coherence, 49–50
cohesion, 55–7
  and voice, 58–60
complement clauses, 112–24
  complementisers, 112–13
  embedded interrogatives, 114–21
  gerund, 121
  infinitive, 121
  mood and modality, 119–20
  noun complement clauses, 122–4
complementisers, 112–13
  or preposition, 218–20

INDEX

constituent structure, 81–5
construction, 125–40, 180–2
coordination, 57, 82–3
coreference and referent tracking, 56

dangling participle, 133
data, 7
deictics, 164, 201
denotation, 21, 176
dependency relations, 85–91
descriptive grammar, 5–6, 15
desubordination, 45
determinative, 158–63
discourse markers, 61
DO-OO construction, 86–7

ellipsis, 24, 62, 70, 217
enrichment, 163
event time, 225
extraposition, 11

finite, 207, 209, 220
focus, 63–7
  and syntax, 64
  and word order, 67
  given and new, 67–70
free participle (clause), 131–2

gerund, 133–5
given construction, 162
government, 88
gradability, 22
grammaticality, 9–18
  and acceptability, 9
  and intuition, 10–12
  and language change, 16
  and power, 13–14, 120
  descriptive and prescriptive grammar, 15

hanging participle, 133
hierarchical structure, 92–4

indirect question, 11–12, 106
infinitive (clause), 130
insubordination, 45
integrated syntax, 103–6
intuition *see* grammaticality and intuition

left dislocation, 66–7
lexical aspect, 261–7
linearity, 95–100
long-distance dependency, 115–16

main clause, 212
meaning, 4–5, 21, 42–3, 44, 47, 48, 55–6, 121–2, 176–8, 245–6, 261–7, 275–9
middle, 58–60, 232–5
modifier, 283–4n
mood and modality, 119–20, 236–42

new construction, 162
non-finite clauses, 71, 128–40
  gerund, 133–5
  how many types?, 139–40
  infinitival relative clause, 185
  infinitives, 130
  participles, 131–2
  reduced adverbials, 136
  reduced relatives, 137
  verb stem, 137
noun, 141–69
  common, 151–2
  count, 153
  countability, 153
  mass, 153
  number and agreement, 155–7
  proper, 151–2
noun complement clauses, 122–4
noun phrase, 141–69
  determinative, 158–63
  partitives, 155
  pronouns, 164–9
  NP Clause construction, 65–6, 105–6
number, 155, 164

participle, 131–2
particle, 171–2
partitives, 155
passive, 243
past tense, 252
perfect, 245–56
pied-piping, 116
predicate-argument structure, 95–6
preposition, 170–9
  denotation, 176–7
  preposition or complementiser, 218–20
  transitive and intransitive, 173

prepositional phrase, 170–9
  complement of adjective, 175
  complement of noun, 175
  complement of preposition, 175
  complement of verb, 175
prepositional verb, 178
prescriptive grammar, 5–6, 15
pronoun
  wh words as deictics, 201
  which as discourse connective, 202

reduplication, 30–1
reference time, 225–6
relative clause, 180–204
  contact, 182
  free, 183
  gapless, 203
  infinitival, 185
  non-restrictive, 188
  non-standard, 186
  propositional, 187
  reduced, 137
  restrictive, 188
  resumptive, 190
  shadow pronouns, 190
  th, 193
  wh, 198–200
relativiser, 180
  unattached, 195
  unintegrated, 197
  wh, 198
  which as discourse connective, 202
resultative, 249–51
  right dislocation, 66

second object construction, 87
sentence, 206–23
  clause, 208
  complex, 210
  compound, 211
  fragment, 216
  simple, 218
  system, 220
  text, 220
simple past, 252–3
simple present, 257–60
situation
  dynamic, 27

stative, 27
situation aspect, 261
spoken and written text, 6–7, 72–4, 103–6
subject, 90, 97–100
  understood, 128–39
subordinate clause, 212
  and main clause, 45–7, 57
  preposition or complementiser, 218–20
substitution, 82
syntactic linkage, 88

tense, 224–8
  future, 229–31
  past, 252
  present, 257
theme, 75–80
  and given information, 77–8
  and new information, 78
  and subject, 75
  marked, 77
  outer, 80
topic time, 226
trace, 115–16
transposition, 81–2

unintegrated syntax, 103–6, 108

verb, 224–67
  criteria, 279
verb phrase, 101–2, 224–67
  middle, 232
  mood and modality, 236–42
  passive, 243
verb stem (clause), 137–8
voice, 58–60, 243

which as discourse connective, 202
with + NP (clause), 138
word class, 268–80
  criteria, 26–7, 170–2, 279
  gradience, 270
  major, 268
  meaning, 21, 176, 275–9
  minor, 268
  sub-classes, 170

EU representative:
Easy Access System Europe
Mustamäe tee 50, 10621 Tallinn, Estonia
Gpsr.requests@easproject.com

www.ingramcontent.com/pod-product-compliance
Lightning Source LLC
Chambersburg PA
CBHW051049230426
43666CB00012B/2621